THE GREAT CHALLENGE

BOOKS BY LOUIS FISCHER

Oil Imperialism

The Soviets in World Affairs (2 vols.)

Why Recognize Russia?

Machines and Men in Russia

Soviet Journey

The War in Spain

Men and Politics, an Autobiography

Dawn of Victory

A Week with Gandhi

Empire

The Great Challenge

THE GREAT CHALLENGE

LOUIS FISCHER

New York

DUELL, SLOAN AND PEARCE

D
825
.F5
c.1

68645

Contents

Part One: *Men, Politics, and War*

Part Two: *Journey through War to Peace*

Part Three: *Double Rejection*

Part One

Men, Politics, and War

1. *Up from Dunkerque*

WAR is politics stained with blood. Before the war, the struggle is fought with words by men in striped trousers. When the diplomats fail, men in uniform take over with bombs. The second world war was the child of pre-war politics.

The war settled one thing: Germany, Italy, and Japan will not rule the earth. It left many other problems unsolved. Those problems will be solved politically or they will be handled militarily.

The increasing deadliness of armaments is no guarantee of peace. The second world war was longer than the first and cost more lives and wealth. A third world war would be still more expensive. Each war has been more expensive than its predecessor. But this well-known fact has not prevented wars. The mounting horror of war merely makes some governments hesitate to go to war. That is the aggressor's chief asset. The normal person's dread of war is so great that a government by the people will happily clutch any straw, any conference or speech or letter which seems to promise peace. This is an important source of appeasement.

Between 1931 and 1940, all the major dictatorships were guilty of aggression. Only the dictatorships were guilty of aggression. No democracy committed aggression. Modern democracies have to reckon with the emotions of their people. Dictatorships are under no such compulsion.

The prevention of war revolves around the future relationship between democracies and dictatorships. A dictatorship is swift to action because its decisions are not impeded by moral scruples or public opinion. Democracies decide slowly, and when several of them concert their diplomacy they may never decide at all, or they may decide to do nothing. This happened often before 1939.

It is not a matter of strength. The democracies, whose peace was threatened and finally destroyed by totalitarian aggression, had more than enough strength to stop the attacks of Japan on China, of Italy on Abyssinia, Albania, and Spain, and of the Nazis on Austria and Czechoslovakia. France alone had the strength to thwart Hitler's remilitarization of the Rhineland in March, 1936.

3

The dictatorships were impressively stupid in not recognizing that aggression and expansion would be their undoing. Democratic governments displayed a monumental incapacity to cope with their problems.

Some statesmen in the democracies did not see the danger. But President Roosevelt, for instance, did see it; early in 1936 he publicly pointed to the coming war. Occasionally, the statesmen were deterred by the reluctance of their parliaments and voters to move in the direction of armed conflict. More frequently, however, military action was not involved. Political or economic action alone could have been effective, and in that field, foreign offices and state departments enjoyed wide latitude. They blundered because diplomacy was then, and still is, a process of detailed bargaining, of give-and-take, and it therefore focuses so much on small, short-range national objectives as to lose sight of the long-range international goal which is peace. Moreover, diplomats and many laymen rejoice when a situation "blows over," when a crisis is "passed." Whether a problem is solved concerns them less than the immediate relaxation of tension. Then some day the unsolved problems come home to roost.

In the inter-war years, no non-Axis government directed its efforts solely or even primarily to war prevention. Instead, the politicians said: Hitler is warlike and we must yield to him, but when he ultimately settles down his friendship will be valuable to us as a counterweight to Russia. They said: The rape of Abyssinia is a crime and a nuisance, and yet if we do not press Mussolini too hard he might side with us against Hitler. They said: A leftist Spain will encourage leftism everywhere; Franco may be a creature of Rome and Berlin but we can buy him with credits, kindness, and "Non-Intervention." Their guide was immediate advantage, never principle.

These tactics of appeasement enabled Hitler, Hirohito, and Mussolini to win bloodless victories which made the war bloodier and longer.

Politics can make a war and can make a war longer. (Politics can also waste a victory.)

Pre-war political hesitations lingered on into the war. Appeasement was contagious. When one government dropped it another took it up. With the exception of France and Great Britain, no non-Axis country declared war before it was attacked. France went to war at 5 P.M. on September 3, 1939, because England had declared war at eleven that morning. France, as always, was afraid to be alone. Only in Great Britain was there sufficient, though belated, popular understanding of national and imperial interests to force the none too anti-Fascist government of Neville Chamberlain to enter the war before the Nazi blow actually fell on British soil and British men. Yet having declared war, England and France likewise waited. For months, the British Royal Air Force, which had bombs, dropped nothing more harmful than paper leaflets. On February 2, 1940, the war news in *The New York Times* occupied six inches of space at the bottom of column two on page two. The headline read, "Activity Increases on Western Front." Three days later, again on page two, the same paper announced a "Skirmish Victory Claimed by French." "British Down Three Nazi Planes and Rout Twenty in Fiercest Battle Yet Over England," read a headline on February 10. No wonder Neville Chamberlain complained in Parliament on January 31, 1940, that "if one were to read only the debates in the House of Commons and some of the more sensational columns of the press, it might be supposed that the Government is making very little effort to win the war."

It was the "phony war." The Nazis and Bolsheviks had crushed Poland. Thereupon the German war remained in a state of pause until Hitler turned on Scandinavia and western Europe.

The only real war was being fought in the snow of the north, between the Red Army and Finland. The Russian attack on Finland on November 30, 1939, and the bombing of Helsinki that night unloosed a flood of anti-Soviet sentiment throughout the world. Within forty-eight hours, President Roosevelt placed a moral embargo on trade with Russia. The League of Nations expelled the Soviet government. After closing its eyes to Fascist aggressions in China, Spain, Austria, and Czechoslovakia, it acted resolutely against the Russian aggressor. In New York, Bishop Manning appealed for aid to Finland. The Lutheran church opened a drive to collect half a million dollars in February, 1940. Herbert Hoover, silent when the Spanish people were under Fascist attack, proposed all-out aid to the Finns.

The Finns, battling their big neighbor, beat back heavy attacks and took a heavy toll of Soviet young men. Finland's President, Kyosti Kallio, on February 1, 1940, begged for "an honorable peace" to end this "barbaric, senseless attack."

"The Finnish bandits will be destroyed and exterminated," the Moscow *Pravda* replied. "We will achieve victory over them under our great leader Stalin," the paper continued. "He is a man with the heart of a scholar, the face of a workingman, the appearance of a soldier." But *The New York Times* called Stalin "a cruel Oriental despot." "Stalin is a cruel and vindictive man," wrote Walter Lippmann; he urged help for the Finns. Joseph Barnes, on December 1, 1939, stated in the *New York Herald Tribune*, which he had represented in Moscow, that Finland "is a cohesive democratic state with a long national tradition. It is not Fascist, even in the elastic Soviet use of that word."

A British Gallup poll in February, 1940, revealed that 74 per cent of the people interviewed wanted arms sent to Finland; 33 per cent wanted men sent.

A number of intellectuals resigned from the Communist party; they "got off the train," as they put it, because the Soviet Union had become an aggressor. In Helsinki, Sir Walter Citrine, head of a British trade-union delegation which had spent ten days visiting Finnish cities and the front, said Finland needed "extensive assistance in material and perhaps manpower, too."

Citrine had written a book in 1936 that was sharply critical of the Soviet regime and its methods at home. Now he was anti-Soviet on account of Finland. Later, when Hitler's attack brought Russia into the war, he turned pro-Soviet. In politics, expediency and patriotism are stronger than principle. Despite Hitler's aggressions, anti-Semitism, and atrocities, many titled and untitled British appeasers found him quite acceptable until September 3, 1939. Then wartime requirements of patriotism altered their attitude. They followed their government, not their convictions.

Sir William Beveridge, father of Britain's cradle-to-grave security scheme, said in the House of Commons on February 27, 1945: "We must stick to principle. We must stick to principle in international affairs and if it happens that one cannot both stick to one's friends and stick to principle, one must stick to principle; because principles do not change, but friends, even if they appear for the moment to be unreasonable, may change and become reasonable. Opportunism, appeasement, self-regarding policies, power politics, all lead to the grave of our hopes."

The bulk of humanity, however, forgets principles and therefore succumbs to confusion and propaganda.

On foreign policy, the lay mind often resembles a jumble shop. I spent an evening in 1937 in conversation with the personnel of a New York settlement house. They were intelligent people. They read the press. They read Soviet Commissar Maxim Litvinov's eloquent pleas for collective security and they favored collective security. They read Prime Minister Chamberlain's speeches apologizing for appeasement and they could readily understand why an unprepared Britain, which wanted nothing but peace, should try to avert war. They read Hitler's speeches, and they felt there was some truth in his argument that Germany lacked *Lebensraum* and markets and had been wronged at Versailles.

The susceptibility of the modern brain to foreign and domestic propaganda is a major problem of politics. In democracies, the citizen is increasingly bewildered by what he hears and reads. In a dictatorship, where the government censors and funnels all news and views, the individual gradually becomes completely receptive and submissive.

Governments, autocratic as well as democratic, manufacture all kinds of weapons to win a war and to make men fight. Arsenals pour out weapons of steel and iron. Simultaneously, other arsenals beat history into a sword. In the process, they bend and flatten history. By the same political metallurgy, facts are distorted. Ultimately, minds are distorted. The peace has inherited these evils.

Government control of minds is a growing world menace. Dictatorships achieve that control through crude methods. But in all countries, powerful forces are passionately trying to twist and kill the truth.

"England wanted this war," Marshal Hermann Goering said on January 2, 1940. "The German people are engaged in a difficult war for the freedom of Greater Germany," he declared. Poland was the aggressor, the Nazi party calendar for 1940 asserted. "The Reich," it lied, "sees itself compelled to answer with force the force used (by Poland) in numerous frontier attacks."

On January 1, 1940, the *Voelkischer Beobachter*, Hitler's own daily, listed the benefits of Nazism: Workers' rights, price control, aid for mothers, health care, children's insurance, factory sports, Strength Through Joy tours, classical music concerts for German workers. These, it said, explained the war; "the propertied classes of England and France began to fear that in the near future their workers . . . would demand similar rights. This was unthinkable to them. The development had to be nipped in the bud."

This was utter nonsense. But all dictatorships have a way of attributing to other countries motives and intentions that do not exist. It is part of their technique of attempting to win friends at home by finding enemies abroad.

The *Voelkischer Beobachter* set the tune and all Nazi papers and radio commentators danced to it. The *Beobachter* of January 2, 1940, displayed a banner headline, "Europe's Liberation from British Threat." On January 4, 1940, the same paper published an article on "Our Socialism." January 7, 1940: "France's goal for a thousand years has been the destruction of German unity." January 8, 1940: "There is no unemployment in Germany." January 9, 1940, the biggest front-page headline: "Polish Murder-Beasts Tortured Severely-Wounded German Airmen." That same day: "England is the fortress of unscrupulous capitalism."

Hitler was striving to win the support of the German people. They heard his lies only. He sold the workers "Socialism"; he sold the whole nation hatred of England and France. To France, he sold anti-British propaganda, to Britain anti-French propaganda, to America anti-European and isolationist propaganda.

The bigger the scoundrel the more unscrupulous his arguments. Someone always believes him.

Many Frenchmen on the Right listened to Hitler's siren voice. French Communists listened to Moscow's voice and Moscow said this was an imperialist war.

Having softened up France, having applied the "strategy of terror" to all Europe, the Nazis wheeled their army and struck down Norway, Denmark, Holland, and Belgium. On May 21, 1940, the Reichswehr was blitzing its way to the English Channel; the RAF bombed Aachen heavily; President Roosevelt asked Congress to speed America's defense program and appealed for unity; and Queen Wilhelmina fled to London from Holland.

"This is not our war," said a long editorial in the Communist *Sunday Worker* of May 12, 1940. "This is not our war—this battle between two gangster groups—the British-French and the Hitlerite. Let us keep out of it." An anti-war rally took place on Times Square in New York on May 22. "Roosevelt, Dewey, and Hoover are United for War," "La Guardia, Stop Stooging for Wall Street," "Let God Save the King," and "The Yanks Are Not Coming" were some of the slogans on Communist party placards.

On the other hand, Senator James F. Byrnes delivered an address against Colonel Charles A. Lindbergh's defeatist isolationism. Wendell Willkie said: "Hitler knows only strength. He will stand aghast when we start the wheels of our industry and put ten million men back to work." Senator Pepper of Florida urged the sale of American planes to Europe's democracies.

America argued. Europe shook with the tread of Hitler's legions, with the roar of his dive bombers, with the thunder of his racing tanks.

Then came Dunkerque. King Leopold of Belgium surrendered his army on May 28. The British and French armies were consequently in grave peril. "The House must prepare itself for hard and heavy tidings," Winston Churchill told Parliament. In the moment of deepest gloom, he had been made Prime Minister. A little British-French armed force, its back to the sea, stood firm inside Dunkerque, so that 350,000 British soldiers might try to get back to England. The Luftwaffe machine-gunned them while they waited on the beach at Dunkerque. Ships came out from Britain, destroyers, cutters, pleasure steamers from the Thames, private yachts, fishing smacks, rowboats manned by boy volunteers. The Luftwaffe machine-gunned and dive-bombed them as they approached Dunkerque. Soldiers waded neck-high to climb into the smaller vessels. Wounded men were carried out to sea and then helped aboard. Ships listed with heavy loads. They raced to British shores. Again the Luftwaffe attacked. In one morning —June 1—six ships, several of them full of troops, were bombed and sunk. Men kept their steel helmets while discarding practically everything else. The sea was full of mines and torpedoes. Hospital ships were machine-gunned from the air. Arrived in English ports, some soldiers, in rags and dirty, bloody bandages, were carried down the gangplanks amid tears and cheers. England cheered. America cheered. Ships went to and fro several times. Every boatload safely anchored in home waters aroused delirious excitement. Britain counted the rescued. They were Britain's only army, her only defense against Hitler's invasion, an army without arms.

A thousand ships had brought 325,000 "from the jaws of death back to their native land," Churchill told an enthusiastic and grateful House of Commons on June 4. One hundred and ten thousand French soldiers had been evacuated. It was an achievement, Churchill warned, not a victory. He knew what impended. The battle for the life of Britain.

England stood alone. But "we shall not flag," Churchill promised the House, and the world, on June 4. "We shall not flag nor fail. We shall go on to the end. We shall fight in France and on the seas and oceans. We shall fight with growing confidence and strength in the air. We shall defend our island whatever the cost may be. We shall fight on the beaches, landing grounds, in fields, in streets, and on the hills. We shall never surrender. And even if, which I do not for a moment believe, this island or a large part of it were subjugated and starving, then our empire beyond the seas, armed and guarded by the British fleet, will carry on the struggle until in God's good time the New World, with all its power and might, sets forth to the rescue and liberation of the Old."

Churchill's optimism was in his mental and temperamental make-up. It fed on his belief that the United States would ultimately enter the war.

Dunkerque marked Britain's lowest ebb. But by opening up the country's untapped resources of stamina and will power, it marked the beginning of victory. For weeks after Dunkerque, British working men and women labored at their lathes until they collapsed from exhaustion. They ate lunch at their machines. They worked all day, slept on the floor near their benches, and then stood up to make more shells and guns. Individuals frequently rise to extra effort in order to survive. Here a whole nation was lashed into almost superhuman exertions by the will to live.

The Channel and Churchill saved England. So did the RAF. Churchill's speeches galvanized the people into action. Because governments are more powerful than ever, this has become the age of "big men" who wield tremendous power and exercise tremendous influence. In a dictatorship, the big man exercises influence because he wields power. In a democracy, he wields power because he exercises influence, and he uses his power to prolong his influence. Churchill helped the British people to be what they are at their best.

Little men despaired. Colonel Charles A. Lindbergh gave England up as lost, and he seemed not to regret it. Marshal Pétain, hero with a frightened soul, did not believe in France or in England. But Churchill, Roosevelt, Charles de Gaulle believed, and with them were millions of little people with big hearts.

Four years after Dunkerque, on June 6, 1944, the British Army, with the United States Army, returned to France. Five years after Dunkerque came V-E day. Five bloody, hungry, cold, anxious years for tens of millions of women, men, and children. The human animal is a remarkable contrivance, and deserves a better fate.

Man deserves at least a world without war. Having seen the horror of war, I translated each day's war bulletins into men's flesh ripped open by bullets and men's bodies broiled black in burned planes and tanks. When the communiqué said, "Only two of our aircraft failed to return," I saw twelve boys dead and twelve mothers and fathers, twelve families and many friends who would always remember, and, remembering, get a cold, empty feeling under their hearts. War must have some very great, ennobling end if it is to be worth all this suffering, pain, and death.

If the second world war was to have any sense it had to become a world civil war, a war against slavery, a war to establish one world indivisible, with liberty and justice to all. A war to give one nation another's territory or oil field or market is a supreme and senseless crime.

2. *America Becomes Involved*

NO STATEMENT by Winston Churchill will look more important to historians than his offer to pool the sovereignties of England and France. It was June 16, 1940. France stood on the verge of collapse. Churchill wanted to help France and his own country. The French and British governments, he proposed, "declare that France and Great Britain shall no longer be two, but one Franco-British Union. . . . Every citizen of France will enjoy immediately citizenship of Great Britain. Every British subject will become a citizen of France."

Super-nationalist and imperialist, Churchill's instinct for survival nevertheless led him, in crisis, towards internationalism and the submergence of national sovereignties. Churchill recognized that security and self-preservation are best served when separate sovereignty is not preserved.

Years later, shortly before victory in Europe, Churchill was asked whether his offer of union with France remained valid. He said no. What he was ready to do in a desperate last-moment effort to prevent defeat he refused to do when victory was sure. In 1940, Churchill was idealistic for the most realistic reason, to ward off disaster. By 1944, this idealism had evaporated. Churchill was good when things were very bad.

The ugliness of war generates idealistic hopes of a beautiful peace, and then it generates poisons which attack to kill the idealism. Apparently, it is illusory to expect progress via suffering. If suffering produced wisdom, there would be so much wisdom in the world there would be no suffering.

It did not lie in Churchill's power to rescue France. Had a million British or American troops, fresh and well-equipped, landed in Normandy in June, 1940, or had the Russians attacked in the east as the Tsar did in August, 1914, France and much subsequent bloodshed might have been saved. But this could not be. Instead, the Nazi legions moved on inexorably. Paris yielded without a fight. On June 10, Italy entered the war.

Count Ciano, Italy's Foreign Minister and Mussolini's young son-in-law, tried to keep his country out. Later, the Nazis executed him for it. President Roosevelt sent three personal messages to Mussolini in the month of May, 1940, urging abstention from hostilities. Pope Pius XII wrote Mussolini a letter, dated April 24, 1940, counseling against participation. These measures, as well as popular demonstrations against war, were unavailing because Mussolini wanted to be in at the kill. He felt certain that soon France, and in a few weeks Britain, would surrender; then Italy would reap the sweet fruits of a cheap victory. But what a mistake he made! Not victory in 1940 but defeat and death in 1945 were his fate.

The mistakes of governments cause most of humanity's misery.

Mussolini and Hitler had met at the Brenner Pass in February, 1940, and decided to bring Italy into the war. Colonel General Gustav Jodl, who for ten years was the brains of the German General Staff, testified after his arrest in June, 1945, that the high command did not want Italy in the war. Field Marshal Keitel gave similar evidence. Actually, Italy neutral and friendly, and shipping goods to Germany, would have been an asset to Hitler rather than the liability she soon became. But Hitler, more political than military, must have thought that Italy's entry into the war at the proper juncture would help administer the *coup de grace* to France and, he hoped, discourage England and hasten her collapse too. Hitler was gambling on breaking Britain's will to resist. He expected Italy's belligerency to be the last cruel blow.

France's fall in 1940 began in 1914. France lost too many young men in the first world war. The poppy fields of Flanders, fertilized with rich, red blood, grew a large crop of pacifists. Victory was disillusioning. America refused to guarantee French security. Britain, as some Frenchmen saw it, had become pro-German; at any rate, they said, British statesmen took Germany's side against France in such questions as reparations and the occupation of the Ruhr. This mistrust of England played a decisive role in the Pétain government's readiness to sign an armistice with Hitler on June 21, 1940. Some Frenchmen expected, and some Frenchmen cynically hoped, that Britain would succumb without much delay. Then why not capitulate quickly and perhaps earn a premium for promptness?

France doubted England's endurance. The Nazi-Soviet pact of August 23, 1939, was like the sound of doom, for with Russia and America neutral, and Britain unprepared, how could France win? In that case, Frenchmen thought, what was the use of fighting at all against a Germany that was bigger, stronger economically, and better equipped militarily? That in itself would explain the fall of France.

General Charles de Gaulle knew that his countrymen had lost faith in the rest of the world; he addressed himself to this question in his first famous broadcast from London on June 18, 1940. "For France is not alone. She is not alone—she is not alone," he exclaimed. This was the psychological nub of the French tragedy. "France has a vast empire behind her," De Gaulle continued. "She can unite with the British Empire, which holds the seas and is continuing the struggle. She can utilize to the full, as England is doing, the vast industrial resources of the United States. . . . This is a world war. . . . There are in the universe sufficient means to enable us one day to crush our enemies. Shattered today by mechanical force, we shall conquer in the future by stronger mechanical force. The fate of the world depends on it."

When Russia and the United States came into the war and when Britain gave tangible proof of her immense air power, French hopes revived and underground resistance to Hitler mounted.

France's inner strength was as inadequate as her outside support. A powerful wing of the Socialist party was pacifist and had applauded the vivisection of Czechoslovakia at Munich in 1938. Many workingmen, on the other hand, felt that the bourgeois leaders of France were corrupt and pro-Fascist and had betrayed France by selling Czechoslovakia and Spain down the river. Uncounted Frenchmen were vocally mistrustful of their statesmen and generals. The nation boasted of its army, but experts knew how obsolete was the army's mechanical equipment. France lacked enough good planes to stop the Luftwaffe, but the French national exchequer was weighed down with idle gold which might have been used to buy planes in America. The Ministry of Finance had refused the money. Observers suspected that French industry wanted the orders. When the war started, pilots, pathetically patriotic, took "crates" up into combat knowing it was suicide. Charles de Gaulle, then still a colonel, had urged the building of tanks. But, during the Riom trial, in March, 1942, former Premier Daladier revealed that the check suffered by Italian armored units at Guadalajara, Spain, during the civil war "was taken by the French technicians as a proof that the conception of armored motorized warfare was invalidated." French generals believed in the Maginot Line, not in tanks. At the same Riom trial, Guy La Chambre, French Minister of Air at the outbreak of the war, blamed the Communists for obstructing work in French aircraft factories after the signing of the Soviet-Nazi pact and he blamed the aircraft manufacturers for delaying the plane-building program. Daladier, on the witness stand, intimated that the manufacturers' sabotage was designed to prove the folly of nationalizing aircraft plants. The result was, as Paul Reynaud, French Premier from March to June, 1940, puts it in his memoirs, that "We lacked a tank corps and we lacked an air force."

These and a thousand other facts demonstrate that for years before the second world war France had been waging a bitter civil war which left her divided, depleted, defeatist.

The French, with their fleet, could have continued the fight in Africa and Asia. But Pétain was neither a democrat nor an anti-Fascist; he therefore had no inner need to fight Fascism.

Pétain said in his 1942 New Year's broadcast: "I do not want for my country either Marxism or liberal capitalism." That left only Fascism. A leader with such Nazi ideas could not resist the Nazis.

France fell because of internal rottenness and insufficient foreign assistance.

The capitulation of France seemed to reveal basic faults in democracy as a form of government. The French surrender was widely regarded not as the death of a democracy but as the beginning of the death of democracy.

I discussed this question on June 22, 1940, at the annual summer Institute of Public Affairs of the University of Virginia in Charlottesville. We had just read the news of the French armistice. "It is too early," I commented, "to bury the democracies and democracy and unfurl the swastika throughout the world. . . . Fascism has not triumphed until all the democracies are defeated, and before that has happened England and America must be defeated."

Despite the news, I was optimistic. "If Germany cannot crush England soon . . . there may be a stalemate in this phase and an Allied victory ultimately, for if Germany cannot win now she cannot win later, whereas if the Allies cannot win now they can win later with American assistance."

I stated my peace aims. "Democracy," I declared, "is far from perfect. But it is better than any dictatorship I know. No dictatorship has given its people either liberties or groceries. The world is not divided into white and black. There is no white; unfortunately there is a lot of black. If you insist on white and will support no other, you can sit in your ivory tower until doomsday waiting for it to arrive. The choice is between democratic gray and totalitarian black. The greatest peace aim is to banish the black and simultaneously make the gray whiter." This is still my program. More concretely, I suggested that, when the Allies win, "Europe must be organized into a federation. Federation is the negation of economic nationalism and narrow political nationalism. History has demonstrated that the only protection of nations lies in internationalism. There is no individual security for man or country."

My manuscript ended with a little allegory, but I ran over my time and had to leave it unspoken. "Mr. X," I wrote, "built himself a fine stout house and called it Democracy. After a while, a Mr. A applied to occupy the house next door. The landlord consulted Mr. X and told him that A was a well-known pyromaniac and had been convicted of arson. But Mr. X vouched for A and said he knew him as a gentleman, and so Mussolini moved in. Soon afterwards, Mr. B occupied the house on the other side of Democracy. Mr. B experimented in bomb-making and other explosives, and the neighbors warned Mr. X that Democracy was in danger. But X laughed and announced that he, in fact, was financing the laboratory which Mr. B had just set up next door. One day, Mr. A and Mr. B came to Mr. X in Democracy and asked whether he would mind if a business associate of theirs, Mr. C, camped for a while on his roof. Mr. X said he would be delighted. So Franco set up a tent on the roof and he drained the big water tank and filled it with sawdust. Finally, fire broke out in Democracy and Mr. X, his wife, and his children were trapped and burned to death. Would you say that Democracy was a badly built house? No. You would say that Mr. X was a fool."

The fall of France made a difference to most Americans, including numerous isolationists. The average isolationist looked to the broad oceans for protection and therefore saw no reason to become involved in trans-oceanic messes. Actually, it was not the oceans that mattered but what happened on the other side of the oceans. As long as the French Army and the British Navy kept an aggressive power from entrenching itself on the Atlantic coast of Europe, the ocean acted as a barrier. With the Germans at Dieppe, Calais, and Brest, however, the ocean might ultimately become a carrier. After the fall of France only the British fleet stood between Germany's armed might and America's armed forces at home. This was a powerful argument for American aid to the British fleet and to the British war effort generally.

Accordingly, President Franklin D. Roosevelt gave orders to scour the arsenals and warehouses of the United States for weapons for the

British Army. Between June, 1940, and the early spring of 1941, "we had ferried over the Atlantic," Winston Churchill disclosed on May 14, 1945, "a million rifles and a thousand cannon from the United States, with all their ammunition." Planes were shipped too. This material helped safeguard Britain against invasion, for Dunkerque left the British Isles with less than one equipped army division.

President Roosevelt's guiding thought in this crisis was stated by him in a letter, dated December 20, 1940, to Admiral Leahy, United States ambassador to Pétain's Vichy government, and published by the State Department on October 7, 1943. "The primary interest of the American people," the President wrote, "and an interest which overshadows all else at the moment, is to see a British victory." Neutrality had been abandoned.

The United States was at war before Pearl Harbor, not officially but in fact. On September 3, 1940, the first anniversary of the war in Europe, President Roosevelt announced an agreement with Churchill whereby the United States gave Britain fifty "over-age" destroyers and Britain gave the United States military and naval bases in the Atlantic. If the destroyers were too old why did the British want them? They were in fact good warships and performed well throughout the war. On March 11, 1941, the President signed the Lend-Lease act whereby billions of dollars' worth of arms were given to nations fighting the Axis. The moment Hitler or Mussolini invaded yet another country Lend-Lease was extended to it. On April 5, 1941, the United States took over the protection of Danish Greenland. On July 7, 1941, the United States joined England in the occupation of Iceland and undertook to "supplement" and "replace" British troops stationed there. In 1941, the American Navy was convoying ships in the Atlantic and actively cooperating with the British in hunting down Nazi submarines. American diplomacy, too, worked against Germany, Italy, and Japan. Repeatedly, for instance, the State Department warned the Pétain regime at Vichy against letting Hitler use the French fleet. Steps were taken in Latin America to frustrate the Axis militarily and commercially. In innumerable declarations, Roosevelt, Secretary of State Hull, and lesser officials showed their un-neutral anti-Axis sympathies.

Many months before Pearl Harbor, the United States military authorities had prepared a detailed, practical and far-flung and imaginative plan for American participation in the defeat of the Axis powers.

Simultaneously, the Roosevelt administration, against the votes of isolationist Senators and Representatives, strengthened the armed forces and other defenses of the country.

These measures as well as all-out aid to England had the support of the vast majority of Americans. But the popular resistance to sending American men into combat continued strong, and in the Presidential campaign in the fall of 1940, both Roosevelt and Wendell L. Willkie promised that no boys would go overseas unless the nation was attacked. On December 7, 1941, Japan solved that dilemma by attacking. History may put this down as the first Japanese suicide attack of the war. It destroyed American lives and property; it spelt death to Japan.

From September 3, 1939, but more particularly from the fall of France to Pearl Harbor, the great debate between isolationists and interventionists raged up and down America.

I have strolled on quiet forenoons through the silent residential streets of Lincoln, Nebraska, of Anderson, Indiana, of Canton, Ohio, and many other towns. . . . The white, wooden home surrounded by a garden, the rockers on the porch, the shade trees, the flower pots in the windows—all added up to a picture of self-contained, pleasant, and comfortable existence. But in the window was a flag with a service star, or two service stars, and sometimes the blue of the star had turned to the gold which denotes death. I can easily imagine a mother, or wife, sitting there inside the house waiting for another V-mail letter or re-reading an old one for the fifth time, and thinking: Why did my boy have to go from this wonderful place to a land I never heard of before and lie in the mud and be exposed to shells and bullets and maybe die? What did Anzio, Bastogne, Iwo Jima mean to her except heartache, longing, and loneliness?

Once I went to see Mrs. Eleanor Roosevelt in her New York apartment. After our talk, she took me to the door. On the floor of the corridor outside lay the afternoon paper. I picked it up for her and we read the big headline about the first landing of the Marines on Guadalcanal.

"I have a child in that," Mrs. Roosevelt said. It was her son James. Neither little white home nor White House is spared.

Guadalcanal, Sicily, Okinawa, Cassino, Normandy—they seem so far away from Kansas and so unimportant to Illinois. How strange that many thousands of Americans should lie under crosses or stars of David in those distant lands and that so many others should have earned Purple Hearts for eyes or limbs lost there! It is strange. And, if you will, it is mad. Yet in this mad world the United States had a part to play in the war and could not shirk it.

The man who said "Am I my brother's keeper?" was a murderer. We live on a small island called the earth. Every country's problems are not the business of every other country, but they become that unless they are solved. If Abel is not our concern, Cain kills him.

Colonel Lindbergh and the America Firsters maintained that a well-defended United States could not be invaded, so it did not matter what foreign nations fell as long as America was strong militarily. That being the case, it was unnecessary and un-neutral to help one side in the war. Isolationists in Congress therefore voted against Lend-Lease and similar enactments.

Lindbergh urged ten thousand planes for the American air force. "That number," he told the House of Representatives Foreign Affairs Committee hearing on the Lend-Lease bill on January 23, 1941, "would, I believe, be adequate to ensure American security regardless of the outcome of the present European war. . . . Accompanying this expansion of our air force should be the construction of aviation bases in Newfoundland, Canada, the West Indies, parts of South America, Central America, the Galapagos Islands, the Hawaiian Islands, and Alaska."

But why these bases? Lindbergh must have thought they would serve to stop or frighten off an enemy. The moment one concedes the possibility of an attack on the United States—and Lindbergh by this plea for bases did that—then the only question is how best to cope with that potential enemy. The internationalists believed that it was wisest to cope with the enemy before, and not after, he succeeded in conquering all of Europe and Asia.

Without American supplies and the hope of further American help, Britain would have succumbed. If, then, Hitler had attacked Russia when there were no British bombings of Germany and no American Lend-Lease to the Soviets, Russia would have been defeated. China's fate was sealed in these circumstances.

Germany, Italy, and Japan would consequently have been in secure possession of Europe, Africa, and Asia. Supported by Franco Spain, they would have filtered into Latin America through trade and propaganda channels.

Watching this development, every American would have wanted his country armed to the teeth. America would have lived like a garrison town, like a walled fortress, ever on the alert, ever under a strain.

Fascist military success would have made converts for totalitarianism in the United States. "That fellow Hitler's got something," people would have said. Some did say it.

The United States would have had to do business with Hitler, Mussolini, and Japan on their terms or become an isolated island. Isolationism would have led to dangerous isolation for America.

Fortunately, the bulk of Americans decided in favor of aid to the foes of the Axis. To put it bluntly, crudely, and correctly, it was better for the United States to fight future enemies on other peoples' territory and in cooperation with other peoples' armed forces than to wait till the enemy, triumphant, faced an America standing alone. Lend-Lease was an ingenious and historic device to give American steel and spare American flesh. More Germans killed by British and Russians meant fewer Americans killed by Germans.

Americans understood; and beginning with the fall of France, the trend to help England grew steadily.

William Allen White, editor of the *Emporia Gazette*, in the spring of 1940 organized the Committee for American Defense through Aid to the Allies. Hundreds of Americans joined the committee. On May 26, 1940, I wired Mr. White asking him to include me. He sent me several telegrams and letters. In a letter of June 13, 1940, he wrote: "I am glad to notice that we are getting the airplanes moving and guns and munitions in fairly large chunks. We may be able to help the Allies to hold on." He underlined the word "may" in ink.

Mrs. Wales Latham launched "Bundles for Britain" in January, 1940, and before long this had become a collecting agency, not only of clothing, surgical instruments, and other urgently needed commodities but also of the zeal of thousands of persons in American towns and hamlets eager to assist and encourage a valiant nation standing alone under the bombs. Bundles worth $5,500,000 were sent across.

The American people were not merely following. "The common people are a lot smarter than their political leaders and a couple of jumps ahead of them," William A. Lydgate, editor of the Gallup Poll Institute, wrote me in 1941. "For example," he said, "our polls here have shown that (1) the American people wanted to lift the Spanish embargo, (2) they condemned the Munich 'peace' before leaders in Paris and London perceived its folly, (3) they voted in favor of lifting the arms embargo in the Neutrality Act *five months* before Congress voted it, (4) for seven years (since November, 1935) the American people have favored a larger army, navy, and particularly a larger air force. . . ."

"Maybe," Mr. Lydgate mused, "the trouble with the world is that nobody has paid enough attention to the ideas of the common people." Maybe? Undoubtedly. Congress undemocratically paid less attention to the majority than to a vociferous, lobbying minority.

The nation, however, was pushing the Federal administration to help win a war which was our war though we were not yet in it.

One evening in 1944, at the home of John Gunther, popular author of the *Inside* books, some foreign correspondents, Cass Canfield, president of Harper, Hamilton Fish Armstrong, editor of *Foreign Affairs* Quarterly, Irita Van Doren of the *New York Herald Tribune*, and Wendell L. Willkie sat around discussing and reminiscing. Willkie told this story:

"In 1941, after I came back from England, DeWitt Wallace [publisher of *The Reader's Digest*] telephoned and asked me to do an article replying to Freda Utley's piece they had carried opposing aid to Britain. He offered to pay me $5,000. I told him I was in court on a case and didn't have the time. Wallace said: 'All we want is 1500 words. We will pay you $6,000.' I told him again I was not in a position to do it. 'Mr. Willkie,' Wallace said, 'I'll pay you $8,000 for the article.' Well," Willkie concluded with a smile, "you know, Indiana boy, $8,000; I promised to do the article." Willkie's ability to tell such a story about himself was part of his great charm.

In that article, Willkie wrote: "The problem that faces the United States . . . is the survival of democratic institutions, of a way of life that means more to us than anything else in the world. . . . We are helping Britain because the fight she is putting up is greatly to our advantage." Hitler's "totalitarian slave system is automatically and irrevocably *against* freedom."

3. *Stalin and Hitler: A Reinterpretation*

THE fall of France brought America closer to England and to war. The fall of France also hastened the invasion of Russia. President Roosevelt foresaw this two years before it happened. Former Ambassador Joseph E. Davies, in his *Mission to Moscow*, reports that he lunched with the President in the White House on July 18, 1939. Rumors of the impending pact between Stalin and Hitler filled the diplomatic air. "The President told me," Davies recorded in his diary, "that he told [Soviet] Ambassador Oumansky, when he was leaving to go to Moscow, to tell Stalin that if his government joined up with Hitler, it was certain as night followed the day that as soon as Hitler conquered France he would turn on Russia, and it would be the Soviet's turn next. He told me to get that word to Stalin and Molotov, if I could."

Here was prophetic statesmanship. Franklin D. Roosevelt understood geography, Hitler, and war. With France conquered and England inaccessible to the German Army, Hitler had to attack Russia.

In 1941, England could not invade the Continent. Later, with American aid, she might. That set the date for the Nazi invasion of Russia. Germany wanted to crush Russia before America entered the war.

There were two things Hitler could not do: he could not invade England, and, in view of the rising tide of American aid, he could not stand still. There were two things Hitler could do: he could attack England through her Empire or he could attack Russia.

Hitler reckoned that Russia would be easier to crack than the Anglo-American combination. He hoped that because Germany had invaded Russia, seat of "the deadly dangers of Bolshevism," the grateful Western capitalist powers might obligingly cancel their war on Germany.

Events often proved Hitler wrong.

Hitler was sure France and England would not go to war on account of Poland. "They are too cowardly," he said in a secret speech to his army chiefs. The main purpose of the Soviet-Nazi pact was to discourage France and England from fighting. The authoritative Moscow *Pravda* said so on August 23, 1940, in an editorial celebrating the first anniversary of the pact. "The news of the Soviet-German pact," it wrote, "was a last warning to the organizers and inspirers of the imperialistic war. The warning, however, had no effect. The war commenced."

Captured German official documents presented to the Nuremberg war criminals trial and cited in the American press on December 7, 1945, show that Hitler did not order the German Army to invade Poland until August 24, 1939, the day after the signing of the pact which, Hitler assumed, had frightened the Western powers out of the war.

Having made this mistake, Hitler hoped the war would end with Poland's military defeat. In September and October, 1939, Hitler several times offered to conclude peace with France and England. Goering told a Berlin audience that after the Polish campaign—four weeks, he estimated—"we are ready for an honorable peace." The Nazis wanted a respite after swallowing Poland. Later, the python could seek other prey.

Russia likewise tried to end the war after the conquest of Poland. Stalin charged in the *Pravda* of November 30, 1940, that "the ruling classes of England and France rudely declined Germany's peace proposals as well as the attempts of the Soviet Union to attain the earliest termination of the war."

The Soviet government saw no sense in a war against Hitler. "To start a war in order to 'destroy Hitlerism' is to commit a criminal folly in politics," wrote the Moscow *Izvestia*, official newspaper of the Soviet government, on October 9, 1939. Foreign Commissar Molotov therefore called France and England "aggressors."

The second world war flowed from the Soviet-Nazi pact. But it is inaccurate to say that Russia expected a major war. Moscow anticipated that the Soviet-Nazi pact would induce England and France to do a "Munich" on Poland and refrain from fighting. The Bolsheviks knew that, failing such an Anglo-French surrender of Poland, Hitler would invade Poland, crush Poland, and divide Poland with Russia. Thereupon, Stalin reasoned, the British and French governments would conclude a reluctant peace with Germany. In the resulting hostility between the West and Germany, Russia would find safety. This is why Stalin concluded the pact with Hitler.

Events proved Stalin wrong.

Stalin did not realize that appeasers no longer ruled in London or, therefore, in Paris. England and France would not make peace. France would fall. In consequence, Russia would suffer as President Roosevelt predicted.

Heads of states and other top officials often engage in the same game of rocking-chair strategy which has such fascination for laymen. I know because I have sat with some and speculated with them on "What would happen if . . . ?" These officials at times judge events correctly. But they also make mistakes for which their people pay.

The eleven-month appeasement interlude that followed the original Munich of September, 1938, no more kept France and England out of war than the twenty-two-month appeasement reprieve after the Soviet-Nazi "Munich" spared Russia the horrors of war. Appeasement makes war more likely, not less likely.

It is mathematically demonstrable that Great Britain and France did not build or buy enough arms during their eleven-month appeasement period to offset the loss of Czechoslovakia's army, arms, and arms factories. It might of course be argued that despite the Chamberlain-Daladier appeasement policy, Great Britain won the war and France was liberated. But at what added expense?

Russia, too, manufactured arms during her appeasement interlude, but not enough to offset the loss of France plus what Germany and her conquered territories manufactured in the same period. In the end, to be sure, the Soviet Union achieved victory. But it has been stated that 22,000,000 Soviet citizens died in the war. No serious foreign estimate puts the figure at less than 15,000,000 military and civilian deaths apart from many more million wounded, diseased, and broken men, women, and children, and the devastation of Russia's rich industrial and agricultural domains. Final victory does not justify earlier appeasement. The cold brain may regard victory merely as a newspaper headline or as an argument to win a parlor debate. But to any civilized person the real questions are: What price victory? and: Would wiser diplomacy have brought the price down?

A wiser Kremlin might have stayed out of the war and out of Finland in 1939 and fought when France was menaced. Roosevelt realized in 1940 that American interests dictated maximum aid to Britain; Stalin should have realized that Soviet interests dictated aid to France.

A Russian second front in the spring of 1940 would have divided the Reichswehr's forces, blunted its blitz against France, and conceivably prevented the fall of France just as the Tsar's offensive into Germany in the summer of 1914 made possible the French stand on the

Marne. Without Russian assistance, France might have fallen as quickly in 1914 as she did in 1940.

Risks attended such a preventive-war policy. For France might have collapsed despite Russian intervention, and then Hitler, after finishing off the Balkans, would have lunged at Russia. But this is what he did anyway. There was at least a chance of saving France if Russia engaged the Reichswehr on an eastern front. Stalin's biggest risk was to have France defeated and then remain alone with Hitler in Europe.

Stalin miscalculated in expecting England and France to appease Hitler before Poland was attacked. Then he miscalculated in expecting England and France to quit the war after Poland fell. Then he miscalculated in failing to help France.

Stalin also miscalculated Hitler's central strategy of the war. On this last miscalculation there is interesting evidence from former Soviet Foreign Commissar Maxim Litvinov who was more consistently correct on the world situation than any other statesman. In a statement to reporters in Washington, D. C., on December 13, 1941, Litvinov said: "My Government did receive warnings as to the treacherous intentions of Hitler with regard to the Soviet Union, but it did not take them seriously and this not because it believed in the sacredness of Hitler's signature, or did not believe him capable of violating the treaties he signed, and the oft-repeated solemn promises he made, but because it considered that it would have been madness on his part to undertake war in the east against such a powerful land as ours, before finishing off his war in the west."

It turned out to be madness. But didn't Stalin know that Hitler had no alternative? Stalin hoped, and therefore believed, that after the Battle of France Germany would remain locked in a death grapple with England until one of them collapsed. The country that won would be too exhausted to bother Russia. Stalin did not foresee that Hitler, after testing Britain's strength in 1940 and 1941 and finding it considerable, would relax his hold on England and drive into Russia.

Stalin misunderstood Hitler and the world situation. That is why he made the pact with Hitler.

The Soviet-Nazi pact and its subsidiary agreements were a bargain with benefits, some real, some illusory, to each side.

The pact "has guaranteed Germany undisturbed security in the east," the *Pravda* affirmed on August 23, 1940. That was true and it meant victories for Hitler in the west.

Appreciable quantities of fodder, grain, flax, petroleum (700,000 tons of oil in 1940), and other products flowed from Russia to Germany and from Japan, through Russia, to Germany.

The Communist parties of Europe, and of the world, suddenly converted to pacifism, appeasement, and isolationism, turned their fire on Germany's enemies and withheld it from Germany. After the pact, this was inescapable. The Moscow press justified Hitler's invasion of Denmark and Norway. In the *Pravda* of November 30, 1940, Stalin said: "It was not Germany who attacked France and England, but France and England who attacked Germany, thus assuming responsibility for the present war." Since Stalin blamed the war on France and England, how could Communists in the democracies be pro-French or pro-British? Throughout the Soviet Union, during the pact period, anti-Fascist and anti-German propaganda ceased. Anti-Nazi films like Friederich Wolf's *Professor Mamlock* and anti-German films like Eisenstein's *Alexander Nevsky* were ordered taken off the screen; but Eisenstein staged Wagner's *Die Walkuere* and Nazi officials in Moscow shook his hand, the hand of a Jew, and congratulated him. All this was inevitable after the Hammer and Sickle flew intertwined with the Swastika from Soviet flagpoles. Had not the *Izvestia* of October 9, 1939, with unwonted detachment, declared: "Every person is free to express his attitude to this or that ideology; he has the right to defend or reject it. . . . It is possible to respect or hate Hitlerism or any other system of political ideas. That—is a matter of taste." With Moscow discarding its anti-Fascism and suggesting tolerance towards Nazis, how could the outside Communist parties be anti-Nazi? To have been anti-Nazi and pro-war in those days was tantamount, in effect, to being anti-Stalin. So Communists in the democracies fomented defense-plant strikes; the American Communist party called off its boycott of Made-in-Germany goods; its White House pickets, till the very day Hitler marched into Russia, carried placards denouncing Roosevelt's anti-Nazi stand. The British Communists sabotaged the war effort even during the murderous air blitz. The French Communists did what they could to hasten their country's defeat. If Stalin signed the pact with Hitler in order to gain time to strengthen Russia, why did the Communists help Hitler and thus weaken Russia by undermining the war effort of the nations that were fighting Hitler?

Finally, the fact that the Soviet government, once the foremost anti-Fascist power and champion of collective security, could, whatever the provocation or attraction, conclude a far-reaching agreement with the Germany of anti-Communist, anti-Jewish, anti-democratic atrocities, with the racist, rapacious, barbarous Fascist government of Germany, helped to promote that cynical disregard of principle and that political immorality which hastened Pétain's surrender to Hitler and which still lingers among us. The Soviet-Nazi pact was the parent of many unprincipled acts and unprincipled thoughts. Any lapse from decency in public affairs was grist to Hitler's mill and is grist now to the mill of totalitarianism.

These were Hitler's dividends from the Soviet-Nazi pact.

What were Russia's dividends?

Russia annexed territory. First, Russia annexed eastern Poland up to the Ribbentrop-Molotov Line or, as most people later heard of it, the Curzon Line. This was done by arrangement with Germany. In a speech at Danzig on October 24, 1939, Ribbentrop affirmed that a few days after the war in Poland began, "Russian troops moved forward on the entire front and occupied Polish territory up to the line of demarcation which we had previously agreed upon with the Russians."

I would not take Ribbentrop's word for anything unless acts bore it out. The fact is that in pursuing the Polish Army the Reichswehr went beyond the Ribbentrop-Molotov Line, and wherever this happened the German armed units withdrew immediately the Red Army presented itself. The victorious Reichswehr would not have done this without prior instructions from the Nazi government to regard the line as the agreed frontier between the Soviet and German zones.

When Hitler began his propaganda barrage against Poland with a view to intimidating Warsaw and forcing it to yield without a struggle, Foreign Commissar Litvinov on November 27, 1938, gave the Polish ambassador in Moscow a solemn reaffirmation of Russia's non-aggression treaty with Poland. This was intended as encouragement to the Poles to stand firm. On June 29, 1939, Molotov, who had meantime become Foreign Commissar, officially assured the Polish embassy in Moscow that Poland, if attacked, would be given Soviet economic assistance and also the right of transit through Soviet territory to Poland from the port of Murmansk. Trade Commissar Mikoyan, a highly placed Communist, repeated this pledge to the Polish authorities. As long as the Kremlin saw the possibility of an agreement with the Western powers it did not raise the question of the passage of the Red Army through Poland, presumably to fight the Germans, because every Soviet official knew, as Litvinov told me repeatedly during the Munich crisis in 1938, that no Polish government could permit Russian troops to enter its country. In the Moscow talks between Russia, England, and France, the Soviets did not bring up the matter of the Red Army's entry into Poland until after August 15, when the Soviet-Nazi pact of August 23, 1939, had already been drafted and when it was clear that Russia would not help Poland. This issue then served as the reason for breaking off the talks.

Stalin knew he could not get a piece of Poland by direct negotiations with Warsaw or by talks with the French and British. He did get a share of Poland from Hitler. The same is true of the Baltic states. In the talks with France and England, the Soviet government demanded special rights in the Baltic states. The British and French regarded the Baltic countries as independent nations and therefore could not authorize Stalin to take their military bases. But Hitler did authorize Stalin.

This procedure was characteristic of Stalin. He tried to get what he wanted in one way and, finding the way blocked, he waited, made a detour, and tried to obtain the same thing in another way. He did this often at home and he did it in foreign policy. Stalin moves straight ahead by zigzags. Blocked by the scruples of the British and French, Stalin broke off his negotiations with them and signed an agreement with Hitler whereby Russia won territory in Poland and established a protectorate over the small Baltic countries. Later, this area was absorbed into the Soviet Union.

On June 22, 1941, in announcing the war on Russia, Hitler declared that during the negotiations leading to the Soviet-Nazi pact, "a special agreement was concluded in case Britain were to succeed in inciting Poland actually into war with Germany." If Poland did not fight, Russia was to get a share of Poland. If Poland did fight, the special agreement provided for additional Russian gains in the Baltics. Hitler said: "Germany solemnly affirmed in Moscow that Esthonia, Latvia, Finland, and Bessarabia, but not Lithuania, lay outside all German political influence." Germany recognized this area as a Soviet sphere of influence.

Documents presented at the great Nuremberg trial corroborate Hitler's version. The facts confirm it. On September 28, 1939, Esthonia, under Moscow's pressure, signed a mutual-assistance pact giving Russia bases on the Baltic Sea. October 5: Latvia signed a similar pact with Russia. October 16: Lithuania signed a similar pact with Russia.

November 30: Russia invaded Finland. With the exception of the occupation of Lithuania to which Hitler agreed after the event, this was in accordance with the Soviet-Nazi understanding of August, 1939, and to fulfill his part of the bargain, Hitler ordered all Germans to return to Germany from the Baltic countries where they had resided for many generations. Hundreds of thousands complied.

The next phase of Soviet expansion opened on June 27, 1940, when Russian troops entered Rumania and occupied Bessarabia and northern Bukovina. On July 21, Lithuania, Latvia, and Esthonia were annexed outright by the Soviet Union. Hitler was preoccupied with France and then with Britain. The German Army faced west. Stalin made hay.

Nazi Foreign Minister von Ribbentrop stated on June 22, 1941, that Russia's bolshevization and annexation of the Baltic nations were "contrary to the express assurances given by Moscow." Molotov corroborated this; Russia's new treaties with Esthonia, Latvia, and Lithuania, he said, "firmly stipulate the inviolability of the sovereignty of the signatory nations as well as the principle of non-interference in the affairs of the other nation." And he added emphatically: "The chatter about the sovietization of the Baltic countries is profitable only to our mutual enemies and all anti-Soviet provocateurs." This very explicit statement on October 31, 1939, did not prevent Molotov's government from annexing and sovietizing the Baltic countries on July 21, 1940. Nor did the act prevent Molotov from asserting that the Soviet government always kept its promises.

The German campaign in Poland yielded Russia a dividend in Poland and the Baltics. The German campaign in western Europe yielded Russia a dividend in Rumania and the Baltics. It was to gain territory and not to gain time that Moscow signed the pact with the Nazis. With the dismissal of Litvinov and the conclusion of the Soviet-Nazi pact in 1939, Russia launched on her career of expansion which still continues.

In June, 1936, Stalin had said: "We want not a foot of foreign territory but we shall not relinquish an inch of our own." This had always been the guiding principle of Soviet foreign policy. Stalin did not say: We want not a foot of foreign territory except eastern Poland, or except the Baltic states, or except a piece of Finland. He said: "We want not a foot of foreign territory." The apologists for Stalin will have to decide whether he really believed in this principle or whether he enunciated it in 1936 because Russia was too weak to be an aggressor and dropped it in 1939 when Russia became strong enough to make annexations.

Although in the wake of revolution Russia lost eastern Poland, the Baltic states, Finland, and Bessarabia, she was not invaded after 1920. She was invaded in 1941 when she had regained them. She was invaded by Germany with whose help she had regained them.

It is a natural law of world affairs, today perhaps the most important law, that the appetite for expansion comes with expansion. Expansion breeds more expansion. By the summer of 1940, Russia had taken most of the lands which once belonged to the Tsar's empire as well as East Galicia and northern Bukovina which had never belonged to Russia. Nevertheless, Defense Commissar Timoshenko declared in Moscow on November 7, 1940: "The Soviet Union has extended its frontiers, but we cannot be contented with what has already been achieved." Russia accordingly tried to expand farther into the Balkans.

In September, 1940, France lay prostrate under the heel of Hitler's black boot. But the air blitz raged furiously over Britain. The U-boat campaign had become a serious menace in the Atlantic. This seemed to Stalin a perfect moment for another great effort. However, Germany was alert in the east despite her activity in the west. Leland Stowe, consistent anti-Nazi journalist, telegraphed from Bucharest to the *New York Post*, September 20, 1940: "Berlin has successfully checkmated Russia's recent designs for further expansion into Rumania. . . . There can be no doubt that the Kremlin's hopes for a September occupation of Bulgaria, and perhaps of a Black Sea strip of territory down to Bulgaria, received an ice-cold douche. . . . This does not mean that Moscow has abandoned its expansionist aspirations in the Balkans." In another dispatch dated October 14, 1940, from Budapest, Stowe confirmed his Bucharest findings. "Stalin's Red Army," he wired, "is now frozen out of the Balkans."

Having won this bloodless political war, Hitler invited Foreign Commissar Molotov to Berlin. Molotov was there on November 12. Newsreels of his arrival at the railway station show him tipping his felt hat to every Reichswehr officer he passed. But his flat face looked grim. He was about to conduct fateful conversations with Hitler.

There was a story in circulation at the time about microphones hidden by the Gestapo in the couch on which Molotov sat during his talks with Hitler. Subsequently, the tale ran, the Germans played the microphone records to Turkish and other officials in order to prove how Hitler protected their interests against Russia. This may not be true but no one would put it beyond the Nazis.

Regarding the contents of the historic Hitler-Molotov interviews, we have only the versions which Hitler and Ribbentrop gave on June 22, 1941. Hitler said: "The Soviet Minister for Foreign Affairs then demanded Germany's clarification of our agreement to the following four questions:

"Point one was Molotov's question: Was the German guarantee for Rumania also directed against Soviet Russia in case of attack by Soviet Russia on Rumania?

"My answer: The German guarantee is a general one and is unconditionally binding on us. Russia, however, never declared to us that she had other interests in Rumania beyond Bessarabia. . . ." In other words, Hitler was saying that Germany would defend Rumania against Russia.

Hitler's version proceeds: "Molotov's second question: Russia again felt menaced by Finland . . . Was Germany ready not to give any aid to Finland?

"My answer: Germany continued to have absolutely no political interests in Finland. A fresh war by Russia against the small Finnish people could not, however, be regarded any longer by the German government as tolerable, all the more so as we could never believe Russia to be threatened by Finland. . . .

"Molotov's third question: Was Germany prepared to agree that Russia give a guarantee to Bulgaria and send Russian troops to Bulgaria for this purpose in connection with which he—Molotov—was prepared to state that the Soviets did not intend on that account, for example, to depose the King?

"My answer: Bulgaria was a sovereign state, and I had no knowledge that Bulgaria had ever requested Soviet Russia for any kind of guarantee such as Rumania had requested from Germany. . . .

"Molotov's fourth question: Soviet Russia requires free passage through the Dardanelles under all circumstances, and for her protection also demands occupation of a number of important bases on the Dardanelles and the Bosporus. Was Germany in agreement with this or not?

"My answer: Germany was prepared at all times to agree to alteration of the Statutes of Montreux in favor of the Black Sea states. Germany was not prepared to agree to Russia taking possession of bases on the straits."

Hitler's assumed tone of innocence and his pose as the defender of the Balkan nations and Finland will deceive nobody. Hitler had his own designs on the Balkans and resented Russian interference. But Molotov and Hitler did discuss Balkan problems. Indeed, Hitler's outline of Molotov's demands resembles the policy which Russia actually adopted after the Red Army's smashing victories in 1944.

Molotov returned to Moscow on November 16. Hitler immediately ordered the representatives of Slovakia, Hungary, and Rumania to appear before him and join the Axis. They obeyed. When Hungary obeyed, the official Soviet telegraphic agency *Tass* declared on November 22 that Hungary had acted without Moscow's approval. *Tass* was thus indicating Moscow's disapproval. But Hitler paid no attention. Amid applause from Mussolini but with little Italian help, Germany was making the Balkans a rampart. For what purpose?

A big development impended. This time Hitler prepared slowly. He did not occupy Bulgaria until March, 1941. On March 3, the Soviet government officially condemned the occupation. Relations between Russia and Germany had visibly deteriorated after Molotov's trip to Berlin, and now they were critical.

Hitler was locking his back door in the Balkans before crashing Russia's front door. But he still had to clean up Yugoslavia and Greece. Yugoslavia was Germany's corridor to Greece where in January and February, 1941, the great Duce's army was being humiliated and mutilated by poorly-equipped Greek forces.

Accordingly, late in March, 1941, Hitler applied his well-known squeeze-and-terror technique and forced the Yugoslav government to join the Axis. Reactionaries and royalists in Belgrade did not object. But the people objected, and military circles objected. Together they staged a revolt and overthrew the Cabinet, which had signed on Hitler's dotted line. Official American sources regarded this *coup d'état* as British-made. The Nazis said it was Soviet-made. Britain as well as Russia wanted to make Yugoslavia a running sore for Germany. In Yugoslavia the British were defending Suez and India; the Russians were defending Moscow.

On March 27, a new anti-Axis government led by General Dusan Simovich seized power in Yugoslavia and started fighting the Reichswehr. On April 5, the Soviet government signed a treaty of amity with this new Yugoslav cabinet. That was open defiance of Hitler.

The *Red Star*, Russia's army paper, stated on April 9 that the Reichswehr was experiencing trouble in Yugoslavia and stressed the traditional martial qualities of the Yugoslavs. "The British command," it added, "headed by General Sir Archibald Wavell, has taken serious measures to help the ally."

The Kremlin looked for sustained Yugoslav and Greek resistance to Germany and expected the British to aid both countries.

The fighting in the Balkans meant war or peace for Russia. There was a possibility that the Reichswehr, after smashing Greece, would keep going in the same direction—to Crete, to Egypt, to Syria, to Iraq, and on to India. Many German generals advocated this strategy. Russia would then be in no imminent danger.

In April, 1941, Rashid Ali rose against the British in Iraq. The next month, the Vichy authorities gave the Germans permission to use the French airfields in Syria. One field, at Aleppo, was placed entirely at the disposal of the Nazis. From Syria, the Germans supplied Rashid Ali. Meanwhile, an Italo-German force fought the British in North Africa.

Would Hitler move on India and join the Japanese? Unsuccessful in the direct assault on the British Isles, Hitler might try to break the British Empire. Germany's attention would be diverted far away from Soviet territory.

These Russian hopes proved vain. Hitler threw concentrated strength against Yugoslavia and Greece and by the end of April both countries were overrun. Soon Europe throbbed with reports and rumors of German troop transfers from the Balkans and France to the Russian frontier. Reichswehr units appeared in Finland.

Alarm swept Moscow. Stalin acted with the vigor and dispatch which have given him power and eminence. On May 6, he removed Molotov and made himself Chairman of the Council of People's Commissars, or Premier—head of the Soviet government. Stalin was then sixty-two.

In a letter dated May 8, 1941, addressed to Sumner Welles, Under-Secretary of State, I wrote: "An attack by Hitler on Russia, or Nazi pressure on Russia to yield more goods for Germany's prosecution of the war would demonstrate the bankruptcy of appeasement as initiated by the pact of August 23, 1939. In the event of war or if events proved recent Soviet diplomacy a failure, Stalin would want to have all the reins of power *and office* in his hand, and he would wish no such reins in the hand of another." In a crisis, the occupation of the highest seat by a puppet like Molotov might constitute an element of weakness. So Stalin took the seat.

Simultaneously, Stalin prepared his army for war. But he had not yet abandoned hope of appeasing Hitler again and deflecting Hitler's efforts towards the British East. The Kremlin's mood changed abruptly from defiance to compliance. On May 9, the Soviet government withdrew recognition from the governments of Norway and Belgium and canceled the diplomatic privileges of their diplomatic representatives in Moscow. Norway and Belgium had been living under Hitler domination for a year. Nevertheless, the Kremlin continued to accept their ambassadors. Now it rejected them. The Soviet government also withdrew recognition from Yugoslavia with whom it had signed a pact of friendship only a month earlier. And, as a special gesture to please Hitler, the Soviets recognized Rashid Ali, the anti-British rebel of Iraq.

Things were coming to a head.

Suddenly, the world, dulled by an excess of sensational events, thrilled to a super-sensation. Rudolf Hess, Hitler's deputy, flew to Scotland and on May 10 descended by parachute near the vast estate of the Duke of Hamilton. A surprised Scot farmer, wielding a two-tooth pitchfork, captured the Number Two Nazi.

Several months later, in London, I discussed the Hess riddle with Foreign Secretary Anthony Eden, Home Secretary Herbert S. Morrison, Clement R. Attlee, Deputy Prime Minister, Professor Harold J. Laski, Labor leader and publicist, and others. Here is my conversation with Eden:

He: "We told the Russians of the coming German invasion three weeks before it took place."

I: "They must have known earlier. When Hess flew to Scotland they must have been sure of it."

He: "Why?"

I: "He made his flight on May 10. By that time the preparations for the attack of June 22 were certainly under way. One doesn't mount such an attack in less than six weeks."

He: "Do you think Hess was opposed to the attack on Russia?"

I: "No. But he wanted you to call off your war on Germany."

At this an eloquent silence ensued and I felt that I had hit the mark.

The pieces of evidence I gathered made the picture quite clear. Hess knew of the coming assault on the Soviet Union. Hitler's *Mein Kampf*, which Hess helped to write, was not anti-British. It stressed Germany's need of the Ukraine and of an arrangement with Britain by which Germany could seize that rich area. What was more natural, then, than that the Nazis should seek an arrangement with Britain when they were about to attack Russia?

Hess, pathologically high-strung, thought Britain had had enough of the war with Germany. No totalitarian understands how democracies operate. Hess remembered the appeasing British lords who visited him before the war. He believed they still had influence. He did not know that appeasement of Germany was dead for the duration. He imagined he could revive it by telling the British of the forthcoming invasion of the Soviet Union. He was wrong. Churchill merely passed the important news on to Stalin, and Hess stayed in a British jail.

Churchill's telegram was not the only concrete advance notice Stalin had of the Nazi invasion. Between April 21 and June 21, German planes crossed the Soviet frontier 180 times and some of them penetrated nearly 400 miles taking photographs. Correspondents in Moscow were given this information on June 28 by Solomon A. Lozovsky, Assistant Commissar of Foreign Affairs.

The Nazi invasion nevertheless found Russia psychologically unprepared.

Maxim Litvinov, flying the Pacific to take up his new post as Soviet ambassador in Washington, D. C., stopped in Honolulu two days before the Japanese assault on Pearl Harbor. Entertained by the highest American Army and Navy officials, he told them about the unexpectedness of the Nazi blow against Russia. He said a country at peace cannot get accustomed to the idea that it may soon be attacked and so it is caught unawares. At this very moment, he stated, the Japanese may be planning war on the United States; they might strike Honolulu. Litvinov advised the American officers to be vigilant day and night. He had learned wisdom from Russia's "Pearl Harbor."

At 4 A.M. on June 22, 1941, the Nazis struck without warning. That first day, the Soviets lost one thousand planes, most of them on the ground. "When Hitler invaded Russia he did so without a word to Stalin, not a hint," Harry Hopkins wrote in the *American Magazine* of December, 1941, after his visit to Russia as President Roosevelt's special emissary. Hitler made no demands on Russia. Demands would have been a warning. Hitler did not want anything from Russia. He wanted Russia. "In Moscow, in the Kremlin," Hopkins continued, "it aroused a hatred of Hitler that nothing but the death of the German Chancellor could lessen. . . . The invasion was regarded in Moscow as the treachery of a partner who had suddenly revealed himself as a rabid dog."

"Suddenly."

Hopkins stresses Stalin's disappointment over Hitler. "Once we trusted this man," Stalin said to Hopkins. "Stalin told me," Hopkins writes in the article, "that he had no intention of doing anything but be straightforward in his dealings with Germany." The Soviets would not have attacked Germany.

Stalin had believed to the end that Hitler would remain loyal to the Soviet-Nazi pact and try to crush the British Empire. That is why Stalin persisted in appeasing Hitler. Instead, Hitler was loyal to *Mein Kampf* and to the ideas of Hess, and tried to crush Russia.

4. *I Predict*

I FIND it endlessly exciting to look back over the recent past. The same events become different. Pearl Harbor was one thing on the morning of December 8, 1941, when every American felt as though he had fallen and hit his head against a hard pavement. But remembering Pearl Harbor years later brings pride in subsequent achievements.

On reading the speeches of Molotov, Hitler, Lindbergh, Stalin, Roosevelt, and others a few years ago I had one impression. My impression on reading them today is very different, for I now understand those speeches better than those who delivered them could have understood on the day of delivery. I have years of events to check against their words.

History always lends perspective. But history of half a century ago deals with happenings which, though they continue to affect our lives, are in themselves ended, as, say, the American war with Spain is ended or President Cleveland's administration is ended, whereas events that occurred two or three years ago may still be incomplete. Despite V-E day, for instance, the war in Europe is not over. We do not know its political results. Hitler has gone, but which way is Germany going? The future will change the meaning of the past.

A statesman making policy often relies chiefly on his ability to predict the future. He assumes certain developments and assumes that the measures he advocates will adequately meet those developments. Nothing, they say, is certain about the future except that it is uncertain. Yet occasionally it is certain. In 1940 Franklin D. Roosevelt could not have foreseen Britain's fate, but he was certain that with American help that fate, and America's, would be better. In such circumstances, policy-making is easy if the policy-maker gets public support.

An element of the past is always present in the future; it is on this element that predictions and policy are based. Prophecy that is merely wild guessing—the common variety of prophecy—is not creative and has no value. Worthwhile prophecy analyzes the known in order to grope for the unknown. It fits together the available facts of the past. From this the shape of the missing puzzle piece becomes apparent. And not only the general shape. By studying the pieces that touch this missing piece you may see that there would have to be a red

37

sleeve and a button in the missing space. In every capital of the world, statesmen and journalists are constantly playing with political jigsaw puzzles.

"When will the war end?" everybody used to ask. Only a charlatan or fool would try to reply. Too many unknown quantities entered into the answer. Many political situations are likewise so opaque as to defy analysis and therefore serious prognostication. But some do yield to prophecy.

We all make predictions either to ourselves or audibly to others. We boast of those that come true; we forget those that are wrong.

Early in 1941, the enigma of Japan and the riddle of Russia tormented American observers. Washington needed clues to the future policies of Tokyo and Moscow. The United States government, very properly, sought to improve relations with Russia in the hope of thus weaning Stalin from Hitler. President Roosevelt had imposed a moral embargo on Russia on December 2, 1939, because of Soviet air attacks on Finnish cities. More than two years later, on January 21, 1941, Under-Secretary of State Sumner Welles informed Soviet envoy Constantine Oumansky that the embargo had been lifted. This looked like a minor measure which would enable a few American businessmen to export to the Soviet Union.

It occurred to me, however, that it might be a very mistaken move. Its significance, I thought, had been misjudged in some comments I had seen. For instance, Arthur Krock wrote in *The New York Times* of January 23, 1941, that "realists will welcome the gesture, the further proof that the Washington government is looking to its Far Eastern rear as well as to the Atlantic front when undertaking the all-out policy of British aid. . . ." It seemed to me, on the contrary, that Washington was exposing its Far Eastern position to serious dangers. I therefore decided to volunteer my views to Sumner Welles. I had never seen him or written to him and I could not gauge what his reaction might be. But I would take a chance.

I accordingly sent the following letter:

Jan. 24, 1941

Mr. Sumner Welles,
Under-Secretary of State,
Washington, D. C.

Dear Mr. Welles,

I was for 14 years an American journalist in Moscow and wrote a two-volume history of Soviet foreign relations. This letter will deal with the recently announced decision of the United States government to lift the moral embargo on shipments of certain commodities to the Soviet Union.

I think the decision is a bad one chiefly because it may achieve a result detrimental to American interests. It could easily contribute to an improvement of Russo-Japanese relations.

This is how I arrive at my conclusions: Russia's present embarrassment and difficult international situation arise from the exposure of its western frontier to German pressure and of the eastern expanses to simultaneous Japanese pressure. Russia is too weak to cope with Germany or antagonize Germany. But if it could weaken or divert Japan its position would be improved and the fear of Germany lessened.

Russia can weaken Japan by supporting Chinese armed resistance. It has done this. But it is expensive. . . .

A better way of relieving Japanese pressure on Russia would be for Moscow to try to direct Japanese expansion southward towards Siam and the Dutch East Indies. This would also serve Germany's interests. Even a great Japanese victory in China would not help Hitler soon in Europe. But the end of the Chinese war would help Hitler by enabling Japan to concentrate on areas to the south of her where we and the British get vital materials. The Bolsheviks would hope that Japan's efforts in the South Seas might involve her with the United States and the British Empire and thus enfeeble Japan. . . .

An agreement with Russia becomes all the more important to Tokyo since we are helping Chiang. Help from America and Russia to Chiang might spell disaster to Japan. If Russia dropped Chiang our help would not be effective. Similarly, an agreement between Russia and Japan is facilitated by any appearance of improvement in the relations between the United States and Russia. Fearing such an agreement, Japan will court Russia more. If we could get Russia to quit Hitler everything would be worth while. But Russia is too exposed and too much in doubt about the outcome of the war to be actively or openly anti-Hitler. Accordingly, our friendlier attitude towards Moscow can only frighten the Japanese into coming to terms with Russia.

For Oumansky, whom I have known well for 10 years, the lifting of the moral embargo is a cap feather, and that is probably why he urged it with such insistence. But you recall, of course, that in the summer of 1939 the Russians used every concession and friendly gesture by London and Paris to sell themselves more dearly to Hitler. And the real objection I would have to the recent steps towards a *rapprochement* between us and Moscow is that Moscow might easily use them to intimidate the Japanese into signing a pact which would channel Japanese aggression southward, undermine Chiang's position, give the Russians a Communist zone of domination in China—partition of China *à la* Poland—without, however, freeing Stalin from Hitler's grip.

Well, this has become much too long and I shall stop. I hope I have conveyed my thought.

I would be pleased to discuss this in person with you, this and other questions. It is not the reason for this letter. But I will be in Washington as part of a lecture tour and I would appreciate the opportunity of meeting you. It would not, of course, be an interview for publication or quotation. Unfortunately, my schedule allows me only February 3 from 9:30 A.M. to 11:15 A.M. Could you see me then? Or I could break a trip and be in Washington on February 11, but I prefer February 3. I hope you can fit me in.

> Very respectfully,
> (*Signed*) Louis Fischer

This, if I say so myself, was good prophesying. When I wrote the letter, no Russo-Japanese agreement was in the news and the likelihood of a Japanese attack on Britain and the United States seemed remote. But on April 13, 1941, the Soviet and Japanese governments signed a far-reaching pact pledging the parties not to fight one another for at least five years. And that was the beginning of the Japanese assault on Singapore, Malaya, and Hawaii.

Sumner Welles replied on January 30, and asked me to come see him on either of the dates I had suggested. I chose February 11 because I thought he would have more time then. He received me in his office in the State Department across the street from the White House.

Sumner Welles is tall and straight with a sort of ramrod straightness. He is broad-shouldered, well-built, and an immaculate dresser. His head is long and distinguished. He speaks with a deep, throaty voice. The requirements of diplomacy have added to his natural reserve. He seems to be completely incapable of small talk but he likes intellectual adventure and when engaged in it his desire to probe a problem to its depths may overcome his great inner restraint. He is very frank when he knows he will be understood. His brain is a precision instrument and his memory phenomenal. There is no arrogance in him, though to an unsympathetic eye he might give a contrary impression. He has a sense of humility about his writings.

As I entered his office for my first conversation with him, he gave me his hand across a clean, flat desk, asked me to sit down near a window, eyed me for a long moment, took out a cigarette and bounced it on a gold cigarette case and, after saying, "Mr. Fischer, I was exceedingly interested in your letter," proceeded straight, in the very first question, to the heart of the subject matter of my letter. When I returned from the State Department to my hotel room I made a practically stenographic record of our talk. I have formed a habit of keeping a diary of important political interviews. Usually I write them down the same day and I think the entries are verbatim reproductions.

"What, in your opinion," Welles began, "is Russia's objective in the Far East?"

I took a long moment to formulate my reply, and said: "The weakening of Japan."

"And what is the long-range objective?" he asked.

"The domination of China," I said.

"Do you believe," he continued, "that Russia wants to dominate all of China or would she prefer to partition China?"

I liked this undisguised cross-examination; his questions would tell me what was in his mind. Later, I thought, I might try to question him.

Moscow, I suggested, hoped first to control the Chinese Communist provinces near the Soviet Union but that did not preclude Russian influence in other parts of China.

"I think that is correct," Welles declared.

He paused and puffed on his cigarette. "To return to the original point," he went on, "do you think it is Moscow's purpose in the Far East to involve Japan in a war with the United States?"

"Yes," I said, "as a means of enfeebling Japan."

"I agree," he announced.

"The Bolsheviks," I remarked, "have usually taken the long view in foreign affairs, but I don't see them doing that now. Since their pact with Hitler they are working on short order and I don't believe they are seeing as far as the end of their present line." He was lighting another cigarette; he is practically a chain smoker. "My chief objection to the lifting of the moral embargo against Russia," I said, "is that the Russians might use our friendly gesture to get an agreement with Japan."

Welles: "That is sure to happen."

L.F.: "Do you know what Stalin wants from Tokyo?"

Welles: "Moscow has asked for southern Sakhalin and the Chinese provinces you mentioned."

L.F.: "Do you think the Japanese will put any faith in Soviet promises to keep out of Manchuria?"

Welles: "If you call it faith it is compounded of various factors: for instance, Japan's trust that the Germans will check Soviet activities in Asia by pressing Russia in Europe. Also, it is a fact that in the last two months, Russia has sent more arms to Chiang Kai-shek than at any time in the last two years."

L.F.: "Do you think that might be pressure on Japan to come to an agreement with Moscow?"

Welles: "That is how I have understood it. The Japanese Navy, which would have to carry out the expansion southward, is the least desirous of undertaking it. But the army is stronger politically."

L.F.: "Why is the navy reluctant?"

Welles: "If you want me to be frank I will say it is because the admirals are better educated politically and have a keener grasp of world affairs."

L.F.: "I think nowadays the factor which shapes policy most is the opportunity to act. Events in Siam and the collapse of the French in Indo-China created opportunities for Japan, and the existence of those opportunities was more decisive than any cogitation or planning in Tokyo."

Welles (with emphasis): "I am sure you are very right."

We then discussed the American and British attitudes towards the Chinese and Indian peoples. I mentioned Jawaharlal Nehru, the Indian nationalist leader.

Welles: "We know Pandit Nehru and respect him highly. How would Nehru react if Japan made war on England and the United States?"

L.F.: "I believe Nehru would be very anti-Japanese. That would be his emotional reaction. His policy, however, would depend on what the British did. The British can be democratic at home, but in India they have been pretty stupid. India is the last outpost of British reaction and I suppose the Tories will hold on to it as long as possible."

Welles: "There is much sympathy here for a liberal attitude towards India. When did you see Nehru last?"

L.F.: "In Geneva in September, 1938, and before that in Paris and London."

With no transition, and quite suddenly, Welles said: "What do you think is the situation in Russia, the strength of the Red Army?"

L.F.: "It would be a mistake to underestimate the Red Army and Air Force. But if the Germans wished they could probably take the Ukraine and part of the Caucasus."

Welles: "Why should they want to do that?"

L.F.: "If Hitler cannot invade Britain, he may anticipate a long war and might therefore decide to clean up Russia first."

Welles: "Wouldn't that give Germany a two-front war?"

L.F.: "No, Hitler's assumption is that though England could not be successfully invaded, neither could she invade the Continent for at least a year and Hitler's attack on Russia would be designed to push Russia back so she could not create a second front during a future British invasion of Occupied Europe."

Welles: "But that wouldn't be the end of it."

L.F.: "No, but it might postpone Hitler's troubles."

Welles: "If Germany tries an invasion of England wouldn't that enable Russia to apply more pressure to Japan?"

L.F.: "It might also have the opposite effect, for if Germany tried an invasion of England and failed, Hitler could concentrate on Russia and then Japan would be better off."

Welles: "All this is of course conjecture. Events of the next few months will show who is right."

L.F.: "There are also other factors to be considered. A German conquest of Bulgaria would likewise weaken Russia and that would help Japan."

Welles: "That is correct. I don't suppose Russia would do anything to oppose a German occupation of Bulgaria."

L.F.: "I have been saying just that in my lectures. But doesn't Bulgaria raise the Turkish question? The Russians and Germans might decide to partition Turkey."

Welles: "Germany made that offer to Moscow last October."

L.F.: "I don't see where the line of demarcation would be. The important spot is Istanbul and who would get that?"

Welles: "I cannot answer that one."

L.F.: "I once wrote a history of Soviet foreign affairs . . ."

Welles: "An amazingly fine book . . ."

L.F.: "I left out of it some material which Rakovsky [Christian G. Rakovsky, once Soviet ambassador in London and Paris] gave me because it might have embarrassed him with Stalin. Rakovsky told me of Stalin's special interest in Turkey and Iran. It is remarkable that Stalin, a Bolshevik, should be influenced in the formulation of foreign policy by the geography of his native Georgia. Ever since 1919 all Bolsheviks have been pro-Turk because Kemal Pasha was anti-imperialist and anti-clerical. But the Georgian Bolsheviks had their doubts, for they remembered that in March, 1921, the Turks seized the

Georgian port of Batum, and the Georgian Communists therefore want to push back the Turkish frontier. Stalin has also been interested in northern Iran which borders on Georgia."

Welles nodded assent. I did not know how much longer he would let me stay so I brought up the matter of the moral embargo. I said: "In view of Stalin's necessity to work with Hitler and since our friendly gestures towards Russia might facilitate a Russo-Japanese agreement, I do not see why we lifted the embargo."

Welles: "For thirty-six months prior to July, 1940, conversations with Moscow were impossible. I believe in the necessity of contact and I still think contact is desirable."

L.F.: "I suppose Oumansky is pleased. He is a small man."

Welles: "He may be a small man but he is acute and he knows that in material goods the lifting of the embargo will mean nothing."

L.F.: "He is very acute. You recall that in my letter to you I did not even mention the goods which Russia might get in the new situation. I don't think she will get much. But I am afraid that she will use our friendship to put pressure on Japan."

Welles: "To return to an earlier point, you said that if Germany could not invade England the war would be long and England could not invade the Continent. England might invade through Italy."

That made me sit up. Was he revealing something? I said that Hitler would be by Mussolini's side and try to prevent the invasion.

Welles: "But it is difficult to guard an entire seacoast."

He put his hands on the arms of his chair and asked me whether I came to Washington regularly. I got up to go. He suggested that I write to him before my next visit to Washington. "I will be glad to see you again," he said.

This was the first of many extremely interesting and rewarding talks I have had with Sumner Welles in and out of office.

Japan saw a unique chance—while Britain was at war in Europe—of moving south into Dutch imperial and British imperial areas. Tokyo therefore wanted an agreement with Russia which would give Japan safety in the north.

Germany wanted to direct Japan southward because that would divert some British strength and some American help from Europe. Germany therefore helped Tokyo achieve a Russo-Japanese agreement. Hitler was not worried over the resulting reinforcement of Russia's position; he thought he could handle Russia alone.

The United States wanted to improve relations with Moscow in the hope of ultimately getting Russia to break with the Axis. The American government accordingly made a good-will gesture to the Kremlin by lifting the moral embargo.

Stalin used the improvement in his relations with America plus Japan's urge to go south plus Germany's wish to have Japan go south and succeeded in getting a neutrality treaty with Japan. Stalin wanted that treaty because Japan's involvement in the South Pacific left Russia with only one active threat, Germany.

By the terms of a frontier protocol attached to the Russo-Japanese treaty of April, 1941, Moscow recognized Japan's seizure of Manchuria which Russia had previously protested, and Japan recognized Russia's protectorate over Outer Mongolia, an important strategic area which China regarded as hers but which the Chinese had not ruled for many years. The treaty, in other words, was an accommodation between dynamic empires at the expense of China.

When Japanese Foreign Minister Matsuoka left Moscow after concluding the treaty, Stalin went to the railway station to see him off. It was the first time in history Stalin had done such a thing. Each of his deeds is carefully planned for effect. Henry C. Cassidy of the Associated Press, who was present at the station, reports that Stalin kissed Matsuoka good-bye. Then Stalin found Colonel Hans Krebs, the assistant Nazi military attaché who was on the station platform, shook his hand and said: "We shall be friends."

In a second interview with Sumner Welles on March 26, 1941, we again canvassed the possibility of a Nazi attack on Russia and delved again into the tense Pacific situation. When I talked with him on May 19, the Russo-Japanese pact had been signed, Hess had flown to Scotland, and stories of military preparations on both sides of the Russian frontier poured in from every European capital. Six days after the beginning of the Russo-German war, I had another hour with Welles in the State Department. We surveyed many aspects of the changed world situation. Before leaving, I asked him to help arrange my trip to Great Britain.

5. *Litvinov and Joseph E. Davies*

IN MY talk with Winston Churchill in London in October, 1939, we spent half an hour discussing how Russia might be won over to the British side. It was not given to any anti-Nazi, however, to bring Russia into the Allied camp. Hitler did that.

The outbreak of the Soviet-Nazi war provoked a word duel between Stalin and Litvinov. A revolutionist is generally assumed to be a rebel and non-conformist. But Soviet citizens are the strictest conformists on earth. In a dictatorship you conform, or else. . . . In a dictatorship, no one criticizes the government. Or rather, no one criticizes the government twice. Maxim Litvinov is the exception to both these rules.

Litvinov is a symbol and Stalin knows its value. Litvinov's name stands for collective security, anti-appeasement, and anti-aggression. When Moscow saw the prospect of linking up with Hitler it shelved Litvinov, its most militant anti-Hitlerite. When Hitler attacked Russia, Stalin took Litvinov from the shelf, brushed him off, put him on the radio to talk to England in his, fortunately, inimitable English, and later sent him to Washington as Ambassador.

Litvinov, unemployed for over two years, was playing cards with his wife Ivy in a log cabin near Moscow when the Nazis invaded Russia. Restored to use by Germany's wanton assault, Litvinov nevertheless refrained from the normal Soviet self-flagellation. He has never, by word or hint, approved of Stalin's pact policy with Hitler. Indeed, when Sir Stafford Cripps was British ambassador in Moscow in 1941 Litvinov said to him: "We burned our fingers" by signing with Germany. Over the Moscow radio on July 8, 1941, Litvinov subtly rebuked Stalin. "No agreements or treaties," he affirmed, "no undertaking signed by Hitler and his henchmen, no promises or assurances on their part, no declarations of neutrality, no relations with them whatsoever can provide a guarantee against a sudden unprovoked attack.

"In his diabolical plans for attacking other countries in order to fulfill his dream of world domination," Litvinov proceeded, "Hitler has always been ruled by the principle 'divide and attack.' He uses the most insidious means to prevent the intended victims from organizing common resistance, taking special pains to avoid war on two fronts against the most powerful European states. His strategy is to mark down his victims and strike them one by one in the order prompted by circumstances." This exact description of Hitler's policy towards Russia is a criticism of Stalin for having helped Hitler carry it out.

Hitler "intended first to deal with the Western states so as to be free to fall upon the Soviet Union," Litvinov continued. This was the brilliant Foreign Commissar's rebuttal to all those parlor diplomats who said Stalin had to sign the pact with Hitler in order to keep Germany from invading Russia after conquering Poland in 1939. No, you are wrong, Litvinov tells them; Hitler's plan was to go west first. That was obvious at the time, to Roosevelt among others.

But, Litvinov added, "There was a hitch somewhere. Hitler has not the training for a Channel swimmer yet." The Reichswehr was unable to invade England. "And so another plan matured in his brain. Believing that he had secured himself a *de facto* truce in the west, he decided to have a 'blitzkrieg,' a lightning war, in the east in order immediately afterwards to fall with added strength upon Great Britain and finish her off."

Litvinov understood.

Litvinov's broadcast of July 8 contradicted Stalin who had spoken on the radio in his Georgian-accented Russian on July 3, in defense of the Soviet-Nazi pact. Other Soviet contradictors and non-conformists are shot or exiled. But Litvinov was irreplaceable abroad and without influence at home. He came out of involuntary obscurity when Hitler attacked and Stalin wanted good relations with the West. He went back to semi-retirement as soon as Russian military victories made Stalin less dependent on London and Washington. He remained inactive but available in case Moscow ever wished to reassure the United States or Great Britain of its friendly intentions. President Roosevelt always thought Stalin disliked Litvinov. The reason probably was that Stalin needed Litvinov.

The Nazi invasion of Russia confronted the American government with the difficult task of supplying arms to the Soviet Union and with the delicate task of working up a pro-Russian public opinion at home. Towards this latter end, the State Department encouraged Joseph E. Davies, ex-Ambassador to Moscow, to write a book on the Soviet Union. The State Department assisted him in various ways; among other things it let him publish a sheaf of his secret diplomatic dispatches. Governments frequently try to manipulate public opinion; the temptation to do so is especially strong in wartime.

Joseph Davies' book achieved great vogue.

One day, Ambassador Davies took his beautiful, rich wife for a walk in the streets of Moscow. They passed several flower shops. The sight stimulated a flow of philosophy. "The male youth of the country, under the biological urge," mused the Wisconsin innocent abroad, "all wanted to prove to his particular lady love that he was better and bigger than his rival. To the degree that he could send better and bigger flowers—to that degree he was competitively demonstrating his greater desirability. He therefore had to make money. He could do so only through the application of the profit motive, the bane of pure Communism. The very essence of Communism, moreover, is a classless society. Here was a stimulus to create a class society. . . ." So, according to Davies, it is Love versus Socialism; big flowers win fair lady. Mr. Davies should have been told that Russians do not say it with flowers. Russians often bring flowers or flower pots to their hosts. But the average Soviet woman does not succumb to the bigger flower pot. If classes or castes are arising in the Soviet Union the reason is not the capitalistic necessities of courtship.

Mr. Davies often amused Moscow, especially Litvinov who has a highly developed sense of humor. After the execution of the Red Army's top-rank generals in June, 1937, Davies discussed the matter with Litvinov. "I asked him the direct question," Davies reports in his book, "as to whether the Government felt positive that it could rely on the support and loyalty of the Red Army." And what do you imagine Litvinov replied? He said: Yes, the Soviet government can rely on the Red Army's loyalty. Did Davies expect Litvinov to say that the army was disloyal?

The Bolshevik leaders liked Davies. He believed in good relations with Russia and that is the prime requisite of a good ambassador. The Kremlin prefers business or professional men like Davies, who are convinced capitalists, to a left-wing intellectual like Sir Stafford Cripps. Russia, of course, did not convert the capitalist Davies to Socialism. His *Mission to Moscow* is an anti-Soviet book. For instance:

"Realistically," writes Mr. Davies, "the Government is in fact one man—Stalin the 'strong man,' who survived the contest, completely disposed of his competitors, and is completely dominant."

"The terror here," Davies telegraphed the State Department in code, "is a horrifying fact. There are many evidences here in Moscow that there is a fear which reaches down into and haunts all sections of the community. No household, however humble, apparently but lives in constant fear of a nocturnal raid by the secret police (usually between one and three in the morning). Once the person is taken away, nothing of him or her is known for months—and many times never thereafter. . . . It is commonly alleged that the secret police of this proletarian dictatorship are as ruthless and cruel as any during the old Tsarist regimes."

"Communism won't work," Davies likewise writes in his book. "It hasn't worked here."

Further in condemnation of the Soviet regime, Mr. Davies affirms that "there are no considerations of honor or loyalty which control as against duty to party. The result is that there can be no confidence or faith between these men, in leadership. No man can trust another. It is a serious and basic weakness." Moreover, Soviet economy has been successful, Davies writes with italics, "not *because* of government operation of industry, but *in spite of it.*"

Why then has *Mission to Moscow* been hailed by Communists and partisans of Russia? That they welcomed it despite its rejection of Soviet principles and methods makes the book an interesting key to present pro-Soviet thinking. The Davies volume excoriated Stalin's personal dictatorship, but it lauds Stalin, extols Russia's industrial achievements, and supports Russia's foreign policy. Moreover, since writing the book Davies has sought to justify the Moscow trials, and he allowed *Mission to Moscow* to be distorted into a film which tries to demonstrate the guilt of the accused. This endeared him to the Stalinists.

The Moscow trials took place in 1936, 1937, and 1938. But they were a most crucial chapter in Soviet history and they were Stalin's handiwork. The Kremlin therefore still hopes to see the trials accepted by world public opinion as something other than a frame-up. So the debate on the trials and purges continues.

Now the Soviet secret police keeps a close watch on front-rank Soviet leaders. It observes their movements, telephone calls, and mail. Yet at the Moscow trials the state prosecution produced no jot of evidence. The sentences were based solely on self-incriminating confessions.

The puzzle of the confessions in the Moscow trials vanishes after a careful reading of the trial procedures which are available in English.

They show clearly that an agreement existed between the prosecution and the accused. The defendants confessed what the Government wanted them to confess. Many of the Soviet leaders, for example, were bitter opponents of Stalin. They felt that Stalin was ruining the Revolution and making Russia nationalist instead of internationalist, reactionary instead of progressive. In the Soviet Union, however, Stalin is considered infallible and inviolate. Since he can do no wrong nobody can charge him with mistakes. The accused at the trials adhered to this custom. Although any defendant in a Soviet trial may speak his mind freely, the accused in the Moscow trials did not speak their minds on Stalin. They glorified him after the manner of official Soviet spokesmen rather than pillorying him as they would have had to do in order to be true to their convictions.

The confessions were usually elicited after months—sometimes as many as ten months—of confinement in GPU prisons, during which the accused refused to confess. They refused until their will power was broken. Finally a compact was reached between prisoners and Government. The men on trial would be sentenced to death or long years of incarceration but would receive mercy in consideration of their proper conduct at the public trials. It is my belief that the accused were promised their lives and the lives of their families. Whether they were actually spared I do not know; neither were they sure that the GPU would keep its promise. Some children of the accused did remain alive; this is known. In any event, a person who realizes that he and his dear ones face instant death unless he plays the game will be inclined to take a chance.

The question is often asked why the accused at the Moscow trials did not choose death as so many revolutionists did under the Tsarist regime and in Nazi Germany. It was easier for a Bolshevik to defy the Tsar's police than to defy the Bolshevik government he himself helped to set up and which he preferred to any other despite his objections to its policies. When such a government asks him to sign a confession it knows is false, he becomes cynical and loses his desire to fight the injustice. This is part of the explanation. For the rest, it must be remembered that more Bolshevik leaders were executed without trials than confessed at trials. Only those who confessed were tried. Less than fifty were tried in Moscow. But thousands refused to confess and paid the supreme penalty.

The confessions falsify Soviet history. In this they merely follow a confirmed Soviet pattern. Every recent Soviet history book and every volume of the new Soviet encyclopedias falsifies history either by suppressing numerous important and proven facts which appeared in earlier editions or by inserting numerous pure unprovable inventions. The big lie is a treasured weapon of all dictatorships. It is used in books, in the press, in diplomacy as well as in trials.

In addition to the public trials of civilian Bolshevik leaders a court martial of the head of the Red Army, Marshal Tukhachevsky, and seven other marshals and generals, took place on June 11, 1937. This was a secret trial, the most important of all the Moscow trials. No outsider knows what happened there. The eight marshals and generals were tried by nine marshals and generals. Within a year, the majority of these judges were themselves executed. Information on the trial is completely lacking. Indeed, it has been said—but who can know such things in Russia?—that there never was a trial. All we have to go by is a brief bulletin in the Soviet newspapers stating that the accused were tried, confessed to treason, and were sentenced to death. The trial was followed by the liquidation of thousands of Red Army officers.

Davies wired the State Department on July 27, 1937, that "as to the alleged guilt of these army generals of overt acts—actual conspiracy with the German government—the general opinion is here that the charge is not justified. . . . Facts are not now available, and it is doubtful whether they will be for a long time to come, which would justify a statement as to exactly what happened and just what constituted the 'offense' of these officers of the Red Army. Opinions must be based on deductions from known facts and these are few."

In an article in the December, 1941, issue of the *American Magazine*, Mr. Davies made a confession of his own. He said he had "missed the boat" at the Moscow trials; he had attended the trials and not grasped the guilt of the accused. What was Davies' confession based on? Not on new evidence. No one has presented any. Neither the Soviet government nor its apologists have ever published the slightest proof that the Red Army generals, two of whom were Jews, conspired with Nazi Germany or Japan against their country. Not only proof but even the most elementary facts about the case are missing. Nor has anybody inside or outside the Kremlin given the world one iota of information on the guilt of the confessed civilian leaders. In all the years that have passed since the trials, Moscow, for reasons easy to comprehend, has revealed no facts that would corroborate the confessions.

At the Moscow trials, defendants stated that Leon Trotzky had personally conferred with Rudolf Hess, Hitler's deputy, and conspired to overthrow the Soviet government. This is a serious charge against Hess. Why was it not included in the indictment against Hess at the Nuremberg war criminals trial? There was a Soviet government prosecutor at that trial. Why did he not ask Hess about those talks with Trotzky? Was it because he knew they never took place?

Many secret Nazi documents have been published since Hitler's defeat. The United States government has published innumerable German state papers which cast invaluable light on hitherto unknown and very confidential matters. The Red Army conquered half of Germany; it conquered Berlin, the capital of Germany. Did it find no documents which proved that Tukhachevsky and his generals conspired with the Nazis to make war on Russia? Is it not interesting that Moscow has revealed no documents which would prove its charges against the accused or their confessions?

What then brought forth Davies' *American Magazine* true confession? He tells us it was the circumstance that Russia had no "fifth column." Mr. Davies is of course entitled to revise his opinions in the light of events. But how does the absence of a "fifth column" in the Soviet Union prove that those who were executed were "fifth columnists"? Many other countries, democratic as well as totalitarian, did not have a "fifth column." Perhaps Russia had no "fifth column" before the purge?

Some commentators found warrant for the Moscow trials and purges in the Red Army's triumph over the Reichswehr. Russia had a purge, they said in effect; Russia fought well against the Nazis; therefore Russia fought well because she had a purge. One might as well argue: Russia had a famine; Russia fought well against the Nazis; therefore Russia fought well because she had a famine.

The fact is that Russia paid a horrible price for the military purge. Why did little Finland hold up the Red Army so long? Why did it inflict such heavy casualties on the Soviet forces? The Kremlin thought Finland would be a pushover. Maybe the executed Tukhachevsky would not have been beguiled by the illusion that a Finnish revolution would open Finland to the invading Russians.

The weaknesses displayed by the Red Army in Finland encouraged Hitler to attack Russia and helped him overcome the objections of those of his generals, including Field Marshal Walther von Brauchitsch, who opposed that course.

The Red Army, needless to say, performed brilliantly against the Germans. But in the first months it performed badly and lost vast stretches of territory and hundreds of thousands in killed, captured, and wounded. Indeed, Russia almost lost the war. Marshal Gregory K. Zhukov, savior of Moscow, conqueror of Berlin, said in Moscow's Red Square on June 24, 1945: "There were moments when the situation was desperate." Stalin used the same words on August 24, 1945: "We had moments in 1941 and 1942," he told a Kremlin reception of army officers, "when the situation was desperate."

In December, 1941, the Nazis reached Khimki, a suburb of Moscow, a short bus ride from the Kremlin. And, after all, it was touch and go even at Stalingrad. Political debaters will emphasize only the final victory. But the Soviet people and the Soviet military know the war was not all smooth sailing. It took the Red Army five years to recover from the Tukhachevsky purge.

The Soviet people paid for the purge in blood.

Much has been written about Russia. The most outstanding fact about the Soviet Union is its 193,000,000 people. Having lived badly for centuries their energy is boundless. They are hard. Neither nature nor history has pampered them. They enjoy lusty health and they multiply fast. Nothing gets them down. They quickly recuperate from wars, pestilence, hunger, and the blunders of their leaders. I lived for fourteen years among those people and I love them. They are meek and submissive. They pay. They paid for the trials and the purges.

The Stalin purge also has an intimate relation to the battle now raging throughout the world between freedom and totalitarianism for the minds of men, especially of youth. Joseph E. Davies did a distinct disservice to democracy by praising a dictator's purge. The justification of wholesale executions is propaganda for totalitarianism. If successful it would undermine democracy.

Mr. Davies did not point out that the Moscow trials and purges offer us one of only two choices. Either the victims were innocent, in which case the purges were political murder deliberately planned as a means of getting rid of rivals and inconveniences. Or the victims were guilty, which would mean that some aspect of Soviet totalitarianism had converted all the prominent men who made the Soviet revolution—except Stalin—into traitors to the Revolution and to their country. Neither alternative is a credit to the Soviet system.

6. The British People and Churchill's England

IN JULY, 1941, two weeks after Hitler attacked Russia, I flew to England. The Clipper took five hours from New York to Bermuda, fourteen hours from Bermuda to Horta, an island in the Portuguese Azores, and seven hours from there to Lisbon.

Flying eight thousand feet above the ocean is as comfortable, pleasant, and smooth as a ride in a streamlined Pullman. I lunched on soup, meat, salad, bread, butter, ice cream, and coffee, then strolled up and down the long corridor for exercise. The Azores looked like rocks strewn haphazard by a god into the sea. We began to descend. On both sides were mountains, their heads cut off by clouds. We dived down among them, landed on the water with a few bumps, and taxied to the breakwater. The rusty *Isle de Re*, carrying Red Cross food to Unoccupied France, rode at anchor. A second freighter raised its bright red and black swastika flag as we docked at Horta.

When a low-pressure area develops over Greenland it draws to it the air from western Africa and that stirs up the water around the Azores thus creating swells. One World. The swells delayed us at Horta for twenty-four hours.

We stayed at the Western Union-Pan American hostel kept by an American couple named Fulmar. Rain descended in sheets. I played chess with Captain Winston of our Clipper. Someone turned on the radio.

"Altitude 5000 feet. What is your visibility?" a voice said.

Captain Winston stopped playing. "That's the Clipper coming in from Lisbon," he said.

"Visibility here 1000 feet," the Pan American manager on land replied to the pilot of the incoming Clipper.

"I am landing on estimates," the pilot was heard to say.

"He's landing blind, flying blind," Captain Winston explained.

"Down at 3000 feet," the Clipper pilot announced a moment later.

"Watch out for high swells just outside the breakwater," the Pan American manager warned. "Thick rain down here."

"Gee whiz," Winston said, and nervously lit a cigarette.

The suspense made one's heart thump. Silence. We waited for the sound of the Clipper's motors but heard nothing.

"Where are you?" the manager called.

"Down to 1000 feet. Approaching the breakwater," the pilot replied. "I can see nothing. Are there any ships in the harbor?"

"Watch for the *Isle de Re* in the center of the harbor. Land west of the *Isle de Re*."

"We can see you now," the pilot announced.

"Good," Winston commented. "But it's going to be a mighty difficult landing."

"Mind the swells," the manager warned again.

Winston fidgeted.

"Landed," the Clipper pilot reported. "Taxiing in slowly."

"Phew," Winston whistled with relief and turned to the chessboard.

"Docked," said the Clipper pilot.

The Portuguese in Horta and Lisbon looked small and thin as though the nation which had inherited an empire from intrepid seamen no longer ate enough. Men and women standing at the landing docks seemed to say to us: Why should you come to Europe when everybody in Europe wants to get to America?

During the second world war, Portugal, Switzerland, and Sweden, but especially Portugal, were the haven of international spies. In Estoril, a fashionable resort outside Lisbon, Nazi officials touched sleeves at the roulette wheel with British diplomats; Jewish refugees and Gestapo torturers ate at neighboring tables; Japanese agents, American airmen, Belgian counts, Italian officers, and Turkish merchants politely took one another's money in the Casino. The Japanese were the most nervous gamblers, the White Russians the most serious, the anti-Nazi Germans the quietest, the Nazis the loudest. Americans chuck in a few dollars for the sensation and to be able to write home about it. I discovered that when I played the modest stakes I could afford I got no kick out of it, and when I risked higher sums I got plenty of excitement but lost more than was healthy for a free-lance journalist.

An unarmed Dutch civilian plane took us from Lisbon to Bristol, England, in six hours. We flew parallel to the Nazi-held coast of France. The Nazis knew all about these regular flights to England and did not molest them except when they were out to get an important passenger; the British accorded similar immunity to German non-military airlines.

Bristol had been badly hit by bombs. Homes that were cut open had poured out their innards like animals. The railway station showed ruined walls and a damaged roof. But the people were calm.

"Did you have a smooth flight?" asked the corporal at the airfield where we landed.

"Have a chair," said the sergeant. We were waiting for passport examination.

"Would you care for a spot of tea?" an officer urged. It was almost like arriving at a country estate for a weekend. Everybody was courteous and cooperative.

The scene at the station took me back to 1918 when I was a volunteer in the British Army in England. Uniforms everywhere. Women in uniform too; an "advance" on the first world war. Soldiers sat on their fat kit bags waiting for trains. Crowded trains.

In one corner of the platform, I noticed two men, obviously father and son. The father, about forty-five, wore an army major's insignia and the ribbons of a veteran of 1914–18. The son, twenty-five or thereabouts, wore the blue of the Royal Air Force. I saw nothing sadder in Britain. The two men did not look sad. The father was recounting an experience in France in 1917. Now and then the son smiled. But it was sad that the generation which fought the "war to end wars," and then fathered sons and daughters to live in peace, was today fighting another world war by the side of those sons and daughters.

The London taxi drove through streets I knew so well. Every street had bomb wounds. This was modern war, war on civilians, war that strikes the baby's crib, that kills the family of four at dinner, that smashes the dishes in the kitchen.

Shortly after my arrival in London, I met an old friend, Storm Jameson, the distinguished novelist. I asked about her eighty-eight-year-old father. "He's in Whitby," she replied. Whitby is on the east coast of England just where the Nazis, after crossing the North Sea, often dumped their bombs.

"Hasn't he been bombed out?" I asked.

"Only his windows have been shattered," she replied.

"Why don't you move him to a safer place, inland?" I wondered.

"What!" she exclaimed. "It's his house. He was born in it. Do you think I would leave my house because Hitler might bomb it?"

There were exceptions who fled, but Storm's was the spirit of England. In 1943, Storm's young sister was killed in one of those senseless daylight raids on undefended little towns with no industries, no nothing, only people. . . . "I'll miss her all my years," she wrote me. "After the war I'll get her children and bring them up."

Once, at an evening party, a woman mourned the deterioration in the quality of cigarettes. Another woman alluded to the poorer quality of paper available to newspapers. "Clothing is so much worse too," a guest remarked.

"Everything is worse," a man interjected. "Only the people are better."

The British people were wonderful. They did not even think they were being brave. "Well," Jonathan Cape, my British publisher, said, "what is one to do? You can either yell or go crazy or commit suicide when the bombs fall. Or you can behave and keep quiet."

The British behaved with dignity. Yet when I watched Londoners, tired and probably hungry, groping their way home through the total blackout, I had a feeling that war was not only inhuman, it was an assault on human dignity. This is not the way human beings should live. War brings out the best in man for the worst of all purposes.

I stayed in London with George Russell Strauss, Labor Member of Parliament, whose house guests were Aneurin Bevan, likewise Labor M.P. and a stormy Welsh petrel, and Mrs. Bevan or Jennie Lee, a Labor leader in her own right. Strauss and Bevan published and wrote the *Tribune*, a left-Labor weekly. One Sunday morning I was on Regent Street when I saw a man walking along and reading the *Tribune*. I asked him what he thought of the magazine. We chatted for half an hour. I brought the report to Russell and Ni (Aneurin) and they marveled at my American enterprise. Years ago I was too diffident to do such a thing. But I find that people like to talk and do not mind being accosted and questioned. I have done it in many countries. It is easiest when I can jump straight into a serious conversation as in the case of the man reading the *Tribune*. When I have to start with "Nice morning" or "Looks like rain" I sometimes get tongue-tied.

Usually when I am trying to understand a foreign country I put the same group of questions to everybody I meet and the result is a sort of pulse-taking, my own "Gallup poll." To two hundred people I said: "Suppose Hitler makes you a peace offer. What would you think?" Only one person replied that such an offer would deserve consideration. All others rejected the idea with varying degrees of vehemence and profanity.

Russia was not yet winning. America was far off, though sympathetic and helpful. Hitler might invade any day. But the people were unanimously determined to go on. There were no sixty-forty yes-no replies. Each was 100 per cent clear.

"There will be no flinching here," Churchill had said to me. The people were firm because they believed they would win.

Amid the noise of Nazi bombs, England found national harmony. Harmony, not unity. Unity is totalitarian. Harmony is democratic. Harmony is the cooperation of divergent elements; unity is the forced submission of all. In a democracy a victorious candidate gets loyal acceptance even if he wins by one vote. But Nazi "unity" required a 97 per cent "Ja" election.

Probably the most amazing thing I learned during my stay in England was a case of large-scale sabotage by patriots. Aneurin Bevan, who as a boy worked in coal mines, told me that coal mine owners were working their bad coal seams and keeping the rich seams for post-war exploitation. This was hard to believe, for it meant weakening the war effort. I asked the head of the Government mines department. He confirmed it. I nevertheless hesitated to record it as a fact. Then the *Financial News*, a businessman's daily, a British *Wall Street Journal*, so to speak, wrote: "Given Excess Profit Tax concessions, however, the coal owners would be readier to concentrate now on working the most productive seams."

The owners were working their poor seams because in wartime anything sells, even poor coal, and because the British government was taking practically all their profits to finance the war. Then why exhaust the good coal? Keep that for the peace period when quality would bring customers and retainable profits. The owner who indulged in such practices might have had a son in the RAF and was ready to give his son's life for the nation. But not his good coal.

Employers and labor, rich and poor, nobility and plebs supported the war. Class barriers broke down among fire-watchers and air-raid wardens. In the Home Guard where civilians trained to repel an invasion, the office boy marched next to his boss. With all citizens engaged in saving the nation, Britain became a nation of friends. Hence the harmony. Friendship and harmony brought happiness.

The coal owner nevertheless worked his poor seam, and the boss remained the boss.

War multiplied the contacts between the social classes; the traffic across class barriers increased. Bombs did not discriminate; why should men?

Yet except as the British government participated in wartime production and set up wartime controls, economic power stayed where it had always been.

When people have been equal in face of the threat of death they resent being unequal in the enjoyment of life. There will always be an England, the common man repeated after Churchill. But what kind? Would there be homes or slums? Jobs or the dole? Security from the cradle to the grave or security only in the grave? The war which stimulated cooperation in the present aroused protest against the past.

A young fighter pilot, leader of a night-fighter squadron, showed me the gadgets in his new Hurricane pursuit plane after flying me above the Channel. There were fifteen little yellow swastikas painted on the fuselage for the "fifteen Jerries I've shot down so far." He patted the side of the plane affectionately as one would a horse. Suddenly he said: "Do you think we shall be unemployed when it's all over?" He was not so much worried as puzzled. Would the country he had served in war find nothing for him to do in peace? He admitted an interest in the Labor party.

Noting the reluctance of the possessors of economic power to part with it, and knowing the limitations of their own economic power, workers and protesting intellectuals, and members of the middle class turn to government for social and economic improvement. Essentially, modern movements for a better life are movements to influence and direct the state. Hence labor's urge to enter politics. Through their votes the millions aim to wrest political power from those who have economic power.

Thus the war which produced social harmony in England carried within it the seeds of social conflict.

While I was in England the newspapers printed a photograph of Churchill on a visit to the much-bombed city of Plymouth. It showed him walking down the center of a narrow street, the inevitable cigar in the corner of his mouth. He wore his best grin. In front of him, immediately behind him, and close to him on both sides walked men, women, and children. He was in the midst of a spontaneous popular demonstration. Almost above his head some folks were cheering him from a first-story balcony, and he had taken off his hat, put it on his cane, and was waving it to them high in the air. This was a photograph of democracy. It is many years since any dictator has been seen among unknown, uncounted citizens who just happened to be around. Walls of stone and fear separate the dictator from his people. Churchill did not fear the British people nor did they fear him. Fear is the pedestal of dictators.

Yet Churchill was not of the people. Before the war and during my visit in 1941, Britons frequently told me that their casualties in the first world war explain the political anemia of the inter-war years. Today's leaders, they said in effect, died in yesterday's trenches. That is a fraction of the truth. The London *Economist*, serious financial weekly, dealt with a bigger fraction when it wrote in 1942: "It is an undeniable fact that the majority of the leaders in every walk of life in this country are drawn from a class which includes barely one-twentieth of the population." What is more, according to the respectable *Economist*, these leaders are "not selected on the basis of ability."

"The United Kingdom, with a population of 48 million inhabitants," continued the *Economist*, "is being run by such brains as can be found in a population of two million plus the few exceptional individuals who crash the barrier." Which barrier? The barrier of wealth and social privilege. "This cannot be an efficient use of the native talent of the country," the *Economist* concluded. Britain's manpower scarcity is partly man-made. The very fact that ten years of major war between 1914 and 1945 (ten out of thirty-one!) have depleted Britain's manpower pool makes it all the more imperative to use the abilities of all who survived. Hence the demand to remove social barriers.

In Russia, in 1917, the barrier between the tiny group of aristocratic, plutocratic rulers and the scores of millions of poor, oppressed workers and peasants was very high. It was also thin and fragile. A few blows with rifles, grenades, and words shattered the barrier into a billion unrecognizable splinters. In Russia, befitting her backwardness, the barrier was made of wood. Elsewhere, it is built stoutly of concrete and steel. The privileged classes in England are entrenched behind records of service to the nation, learning, administrative skill, business experience, and pillboxes of industrial, banking, and trade enterprises which dominate the economic life of the country. They will not easily be dislodged. But the 46 million on the wrong side of the barrier, taught by the Baldwin-Chamberlain appeasement blunders to have less respect for the ruling classes and taught by the war to have more respect for themselves, clamor for opportunities hitherto denied them by the 2 million on the right side of the barrier.

The British ruling class knew how to fight the war. But it had not prevented the war. Therefore, as early as 1941, one heard the opinion that the Tories should not be trusted with the task of making the peace.

When I returned from England in 1941, I wrote: "The British are as one in fighting the Nazis. But some, a minority, are also fighting to preserve the old Britain which was very good to them, and some, a majority, are fighting to create a new Britain. . . . Britain is actually engaged in two wars, a war against the New Order of Hitler and another against the old order of Neville Chamberlain." And of Churchill, I might have added.

J. B. Priestley, the left-wing British playwright, wrote in his book *Out of the People:* "You have no right to use the real Britain to fight a war and then announce that you are doing it to preserve a quite different and much less real Britain." Priestley was taken off the air. So was Harold J. Laski. Laski told me he had asked Churchill for the reason. "Because the England you want is different from the England I want," Churchill replied. Nevertheless Laski, Priestley, and other rebels talked at army and air force camps, wrote articles and books, and broadcast to the Dominions what they could not say to England. I had the same experience of being asked by the BBC to broadcast from London to the Empire and to North America but not to the United Kingdom.

The war of course curtailed some liberties in Britain but not many. England remained free. I visited John Strachey at an RAF airfield near Bath. Strachey had been an advocate of Communism. After the Stalin-Hitler pact, he, like the Communists, became anti-war. But the invasion of Norway in the spring of 1940 changed his mind. He volunteered to be an air-raid warden and "dug for Mrs. Miller" when a bomb buried her. Then he joined the air force and was appointed adjutant of a night-fighter squadron. In his sleeping quarters he had a library which included several volumes by Karl Marx, Lenin, and Trotzky, and his own Socialist books. The authorities knew and did not mind. The British are tolerant. That is a mark of civilization. Without tolerance of differences—differences in thought, skin color (blood is always the same color), race, religion and politics—democracy is a mockery.

Despite the political differences between them, Tories and Labor collaborated in the Coalition Government to fight the war. Even when Labor leaders disliked Churchill's policies, they deferred to him. He dominated Cabinet meetings. Ministers told me that he talked more than any other member of the Government and sometimes as much as all of them combined. They enjoyed his language flow. They found, what I also found in my interview with him, that the sentences which come from him in ordinary, unprepared conversation, seem as polished and classical as his most carefully prepared perorations.

Churchill was an indispensable war leader because the people were energized by his energy and speeches. But he neglected production and allied problems; he had no mind for economics. Sometimes he admitted that himself. He preferred to pore over maps and globes with admirals and generals and chat with chemists about new explosives.

Nor had he much interest in the future. His public utterances on peace problems prove it. He was bound to the past. He was a product of the nineteenth century and he loved it. He loved Empire, royalty, and caste. Though he laid bricks, he could lay no social bridge to the bricklayers. He was an aristocrat. Lloyd George despised the British upper classes, the generals, and the nobility. He fought them. Churchill wanted to perpetuate them. This was strange for he was their superior; indeed they feared him for that reason and kept him out of power until the national crisis of 1940. Yet he tried to save their privilege and wealth. His attachment was not so much to them as to the England of the nineteenth century that made them. The nineteenth century was, *par excellence*, the British century, the century of Pax Britannica after the defeat of Napoleonic France and before the rise of Kaiser Germany, the century of the rounding out of the British Empire under Queen Victoria. Britain's past glory was Churchill's god. The upper classes were synonymous to him with the greatness of his country. So was India. So was the parliamentary democracy of nineteenth century England.

Churchill fought to preserve the heritage of England.

The contradiction between democracy and poverty did not torment Churchill. The contradiction between freedom in England and the bondage of India did not bother him. Nor did he hesitate to praise Mussolini before that Fascist became Britain's enemy. He also had "kindly words" for Generalissimo Francisco Franco. Churchill abhorred the barbarism of the Nazi regime. But Hitler, to him, represented above all a German threat to Britain. He saw it from the very beginning and warned a deaf Britain.

The key to Churchill's character is his enjoyment of leadership. As leader, he sprouted wings. He was having a wonderful time. He knew people loved listening to him. I have seen Churchill chuckle with delight when the House of Commons enjoyed one of his witticisms. There was much of the actor and something of the Puck in him. He was boy and statesman. He relished being photographed. He liked the role and pose of central figure on a big stage. Having written some of the most masterful histories ever penned by a modern author, he was now master of history-making. Unquestioned supremacy and popular adulation tapped new pockets of physical strength in him.

Churchill felt the romance of the past and the adventure of the present but had no vision of the future. He was the poet in politics, a Byronic Napoleon. He loved words and he loved action. In the modern age, this is a rare combination. Hitler had it.

Churchill had animal zest and many passions. He also had initiative. Some leaders of democracies wait for a ripened public opinion to prepare the country to follow. President Roosevelt was that way on occasions. But Churchill plunged precipitously and hoped England would wade in after him. Never, for instance, has a man molded world opinion as Churchill did the day Hitler invaded Russia when he took to the microphone and promised the Russians immediate aid.

Churchill subordinated everything to victory. He had organized armed British intervention against the Bolshevik regime in 1918, 1919, and 1920. He remained anti-Bolshevik. In December, 1941, he said to a neighbor at dinner in the White House that Russia was a "horrid autocracy." It did not matter; Russia was necessary to victory. The people knew his passionate concentration on winning the war. It was contagious. It induced his opponents to temper their opposition. Men like Aneurin Bevan and Harold J. Laski sniped at him continuously and he fired back. But Labor as a party backed him loyally and some Labor members of the Government, Ellen Wilkinson, for instance, succumbed to his charm.

The Labor ministers meanwhile were studying the art of ruling the country. I went to Herbert S. Morrison's office in the Home Office one day and then we drove to the country in his car to spend a weekend at Ellen Wilkinson's modest cottage. He said he found enough leisure to read a few books—he mentioned Hemingway's *For Whom the Bell Tolls* and Jan Valtin's *Out of the Night*—but devoted as much time as possible to studying official documents, especially Foreign Office dispatches, in order better to understand the technique of government. No doubt other Labor ministers took similar advantage of their membership in the Cabinet. After five years of active participation in the government which led Britain to victory, Labor could no longer be accused of unfitness to rule. This deprived the Tories of an argument they had used with considerable effectiveness in previous electoral campaigns; it accounts in part for Labor's sweeping triumph in July, 1945. "Labor believes," I wrote in *The Nation* of August 16, 1941, "that it is making converts in the white collar and middle classes, which never trusted its patriotism and were never convinced of its abilities."

Morrison was 53. He has a keen, quick mind, wit, and warmth. London knows him; he is " 'Erbert" or " 'Erb" to his fellow Cockneys. He used to be an errand boy and then a telephone operator. He became leader of the London County Council and, in 1940, Home Secretary in the Churchill cabinet.

Once, sitting in Morrison's waiting room in the Home Office, I saw on the marble mantelpiece a red frame about five by nine inches, with a white sheet of paper inside it on which DEATH SENTENCES was printed in large red letters. Below the headline was a list of names and columns of data. I thought it was none of my business to examine it more closely. But when I got into Morrison's inner office, he said to Miss MacDonald, his secretary: "Show him the death sentences," and she showed me a list of twelve names. Opposite each name was a remark on the nature of the crime, the date the sentence was passed, the date of the appeal, and the name of the court. A red line had been drawn by hand through the first two names and their particulars, and in the last column opposite these two names was written *Executed* in red ink. Morrison said: "In the beginning I found it difficult to sign 'H.S.M.' when I knew it was all that stood between a human being and his death. But I ultimately came to the conclusion that, especially in wartime, some persons had to be killed by the state and that the longer I delayed initialing the final order the more sleepless nights I would have."

"Just initials?" I asked. "Don't you have to sign your name?"

"Well," he said, "the tradition of the Home Office requires initials but not a signature." Even after the King has refused mercy, the executioner still waited for Herbert Morrison's "H.S.M."

Morrison is a fighter. He sees only with his left eye, but he sees a lot. He hates the poverty in the midst of which he was born. He lives simply. He does not put on airs. But for the tension between him and Ernest Bevin, he would have been the leader of the Labor party, his friends say. Since, in the circumstances, neither he nor Bevin could occupy the office, it went to Clement R. Attlee.

Ernest Bevin is a bull-headed man with a powerful body. He is tough, stubborn, and frankly prefers workers to aristocrats. In the Churchill government he was the organizer of production and did a brilliant job. Even his enemies conceded that. Before he joined the Government he led England's biggest labor union, the Transport Workers' Union, and held it in his iron grip. I had my most unsuccessful interview with him. I must have rubbed him the wrong way with some criticism of Britain's pre-war foreign policy. He was patriotic and responded unfavorably to strictures against his country. For over an hour, I struggled to make him talk freely instead of quarreling. Then I gave up.

Morrison and Bevin, as well as Hugh Dalton, President of the Board of Trade, whom I had known for many years because of his special interest in foreign affairs, have been made bitterly anti-Communist by the irritating, disruptive tactics of the Communists in trade unions and Labor party organizations. But the anti-Communism of British Labor leaders and the Labor rank and file stems chiefly from their devotion to freedom. Many Laborites believe in Socialism without being doctrinaire Marxists. They would nationalize certain key industries and banks and use the state to redress the grievances of the poor and insecure. Their socialism could be translated, Human Welfare. It is no dogma with them; it is a means to the improvement of the lot of mankind.

The Laborites are Social Democrats. They are Socialists who believe in democracy as distinguished from the Communists who are Socialists but do not believe in or practise democracy. The Communists therefore detest the Social Democrats, and the antagonism between Labor and Communists has often been fiercer than the hostility of either to capitalists.

It isn't that the Communists were too left. The Aneurin Bevan "Ginger Group" in the Labor party considered the Communists far to the right of themselves. Bevan, Russell Strauss, and their friends had no love for Churchill, but the Communist slogan was "Support Churchill Without Reserve." At an open-air meeting outside the Ministry of Information in London I heard Harry Pollitt, leading Communist, speak under a banner which read "Strengthen the Government." In several by-elections, the Communists backed Tories against Labor candidates.

The British Labor party's brains and brilliance are in its left wing, its weight and power are in its right wing. "Clem" Attlee is the dead center of the Labor party. The mass of the party is to right of him; but those to the left can build fires under him and events do the rest. I had seen Attlee over the years in his office in Parliament (as leader of His Majesty's Opposition he got an office and a salary from the Government) and in the dining room of the House of Commons. We were in Spain together during the civil war. In 1941, I visited him at 11 Downing Street, next door to Churchill's official residence. Attlee was Deputy Prime Minister, and the Prime Minister was away seeing President Roosevelt in a bay of the Atlantic where, on the cruiser *Augusta*, they drafted the Atlantic Charter. It was August 14. That morning, the press and radio had announced mysteriously and with great solemnity that Attlee would make an important declaration in the afternoon. I lunched with a British friend at the Reform Club. Speculation was rife on what Attlee would say. Some hoped the United States would come into the war. Most thought Roosevelt and Churchill would state their war aims. In the lavatory, after lunch, an old man, a sort of thin Colonel Blimp, said: "They say he's going to tell us what we're fighting for. We know. We want to beat Hitler." A group of fifteen men listened in the billiard room. Attlee spoke in a flat, uninspiring voice. The British were spoiled by Churchill's fine radio performance. Attlee read the eight points of the Atlantic Charter. The moment he finished everybody started to leave. No one applauded. No one made a single comment. No one seemed moved. They seemed let down. They *had* expected America to join Britain and fight the war.

I went from the club to Attlee's office in 11 Downing Street. He came towards me down the long room with a sprightly, undulating gait. I said his statement had come over the air "distinctly," at which he gaily smiled. He was not sucking his pipe and saying "right" and "quite" this time. He was in a talkative mood and on the offensive. We talked about American critics of British policy at home and in the Empire.

Attlee is a tenacious debater. If he has a point he keeps a bulldog grip on it. Others are bored but he is still fighting in his unspectacular way. Speaking of Attlee, Ellen Wilkinson says: "I have seen him at a stormy party meeting when men of great emotional force were making passionate speeches. The whole atmosphere would be electric, with a crisis at hand and the party in danger. . . . Then Mr. Attlee will get up rather slowly and casually and in a quiet, reasonable voice he will make one of his unemotional, sensible speeches. . . . I have seen 200 angry men after such a speech leave the room wondering what they had been making a fuss about."

Clement R. Attlee would be difficult to glamorize. His Labor followers do not mind that; they trust him more because he is colorless. The British working class is afraid that its leaders will be suborned by the subtle bribery of titles, wealth, and invitations to meet the titled. It considers Attlee immune. He is not the lion of salons like Ramsay MacDonald who, having been Labor Prime Minister, joined the Conservatives in 1931.

Harold J. Laski, Attlee's adviser at 11 Downing Street, told me this story. He said: "Once I was talking with FDR in the White House. 'Harold,' he said, 'how do you like Bingham, our Ambassador in London?' I answered that I had never met Bingham. The President was surprised. I informed him that Bingham did not mingle much with Labor people. Shortly after my return to England, I got an invitation to dinner at the American embassy. Attlee was there too, sitting at Bingham's right. The conversation lagged. 'Major Attlee,' said Bingham, 'have you been doing any shooting of late?' 'The last shooting I did was in 1917,' Attlee replied. 'And what did you shoot?' Bingham asked eagerly. 'Germans,' Attlee whispered."

That would never do in a drawing room of a manor house or in a Mayfair parlor.

Several days after the Atlantic Charter was announced on the radio by Attlee, I said to Brendan Bracken, Minister of Information: "Do you agree that Churchill, on his own, would never have thought the Atlantic Charter necessary? Nor was he under any public pressure to formulate war aims. The initiative then must have come from Roosevelt." Bracken agreed. Churchill did not need the Charter to bolster war morale. Roosevelt needed it to create one.

The weakness of the Atlantic Charter was in its conception. It was conceived not as a set of basic principles on which to build the peace but as a means of psychologically preparing America for war. It was propaganda for war, not politics for peace. When peace-making commenced, the Atlantic Charter was first ignored or infringed and then forgotten.

Foreign Secretary Anthony Eden was more concerned with post-war problems and with social questions than Churchill. But even he would not have talked so much in 1941 about the peace settlement had he not known America's interest. Eden realized that America was not yet in the war because, for one thing, we were still fighting the last war. Those who thought the peace of 1919 had been lost were loath to participate in another war and wanted reassurance on the nature of the coming peace.

Eden is able and affable and his affability is emphasized by six prominent front teeth. Next to Churchill he was the most popular politician in England and was regarded as Churchill's most likely successor. (No one thought then of a Labor victory.) Born June 12, 1897, Eden belonged to a younger generation than Churchill. Eden's "You will not get peace without social security" is a twentieth century sentiment.

Anthony Eden's older brother John was killed at the front in the first year of the first world war. Another brother was killed in the British Navy two years later. He himself fought in that war. War deaths and war service linked him with new trends. His grandfather was Governor of Bengal and his mother was born in India. The family, one branch of which was prominent in colonial Maryland and North Carolina, had titles and wealth. These linked him with the Conservatives.

Conservatives considered Eden "weak," perhaps because he had too many "queer" social ideas, and Labor thought him "weak" because he was a Conservative though he should have known better.

A young British Conservative, however, is not necessarily less conservative because he is young. As a matter of fact, the assaults of the twentieth century on the citadels of conservatism induce their warders to build stouter walls. They dig in more firmly so as the better to resist dislodgment. Brendan Bracken, Member of Parliament, Minister of Information, rich, red-headed, temperamental, quick-witted, a former secretary of Churchill and a friend and disciple of Churchill, was one of the most militant of the Young Tories. I had known him before the war. On my first wartime visit to Britain in 1939, he facilitated my interview with Churchill. During this stay he helped me get interviews with a number of officials. On September 18, he invited me to lunch in his private lunchroom at the new, modern Ministry of Information building. There were four of us; Bracken, Lord Moyne,

Secretary of State for Colonies, Viscount Cranborne, Dominions Secretary—all Conservatives—and I. We met at one-thirty; I left at four. Bracken told me that Moyne, who belonged to the Guinness brewery family, had retired before the war and devoted himself to his many cultural interests, among them medicine and prehistoric animals. (He was assassinated later in Egypt by two Palestinian terrorists.) Cranborne, son of the Marquess of Salisbury, is a member of the ancient and influential Cecil family.

Someone mentioned the Munich surrender. "Munich was a disaster. We should have fought to save the Czechs," Bracken said.

"We had no anti-aircraft guns," Moyne protested.

"Walter, if you could see our pitiful plane and gun production figures between September, 1938, and September, 1939," Bracken replied, "you would know that a nation never prepares for war before going to war."

I suggested that in the Munich crisis Russia would have fought on the side of the Western powers. Bracken agreed. He added: "Czech tanks were used by the Huns"—he always said Huns—"to take Paris, and there is nothing in Germany as good as Czechoslovakia's Skoda works."

"However," the studious, bespectacled, empty-cheeked Cranborne interjected, "it was foolish to guarantee Poland without consulting Russia."

I said that that was an insoluble problem because no Polish government could admit Russian troops. They all agreed.

"Bobbity," Bracken said to Cranborne, "I know you differ with me on Spain. I think, owing to religious questions, we could not have done anything there. But when we were firm at Nyon [September, 1937, when the British and French decided to patrol the Mediterranean to stop Italian submarine sinkings of ships carrying arms to the Loyalists] they took notice."

"It was silly," Cranborne interrupted, "to say as Chamberlain did that a maritime nation like England would not protect its ships. We should have told Mussolini and Franco that we would protect our ships and sink all that attacked them even if it meant war."

"We should have stopped the Italians in Abyssinia and the business in Spain might never have happened," Bracken affirmed.

"I agree there," Cranborne remarked.

Moyne demurred. He had been a consistent appeaser.

They asked me about Stalin. I said: "Stalin is ruthless and opportunistic, but a great man."

"That's just what Harry Hopkins reports," Bracken declared.

"Is he impressive?" Cranborne asked.

"No, not impressive looking," I replied.

Moyne asked about the terror. I described some of the acts of the Soviet secret police.

"What about generals like Budenny and Voroshilov who have been doing such a bad job?" Bracken inquired.

"They are political generals," I said. "The staff work is done by generals of whom the outside world has not heard."

"You don't think Tukhachevsky was actually guilty of collusion with the Nazis, do you?" asked Bracken.

"I do not believe it because I have seen no proof," I answered. "The soldiers have been fighting bravely; Russian soldiers always fought bravely. But the staff work seems to be poor."

"At Leningrad," Bracken noted, "they have von Leeb to contend with and he is the best staff man that ever lived."

We discussed the possibility of a winter campaign. I volunteered the view that weather and terrain did not preclude winter fighting in Russia. We also canvassed the question of oil, the defenses on the Volga, and kindred matters.

I said: "I think Hitler's purpose in attacking Russia was to get a negotiated peace with England. He knows he has another year before you and America begin to produce on a really big scale. In that year he hopes to crush Russia and then face you with a situation in which you could not win and therefore might negotiate."

"That's right," Bracken said, "Hitler's timing was perfect."

At three o'clock, Cranborne and Moyne left; Bracken went with them to the elevator and said to me: "Don't go." We talked for another hour.

When Bracken came back, he told me that "the possibility of Stalin's making a separate peace with Hitler is the Government's constant concern." Such a move was being talked about everywhere in London. He said: "The war has been like a game of shuttlecock. First, Poland in the east. Then the Low Countries and France in the west. Now Russia in the east. Is it coming west again?"

Bracken settled down over a whiskey and soda and asked what the British government might do to keep Russia in the war. I said: "Supply Russia with arms, see to it that the Turks don't join the Nazis against Russia, save Spain from the Nazis, and convince the Kremlin that you won't appease Hitler. I am sure," I declared, "that Stalin thinks you are like Moore-Brabazon who wants the Russians and Germans to kill one another off."

"But we will never appease," Bracken exclaimed. "We've learned that much."

We discussed the establishment of a second front on the Continent, and Bracken listed all the arguments against it. I had heard those same arguments from Sir John Anderson, Lord President of the Council, and from Labor ministers. They were purely military. Britain alone just did not have the men and equipment to cope with the Reichswehr even while the bulk of Germany's forces were occupied with the Red Army.

"Despite everything," Bracken said, "we are getting on better with the Russians. In the beginning, we didn't get on at all. Cripps was too left for them. Moscow would have preferred the Duke of Devonshire or someone like that. But now Stalin and Cripps are getting on fine. With Molotov the relations are not so good but he's not so important."

Apropos Cripps I mentioned Halifax, the British ambassador in Washington. "Ah," Bracken said, "Halifax and Roosevelt are good friends. They're both high Episcopalians and they talk religion." He added that he was trying to keep British lecturers from going to the United States.

"America has come as close to war as we can expect," Bracken stated, "and we don't expect troops."

"This is what Hitler banks on," I suggested. "He will make a peace offer to Britain and simultaneously say to the United States that England cannot win unless America sends over five million men."

"That's what America will never do," Bracken said.

"Then your victory depends on Russia," I said.

"Well," Bracken snapped, "we have been helping Russia as much as we can. In the beginning Stalin asked for as many planes each month as we manufacture in a year. When we brought him down to earth, he halved it. We will give him everything we have even at the risk of exposing ourselves. You know," Bracken recalled, "when Cripps brought Stalin the news of the impending Nazi invasion Stalin refused to believe it."

"I think Stalin knew it was coming," I said, "but that was the period when Russia was on her belly before Hitler, and Stalin did not wish to feed British hopes that Russia might soon be fighting Germany."

"So you think Stalin knew," he repeated. "Winston and Stalin get on famously, you know," he continued. "At Cabinet meetings, Winston says 'I had a telegram from Uncle Joe today,' and he chuckles."

I inquired whether the British government had any reliable figures on casualties in the Russo-German fighting. Bracken replied: "Russia, three million casualties in the first ten weeks of the war; Germany, two million, with a greater proportion of killed than in the first world war. There are relatively few prisoners; no quarter is given. American generals," he added, "think the German Army is invincible and that Russia will be defeated. They are from the Middle West and they respect the Germans. It will be very bad for all of us if the Russians collapse."

"Just because a Russian collapse would spell disaster for you," I argued, "you should be ready to pay a lot to prevent it."

"If it would cost us 100,000 lives," he said, "we wouldn't mind. We would mind, but we would do it. But are you sure that anything we do will divert a single German soldier from the east? Hitler has reserves in France and Holland. We have explained this to Stalin and he is satisfied."

Bracken had to work, so we broke it up with friendly handshakes.

The Munich surrender to Hitler in 1938, like the Soviet-Nazi pact of 1939, and the Stalin purge which began in 1935, continues to be the subject of discussion where politically-minded people gather. Munich was argued at Bracken's luncheon. Munich was of course uppermost in the mind of Eduard Benes, the President of Czechoslovakia, when I talked with him in London on September 23, 1941.

"How are you?" I said as I entered his London government-in-exile headquarters.

"Good," he replied.

"Why?" I asked.

"I lived through hell," he said. "Now it is better. Now we are fighting. Munich time would have been the proper time to fight. It is not at all certain that the Nazis would have gone to war over the Sudetenland. I had reports that they were not ready. But if they had attacked us we could have held them back for four or maybe six months. Our fortifications in the Sudetenland were better than the Maginot Line."

"But wasn't your frontier with Austria exposed?" I asked.

"It was not so good but it was good enough," Benes answered. "Of course Prague would have been destroyed. But we could have destroyed Dresden and Leipzig and bombed Berlin. Instead, now the Skoda works and other Czechoslovak factories are working against England and Russia. We had 1700 planes and they were as good as the German planes. France had 1500 planes; England between 1500 and 2000, all front line. The Germans had 3000. The fall of Czechoslovakia was also bad for French morale and for relations with Russia. Munich was a European disaster. We were prepared to fight in Bohemia, then retire into Moravia, then into Slovakia, and then through Rumania into Russia. We had built a railroad through Rumania towards the Soviet frontier."

I asked him to show it to me on the map and he did.

"We built the railroad ostensibly for Rumania on a credit basis," he continued. "But it was actually our prepared avenue of retreat. We had 300 Soviet bombers flown from Russia by Czechoslovak crews and we were beginning to manufacture similar types ourselves. They flew over Rumania. On this and other questions King Carol was very loyal and said 'Don't ask for permission.' Carol would have let Russian troops through into Czechoslovakia. Not the Poles. But the Red Army could have come through Rumania and kept the Poles neutral.

"Three times," Benes declared, warming to his subject, "the Russians promised us help in September, 1938. Early that month, in response to our query, Moscow replied that it would help if France helped. This was unsatisfactory because we suspected that France would not help. So we asked again and Moscow advised us to take the matter up with the League of Nations. But I was afraid that the League, perhaps under British and French pressure, would vote against resistance to Germany and then, if we had fought, we would have been in the position of acting contrary to a League decision. Finally, Moscow told us to fight irrespective of any consideration and promised to help through Rumania and by air."

The lines and folds in Benes' face seemed deeper as he remembered that terrible September. For under threats from London and Paris he agreed not to fight. Munich killed Czechoslovakia. Benes foresaw this but would not defy Britain and France. "I did not want my country to become a second Spain," he said to me. "If we had accepted Soviet aid and gone to war, I would have been called a Bolshevik."

He hinted that his government also encountered opposition from domestic appeasers.

He sighed. "France might have been saved," he said, "if the war had started in 1938 instead of eleven months later. Hitler's Westwall was not yet built and Loyalist Spain was still fighting."

He agreed with me that there was a parallel between Anglo-French appeasement of Hitler in 1938 and Stalin's appeasement of Hitler in 1939. "Russia," he said reluctantly, "should have saved France."

One Saturday afternoon I took a train into the beautiful green English countryside and got off at a small station. I was met by Mr. White, secretary to David Lloyd George, Britain's Prime Minister in World War I. Enroute he gave a lift to two Canadian soldiers who said they had enlisted to fight and were bored by months of inaction. They were thrilled to know they were riding in Lloyd George's car.

After visiting Hitler at Berchtesgaden, Lloyd George had remodeled the main parlor of his farmhouse at Churt and built in a giant window like that in the Fuehrer's eyrie. The view of the valley was now much more beautiful than the one I had seen on my 1938 visit. Hitler's autographed photograph was gone from the top of Lloyd George's piano and so was the photograph of Lord Lothian, late British ambassador in Washington and a former secretary of Lloyd George. There remained many framed pictures including one of Woodrow Wilson dedicated "to my friend" Lloyd George, although little love or friendship was lost between them, Field Marshal Smuts, Foch, Clemenceau, Lord Birkenhead, and "Mam," Lloyd George's mother. On a long couch lay copies of the weekly *New Statesman and Nation*, many left-wing pamphlets, several issues of the weekly *Picture Post*, and several books.

Lloyd George came into the room with a springy walk. But his skin did not look as pink and healthy as when I had seen him in 1938 and his long silver hair that fell to his coat collar was not as lustrous. He remembered that we had talked chiefly of Spain on my last visit. "Alas," he said, "this war might have been prevented by timely action there. The war did not start in Spain. There were Abyssinia and Manchuria. But Spain was the best chance we had to stop the dictators." He immediately brought up the subject of Russia. "Stalin will not make peace," Lloyd George said firmly, "he knows what that would mean." He urged a second front in France to relieve Nazi pressure on Russia. I told him all the ministers I had talked to, including Sir John Anderson, Churchill's right-hand man, were convinced Britain could not do it now.

"Why not?" he snapped. "They say they haven't enough shipping. Shipping! Bah! When our army broke in France in March, 1918, I called the Food Controller and said 'Take your ships off the Atlantic.' We poured troops into France and saved the army and the situation. I would send 100,000 or 200,000 men to France right away. If there is no equipment what have we been doing these last twelve months? From June, 1915, to July, 1916, I was able to arm and send into France 1,300,000 men."

I remarked that this war was different, that armies nowadays need heavy equipment like tanks, and also planes. "Yes, tanks," he said. "We've had plenty of time in which to make them. Winston has no sense of adventure. It was broken by his bad adventure at Gallipoli in the first war. Winston hasn't wanted to do anything on the Continent. When Germany invaded Russia, he went off to see Roosevelt. He wanted to be out of reach of pressure to do more."

A maid wheeled in a refreshment trolley loaded with tea, bread, butter, and honey. Lloyd George took a glass of buttermilk and remarked: "Buttermilk, that's my drink." His hand shook as he drank. He was 78. I noticed he did not smoke any more.

I alluded to a report that Roosevelt had played with the idea, back in 1937 and 1938, of inviting Hitler, Stalin, Mussolini, Chamberlain, and Daladier to the White House to settle the world's problems. "Why didn't he?" Lloyd George exclaimed. "A fine idea." Then he made a grimace of skepticism. "No," he added, "Stalin would not have come. He would have sent Litvinov. Then Hitler would have sent Ribbentrop and nothing would have come of it."

I asked him his opinion of the Atlantic Charter. "What does it amount to?" he argued. "Free trade?" He made gurgling "kh-kh" sounds at the back of his mouth and rolled his head merrily. He did not believe the Charter meant free trade. "Besides that, there is disarmament," he chuckled. "We had that in the Versailles Treaty, but it didn't work. The French refused to disarm. Only we and the Americans took disarmament seriously."

Lloyd George's son, Gwilym, Member of Parliament and assistant to Lord Woolton in the Food Ministry, came in for tea with his tall wife and their son, David. Lloyd George asked about American sentiment for going into war. "Only a country at war," he commented, "is ready to make the effort and submit to the strain of all-out production for war."

"Do you think Russia will collapse before America comes into the war?" he asked anxiously. We discussed that double-barreled guess-question, and then moved on to another: Could Britain win by bombing Germany?

"Bah," Lloyd George exclaimed, "we can no more defeat them by bombing than they could get us down by air raids. Bombs cannot do it."

I mentioned the relaxation I had noted in England. "There is no feeling of urgency about helping Russia," I suggested.

"I suppose it's because we are not being bombed," he said. "People feel gay when they come out of the firing line. After our army broke in 1918 I went over to France to see Clemenceau. I met him at Beauville. It was in April, 1918. As I drove through, some of our regiments were coming out of the line. They had been in the trenches for weeks and had taken a fearful drubbing from the Germans. They were not far behind the battlefield. You could hear the guns firing. But they were bright and cheerful, singing and cheering."

I inquired whether he thought England could hold out for two more years. "Yes, why not?" he replied quickly. "I don't believe in an invasion, you know. Much depends on the Russians. Their casualties have been frightful. They have been fighting by counterattacks, and that is always expensive. The Germans have used tanks and Panzer divisions which saves lives. I was reminiscing with Winston the other day about World War casualty figures and we recalled that when we were skeptical about the reports from our General Army Headquarters on German losses we checked them against official German reports and found the latter to be more correct. In the battle of Passchendaele, for instance, Haig [the British commander-in-chief whom Lloyd George disliked violently] reported that fifty-eight German divisions had been wiped out, but we knew this to be untrue and we know now that the German staff communiqués gave a more accurate picture of German casualties."

Gwilym Lloyd George, who had remained silent all the while, said: "The Germans lie in this war about their U-boat sinkings." The father admitted that and also that they understated their air losses.

He reverted to America and said: "Victory depends on American industrial output." I said it was rising steeply. "Yes," he agreed, "but you didn't do so well in the last war, you know. Your army was using French guns and, in places, even British guns because it had arrived in Europe inadequately equipped." I thought that was not likely to happen in this war.

Lloyd George was to me the embodiment of history and that was exciting. His grasp of problems was amazing and he seemed to have more imagination than any three members of the Cabinet rolled together. Our talk was a shuttle between America and Britain. He preferred to discuss America; I wanted him to talk about England. Speaking of America, he inquired about isolationism. "I liked the Midwesterner when I visited the U. S.," he remarked. "He's a healthy type."

I paused a moment and said: "Why hasn't your Cabinet big men in it?"

"Why hasn't yours?" he countered. "FDR hasn't. Neither had Wilson."

"Is it because Churchill is afraid to nourish a rival?" I wondered. "All big men dislike to have big men around them."

"Not if they are really big," he said, and I felt sure he was thinking of himself. "Churchill need have no fear of rivals. The country wants him and only him."

This interchange must have turned his mind to Russian leadership. "Russian staff work seems to be bad," he remarked. "Budenny is a sort of Murat, a dashing cavalry officer."

"Budenny is a sergeant-major holding a marshal's baton," I said. He laughed. He asked what kind of a man Stalin was. A few minutes later he rose and asked me to sign his visitor's book. Michael Foot and Frank Owen, British gadfly journalists, had signed before me. At the top of the page were the names of Ivan Maisky, Soviet ambassador, and Mrs. Maisky.

I walked about the farm with Gwilym and his wife. We picked and ate apples and plums. Deep in one of the orchards we encountered Lloyd George, wrapped in a greenish woolen cape, striding vigorously and inspecting his property. He looked the great man he was.

I sat in the spacious garden behind the Strauss home absorbing the cuddling warmth of the sun and reading the Sunday newspapers. There were no phone calls. My host and many other Londoners had gone to the country for the weekend or day. Classic music broadcast by the BBC came from inside the house; Ella, the housekeeper, was listening and so did I in the intervals between the book reviews and the financial page of the *Observer*. To limber up, I now and then sawed some wood for use in the fireplace next winter. Giant chrysanthemums, dazzling dahlias, and marigolds bloomed on the edges of the huge lawn. It was September 7, a quiet idyllic day. Exactly a year before, 350 Nazi planes flew up the Thames estuary, broke through the RAF screen, and rained death on London. 103 German raiders were shot down that day. The Germans were stunned, but the struggle for control of the air over the capital continued until October 31, when the Luftwaffe desisted, apparently exhausted. It came again, intermittently; it came, for instance, on May 10, 1941, and staged the worst raid of the war. "London would have been crippled by ten such raids," Sir Warren Fisher, in charge of the city's defenses, told me. But six weeks after that biggest raid, the Luftwaffe commenced to concentrate on Russia. During my nine weeks in England, London underwent only one, very minor, attack. All the time of course, the defenders remained on the alert. Thousands of barrage balloons, looking like whales from the front and moose from the rear, floated high in the sky. They were held in position by long strong steel cables attached to heavy trucks. The balloons were so numerous that no attacking plane dared to penetrate under them for fear of being cut in two by the cables and so it had to stay up where it came within range of the anti-aircraft guns.

Nevertheless, nothing gives immunity to a big target. One day in 1940 three German bombs penetrated forty feet into the Underground where many people had gone for safety. One bomb in the Victoria district ripped 58,000 telephone wires. In January, 1941, London recorded 8000 breaks in the gas mains. In October, 1940, bombs had reduced the Southern Railway to chaotic operation. Two million British homes were completely or partially destroyed during the blitz.

But this was a closed chapter now. When I began reading the *Observer* that peaceful war Sunday, medium bombers flew overhead going east. When I had finished lunch and the four newspapers, they were roaring homeward after visiting Germany and the Nazi-held Continent. England had turned the tables because Germany had turned to Russia. The respite lasted until the buzz bombs deluded Hitler into again believing that the war could be won by blasting England from the air.

Yet even during the lull in the summer of 1941, many hundreds of elderly women slept in the London Underground every night in wooden bunks built by the Government. They were too nervous about bombs to fall asleep at home. Where bombs had leveled innumerable blocks of houses, as in East Ham and other dock and factory areas in London, whole communities slept, indeed lived, in subterranean shelters which were provided with running water, lavatories, canteens, electricity, and radio. People slept in two-tier or three-tier bunks. Children were put to bed in lowers while adults moved around and visited one another. In the morning, the children were sent off to school, and in the afternoon they came "home" to these smelly, noisy caverns where nobody was ever alone. Women cried when they told me how abnormal family life had become under these circumstances. London paid for the war not only in lives and ruined houses, in short rations and bad clothes. It paid in nerves, and when one pays in nerves one pays in installments until death, and even the next generation pays. It was better but not essentially different in York, Bath, Rotherham, Sheffield, and other small British towns I visited. It was much worse on the Continent.

Postwar Europe is a continent of nervous men, women, and children. It is they who must rebuild countries. Simultaneously, they must rebuild themselves and restore their faith in man's decency.

I flew from Bristol to Lisbon. There I waited eight days to get a seat in the Clipper for New York. I knew it was merely a matter of time. Yet I chafed. I was irked by having to be where I did not want to be. The thousands of refugees, most of them Jews, who waited in Lisbon for many many months, had no assurance that they would ever get out. And they knew, as Jay Allen, American foreign correspondent, once said, that "Hitler could take Portugal by telephone."

With Captain Gail Borden of the U. S. Air Force, formerly of the *Chicago Times*, Eugene Meyer, owner of the *Washington Post*, and Sam Herbert, Mrs. Herbert, and Michael Stewart of the British embassy, I drove out to Vila Franca de Xira to see a bullfight. Spanish bullfighting is exciting; Portuguese bullfighting is dull. The toreador fights from the back of a beautiful horse whose footwork is fantastically delicate. Unlike Spain, where every bull is killed, the bull in Portugal is dragged out after it has been thrown by several brave men who clutch its head and tail and flanks.

The Portuguese on the streets were pro-British; one could see that from their wearing of V-buttons and their favorable reactions to Nazi defeats. The clerical-Fascist government of Dictator Salazar was pro-British because it knew England had no sinister designs on Portugal. But it was worried lest it be unseated in case of an anti-Fascist victory in Europe. So it played with England and Germany and made money by selling to both.

In Lisbon, Nazi publications as well as the British press were sold at numerous corner kiosks. I devoured the German dailies and weeklies. All emphasized the difficulties facing the Germans in Russia: mud, wet clay soil, sandy roads, bad transport. There was everywhere an implied admission that Russia was stronger than the General Staff had thought.

The Portuguese I saw in streets, restaurants, and cinemas appeared to have less color, temperament, and vitality than Spaniards. But they made just as much noise and the men slapped one another on the back just as frequently. It was a man's world; women rarely go to cafés or restaurants.

7. The Future Arrives

"I LEFT Europe at 9 A.M. Sunday. I arrived in New York at 3 P.M. Monday." The State Teachers' Association convention at New Castle, Pennsylvania, seemed to gasp. It felt the proximity of the war.

"I came away from Europe," I told the educators on October 24, "with a carefully considered summary of the war situation. It is this: England cannot win; Germany probably cannot win and the British will not end the war by a compromise peace." The conclusion? "Only the United States can end the war and end it with the defeat of the dictatorships." (A stenographer took down my speech and sent me the transcript which I kept.) "Therefore," I said, "measures short of war lengthen the war."

Japan settled the isolationist-interventionist argument. At Pearl Harbor the Japanese told us that there were airplanes in the world and that we live in the twentieth century.

On the afternoon of December 7, 1941, I visited Arthur Upham Pope, authority on Iran and author of letters-to-the-editor about Russia. We had tea among his cats and cushions. "The Japs have attacked us in Hawaii," the liveried elevator man told me as I left. That evening a lounge-carful of men, all civilians, listened to the radio while the train raced from New York to Cincinnati. Their silence revealed their sadness.

Pearl Harbor was obviously a suicidal blunder. What prompted the Japanese to make it? The blow of December 7, 1941, was without doubt designed to destroy or to cripple the bulk of the United States Navy. Did Japan's leaders so underestimate America's industrial capacity as to suppose that we could not quickly replace the losses? Did they so underestimate America's spirit as to imagine that this country would pocket the blow and do nothing about it? Was Tokyo that stupid?

The question is not why the Japanese invaded the Dutch East Indies, Malaya, and Burma. There they saw an opportunity to steal valuable possessions from two empires weakened by the war in Europe. But why, in addition to that, did they drag the United States

81

into the war? What was the sense of gratuitously aligning American military power against Japan?

Tokyo had two alternatives: it could push north and acquire new domains at the expense of Soviet Russia or push south to seize British, Dutch, and French soil. A large school of Japanese political thought regarded Russia as the principal threat to Japan and preferred a thrust into Siberia in coordination with Hitler's advance on Moscow and the industrial areas of the Ukraine in October, November, and December, 1941. Such military action would have been carried out by the Japanese Army.

The Japanese Navy could argue that a southern drive would give Japan endless raw material and manpower resources—more than the Soviet Far East possesses—and also end China's resistance.

That explains why Japan went south towards Hong Kong, Malaya, and Singapore. It still does not explain why the Japanese Navy provoked the United States into war! Were its admirals dizzy with the prospect of easy victory? That may be so. Fanatics are fanatics because they disregard the results of their deeds. Pearl Harbor may just have been a mistake, not the first by power-crazed officials. It may have been an aberration of the medievally-minded Japanese warrior armed with modern weapons.

And yet, Pearl Harbor was a logical necessity for Japan. If Japan was not to miss the boat she had to strike sometime in 1941 while her Far Eastern rivals and potential victims—Britain, Russia, and Holland —were deeply involved in, and seriously incapacitated by, their war with Hitler.

June, 1940, when France fell and England tottered, would have been a better time for Japan to take the offensive southward. Unpreparedness is the presumed reason for Japan's failure to swallow more than French Indo-China in September, 1940. Russia was another consideration. While Hitler was busy elsewhere, neutral Russia had taken steps to regain former Tsarist positions in Europe. Japan was the mistress of several former Tsarist positions in Asia. Tokyo wondered whether Moscow might try to reoccupy those positions if Japan went south. But the Russo-Japanese treaty of April, 1941, and Hitler's invasion of Russia in June, 1941, ended the danger of any Soviet action in the Far East. This paved the way for Japan's big drive in December, 1941.

During 1939, 1940, and 1941, diplomatic relations between the United States and Japan had steadily deteriorated. On July 10, 1939,

Secretary of State Cordell Hull told the Japanese ambassador in Washington that America did not want to see all of China and the Pacific islands "Manchurianized." Simultaneously, the United States started putting economic pressure on Japan, and the bulk of the American Navy was transferred to the Pacific. In August, 1940, the export to Japan of American aviation gasoline and most types of machine tools, and the next month the export of iron and steel scrap, were prohibited. On July 26, 1941, President Roosevelt issued an executive order freezing Japanese assets in the United States. Two days earlier the President had asked Japan to respect the neutrality of French Indo-China; Nipponese forces nevertheless continued to occupy that wealthy colony. On August 17, 1941, straight from his Atlantic Charter meeting with Churchill, the President handed the Japanese ambassador a note which declared that if Japan continued her policy of "military domination by force or threat of force of neighboring countries" the United States "will be compelled to take immediately any and all steps that it may deem necessary toward safeguarding the legitimate rights and interests of the United States. . . ."

This was probably the crucial date. The Japanese Navy was ready to annex vast new territories in the Dutch and British empires. The Roosevelt administration's fierce opposition to Japan's occupation of Indo-China gave Tokyo the impression that any new Japanese aggression, especially against such vital raw-material and strategic areas as Borneo, Sumatra, and Malaya, would invite serious American reprisals. America's attitude was becoming increasingly belligerent.

President Roosevelt hoped by negotiation to stop aggression. This was laudable. But in view of America's naval and military weakness at the time, Mr. Roosevelt overplayed his diplomatic hand. History must decide, however, whether it was worth the price of Pearl Harbor to get the United States into the war a few months earlier.

Japan could not yield to Roosevelt's demands without giving up Japanese expansion and ultimately surrendering all former gains in China. Japan's imperialists could not picture themselves in such a peaceful role. They saw 1941 as a unique opportunity to erect an empire to rival England's. They believed they would be invincible behind the ramparts of Greater Asia.

Japan accordingly decided to cripple the American Navy in a surprise attack instead of waiting until better-prepared American armed forces entered the war in their own time. Convinced by the negotiations in Washington in the summer of 1941 that our entry into the war was inevitable, Tokyo wished to mark that entry with a major United States disaster. Hence Pearl Harbor.

To win and keep an empire, Japan planned to build a huge arc enclosing Burma and perhaps India, Timor and perhaps Australia, the Philippines, Wake, and Guam. Sheltered and supplied by those outposts, Japan hoped to outlast even the most prolonged siege. It never occurred to Tokyo that America would first chip off a bit of the arc at Guadalcanal, then split the arc at Leyte, and finally pierce its center at Okinawa meanwhile bombing, atom-bombing, and shelling the home islands themselves until Emperor Hirohito ran up the white flag

Hitler's invasion of Russia could only have been interpreted in Tokyo as an admission of his inability to invade and defeat England. Hitler's assault on Russia was a bid for a stalemate. With Russia under his control, he reasoned, Germany could not be defeated. With Japan in the war, British and American forces would be divided between Europe and Asia thus further insuring Germany against defeat. And an undefeated Germany could divert sufficient Anglo-American forces to keep them from crushing Japan. A stalemate for Germany was accordingly a guarantee of a stalemate for Japan.

Axis domination of Russia, Europe, and the Pacific area would have prevented an Anglo-American victory. A draw was the worst the Axis expected in these circumstances. Some Nazis and Japanese may even have dreamt of ultimate triumph.

These Axis calculations underestimated Russia's strength and America's power.

In lectures delivered during the months following my return from England I constantly emphasized the need of increasing industrial output, of increasing aid to Russia, and of planning the peace. I have stressed the peace ever since. Though I abhor war I was pro-war because I want real peace and know the world cannot have it while strong aggressors prey on small and weak nations.

In the spring of 1942, touring the western states, I found many persons pitifully jittery about Japanese air raids. Some demanded that our arms remain at home to protect America. Rich families were leaving San Francisco, Seattle, and other cities for the safety of Arizona and Nevada. I told audiences that for five cents I would have anybody heavily insured for the duration against death or damage by enemy bombs.

"I'm an optimist about the ultimate outcome—victory—," the San

Francisco newspapers quoted me as saying February 12, 1942, "but I don't feel we're at war yet. There has been no mobilization of civilians. So far it's been left to the soldiers and factories. Civilians must voluntarily reduce their standards of living before the Government does it for them."

I reverted to old habits formed in Europe and visited factories wherever possible. In Seattle I spent a day at an airplane plant. In Tacoma and Portland I inspected shipbuilding wharves. What I saw was encouraging. "Production rose 70 per cent in a single month at a huge plant that manufactures what is probably the most effective modern weapon of war," I reported in *The Nation* of March 7, 1942. That was a reference, then necessarily disguised, to the Boeing Flying Fortress factory. "Pearl Harbor accelerated the assembly lines. The workingmen know from the daily military communiqués that what they do today and every day soon makes a difference at the fighting front."

Managers in unrelated and widely separated munitions enterprises made the same response when I asked what was their chief complaint. "Paper," they said. Washington demands information, they told me, then the state asks similar data, then the region wants more facts, then another department in Washington wires for statistics already compiled for its neighbor around the corner, and so on endlessly.

At one factory, an executive pointed to a building under construction. "That," he said, "will house several hundred wrestlers. They will wrestle with red tape." I had no way of ascertaining whether this ubiquitous grumble was fully justified. But there did seem to be a plethora of Federal and local quizzers and questionnaire-hunters who irritated management and hampered production.

"Absenteeism" had become a national headache and a golden opportunity for labor-baiting. I collected a sheaf of statistics in various industrial units. Most of the absentees were mothers of children. Many defense workers were migrants from distant states. If a child became ill there was no grandmother or aunt or niece to care for it while the mother went to the factory. "Sitters" were a bottleneck. The quest for a home, food, and furniture often kept workers away from work. Absenteeism also resulted from sudden affluence which led to drinking and wild spending and from a relaxation of morals induced by wartime tensions. Empty whiskey bottles strewn over the pavements of big cities every morning meant absentees in war plants that day.

Absentees were tragic cases rather than willful malingerers. In one plant, the opening of a day nursery for children of working mothers drove the curve of absentees steeply downward.

High wages were the focus of attention. I heard soldiers and rich civilians say: "If a fighting man risks his life for $21 a month on a 24-hour day, why should a workingman get $40 or $50 a week?" Above the din of riveting machines and acetylene torches I put that question to war workers. "If the boss is making millions and being exposed by a Congressional committee as a profiteer, why shouldn't I earn a decent wage which will buy me what I need at the new high prices?" a pretty girl in slacks and lipstick replied. A craneman said: "When the boss takes $21 a month so will I." "If I give up double pay for holidays," a welder shouted, "will it go to MacArthur's boys? No, it will go to the company's stockholders." There was no equality of sacrifice in the United States during the war.

American jingoes out west were having a field day. Many of them thought they could win the war by attacking Mrs. Roosevelt or exiling American-born children of American-born Japanese to Colorado. I talked to women who were afraid that Japanese truck farmers would poison their vegetables. The Japanese, I was told, had to be banished from coastal cities because in case of an air raid enraged Americans might massacre them. Sensational newspapers clamored for the wholesale internment of Japanese. Attacks on isolated Japanese farmers multiplied. A Christ in California might have said: "He that hath chosen his parents, let him cast the first stone."

I found a lot of dejection in California. "Far Eastern experts" had predicted that we could "knock the Japs out of the Pacific in three weeks." When citizens discovered the folly of such prophecy they swung from the extreme of frivolous conceit to the extreme of undue pessimism.

But production was going up. "The motor of America is beginning to turn," I said in an address in Milwaukee on March 3. I dealt at length with the making of a peace which would be "curative and not punitive." "The only road to peace that has never been tried after a great war," I affirmed, "is true democracy."

The *St. Paul Dispatch* of March 11, 1942, quoted me as follows: "Knowing he could not knock out Great Britain, Hitler substituted the invasion of Russia for the conquest of England. . . . It is up to the Allies now to keep Russia in the war. . . . Whether Stalin wanted it or not, he is now fighting on the side of the 'angels' in this war, and

if the 'angels' wish to stay alive they'd better jump in and help him.
. . . Russia will need help, much help. . . ."

"Russia is the keystone of the war and India is the symbol of the
peace," I said to an audience in Louisville, Kentucky, on March 15.
Hitler had been stopped by the Red Army but he still had plenty of
fight in him, I affirmed.

Meanwhile, the Japanese were making rapid headway in the Far
East. "Malaya and Burma were lost," I commented, "partly because
of lack of equipment, partly because of the Kiplingesque, reactionary
British idea of imperialism. Britain is weak because the British government is intellectually a generation out of date. Churchill is all the centuries rolled into one—except the twentieth century." I urged the
American government to help India achieve independence. For "we
could win this war and lose the peace. I think it a reflection of our
rising civilization that people everywhere doubt the peace and wonder if it will be good. Versailles did not attack the fundamental social,
political, and economic problems that caused the war. We can have
that kind of peace again—but if we do we will have another war."

The Red Army had regained only one-fifth of the territory which
Germany had seized. Nevertheless, fear of the Soviet Union was
growing in the United States. The New York newspaper *PM* asked
me for an article on *Has America Anything to Fear from a Victorious
Russia?* Introducing the article, Herbert Agar, President of Freedom
House, stated that "some [Americans] even secretly hope for a Russian defeat or, at worst, a stalemate on the Russo-German front."

"What could America fear from a victorious Russia?" I wrote in
the April 27, 1942, issue of *PM*. "A Communist revolution? The idea
is ludicrous. The American Communists are a hated handful. When
they worked for Republican Spain or when they work for the defense of capitalist America and for Russian relief they exercise some
influence. But if they tried to overthrow the United States [govern-
ment] they could not muster a regiment. . . . If not revolution, what
about invasion? Could Russia invade the United States after victory?
That sounds funny. . . . Rather than stress fear of Russia, we should
emphasize that Russia has so far made the greatest contribution to the
defeat of Hitler and therefore to the defeat of his ally, Japan. Our
purpose should be to strengthen Russia. . . ."

However, I added a word of caution. *PM* omitted this warning.
The following sentence was published: "Much will depend on the

mood in which we and the Russians arrive at the end of the war."
The next three sentences were deleted. I transcribe them from my
carbon copy: "If we seek empire or domination or exclusive Anglo-
American leadership, other nations will resent it as much as we might
resent any Russian post-war annexationist wishes. Russia will not find
security in the absorption of unwilling peoples on her frontiers any
more than we will find prosperity or safety by taking over the headaches of the British, Dutch, and French empires. That way lie trouble
and more wars."

What red pencil censored those lines?

Fools think the way to solve a problem is to conceal or ignore it.
As a matter of fact, Russia's role after the war was beginning to give
more and more concern to top officials in Washington. The White
House had learned that in a talk with Foreign Secretary Eden, Stalin
announced his intention to annex the Baltic nations and eastern Poland. John G. Winant, U. S. ambassador in London, with whom I had
several intimate talks in England, told me in his room in the Hotel
Roosevelt in New York on April 25, 1942, under strict secrecy, that
Moscow would absorb all Polish territory up to the Curzon Line but
that the President opposed such frontier changes during the war. This
meant American resistance to Russian expansion. Already, allies who
were helping one another win the war were maneuvering for advantage after the war.

At the Royal Institute of International Affairs at Oxford University
where I delivered a lecture during my stay in England in 1941, a celebrated historian of the Paris Peace Conference had said to me: "After
the war, England will be America's junior partner." He added: "I
won't mind." Two of his colleagues in the Royal Institute concurred.
One of them said: "Britain will be the middle man between America
and Russia." Another suggested that a Conservative Britain might
form an alliance with a nationalistic Russia; the result would be a division of Europe into two spheres. "But we may be uncomfortable alone
on the European continent with Russia," the historian objected.

When I recounted this conversation to a State Department chief,
he said, simply: "America will be the counterpoise to Russia after the
war." In 1942, the anti-Axis powers were not yet winning, yet America's waxing strength and Russia's apparent appetite for territory had
stirred a lively discussion on post-war alignments within the Big Three.

American relations with Pétainist France also aroused much debate.
I said to a diplomat in Washington: "My observations throughout the

country tell me that our boys are going into the army willingly; they will do a good job. But there is no lift, no enthusiasm. Few know what the war is about. People are confused by our friendship for Vichy which collaborates with Hitler. 'What are we fighting for?' " I said, "is a frequent question at meetings. If we broke with Vichy and took a clear anti-Fascist line towards France, Spain, and India." I argued, "our aims would become clearer and the public would believe that Roosevelt and Churchill meant what they wrote in the Atlantic Charter."

The Administration knew that its policy towards Vichy France irritated public opinion. Spokesmen admitted that the French fleet was no longer in danger of falling into Germany's hands. They had previously justified relations with Vichy by concern over the fate of the fleet. "But suppose we want to take the offensive on French territory," a Washington adviser of the President said to me in the spring of 1942 (I made a mental note of that hint), "and suppose our agents on French territory have important contacts. Should we disrupt them?"

Ambassador Winant told me that the British government which had no relations with Pétain hoped we would continue ours with him.

An important clue to the behavior of state departments and foreign offices is their notion that they are in the "business," as I have often heard it called, of maintaining relations and improving relations with other countries and collecting information about them. Hence the ferocity with which diplomats obstruct any rupture of diplomatic ties regardless of the principles involved and the effect on morale.

Recovering slowly from the shock of Pearl Harbor, thinking Americans began, in 1942, to think about the purposes for which the war was being waged. Defeat of Japan, Germany, and Italy? Certainly! Is that enough? After victory, what?

To Felix Frankfurter, Associate Justice of the United States Supreme Court, I summarized some of my impressions of American public opinion. "The country," I said, "is groping for the meaning of the war. Ultimately America will have to choose between an idealistic peace and imperialism. When the nation realizes our great strength it may want to go places and annex new territories. You know: 'American Century,' and all that. Russia's present policy of expansion worries me partly because we may decide to embark on a similar course. The alternative is to pursue a straight anti-Fascist policy of opposition to spheres of influence, empires, and high tariffs, and of loyalty to the Atlantic Charter. That is why relations with pro-Fascist Vichy disturb the gropers. That is why they are interested in India." (I am not at liberty to quote Justice Frankfurter.)

India was front-page news. The Japanese were in Burma. The Nazis might invade Turkey and take Egypt. The only chance the Axis had of winning the war was to establish a junction somewhere in Asia, perhaps in India. And India was seething. President Roosevelt had sent Colonel Louis Johnson, former Assistant Secretary of War, as his special envoy to New Delhi. The British government had sent Sir Stafford Cripps, former Ambassador to Moscow and now member of the Cabinet, to India with written proposals. All Indian parties had rejected the proposals. What now? Would Japan invade India? Would Hitler smash into the Near East?

On Thursday, April 24, I told Mr. Sumner Welles I would like to go to India. He penciled a note on his pad. Exactly a week later he telephoned me in New York and said: "If you can get your 'shots' in the next three days there will be a seat on the plane leaving New York Sunday." I said "Fine" and asked about my passport. He promised to have it put in the mail for me that evening. I received it in the morning. No questionnaires, no applications, no red tape. I got the first installments of my cholera, typhoid-paratyphoid, yellow fever, and smallpox shots, and left in the Clipper on Monday, May 5. (It was the birthday of both my sons.) I anticipated an exciting time but my expectations were mild compared to the time I had.

8. *South to India*

AMONG its fifty passengers the Clipper seaplane carried American engineers going to India to raise the output of mica which the United States needed for war purposes, American officers going to China to organize the Chinese Air Force, State Department officials carrying sealed mailbags from which they never parted, two Americans, husband and wife, enroute to British East Africa on a three years' assignment to fight yellow fever, and a Polish diplomat flying to China via Egypt and Russia. In Miami we picked up several Latin Americans and a group of GIs who would be paymasters for American servicemen stationed on the African Gold Coast.

Next morning, the Clipper landed at San Juan, Puerto Rico. I telephoned Rexford G. Tugwell, Governor of the island, whom I first met in Moscow. He came down and we spent an hour together until departure time. President Roosevelt must have been conducting his own little experiment when he appointed a Brains Trust intellectual like Tugwell to govern Puerto Rico, Ernest Gruening, managing editor of *The Nation*, to govern Alaska, and Robert Morss Lovett, one of the editors of *The New Republic*, to govern the Virgin Islands. "You have criticized what others do," the President might have said. "Now go and do it yourself and see how you like it." I know Gruening liked it very much. Practical administration instead of editorializing and theorizing had not made a conservative out of Gruening or Tugwell or, to judge by the complaints of conservatives, out of Lovett. In fact, intimate knowledge of the corruption of politics and the sinister pressures often brought to bear on politicians confirmed their critical attitude towards governments.

We played poker over Surinam and talked about the American soldiers who guarded that Dutch colony. Surinam's interior is impassable jungle. From the plane, however, it looked like hundreds of miles of well-kept, well-swept forest with here and there a straw hut hugging the low bank of a stream and occasionally a cluster of such huts around a red-tiled house, probably an estate. A Brazilian on board who had combed South America for landing fields for the American Air Force and knew every square foot of the land and water over

91

which we flew said the jungle was actually clean, with little under-brush and few wild animals of prey: some jaguars, leopards, pumas, and smaller cats, and armadillos, tapirs, and ant-eaters, but innumerable wild birds and hosts of long and short snakes. The monkeys, he said, sit conveniently in the palm of one's hand; the largest stand about two feet high.

Forty-five minutes out from our next landing place at Belem, in Brazil, one of the Clipper's four motors went dead. It was rather disturbing to see the three motionless arms of the propeller, but an airplane mechanic on board said the plane could make port even on two motors. We landed smoothly on the Para River amid sheets of rain that shone silver white in the searchlight beams which guided the pilot through the blackness of the tropical evening.

We spent five days at Belem while the motor was repaired. Belem, the capital of the state of Para, is a hundred miles south of the Equator but it was not hot in May. The nights were pleasantly cool and you covered with a sheet and blanket. Before it can get hot in the morning, clouds begin to gather to shut out the sun. A gentle breeze blows most of the time. By early afternoon rain begins to threaten, and it rained every day we were there. I asked whether this was the rainy season. "No," I was told, "that begins in January." This was the dry season.

The insects my mind had always connected with Amazonia were not in evidence. I did not see nor feel a mosquito at Belem. I saw ant-eaters in the zoo but no ants, and no more flies than in American cities. The numerous parks of the city are free from obnoxious things that creep or fly.

What surprised me most was the ancient, dignified culture in a place where I, in my ignorance, had expected a steaming tropical settlement of straw homes on stilts. Para, founded by the Portuguese navigator Francisco Caldeiro Castello Branco on the day before Christmas, 1615 (this I got from a city handbook), has a cathedral, numerous stone churches, and many schools and public buildings. Its wide streets are paved with rounded cobblestones and the sidewalks are of cement. There is trolley and bus service. Most streets are lined on both sides with massive old trees whose foliage meets to create shade. Plant life is so lush that leaves sprout straight from the bark of trees.

Famous explorers like Humboldt, Agassiz, and Martins made Belem headquarters for their researches and explorations in the Amazon region. Belem is today the port for Ford's rubber plantations six hundred miles up the river where, according to U. S. Vice-Consul Hart of Boston, Americans employed on the plantations enjoy all the comforts of home right in the heart of the jungle.

Amazonia was the mother of rubber. Its cultivation, however, was neglected. But "an audacious Englishman," the Brazilians say, evading rigorous government regulations against the export of rubber seeds, carried off 70,000 seeds which were first planted in Kew Gardens, London, and then transplanted in Malaya, Sumatra, Java, Ceylon, etcetera, to start a fabulous industry. Today, aided by American capital, Brazil is attempting to gain a toehold in the rubber world.

Dr. Orlando Lima came to administer the rest of my cholera and paratyphoid shots. "Who are these people in shorts?" he asked in a tone of condescending amusement. The doctor was dressed in an immaculate two-piece white suit with necktie and stud. He thought "North Americans" queer; in Belem they wore shorts and in New York he had seen them carry their jackets on their arms and roll up their sleeves. The first evening I came down to the hotel dining room without a jacket. The head waiter, in black and white tuxedo, sent me back with the polite explanation that they did not serve customers in shirt sleeves. Like all Latins, the Brazilians pay much attention to form.

Dr. Lima told me he had studied at the medical college in Rio de Janeiro and taken graduate courses in Germany in 1908. "You don't look that old," I remarked.

"I am fifty-seven," he declared. His hair was thick and black. When I noted that he did not have a single gray hair, he said: "Naturally. It is because I am brown. I am part Indian," he announced proudly. "We mix the blood. It is good to mix the blood." On the streets one sees obviously white persons with Negroid features, and brown faces with Chinese eyes, for the original Portuguese colonizers came to Brazil when Portugal was likewise exploring the Far East. A tall Belemite is rare; so is a blonde woman. Women wear no hats.

Belem near the Equator reminded me of Russia for only one reason: the ubiquity of President Getulio Vargas' photograph. Among the most widely distributed pictures was one of Vargas lunching with Roosevelt in the White House. Good connections in Washington raise one's prestige, and Latin American dictators have frequently been bolstered by the smiles and gold of the United States. North America's popularity with the people south of the Rio Grande is not enhanced thereby.

The United States government supported South American Fascist dictatorships that helped win the war and opposed Fascist dictatorships that did not help. This did not give Latin anti-Fascists the impression that the United States was anti-dictatorship.

From Belem, the restored Clipper flew to Natal, nearest Brazilian jumping-off point to Africa, and thence it winged effortlessly across the Atlantic in fourteen hours and deposited us in Lagos, Nigeria. This British colony has a population of twenty-one million. How little thought we ever give them. They belong to three tribes or clans speaking different languages. In a canteen near the airfield which served only warm lemonade, three attendants, one from each of the tribes, communicated with one another in primitive English. Lagos has several English newspapers including a Socialist daily. I visited a school maintained by missionaries. Cute chocolate-colored girls of five or six, their wiry hair twisted into scores of tight braids that stood out from their heads like rays of the sun, were learning to read "Christ walked on the waters" in their native tongue. They looked clean and bewildered.

At Lagos, the United States Ferry Command took over and transported some of us north to Kano, making the five hundred and forty miles in two hours and seven minutes. Kano is the capital of a Moslem emirate. The emir or king gets a fat annual subsidy from the British; in return, he behaves and makes his subjects behave. The people resemble Arabs and I was able to exchange some words with them in rudimentary Arabic.

We slept in British barracks at Kano and took off at five the next morning from a new American airfield for Maiduguri, where we landed at seven at another new American airfield. Here a sandstorm enveloped men, machines, field, and huts and it was impossible to go on. An officer said we would have to spend the day and night at Maiduguri. The prospect of twenty-four hours in the accommodations of this African wilderness did not cheer me. But protest would of course have been vain. We entered a rickety bus that rocked over deep-rutted roads. Every time the ancient vehicle stopped to let a bullock cart pass one of the American airmen, boys of twenty-one or nineteen, three months out of Kansas or Virginia or a Midwest university, would shout: "Jersey City, next stop Times Square," or "All out for Union Station." They confessed being very homesick.

Negro men and women, practically nude but wearing huge straw hats, worked under the hot sun in fields of cotton. Everything seemed poor and antediluvian. The airplane had taken us back to the age of Noah.

As guests of the Ferry Command, we stayed in its camp which consisted of a group of large new wooden huts with every window screened and every door double-screened. Each person had a bed with a mosquito-netting canopy. Each hut had hot and cold water showers with large cakes of American soap, modern toilets, plugs for electric razors, electric light, and a huge refrigerator filled with brown bottles of ice-cold water which had previously been boiled. A Negro attendant constantly replenished the supply of bottles.

At the sound of a gong, we went to lunch. The moment we started leaving, some boys began shooting Flit through the air and into all corners to kill any flies and mosquitoes that might have entered. The mess hut was darkened and cool. Electric fans twirled. There was not a single fly. Native waiters, probably just out of the bush, wearing white suits and white cotton gloves, moved noiselessly on bare feet and distributed a typed menu.

The next morning the same mess had new white cloth table covers and napkins. "Corn flakes or oatmeal?" an American Negro waiter asked. My second dish was eggs "sunny side up," then buckwheat cakes with butter and maple syrup and, finally, good coffee with sugar and cream. At Maiduguri, right in the middle of nowhere! If the American boys had to be far away from home in order to help win the war they got as much of home as a solicitous Government could bring them from the United States to the wilds of Africa. It was the same in every newly-established American Ferry Command camp from Nigeria to India.

With Germany and Italy entrenched in southern Europe, the Mediterranean, and parts of the North African coast, and with Japan in control of the Pacific islands and Malaya and Burma, we were moving along the only safe air route from America and England to Egypt, Turkey, Russia, Iran, India, and China.

The planes flying this course were army transports stripped of every convenience. Passengers sat in shallow aluminum pans and leaned against the shivering sides of the plane. If you got tired of that you could sit on the floor or on the crates containing guns or other war equipment. From Maiduguri to Lake Chad in French Equatorial Africa to Khartoum in the sizzling Sudan we traveled over desert which consisted of sandy wastes and rocky ridges. The plane was filled to the brim with cartons of small rubber tires, the kind that goes under an airplane to help wheel it about. The tires were Lend-Lease material for Russia. Some cartons broke open and several of us enjoyed the luxury of sitting in a tire on the bouncing floor. I read a book by Shuster and Wint on India.

I flew from Khartoum to Cairo in a machine piloted by T. F. Collins of San Angelo, Texas (Texans were everywhere), and Raymond Wise, Jr., of Pennsylvania. They told us we would do the nine hundred miles to Cairo non-stop, which was good news because every descent to the earth meant sweltering heat and delay. But just before the take-off, Wise said: "We have to stop at Wadi Halfa, about half way to Cairo. We've got a GI in the hospital up there and he's out of money so we're bringing him $150." Wadi Halfa is a tiny clump of date trees and huts in the middle of the desert and the GI, the only American there, was eleven thousand miles from home. We made up a bundle of magazines for him.

Cairo was civilization which means many things, but on that trip it meant a wonderful hotel room, cool drinks, a bathtub, decent food, and taxis. It meant meeting friends among the foreign correspondents and diplomats. Alexander Kirk, whom I knew first in Rome and later in Moscow, was then United States ambassador to Egypt. Nazi General Rommel threatened Cairo. The British forces were valiant but weak. Kirk had an *idée fixe:* the United States must invade Italy. That would save Egypt and the Suez Canal and turn the entire European war. Kirk is extremely wealthy and those who do not know him could easily regard him as belonging to the aristocratic coterie of American career diplomats and the "Groton-Harvard" State Department crowd. He does delight in entertaining lavishly. But he has a penetrating mind and a keen perception of international politics. He seems supercilious and poses in that role at times; actually, he is not indifferent. He fights for policies he believes in. He incessantly urged the bombing of the Rumanian oilfields.

On arrival at the famous Shepheard's Hotel I collided with Maurice Hindus, an old friend, who had just flown in from Moscow. Then we found Colonel Louis Johnson whom President Roosevelt had sent as his special envoy to India. He was accompanied by Colonel Arthur W. Herrington, an industrialist of Indianapolis, who knew the Near East from having worked in it for long periods. Johnson, with Herrington as aide, had studied conditions in India and closely watched the India mission of Sir Stafford Cripps in March and April, 1942. I met Johnson when he was Assistant Secretary of War—a post he held until 1940—and I had a special State Department letter asking him to help me. I looked forward to the contacts and information I would obtain through him in India. But the climate and conditions of India had made him seriously ill and he was rushing home for a cure. I gathered that his experience in India had made him an advocate of a change of regime. He spoke with high regard and enthusiasm about Jawaharlal Nehru, the Indian nationalist leader.

I waited four days in Cairo for an eastbound plane. I would sit on the hotel terrace with an American newspaperman. "Have you heard what happened here in February?" he asked. I replied in the negative. Mysteriously and with many "off the records" he whispered a cryptic sentence. Alexander Kirk said I ought to look into what happened in Cairo in February. I said: "What?" He disclosed a few particulars and then changed the subject. In this manner, I pieced together fragments that began to make a story. Nobody could write it from Cairo because the strict British censorship was particularly strict on this story. I did not intend writing it but I was curious and wanted to know. So I got myself an appointment with Sir Miles Lampson, the British ambassador, a plump, jovial man. We skipped around many topics and bit into none. Finally I said: "I know enough of what happened in February to be able to talk about it with the assurance that I am not altogether wrong, but some parts of my information must be inadequate or incorrect."

He asked me to tell him what I had heard. I told him and he commented. This is what happened: In February, 1942, relations between the British government and King Farouk of Egypt had deteriorated seriously. The King could scarcely be called pro-British or pro-war. It would not have been unnatural had he entertained a few sympathies for the Axis, not so much because he loved the Italians, still less the Germans; but he may have thought that a British defeat would give Egypt fuller freedom. Things came to a head when the British demanded that code and courier facilities be denied the Vichy minister in Cairo who was suspected of sending secret information on British military affairs to the Pétain authorities. These apparently let it leak back to the Germans. The King had refused to withdraw diplomatic privileges from the Vichy envoy. So Sir Miles Lampson and Lieutenant General Robert G. Stone sought an appointment with the King. On the agreed day, in February, British tanks and soldiers surrounded the royal palace. Then Lampson and Stone entered the King's chamber. Everybody was polite and urbane. The Englishmen suggested that there was an airplane in readiness for His Majesty at the airfield and it could take him to a place far off where he might stay very long—this, however, only in case he did not see fit to issue a certain order about the man from Vichy and change his Prime Minister. The King saw fit.

The Nazis did not bomb Cairo. The Egyptians buzzed through their lives as usual, making profit out of the war but not investing any sentiment in it.

On May 21, I left Cairo, flew over the Suez, over Rafa in the south Palestine desert where I had been a British soldier for several months in 1919, over Gaza now expanded by war, over Tel Aviv, the white Jewish city by the green sea, over the bald hills of Judea, over the snake-like Jordan and over the barren brown desert to the lake at Habanniya, near Baghdad, where we landed. The trip took four and a half hours. Iraqui soldiers showed us the ridge near the airfield on which Rashid Ali's rebel troops had entrenched themselves while fighting the British in 1941.

After a lunch in the mess hut, we hopped to Basra in two hours. Here the Euphrates and Tigris unite to form the Shatt-al-Arab which flows softly along the edge of the beer garden outside the hotel. The hotel is air-conditioned, the electric fans never stopped, I used no covers, and dripped perspiration all night. Africa is cool compared to Basra.

Near Basra, the Russians had a Lend-Lease airfield. We dropped down and unloaded the rubber tires for them and then flew to Sharja in the independent principality of Oman which is part of Arabia. Wild, rough, mountainous country alternated with sea. We slept in a British Eastern Airways hostel in Sharja; next morning, six hours, seven hundred and forty miles, mostly over water, to Karachi, the eastern gate of India. We came down at an American military airfield, manned by Americans only, and looking like any major military airfield in the United States. The informality of the Americans was a delight. Nobody demanded my passport or papers. I asked Colonel Mason, who was in charge: "How soon will you have a plane for New Delhi?" "In thirty minutes," he said. I bought a carton of damp biscuits in the canteen, and climbed in. Late that afternoon, May 23, I reached my destination, New Delhi, the capital of India.

9. *West Meets East*

EAST is the glamor of the maharajah on his elephant and the squalor of the peasant's hut, the hunt for tigers and the hunt for bread, the color of fabric and the drabness of life. East is mystery, intrigue, and romance, and starvation, drudgery, and early death. East is the enigmatic beauty of nature and the obvious ugliness of life.

The West lives. The East gropes for the meaning of living. The West moves madly. The East waits patiently. The West seeks the new, and the antique is a decoration. The East lives with the old. The West reads more and thinks less. The East reads little and considers contemplation the ideal condition.

In the West, it is the machine that has rhythm; in the East it is man.

The West covets wealth, power, strength, and beauty. The East bows to these but respects frailty, simplicity, humility, and self-denial.

The East is different from the West. But is it a difference of space or of time? Is it that Asia is not Europe or that Asia is the fourteenth century and not the twentieth? When Europe was in the fourteenth century it was more like Asia today than like Europe today.

Asia is hundreds of years east of the West.

Asia's problem is to begin living in the present.

India's problem is to catch up with the twentieth century.

The conflict in India is not between East and West but between the seventeenth century and the twentieth.

I left New York in May, 1942, and spent the summer in 1642. However, a three-mile taxi ride or even a three-minute walk carried me three centuries into a world Made-in-Britain. The Portuguese, the French, and the British brought the West to India. The West became a part of India. But the British never became a part of India. They are in India, not of India. The Indians accepted what the British brought; they did not accept the British. Nor did the British accept the Indians. Rudyard Kipling's "East is East and West is West and never the twain shall meet" means, English and Indians cannot mix because master and servants do not mix.

I did not see an Indian or an Englishman at the United States Air

Force field at Karachi where I entered India. I did not see an Indian at the airfield in New Delhi. There were some Indians in the streets of New Delhi and some in the Imperial Hotel. But New Delhi was England in an Indian setting, a British city for bureaucrats. I did not feel like going to bed on my first day in India without seeing India. So I asked the hotel cashier to exchange some dollars for rupees with which I could go into Old Delhi, the native city. It was after hours, he said, and he would have to get the manager's permission. The manager was an Englishman. "You had better not go to Delhi at night," he warned. "They would just as soon stab you in the back there as not." He nevertheless gave me forty rupees and I drove to Old Delhi, saw cows and bullocks sleeping in streets, and half-naked, emaciated people sleeping on pavements, and sat alone in a small native establishment to watch a heavily-dressed girl dance by moving horizontally from the neck and waist. Then I taxied home intact. My impressions were of heat, dirt, dust, and primitiveness.

One can form a deep attachment for the people of a foreign country. I have such an attachment for the people of Spain, England, and the Soviet Union. One can love a foreign country for its beauty: France, Italy. But in India, neither the people, nor the physical characteristics of those parts of the country I saw, nor the nation's culture fascinated me. What stands out in my memory of India is persons I met and problems I studied. The persons talked about the problems. In India there is one topic of conversation: India. Often I tried to channel a discussion towards America or Russia or the war. I failed. The problems of India are so painful and urgent that they absorb all attention. India is sick, and it is like having a sick heart or a sick stomach. You could only forget it if it got well.

India is divided into two parts: an amorphous mass of hundreds of millions too weak physically and too handicapped economically and educationally to lift themselves above their apathy, and, second, a top stratum of several million, perhaps four or five million, who strive nervously to overcome the disadvantages of national poverty, a difficult climate, and the ever-present sense of inferiority born of having a foreign master.

The hard past and the fierce struggle to acquire and keep a foothold on the few rungs of success in a retarded country like India intensify the competition for wealth, power, and position. The competitors develop terrific drive and passion. They seem to feel that time is running out quickly. The fear of failure generates surging energy and deep bitterness in them. Failure brings a desire for revenge even at their own cost. Yet the same persons can be relaxed and philosophical in private encounters and charmingly naive in their frankness about intimate matters.

I heard about "frustration" from the poor, idealistic student and from the multi-millionaire, from the high Hindu official and from the hard-working merchant. They referred only to frustrations resulting from British rule. But I found that frustration is also heaped high around every roadblock built by the caste system and the scarcity of economic opportunity. Indians are indeed frustrated, and their collective conduct consequently strikes one as not a little abnormal. There is something pathological about Indian politics. India needs a doctor.

Gandhi's great following has been ascribed to the fact that he is regarded as a semi-god and that he is an astute statesman. People have debated whether he is saint or political boss. Above all, he is India's doctor.

Jawaharlal Nehru, generally regarded as Gandhi's leading disciple and political heir, stressed this when I talked to him in New Delhi the day after my arrival. Gandhi's achievement in raising the Indian's self-esteem is one of the bonds that tie Nehru to Gandhi. For these two men are very different. Nehru is a bit of the West operating in the East. In 1942 he was fifty-two. Some ten of these years were spent in prisons in India. Other years were spent at Harrow and at Cambridge. British prisons and British schools speak in Nehru. So does the modern world. Everything in Nehru protests against the machine-less backwardness of his country. Gandhi revels in it.

In dress, in food, in the religious allusions he uses, in his philosophy of life, Gandhi is old India. But Nehru concedes just enough to that old India to be accepted by it so he can change it.

I had seen Nehru in Geneva, Paris, and London in European clothes. Now I found him dressed in white linen drawers tight around the legs and reaching down to his ankles, a white shirt which hung down to his knees, and an apricot-colored waistcoat. He was barefoot, but a pair of black leather shoes stood near the sofa on which we sat. He introduced me to his cousin at whose house he was staying. She is the wife of an Indian Civil Service official, and wore a white sari and had a round, bright red spot painted in the center of her forehead; it signified that she was not a widow. She served us orange squash.

At regular intervals I heard the swish of water splashed against a thick straw curtain forming the outside wall of the terrace. The water cooled the sultry air as it came through the straw and kept out the dust which filled the air. The house was low but otherwise constructed and furnished in European style—except for the exquisite Oriental decorations.

Nehru smoked innumerable cigarettes in a long holder. He smiled a lot, showing fine white teeth. His skin is dark sand-brown; he is most handsome though bald with a ring of white hair above each ear.

"Yes," Nehru admitted in response to a question, "the British have given India order and security. But they have also weakened and demoralized us. It is only in the last twenty-two or twenty-three years since Gandhiji [the "ji" is a suffix of respect] launched his program of non-violent non-cooperation that Indian pride and national sentiment have reasserted themselves. Before, when a policeman struck a peasant the others ran away. Now they rush to defend the peasant. The Indian people have learned courage. This is not only a political weapon. We have used it to prevent high rents."

Gandhi is the father of India's defiance and its symbol. Gandhi, thin, in loincloth and sandals, walks to the sea to make salt in defiance of a British regulation that individuals must not make salt but buy it from the Government salt monopoly. Tens of thousands of Indians march behind Gandhi to the sea. It becomes a popular pilgrimage. The idealism of youth spills into it; so does a leaderless nation's yearning for a leader. The Salt March provides Indians with the opportunity physically to follow a leader. And, thanks to Gandhi, his followers feel the elation of standing up to the foreigner who is master in their house.

Gandhi walking up the steps of the Viceroy's great marble palace gives Indians a new sense of importance. Gandhi fasts; the Empire trembles. One of Gandhi's non-cooperation campaigns becomes violent. He fasts to reprove it. The violence stops. Without any of the paraphernalia of power, for he can neither punish nor reward, Gandhi exercises control. Out of the weak shall come forth strength. The weak glory in Gandhi's strength. His strength is theirs. Thousands think of him and address him as *Bapu*, father. He signs himself *Bapu*. He signed himself *Bapu* in a letter to me.

Gandhi is India's antidote to frustration. Indians have walked straighter since Gandhi came to lead. Nehru is grateful. Nehru is proud, temperamental, and tempestuous. "We do not wish dominion status," he said. "We are not a daughter of the mother country like

Canada or Australia. We are ourselves a mother. India has been a cultured country for centuries. The British ask us to unite in a commonwealth of British nations some of which, South Africa for instance, discriminate against Indian residents. We would much rather join an international family of nations, including the British but not only the British, including the Chinese, America, Russia, and all humanity."

I prodded Nehru to talk of Gandhi. "Gandhi," he declared, "is an Indian nationalist leader with a message for the whole world. He is very Indian. But his spirituality is universal.

"There is an element of the dictator in Gandhi," Nehru conceded with a smile, "and there is more compulsion in one of his fasts than in Hitler's terror. Gandhi does not believe in strikes. He prefers arbitration. Yet on one occasion, some textile workers struck and Gandhi went on a fast to compel the mill owners to settle. They of course hastened to settle." What Indian could take it upon himself to endanger Gandhi's life or prolong his pain for a day?

I spent a week with Mahatma Gandhi at Sevagram, a village in the center of India. Nehru was there during the last three days of that week.

I lived in a floorless mud hut with roof of straw, slept under the stars in a bed made of four wooden posts which supported a net of rope, and ate what Gandhi ate: a mess of boiled squash and spinach leaves, boiled potatoes, raw onions, cow's milk, mangoes, tea, honey, and biscuits. The same menu every day. I fared well. But after I had had boiled squash and spinach leaves for lunch and dinner the first day and lunch and dinner the second day, I said "No, thank you" at lunch on the third day. Gandhi, who is very much interested in dietary problems and always watched me at meals, said: "You don't like vegetables."

"I don't like the taste of these vegetables," I replied.

"You must add plenty of salt and lemon," he proposed.

"In other words, you want me to kill the taste," I laughed.

"No," he said, "enrich the taste."

"You are so non-violent," I said, "you wouldn't even kill a taste."

Gandhi is, of course, a pacifist. But my talks with him and a study of his life convince me that his pacifism is political, not religious. He is not an absolute pacifist. He rejects war because he does not believe in the wars which modern nations wage for conquest and supremacy. He would, if he could, have put a stop to World War II because he had no faith in the ability of governments to use victory for the improvement of humanity.

Gandhi's non-violence, when you look closely, is not pacifism; it is not the refusal to fight. It is the weapon with which Gandhi fights. Fasts are weapons, too. The Indian nationalist movement has no other weapons. The people have no arms.

Gandhi told me how he came to adopt the method of non-violent resistance; the whole episode is characteristically Indian. "It began in 1916," he said. "I was in Lucknow working for the Congress party. A peasant came up to me, looking poor and emaciated like any other peasant in India. 'My name is Rajkumar Shukla,' he announced. 'I am from Champaran, and I want you to come to my district.' He described the misery of the farmers of his district and begged me to let him take me to them. Champaran is hundreds of miles from Lucknow but he begged so persistently and persuasively that I promised."

Gandhi, however, could not go immediately. So the peasant followed Gandhi for weeks through the length and breadth of India until, in 1917, he got Gandhi to take a train with him from Calcutta to Champaran.

Gandhi proposed to ask the peasants of the region about their lot. "But in order to get the other side of the question," Gandhi continued, "I also wanted to interview the British Commissioner of the area. When I called on the Commissioner he bullied me and advised me to leave the district immediately. I did not accept his advice and, instead, proceeded on the back of an elephant to one of the villages to investigate conditions.

"On the road," Gandhi said, "a police messenger overtook me and ordered me to leave Champaran. I allowed the police to escort me back to the house where I was staying, and there, for the first time, I offered civil disobedience. I would not leave the district. Huge crowds gathered around the house. I cooperated with the police in regulating the crowds.

"Then I was brought into court on trial," Gandhi recalled. "The Government attorney pleaded with the magistrate to postpone the case, but I asked him to go on with it. I wanted to announce in court that I had deliberately disobeyed the order to leave Champaran. I told him I had come to collect information on peasant conditions and that I therefore had to disobey the British law because I was acting in obedience with a higher law, the voice of my conscience.

"This was my first act of civil disobedience against the British,"

Gandhi observed. "My desire was to establish the principle that no Englishman had the right to tell me to leave any part of my country to which I had gone for a peaceful pursuit. I pleaded guilty."

Government officials implored Gandhi to drop his plea of guilty. They did not want to convict Gandhi. Gandhi refused to change his plea. Finally, the Government had no alternative but to dismiss the case and let Gandhi proceed.

"Civil disobedience had won," Gandhi said.

Since that day in 1917, Gandhi has perfected his system of civil disobedience. The police charge an Indian independence demonstration with staves. The marchers lie down in the road and allow themselves to be beaten until the procedure becomes too scandalous and the British withdraw the police. Indians refuse to buy foreign textiles. Indians refuse to pay taxes. Indians block British officials in automobiles by lying across the streets.

Shrewdly, Gandhi turned the passivity and supineness of the Indian into an instrument of struggle. The docility bred by British rule was used against the British rulers. Only courage had been added. That was Gandhi's contribution.

I once said to Gandhi that England was a very democratic country. He insisted, however, that England could not be democratic at home and imperialistic in India. Imperialism is, indeed, the antithesis of democracy. It is anti-democratic for one country to hold another in prolonged bondage merely because it has the physical strength but was never given the right to do so. Imperialism is might without right. Within this severe limitation, the British in India observed innumerable rules of the democratic code. In any European dictatorship, a Gandhi would be liquidated at three o'clock some morning and nobody would hear another word from him or of him. There could have been no mass civil disobedience in Nazi Germany, nor is non-violent non-cooperation conceivable in Soviet Russia. But Gandhi knew that the British would not and could not liquidate him so long as there was unfettered public opinion in India, England, and the United States. It was freedom of speech in these countries that made possible Gandhi's non-violent battle for Indian freedom.

During my week as Gandhi's house guest I kept wondering what was the secret of his power. The Congress party which he and Nehru lead and over which Maulana Abul Kalam Azad, a Moslem, presided, is a loosely-knit body into whose coffers members pay eight cents a year without however committing themselves to any duties or discipline. Gandhi has no money, no property, and no machinery of compulsion or organization. Yet he has the loyalty of many millions of Indians who never saw him. A considerable percentage of these will make heavy sacrifice, even risk their lives and their liberty, at his call. Gandhi fasts and countless millions turn to his bedside in anxious vigil. Why is it?

In part, the explanation is religion. India is a very religious country, and the Hindus, who form the bulk of Gandhi's following, have a peculiar idea of God. Hinduism is a sponge religion. It includes features of Buddhism, Christianity, and paganism. Gandhi who is very Hindu knows the Koran and believes in some tenets of Islam. In Gandhi's mud bungalow there is only one decoration, a framed black and white print of Jesus Christ under which is written "He Is Our Peace." "I am a follower of Jesus," Gandhi explained to me. Hinduism absorbs all dogma and destroys none. There is therefore no Hindu fundamentalism; all its fundamentals are in a constant state of flux, which means they are not fundamentals.

Hinduism is broad enough to embrace agnosticism, monotheism, and idolatry. Hindus have idols before which they dance and pray. But when I asked those Hindus whether they believe in idols they answered: No, they believed in one God. "If Niagara Falls were in India," Nehru said, "they would be a god." They would be regarded as a manifestation of divinity. Untold Indians regard Gandhi as a manifestation of God, and yet a man. A Hindu financier who told me he loathed the Congress party and did not concern himself with politics, nevertheless declared ecstatically that "A Gandhi lives only once in thousands of years; the gates of Heaven are waiting to receive him."

But why is it Gandhi who is thus distinguished, and why do Moslems and non-believers adopt Gandhi as their leader? On my sixth day at Sevagram I put the question to Mahadev Desai, Gandhi's personal secretary, now dead, who had served the Mahatma for over ten years. "All these days," I said, "I have been trying to fathom the source of Gandhi's great influence. I have come to the conclusion, tentatively, that the chief reason of that influence is Gandhi's passion."

"That is right," Desai said.

"What is the root of the passion?" I asked.

"It is the sublimation of all the passions that flesh is heir to," he affirmed.

"Sex?" I said.

"Sex, and anger, and personal ambition," Desai enumerated. "Gandhi can admit that he is wrong. He can chastise himself and take the blame for the mistakes of others. Gandhi is under his own complete control. That generates tremendous energy and passion within him."

Passion is the indispensable ingredient of all great men. It may be passion for good or evil; it may be harnessed to a Hitler who had it in abundance. It may be intellectual or animal or ethical. But there must be passion.

While groping for the key to Gandhi's greatness I decided to ask Gandhi himself. I used to walk with him mornings at sunrise or evenings as the sun was sinking. One evening, I said to him: "This isn't a personal question but a political question: how do you account for your influence over so many people?"

"I think my influence is due to the fact that I pursue the truth. That is my goal," Gandhi answered. "But truth," he added, "is not merely a matter of words. It is really a matter of living the truth." I assumed he referred to the simplicity of his life. He could have all the millions he desired as gifts. Except on rare occasions, however, his diet, shelter, and attire approximate those of the Indian peasantry who are ninety per cent of the population of India. This has been called a pose for political effect. Since he need not live that way it does seem calculated. But so is all renunciation. Gandhi lives on the earth; more than three hundred million Indians live on the same level. They see themselves in him. His manner of living aids their identification with him.

I pursued the subject further. "Isn't it," I said to Gandhi as we strolled along, "that when you advocate independence you strike a chord in many Indians? A musician does something to the members of his audience. You play a note which Indians are ready to hear. I have noticed that people applaud most the arias they have heard often and liked. Is it that you say and do what your people want you to say and do?"

"Yes," he said, "maybe that is it."

Gandhi's influence is a complicated phenomenon with many causes. One cause is the timing of Gandhi's appearance as India's independence champion. He came into his own as leader in 1919 when a world wave of nationalism struck many underprivileged peoples, among them Indians. Simultaneously, India was swept by disappointment over the slight advance towards freedom after her heavy casualties in the first world war. Gandhi's emergence was the answer to a need and a prayer.

India was again in a trough of disappointment during the summer of 1942. In March, Sir Stafford Cripps had carried to India a written proposal drafted by the Churchill government for wartime and post-war changes of administration. For different reasons, all Indian parties rejected the Cripps offer. The effect of Cripps' failure on India was black dejection and crisis.

Gandhi is temperamentally incapable of despair. He is a fighter. Those who do nothing are more given to hopelessness than those who actively combat the cause of their pessimism. Seventy-three years old when I saw him in 1942, Gandhi was affirmative, dynamic, jolly, and his interest was not in the past. He never once reminisced; Lloyd George always reminisced. Gandhi looked to the future. His life's work, the emancipation of India, still remained undone.

The failure of the Cripps Mission to give India freedom stimulated in Gandhi a desire to do something. Gandhi believes in action as a means to an end and as an end, as a cure. "China should be able to say to America and England: 'We will fight our battle of independence singlehanded without your aid.' That I would call independence," Gandhi said to me. This is wisdom. Independence gained by dependence on others is not independence. The process by which a goal is achieved is part of the achievement. In a true democracy it must be so. In Stalin's Russia, all good and all evil comes from the top. Decisions are always taken at the sharp point of the dictatorial pyramid and are then communicated to the wider strata where they bring automatic responses induced by habitual and unquestioning obedience. In a system based on the principle that the end hallows any means, the means lose all educative and moral value and produce cynicism and political immorality.

But Gandhi, who does not proclaim himself a champion of democracy, is nevertheless a democrat to the core because he is scrupulous about means; he lives in a glass house, has no secrets, is honest with his followers, and believes in action undertaken simultaneously by leaders and followers. In fact, Gandhi's ideal seems to be a political symphony orchestra without conductor. For instance, he forbids Indian nationalists to participate in terror or underground activities. On the eve of a country-wide civil disobedience campaign, he communicates his plan to the British authorities. When the campaign begins the heads of the Congress party invite arrest by standing up in public places and disclosing their intention to practise non-violent non-cooperation. The British immediately arrest those heads of the Party, thousands of them, and clap them in jail. Thereupon, the masses, whether members of Congress or not, enter the leaderless campaign and non-cooperate in their villages and towns. They decline to pay taxes or to sell their grain or to comply with Government regulations. This goes on until the campaign peters out or until Gandhi calls off the campaign when it has accomplished its object or part of its object or when he sees it has failed.

Gandhi's response to Cripps' failure was the civil disobedience campaign which started on August 9, 1942, with the arrest of Gandhi, Nehru, and several thousand others. Nehru was released in 1945.

During my stay with Gandhi, the idea of the coming campaign of non-cooperation was maturing in his brain. The germ was spontaneously generated in May in the course of a weekly day of silence. He thought to himself: "The British Must Go." Having thought it, he wrote it for publication and said it to anyone who would listen. He said it to me. The purpose of the new disobedience movement would be to make the British go.

Each day, in the afternoon, Gandhi gave me an hour's interview. Exactly at the end of the hour he would pull his big nickel-plated dollar watch out from inside the cord of his loincloth, smile, and say "Now," at which signal I would depart. He is very punctual. On the third day, I was sitting on the earth floor of his hut near the thin pallet on which he reclined. We had been discussing his "The British Must Go" idea.

I said: "It seems to me that the British cannot possibly withdraw altogether. That would mean making a present of India to Japan, and England would never consent to that, nor would the United States approve. If you demand that the British pack up and go, bag and baggage, you are simply asking the impossible; you are barking up a tree. You do not mean, do you, that they must also withdraw their armies?"

Gandhi's mind is brilliant and swift. But this time he remained silent for at least two minutes. The silence was almost audible. At last he said: "You are right. No, Britain and America and other countries too can keep their armies here and use Indian territory as a base for military operations. I do not wish Japan to win the war. I do not want the Axis to win. But I am sure the British cannot win unless the Indian people become free. Britain is weaker and Britain is morally indefensible while she rules India. I do not wish to humiliate England."

Subsequently, G. D. Birla, India's millionaire "Textile King" and friend of Gandhi, told me he received a letter from the Mahatma informing him that I had changed Gandhi's mind on this point. Gandhi told the same thing to Rajagopalachari who told me. Many of Gandhi's intimate collaborators, however, disapproved of the compromise he had made in his original plan and hotly expressed their disapproval to him.

"I am essentially a man of compromise," Gandhi said to me, "because I am never sure I am right." That is one facet of this remarkable, complicated man. Then he added: "But now it is the unbending future in me which is uppermost." That is a second facet. He refused to abandon the contemplated civil disobedience campaign.

"Why will it not wait until after the war?" I urged.

"Because I want to act now and be useful while the war is here," he replied. Also, I suspect, he was conscious of his advanced age. It might be the last great act of his career for Indian independence. Nevertheless, he said: "Tell your President I wish to be dissuaded." That is a third facet. Practical politician, he knew that if President Roosevelt induced him to postpone the campaign because it might interfere with the war, the United States would thereby be committed to intervening later on behalf of Indian freedom.

Nehru was at first disposed to oppose Gandhi's proposal of a civil disobedience movement in 1942 because he hoped the United States would use its influence to bring about a change in India. He is an internationalist and an anti-Fascist with a perfect record as an enemy of pre-war Fascist aggression. Nehru feared that popular sabotage of the British government in India would embarrass the conduct of the war. But Gandhi's outlook was chiefly Indian. Deprived of their rights as a nation, many Indians are pathologically indocentric. "It is like having somebody in your own home who should never have been there in the first place and who refuses to depart," a Bombay housewife said to me. They are so passionately eager to be rid of the British that they often see nothing else. Nehru, and the growing group that sees eye to eye with him, has a broader, world outlook, but he could not prevail in 1942. Gandhi prevailed upon Nehru to support the disobedience campaign.

With all his passion and impatience, Gandhi is nevertheless tolerant and mellow. Nehru is not. Nehru loathes the British imperialists on two big counts: as imperalists and as reactionaries. He is conscious of the deleterious effects of imperialism on four hundred and fifty million Chinese and on universal progress. Imperialism, he knew, would waste the war and ruin the peace.

Unless the old imperialisms were destroyed during the second world war, peace would give rise to new imperialisms. That dictated my interest in India. I was interested in Indian freedom as a stepping stone to a free and better world. Nehru's nationalism includes this internationalism. But Gandhi had no difficulty convincing Nehru that the British would not act if they were not forced to act. Bitter over the behavior of his friend Cripps in India and after he left India, only Nehru's great fear of a Fascist victory restrained him. But he had no answer then to Gandhi's argument that a popular upheaval which compelled the British to grant India full self-government would generate enthusiasm for the anti-Fascist cause in India, China, and throughout the world and thus hasten victory.

"I would fight Japan sword in hand," I heard Nehru tell a gigantic open-air mass meeting in Bombay in June, 1942. "But I can only do so as a free man."

On the fundamentals, therefore, Gandhi and Nehru agreed. Freedom for India during the war would have said to Axis peoples: Though you lose the war you gain a better world. It would have said to the anti-Axis nations: Victory will bring peace and human progress.

Any hesitation Nehru may have had about the wisdom of launching a civil disobedience at that time was swept away by Gandhi's insistence. Gandhi was the biggest asset of the independence movement. He was the capital which Nehru would inherit. Nehru could not very well disinherit himself and split the nationalist movement on the issue of supporting a war which was unpopular in India and on which even his heart was divided.

At Sevagram, while Gandhi and Nehru debated the matter, Nehru looked very unhappy. But once he had been won over, he became more intransigent than Gandhi. As I was leaving the village, Gandhi and his secretary Desai asked me to suggest to the Viceroy that he receive the Mahatma. Gandhi still hoped to avoid the painful civil disobedience movement. But when subsequently, in Bombay, I asked Nehru whether he thought it would be a good thing for Gandhi to talk to the Viceroy, he said angrily: "No, why should he?" Nehru's mind was made up.

Gandhi has no bitterness. The British much prefer to deal with him than with Nehru. All the high British officials I met in India spoke disparagingly of Nehru, but not of Gandhi. The British can, without understanding Gandhi, understand why he behaves as he does. But Nehru, the product of British education, high-born scion of a wealthy family? They resent him more because he could have been with them and is so much against them.

Nehru has an incisive mind and a beautiful pen. He is clean, truthful, self-critical, and modest. His outstanding qualities are dignity and indignation. Everything in him rebels against the indignities which modern life imposes on man.

Nehru lived the first part of his life within the shadow of one great man, his father Molital Nehru. He has lived the second part of his life within the shadow of a second great man, Mohandas K. Gandhi. His own greatness will not emerge fully until he comes out of the shadow.

History has assigned Nehru a special function. The Indian independence movement was a primitive urge to be free and to be alone. Now India's emerging emancipation raises new problems for India and poses a crucial dilemma for the rest of the world. The West too needs a doctor. The second world war was a sickness. The failure of the peace leaves the world sick. Will mankind find a doctor or get a dictator? Will it be yogi or commissar? After 1918, Germany turned to the mysticism of Dostoyevsky and to Indian and Chinese philosophers. Arthur Holitscher, a German journalist who knew Lenin, visited Gandhi and wrote a book entitled *Lenin and Gandhi*. Rabindranath Tagore and Nehru, friends of the Mahatma, visited Russia in the same confused twenties. Nehru, at least, was groping for a synthesis of Russia and India, a synthesis of the commissar and the yogi.

Today, many Indians, including Nehru, and Pearl Buck and many Occidentals, incline to the view (or is it the hope?) that India may itself be the synthesis of East and West.

The West is becoming the wild West; it cannot tame its lust for power and wealth. The yogi does in order to be; the commissar, and capitalist, does in order to have. Renunciation and asceticism are normal where life's aim is being. Aggrandizement, imperialism, dictatorship, and monopolies are normal where the aim is having. The yogi is the democrat; he respects means. The commissar pursues ends with any available means. How can words and minds be free if they are harnessed to an end?

Western democracy needs more yogis.

In the East, the yogi must be reconciled to the machine. Gandhi refuses. Nehru will try.

10. *The Problems of India*

AFTER my first seven days in India, all spent in New Delhi, I real-ized that the greatest distance I had walked was across the side-walk from a taxi to a building entrance. So I decided to take a walk. I waited till sunset. But the houses and pavements were giving off so much heat and the air was still so hot that I could barely move my legs and I crossed over into the big park at Connaught Circus. I stood and looked around, then made a few steps and sat down. It was too hot for exercise.

At one place in the park, twelve brown youngsters, all clean and bright-eyed and each with a hockey stick, were sitting on the grass apparently having a caucus about their game. Elsewhere, boys ran in and out of freshly-dug slit air-raid trenches. Adults sat on the sparse, dry grass. Occasionally a flash of lemon-green or rose-pink or tomato-red caught the eye—a woman's sari.

On a path by the edge of the park stood a small wooden platform with two large earthen jars on it. Near it an old Indian sitting on his haunches bailed water out of the jars with a bronze bowl and poured it into the cupped palms of persons who stopped for a drink. I watched for a while and then a man in a white suit who had also been watching smiled and beckoned, offering me a drink. I walked over to him. He spoke English and told me he was a physician. He paid the old Indian to bring the water and serve it. He did it because there was no drink-ing water available to passersby for miles around. He and five of his friends regularly dispensed water in this way on Connaught Circus. It cost each of them fifty rupees, about $15, a month and they did it during the five or six hot months of the year. There were scores of such watering places in New Delhi supported by private persons, he said. Tomorrow, he added, there would be ice and a siphon so the jars could be kept sealed. All the while we talked, people came and drank.

"Why don't the authorities supply water?" I asked.

"I ask you," he replied. "We have petitioned the Government, but they declare it would deface the park to put in drinking pipes and fountains. We do this without permission, and the officials have told us not to do it. We may be arrested." He said he was a member of the Congress party and belonged to the *Kshatriyas* or warrior caste, the second highest, next to the Brahmins. "But today," he remarked, "we have been deprived of our arms and cannot fight."

Captain Culler of the United States Air Force and I stood leaning over the parapet of the second-story terrace of my hotel. Indian men and women employed in the construction of buildings for American military personnel were walking home to Old Delhi. The men were naked except for a narrow loincloth, but the women wore numerous colored skirts like gypsies. Quite a number of women carried small babies mounted on their hips. They had worked for ten to twelve hours in the sizzling sun and now they were walking the four or five miles to the old city. They all looked like emaciated symbols of misery.

"Isn't that terrible," I said to the Captain.

"I call it slavery, that's what I call it," he exclaimed. He was from South Carolina.

A few days later, dining with a British member of the Viceroy's Executive Council, I asked him why enough buses were not available in New Delhi to transport these people. They could not pay the fare, he said.

I found an Indian in my railway car compartment when I got into it at Hyderabad, capital of the native state of Hyderabad which is ruled by the Nizam, reputed to be the richest man in the world. He was a Moslem officer in the Indian Air Force going to Poona to get a new airplane for his squadron. He fought against the Japanese in Burma. Although a volunteer with three years of military service with the British, he denounced the British more vehemently than any Indian I had met. "Look at those people," he said, pointing through the window. "They live like animals." We were passing through innumerable villages where the population lived in huts made of bamboo or of mud or of palm branches. Even older children were completely nude. The women wore rags and the men a loin strap. "The British have exploited India," the officer declared. "I did not know much about it until I read John Gunther's *Inside Asia*. The British keep us ignorant, and poor, and they retard the growth of our country."

One does not have to be in India more than a few days to know that India is heartbreakingly poor and that Indians of all parties, religions, and classes are passionately anti-British.

"Nowhere in Asia or Africa have the British won friends among the natives or introduced modern conditions of life," Sir Firoz Khan

Noon, Member for Labor in the Viceroy's Executive Council, said to me. "Everything one sees in London or Paris, not to speak of New York, has been created in the last one hundred and fifty years. But in India," he added, "little has changed in the last hundred and fifty years. The same rags and poverty. However, it is true that though Indians do not eat more they die less because the British have introduced a health service." Noon is a Moslem landlord, collaborates with the British, and is anti-Gandhi.

The British in India are guilty of "social arrogance and economic exploitation," Sir Homi Mody, Supply Member of the Viceroy's Executive Council said to me. Mody is a millionaire Parsi.

"India was never as anti-British as it is today," Lord Linlithgow, the Viceroy, said to me.

In Bombay, the Indian Journalists' Association invited me to address one of its meetings. We agreed that instead of making a speech I would informally answer questions. Responding to one question, I urged support of the war effort and sketched the bleak prospect for India and all of us if Fascism won.

"For India," a journalist declared, "there is no difference between Japanese Fascism and British Fascism."

"Now look," I began. "England is not Fascist. England is very democratic, and in many political respects more democratic than the United States. I know," I proceeded, "that you dislike the measures of repression which the British occasionally adopt in India. But since I arrived in India, almost every fifth person has told me that he has been in jail. Now I have lived for years in Russia and Germany," I declared. "In those countries one rarely meets anybody who has been in jail; they are in jail, and many of them have been shot."

A second Indian writer rose and said: "The British don't bother shooting us; they kill us."

I asked him what he meant.

"The average length of life in India," he explained, "is twenty-seven years." I later found that figure in the official British statistics. In England, the average life expectancy is sixty years; in the United States, sixty-three.

A third journalist affirmed that "Forty-five per cent of all children born in India die before the age of five." That too is from the British census.

In the *chawls* or tenements of Bombay and in the villages of the Thana district not far from Bombay I saw poverty infinitely more degrading than any I had ever seen in Poland or Russia in the twenties or in the hungriest rural regions of Spain in the thirties. Pearl Buck says that the Indian peasant is worse off even than the Chinese peasant. Industrial labor is only slightly better situated. "The Indian worker," writes the London *Economist*, "lives for a year on what the British worker spends for cigarettes." Mr. J. H. Hutton, the chief of the British Census Bureau, states in his introduction to the census report of 1931 that in Bombay "256,379 persons live in rooms occupied by six to nine persons each. . . . For the majority of Bombay's population the available floor space per head is six foot square." Since then the crowding has increased perceptibly.

Several hundred million Indians are always, literally always, hungry. This permanent gnawing hunger undermines not only physical strength. The brain descends into the stomach. Indian villagers did not know who was fighting whom in the war or on what side the British were fighting. When I asked them how they felt about the war, they answered "We're hungry." When I asked them their attitude towards the British, they answered "We're hungry."

India's politics are made in the stomach.

In the educated, politically-minded few this condition created a fierce animosity towards the British.

When I talked with fabulously-wealthy maharajahs or millionaire Indian industrial tycoons I upbraided them for not doing more to alleviate the distress of their people. They could do more, and some try to do something. But to lift four hundred million persons even as little as one notch upward is a mammoth undertaking; individuals cannot handle it. In fact, Britain alone is probably too weak to deal with it. India's problem requires the kind of international pooling of resources that produced the atomic bomb and beat the Axis.

The population of India is increasing five million each year. "Birth rate," wrote Mr. Hutton in his 1931 report on the official British census of India, "is negatively correlated with wealth." That is one explanation, he adds, for the high birth rate in India, China, and Russia. Assuming no interference from government for political or religious reasons, the success of birth control depends on a certain amount of education, plumbing, and what, for the average Indian, would be expensive paraphernalia. Thus better economic conditions are a prerequisite to a lower birth rate in India. It is also true that fewer births would improve living conditions, but, in India at least, this is putting the cart before the horse.

According to the British census, India had three hundred and thirty-eight million inhabitants in 1931 and three hundred and eighty-eight million inhabitants in 1941—an increase of fifty million in ten years. That is India's central difficulty.

In the Soviet Union, throughout the period of unprecedented industrial expansion when tremendous new cities and vast factory units were springing up over the face of that country during successive Five-Year plans, only one million persons were being absorbed into gainful employment each year. India, however, with five million new mouths to feed each year, has undergone negligible economic expansion in recent decades. Major General Sir John Megaw, Director General of the Indian Medical Service, in an official British publication which appeared in 1933, wrote: "It is clear that the growth of population has already begun to outstrip the increase in the production of the necessities of life so that the existing low standards of economic life must inevitably become still lower unless some radical change is brought about. The outlook for the future is dark to a degree." Subsequent events have justified Megaw's gloomy forebodings. Living standards in India are declining.

During the second world war, India's steel and arms output rose, but her total industrial output dropped.

I gathered in India, and have published, British documents and official British statements which demonstrate that the British government obstructed industrial expansion in India. I told this to friends in Jerusalem where I stopped on my way back to New York. They said it was British policy in Palestine too. It is imperialist policy everywhere to use the colony as a source of raw materials or semi-manufactured products. "The American revolution," wrote the late Raymond Leslie Buell of Fortune magazine, "was in the main a revolt against the mercantilism, against the exploitation involved in the Navigation, Molasses, Sugar, and Stamp Acts. Britain denied the right of the colonies to develop trade, manufactures, and even land when they did not directly enrich the merchants of the home country." The Tory spirit of 1776 still lives. Imperialism changes as little as it has to. Imperialism is an obstacle to economic progress.

India, plus China which is still a semi-colonial country despite her nominal independence, plus the other colonial nations of Asia, of Africa, and much of Latin America constitute an economic desert. A billion and a half human beings live on this desert. They eat little, wear little, and enjoy little shelter. Their production and consumption is shamefully low. They are three-fourths of the human race. They drag down the other fourth.

The Western world suffers economically, politically, and spiritually because the East lives in the abyss. In any community, the poor, the diseased, the criminal are a burden to all. The world is a community.

It is insane that a world capable of producing as mankind produced during the war should count many millions of men, women, and children who are idle, hungry, naked, and unsheltered. It is insane, criminal, un-Christian, and undemocratic.

The great challenge of our time is to adjust the way we live to the way we could live if we took advantage of our mechanical and technical progress. Unplumbed riches lie hidden in the bowels of the earth, and if more are needed the magic of plastics will conjure them up out of sea water, seaweed, coal dust, and sand. The burst atom will surrender undreamt-of wealth. Labor to fashion these materials into usable articles of consumption is in endless supply and grows with every new machine. These inexhaustible reserves of man power, brain power, and matter make a mockery of a civilization which tolerates poverty, illness, and illiteracy.

The fault is in the longevity of centuries. Centuries die but their ideas, their political and economic forms, and their moral standards survive to plague us. Science has given us a preview of the twenty-first century. It has the key to abundance and health; it promises man freedom from gravity and space limitations. Politics, however, is still bogged down in the ancient era when there was no steam engine, electricity, or airplane. Politics sticks in the mud of the Middle Ages and holds man in bondage to want and fear. Politicians make peace in terms of geographic boundaries, of national sovereignties, and of imperial domination.

Politics will either overtake science, or science, its powers uncontrolled by organized man, will blow the earth into smithereens.

The glaring, maddening discrepancy between what life could give India and what it actually gives India is a measure of the country's frustration, unhappiness, and discontent. India is one-fifth of the human race. Asia is one-half of the human race. The population of Asia has doubled in the last fifty years. Asia is aroused. It wants liberty, security, prosperity, and dignity. The world will not be economically or politically normal until the billion inhabitants of Asia, and many millions elsewhere, partake of the blessings which would be theirs but for man-made, obsolete obstacles.

India's problems, whether political, social, or religious, can be understood only against the black background of her destitution and retarded economic growth. The Hindu-Moslem problem, for instance, is strangely and crucially affected by industrial backwardness. Owing to the extremely limited possibilities for employment in Indian cities, government jobs are a major industry. The competition for them is keen and many Indians are involved because the British have needed a large corps of Indian civil servants. The British performed a miracle of administration in India. Their government was practically invisible. Sir John Thorne, the Viceroy's confidential secretary, wrote me on July 13, 1942, after I had met him at dinner and asked for the figures, that the Indian Civil Service (I.C.S.) includes five hundred and seventy-three British subjects while the Indian police includes three hundred and eighty-six British officers and not more than four hundred and fifty lesser British officials. "Therefore," Sir John summarized, "fourteen hundred would be approximately correct as a complete total" of the Englishmen who administered India. British power, of course, was also represented by the British Navy and Army and, less directly, by British business. But the actual machinery of government was manned by fourteen hundred British subjects. The rest were Indians.

Many thousands of specially-trained Indians are enrolled in the I.C.S. and in other administrative units. They hail from all classes and religions, but Hindus predominate. The usual explanation one hears in India is that Hindus have keener brains and better education. I think the explanation is different. When the British arrived in India they displaced the Moslem rulers of the country. Especially after the Great Mutiny of 1857, the British feared the Moslems who had played the leading role in the uprising. Moslems, therefore, were discouraged from entering British government service. Because the Koran forbids usury and for other reasons, moreover, Moslems left money-lending, industrial production, and large-scale commerce almost exclusively to Hindus. As a result, the Moslems were either big landowners or small farmers. A Moslem urban middle class was practically non-existent.

The Hindu middle class of the cities, and the rich Hindu and Parsi industrialists, felt themselves economically hampered and socially snubbed by the British. They accordingly became the spearhead and financial backers of the Congress party, champion of Indian independence. Congress also won the sympathies of most Hindu and Moslem intellectuals.

Since the Hindu middle and upper classes were anti-British, the British, along about the beginning of the twentieth century, commenced courting the Moslems.

The Hindu capitalist wants national independence so he can expand without the competition and interference of the imperialistic mother country. The Moslem landlord, on the other hand, suspects that the first act of a free India might be a land reform which would endanger his tenure and wealth. The Moslem upper class consequently has no passion for independence. Mr. Mohammed Ali Jinnah's Moslem League consists overwhelmingly of upper-class landlords.

To help build a Moslem middle class, a percentage of government jobs was reserved for Moslems even if they were less qualified than Hindu applicants. In 1909, the British introduced the existing system of communal or religious electorates: a Hindu may only vote for a Hindu candidate for public office, a Moslem for a Moslem, and so on. This spurred the ambitions of Moslem politicians, cemented the ties among Moslems, and widened the gulfs between religions.

A new Moslem middle class in the cities began competing with the older Hindu middle class. British encouragement of the Moslems was a bid for Moslem political support; it made the Hindus more anti-British; it intensified Hindu-Moslem antagonisms.

The Viceroy, Sir Archibald Wavell, many key British officials I consulted, Jinnah, Gandhi, Nehru, and Azad, the Moslem president of the Congress party—in fact, every person I talked with in India—affirmed that there was little or no friction between the Hindus and Moslems in the villages of India, and India is ninety per cent village. The Hindu-Moslem problem is a man-made city problem, a mirror of the job-poor city.

Jinnah told me that seventy-five per cent of all Moslems in India were former Hindus converted to Islam several hundred years ago by the Moghul conquerors. Nehru put the figure at ninety-five per cent. In any case, the vast bulk of Hindus and Moslems are of the same racial origin. A Hindu Bengali is indistinguishable from a Moslem Bengali in appearance and language. Ethnographically, India is much more homogeneous than the Soviet Union or Switzerland and probably than the United States.

Religion plays an important part in the Indian's way of life. Nevertheless, and although Hindus worship the cow while Moslems eat it, the friction between the two religions is negligible in the rural areas. It assumes importance in the cities where the segregation arising from strict Hindu dietary laws and from differences in pre-marital and marital customs is enhanced by economic rivalry. If the young man on the threshold of a career had a wider choice of employment in industry the competition for political positions would not be so sharp.

The growing rivalry between the emerging Moslem middle class and the Hindu bourgeoisie opened new vistas for the Moslem politician. Mohammed Ali Jinnah then resigned from the Congress party and became the leader of the Moslem League. Congress embraces members of all religious communities and is, therefore, the only important political party in India. Others, like the Hindu Mahasabha and the Moslem League are religious bodies with political aims.

The members of the Moslem League, in 1942, were almost all landlords. As the tension between Moslems and Hindus in the cities waxed, and as Jinnah, with British government help, demonstrated his ability to get jobs for his fellow-Moslems, social pressure and self-interest sufficed to keep many professional and intellectual Moslems from joining Congress. They nevertheless found it impossible to co-operate with the big estate owners of the League. Nor could the Moslem peasants forget their hostility to their landlords and develop a sympathy for the League.

Since a common religion did not suffice to erase class antagonisms among Moslems, Jinnah needed a device which would form a bridge between Moslem landlords, peasants, and the new urban middle class. He found it in nationalism. In 1940, for the first time, Jinnah proclaimed India's Mohammedans a nation and outlined the goal of a Moslem national home, a Zion. He calls it Pakistan and as projected it would embrace the provinces of Sind, Punjab, Baluchistan, the Northwest Frontier, and Bengal where the Moslems are a majority and Assam where they are a minority.

Religion plus nationalism are a powerful combination and it has given Jinnah additional popular support. The Cripps offer of March, 1942, which recognized the theoretical validity of Pakistan, was wind in Jinnah's sails.

Most prominent of India's ninety-two million Moslems, Mohammed Ali Jinnah lives by the sea at Bombay in a sumptuous and gigantic house with a huge marble terrace. He is tall and extremely thin with a handsome thin face and bad, stained teeth. At my first interview with him, he wore a long, straw-colored tunic, tight white trousers clinging to his bony legs, and black patent leather pumps with no socks. A monocle dangled from a cord. Indians regard him as able and incorruptible.

His argument was: The Moslems do not wish to be a permanent minority; they seek self-determination; true, most Moslems are ex-Hindus, but Islam is a way of life; witness the fact that Moslem dress, architecture, art, food, and language differ from those of the Hindu; Moslem India must be separated from Hindu India and become an independent state or Pakistan.

I remarked that the duty of a civilized human is to reduce existing differences rather than exacerbate them. "I am a realist," he replied. "I deal with what is and not with what should be done."

Jinnah admitted that British policy aimed to divide the religious communities in order to rule India with greater facility. "The British have done much harm to Indian education and economy," he asserted.

I came back for another interview three days later. Jinnah said the Cripps Plan conceded secession and Pakistan in principle, but in practice "only the legislature of Sind would have voted for secession. The Northwest Frontier Province is controlled by Congress. The Punjab legislature might also refuse to vote secession. So the principle was conceded but the method was unacceptable."

"In other words," I commented, "the British government did not give you Pakistan and many Moslems are opposed to it. Now you want Gandhi to give it to you."

"Gandhi has already promised it," he said. "He has stated that if the Moslems wish to secede no one can stop them. If the Hindus and Moslems agree on Pakistan we would get it. We would be neighbors. Hindustan and Pakistan. We would be dominions in the British Commonwealth."

Jinnah advocates Pan-Islamism, a project for a Moslem empire stretching from Morocco to China. A Jewish Palestine, he felt, would interfere with the scheme.

Jinnah talked at length and with vehemence about Nehru and Gandhi. "Nehru worked under me in the Home Rule Society," Jinnah recounted. "Gandhi worked under me. My goal was Hindu-Moslem unity. I began in 1906. I was in Congress. When the Moslem League was organized I persuaded Congress to welcome it as a contribution to Indian independence. In 1915, I persuaded the League and Congress to hold their conferences at the same time in Bombay in order to give the impression of unity. The British, seeing the danger of such unity, broke up the big open meeting, but the closed common sessions continued. In 1916, I again got the two organizations to meet in Lucknow and we drafted the Lucknow pact for Hindu-Moslem collaboration. And so on until 1920 when Gandhi came into the limelight. Then a deterioration set in. At the Round Table conference in London I became convinced that unity was hopeless. Gandhi didn't want it. I was a disappointed man. I decided to remain in England. I did not even go back to India to sell my possessions. I did it through an agent. I remained in England until 1935. I practised law before the Privy Council and, contrary to my expectations, I was a success. I had no intention of returning to India. But each year friends from India visited me, and gave me an account of conditions, and told me how much I could do. Finally, I agreed to come back. I tell you this," Jinnah concluded, "to show you that Gandhi does not want independence. He does not want the British to go. He wants Hindu raj. He is first of all a Hindu."

When I returned to my room in the Taj Mahal Hotel, I read Jinnah's Presidential Address at the Moslem League Session in Lahore in March, 1940. "I think it is a wise rule," he said, "for everyone not to trust anybody too much."

I read other speeches by Jinnah and also his weekly magazine, *Dawn*. Jinnah swears at his opponents and engages in petty polemics. He rarely offers a new or big thought. He does not open vistas. His stuff is thin. He is a thin man. He plays one note: The Moslems want Pakistan. But he does not present Pakistan as the beginning of Islam's renascence, as a great adventure in culture and spirit. He does not even say exactly where and what Pakistan would be. He haggles; he says: I will not tell you the details of Pakistan until you meet me half way. He is a political merchant, not a statesman. "Constitutionally and legally" is his recurrent phrase and it is the key to the man. He has skill, not scope.

I saw Jinnah for five hours. He talked at me. He was trying to convince me. When I put a question to him I felt as though I had turned on a phonograph record. I had heard it before or could read it in the Moslem League's literature. When I asked Gandhi something it was like starting a creative process. I could see and hear his mind work. With Jinnah, I could only hear the scratch of the phonograph needle. Jinnah gave me nothing but conclusions. Gandhi let me watch as he moved to a conclusion. An interview with Gandhi is an exciting intellectual adventure. An interview with Jinnah is dull even when it is important.

Jinnah is the Moslems' lawyer, not their leader. He puts their case persistently and well. But he gives one no suggestion of the great wealth and warmth which Moslem humanity in India possesses. The Moslems are very attractive, in many ways more attractive than the cerebral Hindus; they have energy, love of life; music; poetry. One would not suspect it meeting Jinnah.

In New Delhi at the home of Devadas Gandhi, editor of the *Hindustan Times* and son of the Mahatma, I met another Moslem, Khan Abdul Ghaffar Khan, widely known as "The Frontier Gandhi." He is the Moslem leader of the Northwest Frontier Province, anti-Jinnah, pro-Gandhi, and the organizer of the tremendous following which the Congress party has among the Moslem peasants of his area. Physically, mentally, and spiritually, the Khan is one of the most impressive men I met in India. He stands over six feet with a powerful body and strong, perfectly oval head. Gray-black stubble covers his head and face. He is past sixty but his black, flashing, penetrating eyes are thirty. His appearance is only one-tenth of the impression he makes. I felt his power before he opened his mouth. His home is a village in Peshawar where he lives like the peasants. His father and he were rich but he renounced his wealth. He had on a long blue-gray blouse and a pair of those very wide-seat trousers typical of the frontier Pathan tribe to which he belongs. Most of the color had been washed out of the homespun material and there was a patch in his blouse near the neck. He has big, almost white hands and finely molded feet. After he shook hands with me he touched his hand to his heart.

I asked him what he thought of Jinnah's Pakistan. "I judge it," he replied, "by those who support it in my province. It is supported by the rich khans, the wealthy nawabs and the reactionary mullahs [priests]. Pakistan will give strength to those Moslems who oppress my peasant people."

"Will it strengthen Islam?" I asked.

Angrily he replied: "Jinnah is a bad Moslem. He is not a devout follower of the Prophet."

"Are you religious?" I asked.

"Yes," he answered. "I pray in the mosque five times a day. I live the life of a faithful follower of God. Our movement in the Northwest Frontier Province is called *Khudai Khidmatgar* which means

Servants of God. The movement is sometimes called the Red Shirt movement but the color has nothing to do with our ideas. We urge broader education and higher ideals. When I advocated more schools three years ago I was put in prison by the British government and the mullahs opposed me."

He spoke English with me and carefully chose each word. I thought: How exciting to meet this man from the distant mountains of far-off India and immediately establish a bond with him. If Mahatma Gandhi is of the soil and sand of India, Ghaffar Khan is of its rocks and crags and raging torrents.

Once he offered the British to go into the tribal areas between India and Afghanistan and persuade the lawless, fuzzy-wuzzy Afridis and Wazirs to stop fighting the British and one another. He felt he could win them for Gandhi's peace principles. But the British were afraid he would gain influence among them, he said, and refused permission.

"My people believe in Gandhi," he said, "because Gandhi wants freedom for India."

Jinnah tells the Moslem peasants they are Moslems only and ought to constitute a Moslem nation. Ghaffar Khan, Nehru, and others tell the Moslem peasants they are peasants economically, Moslems religiously, and Indians politically. Hitler told Germans they were Germans only. He hoped nationalism would make the workers forget their class enemies and hate only their racial enemies: the Jews at home and, later, the whole world. The religious racism of Jinnah is equally dangerous.

For a while the British flirted with Jinnah and lent him strength because they wanted a counterpoise to Gandhi's independence movement. To parry a menace to their empire they were ready to nourish a menace to all of Asia.

Gandhi says the vivisection of India into Pakistan and Hindustan is "blasphemy." In more worldly terms, it is stupid. Pakistan would be another poor if bigger Iran or Iraq. Two Indias would mean a hundred headaches for the whole world. Weakened by division and friction, India would become an arena where big powers would intrigue and maneuver against one another as they do in the weak countries of Europe and in China.

In a free federated India, the solution of the Hindu-Moslem problem will require, first, broad autonomy for all provinces, with strict legal guarantees for Moslem minorities in provinces where Hindus are in the majority and for Hindu minorities in Moslem majority provinces; second, the abolition of the present religious electorates which allow citizens to vote only for candidates of their own denomination, and a determined effort to take religion out of politics.

In the Indian Army and in schools, religious segregation and dietary exclusiveness are being broken down. Indian students told me that the youth of India pay much less attention than their parents to religious and caste differences. "Generally speaking," says the British census report of 1931, "there would seem to be no insuperable reasons why the Muslim and the Hindu should not dwell together in harmony, and there are Hindu temples in Madura and Tanjore which have hereditary Muslim trustees." One 1931 census superintendent wrote: "To the generality of English-educated persons . . . religion is now a matter of utter indifference and unconcern."

Poverty, illiteracy, and provincialism go hand in hand with religious obscurantism and church-ridden politics. Hindu-Moslem urban tension would retreat before prosperity and compulsory education. Industrial and agrarian revolutions are urgent necessities in India to raise living standards and improve health. Economic advancement would bring cultural enlightenment in its train, and together they would un-freeze the present rigid communal and caste divisions.

Intolerance of differences is a hardy plant and its refinements persist even in countries that boast loudest of their civilization. India, however, has scarcely begun to attack the problem. India lacks a compulsory public school system which could quickly popularize a common language. Schools where children of Untouchables or outcaste Hindus, whose shadow, not to speak of touch, is supposed to pollute a caste Hindu, would sit with children of Hindus, Moslems, Sikhs, Christians, Parsis, and British would go a long way to proving that the innumerable taboos and ghettos of India are silly. Similarly, an expanding economy and greater opportunities of employment would do much to eliminate the misunderstandings and walls between religions and castes. Today, the Untouchables or "depressed classes" are almost entirely confined, in the cities, to scavenging and street cleaning, and to leather work which is considered unclean by orthodox Hindus. In the present job scarcity, each religious or caste group tries to stake out a monopoly claim to a given type of work, and the Untouchables are thus prevented from invading more remunerative and less menial professions.

The caste system has ancient roots. In modern times, the congealing of castes is part of the stagnation of Indian economy and education.

The bitterest man I met in India was India's most prominent Untouchable, Dr. Bhimrac Ramji Ambedkar. His father and grandfather served many years in the British Army and because of this unusual circumstance, he was able to get an education in India. Later, with a scholarship given him by the Maharajah of Baroda, he took M.A. and Ph.D. degrees at Columbia University in New York. He also studied at Bonn University in Germany and at London University. He is a noted writer, lawyer, and economist. He has a compact body and a firm will, a "tough customer" as unsentimental and rational as most Hindus are philosophical and irrational. He detests Hindus and for good reason. No treatment which human beings mete out to other human beings anywhere in the world is as revolting as the treatment accorded in India to the fifty to sixty million Untouchables. The Hindus, in my opinion, are themselves polluted by the belief that even remote contact with outcastes pollutes them. A religion is dishonored by such barbarous notions.

Gandhi has striven by word and example to improve the Untouchables' lot. He eats food prepared by them, and they live in his village in close proximity to him. Gandhi consequently has a large following among the "depressed classes" and they probably know him better than they do Ambedkar.

Ambedkar is anti-Gandhi, pro-Pakistan, and the most pro-British Indian I encountered. Ambedkar said to the Untouchables' congress in August, 1930: "I am afraid that the British choose to advertise our unfortunate conditions, not with the object of removing them, but only because such a course serves well as an excuse for retarding the political progress of India." The hostility between caste and outcaste Hindus, Ambedkar implied, provided the British with another argument to justify their stay in India. Nevertheless Ambedkar joined the Viceroy's Executive Council in 1942 and became a collaborator. Ambedkar's mounting hatred of the persecuting Hindus causes him to welcome anything the Hindus reject and to reject anything the Hindus want. In Ambedkar, one hears an echo of age-long injustice and suffering which produce irrational emotions in even the most rational person.

I discussed Untouchability with a most orthodox Hindu. He was Sir S. Varadachariar, a member of the Indian Supreme Court to whom I was recommended by Sir Maurice Gwyer, the Lord Chief Justice of India, to whom I brought a letter of introduction from Felix

Frankfurter. "The only political philosopher in New Delhi," Sir Maurice called Varadachariar.

The Indian justice came to his front door to meet me when my taxi arrived. He wore a white, collarless shirt with a gold collar button, gold studs, and gold cufflinks, tight Indian cotton trousers and no shoes or socks. A tuft of long hair on the crown of his head was tied into a knot. The rest of his hair was clipped short, and the whole effect was Chinese. Down the center of his forehead from where his hair ended to a point between his eyes was painted a continuous thin blood-red stripe. Two white stripes, occasionally broken, converged from his temples to the bridge of his nose. The stripes aroused my curiosity. He was about sixty and spoke an excellent English though he had never left India.

He said: "India is a big country; some of its inhabitants still live in trees and others are the cultured products of Oxford. We have divergent races and religions and we need unity, but the unity which has been given us by the British is an administrative one. It begins and ends at the top. There has been progress, but it was undertaken by others for their profit, and the benefits which we enjoy are a by-product. Our education, for instance, has been over-literary because first the East India Company and then the British government needed clerks for their offices. But when the unemployed surplus among these literary school graduates goes into politics and gives the Government trouble, the British do not realize that they themselves are responsible."

His words flowed on with little prodding from me. "The British are birds of passage in India," he continued. "When they build industries they are not thinking of India, they are thinking of themselves. India is an incident in the lives of the persons who rule her. They stay here for five years, like the Viceroy, or for ten or twenty years. Always what comes after India is what they enjoy. So India has been held back and cannot find her place in the modern world."

Those forehead marks intrigued me. I asked him what they were. "I am a Brahmin," he replied. "Hindu is a collective term. Some Hindus pay special homage to one of the three heads of the trinity. One of those is Vishnu, another is Shiva. My god in the trinity is Vishnu, and all followers of Vishnu should wear these marks."

"Always?"

"Yes," he said, "but unfortunately many are ashamed to do so." I inquired whether he believed in Untouchability.

"It is not a matter of 'believing' in Untouchability," Varadachariar began reprovingly. "It is necessary to understand its origins. If you believe in the transmigration of souls, then if a soul has sinned in one of its incarnations it may be deposited in the body of an Untouchable in another of its migrations."

I said: "It seems uncivilized to punish a body for the sins of an earlier soul for which the poor fellow is not responsible."

"You are thinking in social and economic terms," he protested. "But if an Untouchable went to London and got an education and came back here he would not suffer any disability except the disabilities of his soul."

"Still," I argued, "most of them are so poor they cannot think of going to London."

"In a railway carriage," he said, "you do not know who is an Untouchable and who is not. Life has a practical way of moderating the effects of Untouchability."

A devout Hindu, Varadachariar was nevertheless on the defensive about Untouchability. Other Indians too expressed the view that city life tends to tone down the differences between caste Hindu and outcaste Hindu.

Yet another great artificial division has weakened India's cohesion: the native states ruled by maharajahs. Of the four hundred million Indians, roughly one-fourth reside in these native states which are governed directly by Indian princes and indirectly by the British. The states vary in size from Hyderabad with a population of seventeen million to tiny enclaves counting only a few hundred souls. They are sprinkled irregularly throughout the length and breadth of the country. Their populations are as mixed as everywhere else in India.

The President of the Indian Chamber of Princes in 1942 was the Maharajah of Bikaner. One day, sitting in my hotel room in Bombay, I received a telephone call from a secretary saying the Maharajah would see me. I had not sought the interview. I wondered why he wanted to talk to me. I had just come from spending a week with Gandhi. Did he wish to find out for himself and the British what were Gandhi's plans about the impending civil disobedience movement? Had he been assigned the task of mediating between the Viceroy and Gandhi?

A retinue of brown men in white jumped to their feet when I came to the low front porch of the Maharajah's Bombay palace. A secretary immediately ushered me into the Prince's drawing room. He was standing—a monumental figure with finely sculptured head. He was dressed in a white linen suit and a purple shirt open at the neck showing a purple undershirt. His thick mustache was curled and black-gray; his very bushy eyebrows were almost black but the fine crop of hair on his head was completely white. Long black hairs grew horizontally backward from the lobes of his ears.

Bikaner's voice was somewhat hoarse. He told me he was in Bombay for a throat operation. "Nothing serious," he said, "just a growth on one of the vocal cords which prevents them from coming together. It will be snipped off and that will be all." (He died several months later of cancer of the throat.) He spoke in perfect English with a broad English accent.

The Maharajah's first question was: "Well, what did the Mahatma say to you?"

I squeezed seven days of conversation into: "Gandhi is impatient and wants a change. I have the impression," I added, "that India is very anti-British."

"British India," Bikaner said, "is entirely anti-British. Generally speaking, the British isolate themselves. Do you know, there are clubs here which Indians cannot join. There is the Yacht Club. They said to me: 'Of course Your Highness may join.' But I replied: 'No, thank you. I have dined with the King in Buckingham Palace, and I do not need your club.'"

"You don't think the British can stay on in India forever?" I probed.

"Britain," the Maharajah said, "has given certain pledges to the native Indian states and she cannot break her word."

"When I was in the native state of Hyderabad recently," I told the Maharajah, "I read the texts of all the treaties between the British government and the native states of Hyderabad and Mysore going back to the seventeenth century, and it seems to me that all these treaties were forced upon the states by the British government. Now the British contend that they cannot break these treaties."

"Well," he smiled, "Mysore is an unimportant state and Hyderabad is a special case where a Moslem prince rules over a Hindu majority. I will show you my treaty." He rang a bell and a man in a bulging orange turban came in. He was instructed to summon the private secretary. A moment later there was a knock. To save his voice, the

Maharajah whistled, and the secretary entered. Bikaner spoke to him in English. The secretary left swiftly and soon came back with a one-page document printed on both sides. The Maharajah handed it to me and I read it slowly while he sat motionless.

"The two significant words in this treaty are 'subordinate cooperation,' " I said when I finished reading. "You are subordinate and must cooperate with the British."

The treaty is dated Delhi, March 9, 1818, and Article 3 reads: "Maharajah Soorut Singh and his heirs and successors will act in subordinate cooperation with the British government and acknowledge its supremacy and will not have any connection with any other Chiefs or States."

"Yes," the Maharajah agreed, "but it is a good treaty." He picked up a heavy red crayon pencil and marked Article 1, saying: "This is a good article. And this," he added, marking Article 2, "and this," marking Article 9. Article 1 is a general preamble about friendship. Article 2 says briefly: "The British government engages to protect the principality and territory of Bikaner." Article 9 reads *in toto:* "The Maharajah and his heirs and successors shall be the absolute rulers of their country and the British jurisdiction shall not be introduced into that principality."

"We have loyally fulfilled this treaty," the Maharajah declared, "and have given military support to the British government. I myself have fought on the field of battle for His Majesty, the King."

"Gandhi told me," I said, "that if the British consent to transfer political power to Indians, a provisional government would immediately be formed consisting of representative Moslems, Princes, and Hindus."

"We would expect the same protection from such a government as we now receive from the British government," the Maharajah commented.

"But do you think it possible," I asked, "for two such different systems to live side by side?"

"Yes, why not?" he wondered.

"Well," I said, "an Indian national government would introduce universal suffrage and other democratic reforms."

"I am an autocrat," he asserted. "But my people are happier than those of British India. You must come to Bikaner state. We have some of the finest hospitals in India. I have a refugee, a German Jew, in charge of one. We have schools and fine roads. I treat my people well. Naturally, they are more backward than in British India and are not ripe for democracy."

"Do you have any Hindu-Moslem trouble?" I inquired.

"For many centuries we have had none," he said. "But now it is coming in from British India. Mullahs have entered the northern part to tell our Moslems that they must have no contact with Hindus. I must say, and I am speaking frankly to you, that whenever there is trouble it is usually the Moslem who starts it. Mr. Jinnah is a dirty, nasty fellow. I will tell you something about his private life. As a young man he was welcomed into the house of a Parsi, a certain Sir Something Petit. He was treated like a son. Then he made love to the daughter and married her. Now you don't make love to a girl when you have been accepted into her family. It was an unhappy marriage. At present his daughter has left her father and married a Parsi who is a convert to Christianity. That's the irony of life."

I asked him his view of Jinnah's Pakistan. The Maharajah argued at length that it was not practicable and that Moslems really did not want it. It would split India, he argued. "All this started," he said, "from the original mistake of the Aga Khan who went at the head of a Moslem delegation to see Minto, the British Viceroy. [The interview took place on October 1, 1906.] The Aga Khan asked that separate religious electorates be instituted in India."

"Why did the British yield to that request?" I asked.

"The visit of the delegation," the Maharajah explained, "has been called 'a command performance.' The British wanted it. This is the usual tactics of empire: 'Divide and Rule.'"

The interview had now lasted for an hour. He rang for his secretary and asked him to bring me a book about the state of Bikaner. While we waited, the Maharajah said: "We have had a good talk and I am glad you came. But, you know, I was expecting Bill Fisher, of Life and Time, whom I have met on several occasions." We both laughed. His secretary had made a mistake.

"Let us go and see the monsoon come in," the Maharajah suggested. The sky over the sea was fiercely black. He walked me across the broad garden lawn on which an immense blue carpet had been laid. In the middle of the carpet was a circle of wicker chairs. The lawn ended in a wall. Below was the rocky beach. High waves were beating against the wall and throwing spray towards us. The black clouds boiled. Rain was coming soon. The Maharajah introduced me to two women who stood at the wall and we all watched this great turbulent phenomenon of nature. One woman was an Indian physician in a Bikaner hospital, and the other a gray-haired Hungarian Jewess, the painter of the Maharajah's three beautiful grandchildren who just at that moment pushed their shining bright brown faces out of a window to greet him.

The book the Maharajah gave me was entitled *Four Decades of Progress in Bikaner*, an official publication of the Bikaner government, dated 1937. Bikaner covers 23,317 square miles and is slightly smaller than Holland and Belgium combined. It has no rivers. The population was 584,755 in 1901 and 936,218 in 1931. The population of the capital city of Bikaner is 85,927. The Hindus number 725,084, the Moslems 141,578, the Sikhs 40,469, and the Jains 28,733.

The great need of the state is water. It depends on the monsoon which sometimes fails. They have had bad famines.

The Maharajah of Bikaner reigned for 44 years. He was one of the signatories of the Versailles Peace Treaty. He was one of the great figures of medieval India.

The maharajahs know that a new wind is blowing in the world and in India. Mrs. Sarojini Naidu, famous poetess and volatile champion of independence, told me that several of the princes are secretly keeping in touch with the Congress party. A secretary of the Indian Chamber of Princes said to me: "The Indian states will not be India's Ulster"; they would not prefer England to a free India. The princes are becoming reconciled to change. One of the most liberal maharajahs was Indore.

One day, United States General Adler arrived at the palace of the Maharajah of Indore for a hunting trip. Several days later, on May 30, 1942, the Indian papers published an Open Letter to President Roosevelt written by the Maharajah of Indore. In it, the Prince urged the President to arbitrate between Britain and India. "India," he wrote, "is divided and disaffected."

"By accident of birth," the Maharajah stated, "I am a ruling prince," but "I am by conviction an internationalist and a democrat."

The Viceroy sharply reprimanded the Prince for writing this letter. Among his other sins the Maharajah had offered Indore a modern, democratic constitution.

The Indian native states are strongholds of medievalism. To perpetuate itself the British Empire was forced to perpetuate the past. The states are the past. They are the sixteenth century used to hold back the twentieth.

The princely states of India are one of the shrewdest devices of imperialism. I have at least half a dozen enunciations of policy by high British authorities showing the true purpose of the native states. I quote two. Professor Rushbrook Williams, an Englishman who has frequently served as official British contact man with the maharajahs, wrote in the London *Evening Standard* of May 28, 1930: "The situation of these feudatory states, checkerboarding India as they do, is a great safeguard. It is like establishing a vast network of friendly fortresses in debatable territory. It would be difficult for a general rebellion against the British to sweep India because of this network of loyal native states."

Lord Canning, British Viceroy of India, stated on April 30, 1860: "It was long ago said by Sir John Malcolm that if we made all India into zillahs (or British districts) it was not in the nature of things that our Empire would last fifty years; but that if we keep a number of Native States without political power, but as royal instruments, we should exist in India as long as our naval supremacy was maintained. Of the substantial truth of this opinion I have no doubt; and the recent events have made it more deserving of our attention than ever." The "recent events" were the Great Mutiny of 1857.

It is doubtless difficult for fair-minded persons acquainted with the enlightened nature of democracy in England to believe that the British laid aside many scruples in the Empire and exploited and fomented religious, social, and political divisions in order to keep a firm hold on the colony. But it is no simple task to dominate four hundred million people with a small administrative apparatus and an army and navy. It was a difficult task in view of the rising tide of Indian self-assertion. The British therefore took Indian support where they found it. They took it from puppet maharajahs. They took it, during the war, from Communists who received concrete help from the British administration because, loyal to their Moscow instructions, they were the only pro-war party. They utilized Hindu-Moslem differences and Hindu-Untouchable hostility to bolster their position. They ruled because they could divide. If four hundred million Indians were prosperous, educated, and united they would soon discover the means of breaking away from the Empire. The primary purpose of the British in India, accordingly, was not the prosperity, cultural advancement, and unity of the country.

The British, obviously, have introduced railways, irrigation systems, electricity, health services, and so forth. This is, after all, the twentieth century. But the earlier centuries, back to the fourteenth probably, are carefully preserved, and forward speeds are held to a minimum.

The call of the new was the cause of India's revolt.

No one imagines that independence will solve all the problems of India. It will create problems. Freedom merely opens the door to the solution of the problems.

Conditions under slavery are no guide to what conditions could be under liberty. The span between slavery and liberty embraces everything that is good, or potentially good, in man. The use of freedom is learned only in the exercise of freedom.

Freedom is the elixir of growth. Freedom is medicine for the sick. Freedom is a tonic for those who give it and those who receive it. Freedom will help cure India, England, and the world.

India's freedom from foreigners will lead to new struggles, under new leadership, for freedom from want, freedom from caste, freedom from the past.

11. *The British in India*

ALMOST every Indian said: We are frustrated; almost every Englishman said: The Indians are not generous. The British in India
are unhappy because nobody appreciates them. Many British officials
in India are profoundly convinced that they have done a great service
to India. But they know that Indians feel differently.

Members of British families that for centuries have regularly sent
sons to India told me there was no fun, no future, and no satisfaction
in it any more. They worked hard, lost their health in the bad climate,
lived away from home so long that when they went to England on
leave they felt as in a foreign country, and the wages were Indian
animosity. The British in India live on a small barren island in a bitter
sea of hostility. They import most of the worldly comforts but can
buy no real joy.

The British do not associate with Indians as man to man. One of
the highest British officials in India invited me to lunch at his home
with three Moslems. The official would say to an Indian guest: "Tell
Mr. Fischer what would happen if the British left India," and of
course the guest replied that it would be world's end; or "Tell Mr.
Fischer about the Hindus and Moslems," and of course they were
ready to cut one another's throats. Later that day one of the Moslems
contrived to meet me out-of-doors and said: "I had to see you. I
wanted to tell you that I do not believe the statements I made at
lunch." Such Indians acknowledge the supremacy but not the superiority of the British. The Englishman feels this; it robs India of much
of her attractiveness.

After a week in Gandhi's mud hut I spent three days as the house
guest of Sir Claude Gidney, the British Resident of Hyderabad, and
Lady Gidney. I occupied a suite in a great palace located in a vast
park. A silent, barefoot Indian in gleaming white uniform with a
breastplate of red and gold and an unsheathed studded dagger in his
twisted colored belt was in constant unobtrusive attendance. As soon
as I opened an eye in the morning he brought me *chota hazari* consisting of black coffee and fruit. He drew my bath when he thought

I wanted it and took my shirt for laundering the moment I removed it from my back.

I had left New Delhi without a jacket because I could see no use for it in hot India. I did have a tie in my suitcase but it usually stayed there. During cocktails on my first evening at the Gidneys', however, Sir Claude asked to be excused and went upstairs to dress for dinner. Somewhat embarrassed, I believe, at being left alone with a stranger, and just to make conversation I am sure, Lady Gidney started telling me what she did. Charities kept her very busy. She had her war work among British soldiers. And then there was the entertainment of Indians. "This is a delicate matter," she explained. "If an Indian is invited to lunch that gives him status with his own people. It raises his social position and may improve his business. An invitation for dinner is even more beneficial, and an invitation when British guests are present gives an Indian considerable prestige in the community. I must be careful not to stop inviting somebody who has received regular invitations because that would be interpreted as disfavor and he would lose caste among his countrymen."

When invitations to a meal are so potent it is easy to see that titles, decorations, jobs, and favors from the Viceroy and King would recruit a whole tribe of sycophants and puppets. It is easy to see how the tribe could be split into jealous rival cliques. In proud, politically-conscious Indians, these goings-on merely arouse disgust for the native servitors of the foreign raj and distrust of the raj.

One day, the Nawab Kamal Yar Jung came to lunch with the Gidneys. A corpulent, photogenic Moslem in white with a purple-brown face surmounted by a high white turban, the Nawab told me he owned "three hundred and seventeen square miles of land, I think," inhabited by about eighty-five thousand souls. Eighty per cent of the population of Hyderabad, he said, was "dissatisfied" and it was therefore quite impossible for the British to quit India and "leave us unprotected."

British imperialism tied itself to the least progressive and least dynamic forces in India. It became undynamic itself. I asked Sir Archibald (now Lord and Viceroy) Wavell, British Commander-in-Chief in India, what caused the remarkably swift collapse of the British positions in the Pacific after Pearl Harbor. "We had grown fat and lazy in those areas where nothing had happened for centuries except tin mining and rubber growing," he replied.

Wavell is cultured, enlightened, and honest. I met him first at lunch in his home in New Delhi. After a long private talk, he walked me downstairs. On the steps I said to him: "You look tired."

"I am tired after three years of war that consisted chiefly of defeats," he admitted. "Rommel is a great soldier. I know; I fought him." I saw Wavell four times and each time he brought up the subject of Rommel.

Wavell moves like a tank on thick cavalry legs. His face is gnarled and deeply lined. His left eye is closed and blind. He has dense, steel-gray hair. On his left breast are five long rows of military ribbons which make a patch of rich color against the khaki of his uniform. Thirty years ago he served in India as a subaltern. In 1941 he came back as Commander-in-Chief. Meanwhile, he had been in many parts of the world, including Russia. He was in Russia for a year before the first world war and for six months during that war. The Russians, he found, were virile people and fought well for their country even under the Tsar. In 1936, he attended the Red Army maneuvers in White Russia and, he told me, his report to the War Office noted that under Marshal Tukhachevsky the Red Army was becoming a formidable political force inside the Soviet Union.

Once I walked with Wavell in the park behind his New Delhi house. He was relaxed, and reminisced about his experience in the Caucasus during the first world war. He remembered some Russian phrases, and, suddenly, he started singing the famous Georgian ballad *Allahverdi, Bokh Stoboi*.

Wavell's hero is General Allenby, his commander in the first world war. While I was in India, Wavell was working on the second volume of his biography of Allenby. He complained that he found too little time for writing, and then, succumbing to the universal weakness of authors, he pulled out a section of his manuscript and asked me whether I wanted to read it. I took home Part One of the unfinished book. I read it avidly. A short sketch of the career of a certain Banem Aaref shows that English literature lost a fine writer when the British Army found a great general. Many brilliant and courageous pages are devoted to the central episode of Allenby's career as High Commissioner of Egypt in 1922: a dispute between Allenby, who wanted to scrap the British Protectorate over Egypt and give the country a greater degree of independence, and the British government which demurred. Allenby went to London to present his case. Prime Minister Lloyd George, Lord Milner, Lord Curzon, in fact, practically the entire all-star Cabinet, opposed Allenby and, says Wavell, of all the opponents "the most determined had been Winston Churchill."

Finally, Allenby threatened to resign and take the question to the British people. Allenby enjoyed tremendous prestige in the country because his military victories in Palestine and Syria had broken the back of the Turk and started the debacle which quickly ended the first world war. The British government, afraid of a public scandal, was forced to yield to Allenby and give him what he wanted.

Reading the description of Allenby's struggle with the Cabinet in London I had the feeling that in similar circumstances Wavell might take Allenby as his model.

"I am sure," I said in a letter to Wavell when I returned the manuscript, "that Churchill, Lloyd George, Curzon, Milner, and the others adduced as plausible arguments for refusing independence to Egypt as any I have heard here for refusing independence to India. Yet Allenby stood his ground and won. You are convinced he was right and the Cabinet wrong. I share your view; governments are often wrong. The whole history of Europe between 1919 and 1939 is a record of wrong policies. There is little in the recent acts of British cabinets to suggest that London's present attitude towards India is a pillar of wisdom."

At a subsequent meeting, when I complimented Wavell on his write-up of Allenby's contest with the Cabinet, he said: "It was a greater victory than many of Allenby's successful military battles."

Another day, I came to see Wavell in the afternoon, and we talked on into the dim twilight. We sat at his desk. I noticed a little black Bible in one of the pigeonholes. Wavell quoted Matthew Arnold at me—he has published an anthology of poetry—and drew concentric circles on a blotter with red pencil. Again he said: "We had grown fat" in the Empire. Britain, he declared, received little help from colonial peoples in fighting the war. "The Indian soldier," he remarked, "enlists for money and his honor," the honor of his family in which military service is an ancient tradition.

Wavell is the philosophical artist with a perspective of history and not a bureaucrat with his nose in reports on day-to-day events. Linlithgow, the Viceroy in 1942, sat up until late in the night reading hills of detailed memoranda on what was happening in every district of India. He saw India through the microscope, not through the telescope.

On July 4, Lord Linlithgow gave a party in his great, ornate marble palace in New Delhi to celebrate America's independence from the British Empire. At that party, I heard all the arguments against Indian independence. General Winterton, who had been Sir Harold Alexander's Chief of Staff in Burma, said to me: "But could a free India defend herself?"

"Can a free England?" I rejoined.

If only those countries are to be free which can defend themselves single-handed, no country would be free, certainly Sweden, Denmark, Spain, France, and many others would not be free. The General's question merely means that mankind needs an effective international organization which will protect a free India, a free England, a free Russia, and all free nations against all aggressors. The defenseless person and the defenseless country are more valuable to society and more entitled to freedom than the bully and conqueror.

Later that evening, I was invited to sit and talk with Lady Linlithgow, the handsome wife of the Viceroy. She tried to discuss the weather—it was a hundred and ten all evening and everybody visibly dripped perspiration—but we soon switched to politics, and she said: "But are the Indians capable of ruling themselves?"

"That's a queer question to put on a night like this," I replied. "It's exactly what the British Tories said about the thirteen American colonies in 1776."

All Englishmen in India asserted that Britain was getting out. Sir Reginald Maxwell, Home Member in the Viceroy's Executive Council, told me at dinner in his house that "Britain is getting out of India after the war. I always thought it wrong that we did not say when. I believe it will be two years after the war."

"You know," I once said to General Wavell, "that the present order in India cannot last more than five or ten years."

"Quite right," Wavell affirmed with emphasis.

The second time I interviewed the Viceroy he said to me: "We are not going to remain in India. Of course, Congress doesn't believe this. But we will not stay here." Congress did not believe it, and few Indians believed it because, while declaring that they were leaving, the British continually cited the reasons for staying.

I search my records and my memory and cannot find a single instance in which a British official in India or a conservative Englishman anywhere argued in favor of independence for India. Quite the contrary. Outside India, particularly in the United States, the British spent millions on propaganda against Indian independence and stressing India's inability to rule herself. Indians, therefore, had little faith in British promises of independence.

This lack of trust between Indians and British was a basic factor in the Indian situation. Sir Reginald Dorman-Smith, who was British governor of Burma until the Japanese conquest in 1942, discussed the subject in an article in the London *Asiatic Review Quarterly* for January, 1944. Re-examining the East Asia problem in the light of the quick collapse of Britain's power in that area, Sir Reginald wrote: "One thing I can say with some surety, and that is that neither our word nor our intentions are trusted in that part of the globe. The reason for that is not far to seek. We have fed such countries as Burma on political formulae until they are sick of the very sight and the very sound of a formula, which has come, as far as my experience shows, to be looked upon as a very British means of avoiding a definite course of action. Our formulae have puzzled not only our enemies but also our friends because they have been hard to interpret to either friend or foe. . . ."

Burma has been promised independence. Yet Sir Harold R. L. G. Alexander, British Commander-in-Chief in Burma until the Japanese conquest, told the press in New Delhi, according to the Sunday *Statesman* of May 31, 1942: "We must take back Burma. It is part of the British Empire."

Burma will be free. Burma will be part of the Empire. Which is it? Sir Reginald Dorman-Smith wrestles with this dichotomy. Great Britain, he writes, "is committed to a policy of guiding Burma to the goal of full self-government. . . . Our aim therefore must surely be to build up . . . a Burma which will have no wish whatsoever to contract out of the Empire. . . ."

Sir Reginald hastens to explain that the word "freedom" must be properly understood. "I sometimes wonder," he declares, "whether we are not in danger of forgetting that it is a word which can mean different things to different people." He also wonders whether "we should not ourselves tell such countries as Burma more precisely than we have done in the past what we mean by the word."

So there was a British imperialistic lexicon and in that lexicon "freedom" meant staying in the Empire.

Sir Stafford Cripps came to India and, on behalf of the Churchill government, proposed giving India dominion status. The first act of the Dominion, he stated, could be to vote itself out of the Empire. That was in March, 1942. But in November, 1942, Churchill said: "I have not become the King's First Minister in order to preside at the liquidation of the British Empire." He issued that famous declaration apropos India. Consequently, when the British spoke of getting out of India, Indians suspected that the plan was liquidation which does not liquidate.

According to a Chinese proverb, the beginning of wisdom is calling things by their right names.

Australia and Canada, South Africa and New Zealand, and Eire, are free within the British Empire. The war proved it. Eire stayed out of the war. The other four Dominions voluntarily voted to fight by the side of the mother country and did so with heroism and cohesion. This is one of the startling political phenomena of the century.

India, however, has a different attitude towards England. The British record in India has filled Indians with no love for the British. The British know this and are pained by it. India's past created a burning desire for a future unencumbered by political ties with England.

Something else is involved: color. The color question will be the central social issue of the second half of the twentieth century. There are more colored people in the world than white; they are the oppressed majority. They are sick and tired of bearing the white man's burden. They respect the mechanical genius, wealth, and scientific progress of the white man. They do not respect his ethics or his political sagacity. They respect his war-making abilities, but not his peace-making abilities.

Western man can stay in Asia as a friend. He cannot stay there much longer as a master. India and China, never cognizant one of the other, are weaving a network of neighborly contacts. Either India or China, or Russia, will make a bid in the next fifty years for the leadership of colored humanity, more than a billion persons. "Asia for the Asiatics" was an imperialistic nostrum which Japan used for her own aggrandizement. Asiatics could use it against imperialism. It would be a dangerous development.

The East's affection for the West is in inverse ratio to the force which the West has imposed on the East.

The white man is so accustomed to his supremacy that he forgets it offends. He forgets, too, that he is losing it.

Englishmen have said: Indians are incapable of ruling their country. The Indians say: The white man is incapable of ruling the world. Witness two world wars and the unhappiness, intellectual confusion, suffering, and spread of dictatorship between wars.

The Indians also say that Britain is incapable of ruling India. England can keep India quiet, they assert, but she cannot keep her fed or clothed or housed. Recurrent famines are no proof of ability to govern. The Bengal famine of 1943 particularly angered Indians. The number of deaths from that catastrophe has been estimated as high as three million; no one has put it at less than one million. A hundred and twenty-five million cases of malaria in India and a hundred thousand fatalities each year are no proof of ability to govern. Thirteen and six-tenths per cent literacy, according to the 1941 census in which "literacy" was watered down to mean reading only, instead of reading and writing as theretofore, is no proof of ability to govern. Industrial stagnation, iniquitous systems of land ownership, and moral depression from prolonged foreign occupation ("We are the occupying power," Lord Linlithgow said to me) made Indians extremely intolerant of the British, sometimes unfairly so. This is the biggest fact in India.

India has innumerable successful Indian administrators, industrialists, bankers, publishers, economists, sociologists, scientists, jurists, publicists, educators, and statesmen-like political leaders of experience and proved talent. Sir Stafford Cripps has told us that the Viceroy believes India can govern herself. "On the basis of right and justice and principle," Cripps said in the House of Commons on October 26, 1939, "I should have thought nobody could have denied that India today is fully entitled to self-government. What answer have we to give now to that demand, admitting, as the Governor-General [Viceroy] fully admits, the competence of the Indians to govern themselves, unless it be that our selfish desire to continue the exploitation of India as part of our imperial monopoly is to override our conceptions of right and justice?"

So, India can govern herself. The British know it. The British are not wanted in India. They know that too.

If England needs India economically, British subjects can invest in, work in, and trade with a free India. England has large-scale and profitable business relations with Argentina and with many nations outside her Empire. But England's political control of India gave her exclusive economic advantages which were unfair to India and to other countries. Financially and commercially, India was a closed-door country. England held the key. She occasionally unlocked the door for competitors. Usually she unlocked it for herself.

Does England need India to remain a first-class power? If the answer is Yes, that does not make continued British domination more acceptable to Indians. Why should they be dependent so that England can be great?

"In the first and second world wars, England recruited big Indian armies which fought valiantly and helped hasten victory." This argument might be used to justify the retention of India forever. It might have been used to justify Japan's conquest of China; what a wonderful reservoir of manpower that would have been for Tokyo.

"If Britain had not held India, Japan might have seized that valuable colony as she did China." But the answer to this contention is not that India and China should be colonies. The answer is that they should be made strong, prosperous, and independent and therefore better equipped to resist aggression. If England ought to keep India lest some other power acquire possession then France, Spain, Italy, Bulgaria, and every small and weak country should become a colony of one of the two or three big powers. After a while, somebody would discover that England was too weak to protect herself and would do well, therefore, to submit to American or Russian domination. What becomes of the international organization to safeguard the peace by giving security to nations that cannot defend themselves?

Imperialism is the antithesis of internationalism. Empires are consolidated spheres of influence and encourage the formation of rival spheres of influence.

Empires are the incorporation of the principle of might without right. Nobody gave England the right to rule India. Imperialism is therefore immoral.

At an early stage, and in some areas, imperialism helps native peoples. The benefits of Western domination, however, have made Asia conscious of the need of ending that domination especially since, at a later stage, it harms the colonies economically, spiritually, and politically. The imperialist power nevertheless lingers on because it came for selfish gain. The interests of the colony are a tertiary consideration.

"The loss of India would mark and consummate the downfall of the British Empire," Churchill asserted on December 12, 1930. In March, 1931, again considering the question solely from England's viewpoint, Churchill said: "The loss of India would be final and fatal to us. It could not fail to be part of a process that would reduce us to the scale of a minor power."

"A minor power." That is a nineteenth century concept. The purpose of government and of all human endeavor is to make individuals happy. Normally, under peacetime conditions, a Dane or Swede or Swiss is better situated than the average Briton. Does it matter that he is the citizen of a minor power? I have never been able to see the relationship between the acquisition of another piece of territory and the welfare of the individual. Annexations in recent decades have usually led to wars.

It might be argued that the residents of a major power have the advantage in war. This is doubtful; it depends on circumstances. The residents of France, Italy, Japan, Germany, Russia—all regarded as major powers in 1939—indeed of Great Britain when one remembers the air raids, suffered as much or more than the citizens of minor powers. And if there is another war, with atomic bombs being shot across oceans from ramps and with super-Superfortress bombers flying nonstop around the globe, the men, women, and children of all powers, major and minor, will taste the same hell.

Indian independence will require of Britain economic and political adjustments to the twentieth century which she has been too conservative and too handicapped to make. The United States has a twentieth-century industry and therefore needs no colonies. The world wants what America can export; it wants, in particular, American machine tools for new factories, and America's mass-production goods. But England's industry was born earlier and, while it can manufacture articles that are every bit as modern and complicated as those of the United States, there is much in the industrial system of Great Britain which is obsolete. A country that wished to introduce large-scale industry could buy some machinery in England, but it would certainly prefer to get most of the equipment in the United States. America, therefore, would naturally be more interested than England in the industrialization of India. An England with a modernized industry, however, would take a different view of India. As long as British economy has at least one foot and a hand in the nineteenth century it cannot build a twentieth-century India.

A modernized, twentieth-century Britain which stressed the manufacture of machine tools rather than textiles and luxury articles, would have welcomed Indian industrialization and therefore Indian independence. In an India free and industrialized, Great Britain, to be sure, will have to compete for business with the United States and other advanced nations. But if four hundred million Indians began living slightly better than animals the increased demand for all kinds of goods would keep England and America and everybody pretty busy. Somebody once said facetiously: "If every Chinese wore pants there would be enough work in the United States for fifty years." If every Indian and Chinese and Greek and Peruvian had adequate food, clothing, shelter, education, health service, and medical care, world income would rise, world unemployment would fall, world happiness would increase and world peace would be less precarious.

Where would India and China, Greece and Peru, Nigeria and Tunisia obtain the means of thus raising their living standards? Exactly where the United States obtained them. Out of the ground, air, and water, out of the labor of the people.

India's freedom reflects the dawn of a new England.

This is true in politics as well as economics. In the dead past, the fact that Great Britain was not merely an island but an empire with half a billion inhabitants did give England added weight in world affairs. All this is changing as a result of the reduced value of navies in the air age and the expanding industrial might and political scope of America and Russia.

The old game of power politics is immoral and leads to war. One might understand a country's playing power politics if it could win. But why should England play power politics when she cannot win?

In a contest between England and Russia, an unhappy, partially-fettered India would side with Russia. A free India will fear Russian domination in case of Britain's defeat, and will therefore be England's natural ally.

The ability to produce atomic energy will give England greater military power than the possession of India. Imperialism is stupid in the atomic age.

England's choice is precarious imperialism or the internationalism of friendly nations; in other words, insecurity in empire or security through international organization.

In an earlier struggle for empire, Britain won against Spain, Portugal, and France because she was more advanced and stronger. In the coming struggle of empires, England must lose because she is weaker. The British Empire can be maintained only with American support, but it is doubtful whether that support would be beneficial, for the survival of an empire otherwise doomed to die would perpetuate obsolete political and economic arrangements in England and India and thus handicap England, India, and America.

England's best bet is internationalism in place of imperialism. The

British alone cannot achieve this result. They can work towards it and thereby help themselves and help the world.

History has assigned to the British Labor government the task of reshaping Great Britain's economics and politics to meet twentieth-century needs. It is clear now that the British people fought a two-front war. They defeated Hitler with Churchill; then they defeated Churchill in order to move into a new age. It is no accident that the same British government which nationalized backward home industries like coal and iron and steel also moved towards internationalism by loosening the ties of Empire. Twentieth-century economics go together with twentieth-century politics. A free India compels the British to modernize their industries.

No anti-British sentiment impelled me to advocate Indian independence. Great Britain is probably the most civilized, most enlightened, and most democratic power. I urged India's liberty for the sake of England, and of India, and of humanity.

Nor have I advocated Indian independence because of any interest in nationalism or nationalistic separatism. I criticized Indians in India for being indocentric. Narrow nationalism is a disease. Nationalism excludes; it therefore obstructs progress towards all-inclusive internationalism.

Somebody might say: Why make India a nation in order later to merge it with an international system? The answer is that imperialism is an infinitely more serious obstacle to internationalism than are democratic nations.

Because of her diversity India may avoid some of the pitfalls of nationalism. Democracy flourishes on diversity. Dictatorship abhors differences and liquidates them. It insists on uniformity. Democracy is like a rainbow in which seven rich colors merge to produce light. A free India may become truly democratic and then move forward, together with other non-imperialist, non-aggressive nations, into an internationalism that will restore humanity to sanity and, thereby, to peace.

Hundreds of millions in all continents will regard independence for India as proof that a new world can yet be built out of the ruin and rubble with which the modern cave man covered the earth between 1939 and 1945.

12. *Ten Quiet Days in Palestine*

I NEVER thought I would be in Baluchistan. It was a name and a spot on the map. The plane came down there the day we left India. Then on to Arabia and Iraq. I was in a hurry to get back to New York and hoped there would be no long stops.

The timetable said "Lunch at Kallia" on the Dead Sea, the lowest place on the earth's surface, and site of colorful chemical works. From Basra, accordingly, I wired Gershon Agronsky, editor of the *Palestine Post*, an English-language daily in Jerusalem, to come down to have the meal with me. We had been young men together in Philadelphia. I suggested he ask other friends too.

Gershon was in South Africa on a Zionist mission. His wife Ethel made the hour-plus trip to Kallia. With her was Ida Bloom Davidowitz, a dear friend and, like myself, a native of Philadelphia.

They asked about my plans. I pointed to the giant seaplane rocking on the green water a hundred yards away and told them that I was sorry but I had to rush home. I expected to be in New York in five days. Ethel insisted that I come up to Jerusalem for a visit. I said it was impossible. If I gave up my priority on the plane I might not be able to get another for weeks or months. I would have to leave in half an hour, when the plane took off.

My friends argued and coaxed, and I said no. Finally I said to myself "Why not?" With complete irresponsibility, I had my luggage removed from the plane and drove up to Jerusalem, one of the beautiful and exciting cities of the world. Enroute, we saw the British tunneling the wild brown hills and building sandbag defenses. Nazi General Rommel was three hours' march from Cairo and threatened the Suez Canal. If he broke through he would be in Palestine in a few days.

Once more, as in 1919, 1920, and again in 1934, I climbed Mt. Scopus, walked through the olive groves on Gethsemane, followed the Via Dolorosa, stood before the tragic Wailing Wall, and admired the Mosque of Omar. Every dusty stone in Jerusalem speaks ancient history. Some scenes are pages out of the Bible.

A new Jerusalem, modern, comfortable, and clean, now sits by the side of the old. It was built by the Jews who immigrated in the last fifty years to establish a Jewish national home. The Jews are proud of their achievement as builders. I was invited to go north for a tour of the agricultural settlements erected by Jewish pioneers in Galilee and the Valley of Isdraelon. In these areas, Jews from the ghettos of Poland, Tsarist Russia, Rumania, and other countries and, here and there, members of a new Palestine-born generation, have conquered barren rocky wastes or malaria-infested swamps and converted them into fruitful gardens where thousands live in equalitarian farming communities called *Kvutsot* or *Muoshavot*.

I did not travel to these colonies partly because I knew their great accomplishments, partly because I was heavy with the impressions and fatigue of India, and partly because I was more interested in the central political problem of Palestine, the Arab-Jewish problem.

The Arabs had been celebrating Rommel's victories over the British Army. In Arab villages, flags and banners were ready to greet his entry into Palestine. The Nazis and Arabs together could have staged a perfect anti-Jewish pogrom. Yet when I suggested to some of my American Jewish friends, who had the money and passports, that they go to America until the war was over, they looked at me as though I were mad. They would not desert. If Rommel came and if the Arabs tried to massacre Jews, they would fight alongside the half million Jews of Palestine. Several para-military Jewish organizations were armed and prepared to resist. Other Jewish young men had enlisted in the British Army and seen service in Egypt, Libya, and later Italy. The Arabs were anti-British and refused to help in the war against the Axis.

The Jews were brave and resolute but in no sense grim or depressed. They were working and building as usual.

In Tel Aviv, a new Jewish city on the coast of the Mediterranean, I stayed with the Davidowitz family. Harry S. Davidowitz, a former rabbi of Philadelphia and Cleveland, manufactured artificial teeth and translated Shakespeare into Hebrew. Suzanne Davidowitz, nineteen, the elder of two daughters, worked in a new agricultural settlement on the shore of Lake Hulah, a region permeated with malaria. Her parents were wealthy, and this was a labor of creative love and of idealistic devotion to a Jewish Palestine. Many thousands like her had died or permanently undermined their health in wresting such districts from the neglect of centuries.

Suzanne rarely left her comrades to enjoy the comfort of her Tel

Aviv home. But a special entreaty from her parents and me brought a favorably reply.

After lunch one day, Harry Davidowitz and I argued the Arab-Jewish question. Suzanne sat between us at table without uttering a word for at least three quarters of an hour. Suddenly, apropos nothing at all, she said: "Up in the settlement, we have a new potato-sorting machine."

I took this as a completely unconscious but very symbolic Jewish response to the Arab problem. Face to face with the menace of Arab violence, the Jews continued to put brick on brick and to acquire new potato-sorting machines.

Zionism aims to establish a Jewish state, or commonwealth, in Palestine. To do this, it aims to make Jews a majority of the population of Palestine. The population of the country consists, approximately, of half a million Jews and a million Arabs. Experts say that with irrigation, electrification, and industrialization, Palestine could support several million more persons.

"If I forget thee, O, Jerusalem, let my right hand forget its cunning, let my tongue cleave to the roof of my mouth," sang the Psalmist. The Jewish nostalgia for Palestine has survived all the centuries of dispersion. For many devout Jews, Palestine is inextricably connected with their religion. For many non-religious Jews, Palestine is a religion. Zionism stems primarily from the lure of an old home, a birthplace, the birthplace of a people that has lived in many countries but lived the life of other peoples, never its own life with its own government in its own home. The umbilical cord of history ties numberless Jews to Palestine. Millions who were never there and never expect to be there have been moved by the dream of a Jewish national restoration.

This is an emotion and therefore needs no explanation. I used to feel it as a young Zionist in Philadelphia, and I enlisted in the Jewish Battalion of the British Army and went to Palestine in 1918 and remained until 1920. I do not have the emotion any longer. It started to evaporate in Palestine. My interest in Zionism and, indeed, my special interest in Jewish affairs left me completely during the years between 1921 and 1939 which I spent in Europe. I became absorbed in larger social, economic, and political questions. I understand the concentration of Jews on the painful Jewish problem. It cannot be ignored or neglected. But I am not attracted by nationalist movements unless they are part, as the Indian or Indonesian nationalist movements are, of an attempt to end imperialism and its evils. Zionism however is a nationalist movement which is tied to British imperialism.

I hope nationalist problems will ultimately be solved by world solutions. I know the Zionist answer. The answer is: We cannot wait for 'ultimately.' I agree, and I have never said or done anything to interfere with Zionism. My own participation, however, would require a temperamental excitement and an ideological agreement that are lacking.

I exposed myself to Palestine for a month in 1934 and for ten quiet days in 1942, but the emotion of my youth for Zionism was not revived. Moreover, I believe that no nation, certainly not a small nation like the Jews, can solve its problem in isolation. How many nations in recent years have gone to hell on their own territory?

Palestine has beauty, and many of its Jews live happy, useful lives. Their happiness is the product of a sense of creation and of putting down roots. They are building; they are building houses, farms, factories, roads, streets, hospitals, and schools, but all of these material things add up to something spiritual—a national home. The sacrifices they make are impressive. Jewish Palestine is bathed in blood and suffused with idealism. It has its speculators, exploiters, and self-seekers. But these are a minority. Bigness of purpose often makes people bigger than they are. In Palestine one feels that the total achievement is greater than the sum of the achievements of the individuals in the community. The excess is probably what we mean by culture, culture in the sense of civilized communal living.

Other attempts at organized Jewish migration and colonization, in Argentina, the Ukraine and Crimea, and Santo Domingo, for instance, have met with varied success. Palestine has been economically more successful than these because Jews throughout the world have contributed enormous funds running into tens of millions of dollars to help build Palestine. Jews have lavished money as well as love on Palestine. The economic foundation of Palestine is made of gold given by world Jewry. The viability of Palestine's Jewish economy therefore remains to be demonstrated.

Sentimental attachment for Zion notwithstanding, many Jews in Europe would probably choose America if they could. Indeed, some Palestinian Jews might move to America. The United States, whose inhabitants, with the exception of a few red Indians, are the children of immigrants and refugees, is however closed to all but a handful of newcomers. Though under-populated, the United States and most other big, under-populated countries—Australia, Canada, the Soviet Union, Argentina, and Brazil, for instance—do not want Jewish immigrants.

Remains tiny Palestine.

No words are adequate to describe the horrors which Jews suffered in Hitler-occupied Europe. At least five million Jews were killed during the second world war, five out of Europe's seven million Jews. They were killed not in bombings or battles—although these took their Jewish toll too—but by deliberate, cold-blooded murder. "You, you, you, for the gas chamber." "You, you, you, to be burned in the incinerator." "You, you, you, to work until you can work no longer on our starvation diet and then to the furnace with you." Five million human beings efficiently killed. The Nazis killed anti-Nazi Germans with the medieval axe. They killed Jews with modern chemistry and physics.

Small wonder that Jews do not wish to stay in a Europe poisoned by Hitler. For even before Hitler, Jews in many lands were subjected to indecent discrimination. The Soviet Union was the only country where the government frowned upon and punished anti-Semitism, and where racial persecution had all but disappeared as an active social force. Elsewhere in Europe and throughout the world, Jews suffered disabilities and were never fully accepted as equal members of society.

In the United States, Jews have complete legal, political, religious, and economic freedom. They have their geniuses, successes, criminals, and failures. Officially, America recognizes no difference between Jews and non-Jews. But individual Americans and groups of Americans do. Millions of American Christians avoid personal associations with Jews or reduce such associations to a minimum. There are "select" hotels, and hotels for "Christian clientele only." This is not very Christian. The reluctance to associate with Jews has no basis in smell, or color, or wealth, or manners, or education, or talent, or conviviality, or the ability to entertain. On every level, Christians would find Jews who are their equals. Does difference of religion account for the gulf? The attempt of Christians to dissociate themselves from Jews even makes them turn away from names in the Bible. How many Christians are now named Abraham as Lincoln was? or Isaac as Newton was? or Jacob as Astor was? or Benjamin as Franklin was? or Elihu as Root was? or Noah as Webster was? or Sarah, or Leah, and so on and so on? Since Christians regard Biblical names as peculiarly Jewish, Jews now tend to prefer Anglo-Saxon and French names.

One of the worst maladies of our civilization is the desire of people to escape being themselves. Anti-Jewishness strengthens this desire in many Jews. They become pathologically self-conscious. They think a Jew should not become a Justice of the Supreme Court or a radical or a newspaper publisher. The disabilities which gentiles place upon Jews cause the Jews to heap disabilities upon themselves.

Many Jews see the need of at least one place in the world where Jews would be Jews because they want to be Jews and not because others do not want them.

Some Jews contend that Jewishness is exclusively religious. The contention is ludicrous. A large percentage of American Jews are not religious yet they feel Jewish; they feel the tie of blood or of common cultural origin. Or anti-Semitism makes them feel Jewish.

But even among Jews who object to a Jewish political state because Judaism to them is only a religion, an increasing number realize the compulsion of finding a haven for European Jews, and they recognize that Palestine is first choice next to immigrant-shy America. Persons who were anti-Zionists a few years ago not uncommonly class themselves as non-Zionists, or even as Zionists, today. They may still object to political Zionism. They cannot deny the necessity of a new home for homeless, unhappy Jews.

If this were a better world Jews would not have to go to Palestine and fewer would want to go. They could live in Germany, Poland, Rumania, and other countries. But the ruling emotion of European Jews is to leave the scene of Hitler's anti-Jewish horror. With nationalism rampant in the postwar world anti-Semitism is not likely to abate. It was easier to defeat Hitler with arms than to defeat the virus with which Hitler infected a continent, indeed more than a continent.

The broader acceptance of Zionism by Jews and non-Jews is a criticism of the postwar world and of the peace.

When one thinks of the contributions which Jews have made to science, art, learning, industry, and government in all countries it is strange that most countries keep them out. Is it that countries built on competition dislike competition? Hitler perhaps lost the war because he expelled or tortured or shot German-Jewish scientists. The British and American governments had the wisdom to admit them and use them in defense plants and laboratories. In peace, however, we worry about the unemployment that may result from the increases in the population of the country. When Americans had faith in the future growth of America the door was wide open. The United States, land of endless possibilities, is still very under-developed.

The Arabs too combat Jewish immigration. During my sojourn in Jerusalem, I had a daily talk and walk with Dr. Judah L. Magnes, Chancellor of the Hebrew University on Mt. Scopus. A former rabbi of New York, he has lived in Palestine for over two decades. Through him, I met leading Arab politicians.

Dr. Magnes is a Gandhi-esque Jew. Profoundly religious and so-cially-conscious, his constant companions are God and the common man. He has stubbornness with mellowness; the combination reflects his conviction that he is right. Most Zionists think he is wrong. In fact, some Jews in Palestine loathe him, for he would compromise with the Arabs and try to convert them to an acceptance of limited Jewish immigration.

Magnes is probably the one prominent Jew in Palestine who is in touch with Arabs. The Jews and Arabs live in two separate worlds. The hatred and tension between them is great. From 1936 to 1939, and interrupted only by the outbreak of the second world war, a condition of civil war existed in Palestine; Arabs besieged and am-bushed Jews; and many dead and wounded were numbered on both sides. Magnes seeks to remedy the situation by contacts and conces-sions. His opponents say they must first establish a Jewish majority in the country and then they will talk to the Arabs. Concessions, they argue, would be regarded as confessions of weakness and would lead nowhere.

In Dr. Magnes' company, I spoke with Auni Abdul-Hadi, who be-came the outstanding Arab notable of Palestine when Haj Amin el Husseini, the Mufti of Jerusalem, fled from the British and went to see Hitler. I also met Dr. Khalidi and other leading Arabs. Subsequently, I talked again with all of them in an Arab home.

These Arab politicians admitted that Arabs in Palestinian villages were waiting to welcome Rommel. They argued that the Jews had not enriched Palestine but only enriched themselves in Palestine. Above all, they were adamant in their opposition to Jewish immigra-tion, to the sale of land to Jews, and to a Jewish state in Palestine. They declared that they would object less to Jewish immigration if the Zionists were not out to create a Jewish majority with a view to political control of the little country.

This Arab opposition is stubborn. Palestinian Arabs have obviously benefited by Jewish enterprise. One look at an Arab village which abuts on a Jewish colony shows how the Arabs have copied Jewish methods and gained thereby. Arabs have grown rich by selling land to Jews at outrageously speculative prices. Arab living standards, health, and culture have improved by the proximity of Jews. Left to themselves, the Arabs, though irritated by the introduction of Jews into Palestine, might soon reconcile themselves. The intransigent opposition of Arabs to Zionism comes from outside of Palestine.

The Arabs of the Middle East have been overtaken by nationalism. Imperialism always begets nationalism. Zionism, tied to the apronstrings of British imperialism, accelerated the process among the Arabs. The Arab leaders of Iraq, Syria, Lebanon, Transjordania, Saudi Arabia, Egypt, Palestine, perhaps also of the North African Arab lands, dream of unity, of an Arab League which will become a power in world affairs. But although the Arabs belong to the same racial stock and although most of them are Moslems (some Arabs are Christians), they have never been united. Many circumstances divide them. They seek some strong cement to bind them together. They have found it in Zionism. Hitler fanned the flame of German nationalism by throwing Jews on the fire; the Arabs hope to build an Arab empire on the ruins of Jewish hope.

The British authorities in the Middle East frequently make policy and then seek approval in Downing Street. Or several branches of the British government pursue contradictory policies. In Palestine, for instance, one office has been known to connive at or assist the arming of Arabs while another manifests a pro-Jewish tendency.

Generally speaking, however, the British government seems to have courted the Arabs and facilitated the formation of an Arab League. This may have been due to a feeling that the trend was too strong to be stopped, or to a conviction that if Britain did not support it the Russians or the United States or France might. Moreover, the Arabs threaten violence. The British shrink. England also considers India's ninety-two million Moslems.

Sensing the vacillating if not sympathetic viewpoint of the British, and instigated by Arabs outside Palestine, the Arabs of the Holy Land assume a fiercely anti-Zionist position. Civil war is always just beneath the surface in Palestine and often on the surface. The Jews are brave fighters and have won many pitched battles and sieges in Judea and Galilee. I myself participated in the defense of Jewish blockhouses at Tel Hai and Kfar Gileadi in Upper Galilee where, standing guard at night, we could hear the Jordan rushing down from its source in the territory of the tribe of Dan. That was in 1919. The troubles have multiplied since then; so have the armaments; so has Jewish terrorism.

The Jews I talked to in 1942 had no solution except to insist on the implementation of Britain's numerous pledges. Meanwhile, they would literally dig in and hold their ground. In the 1920's there was still time to close the chasm between Jews and Arabs by forming trade unions and merchant associations together and by facing imperialism together. But, as Moshe Shertok, a Laborite and official of the Jewish agency, said to me in Jerusalem in 1934: "We are nationalists first and Socialists after that." The Jews were militant Jewish nationalists and the Arabs were militant Arab nationalists and no Magnes could bridge the gulf. Now it is very late.

My ten quiet days in Palestine were very disquieting.

It may very well be that there is no solution of the Palestine problem by means of the usual procedures of national statehood based on a racial majority. Palestine must aspire to friendly inter-racial, international and inter-religious co-existence of Jew, Moslem, and Christian. It is a difficult goal to attain. It is an idyll that has so far eluded less disturbed and more prosperous countries.

At least Palestine was saved from invasion in 1942. When I arrived in Cairo from Palestine in July, 1942, the city was tense. General Rommel's dark shadow could be seen clearly across the yellow Egyptian sands. The entire Allied world was aroused, for victory hung in the balance. The British, aided by Poles, were battling valiantly, but needed help. "In the summer of 1942, when in a single battlefield Marshal Rommel had destroyed a large proportion of Great Britain's tanks in Libya, General Marshall (U. S. Chief of Staff) unhesitatingly stripped our training forces of medium tanks and shipped them to Egypt as the only means of meeting the crisis.

"One of our armored divisions was at that time in a port of embarkation, ready to sail for further training in North Ireland. That division, too, was divested of its armor and its shipment delayed until the tanks could be replaced. But the important thing was that Rommel had been stopped. The dangerous crisis was met. We know now that Marshall's estimate of this situation was correct. Hitler intended to break through Egypt to the Near East. Had he succeeded, the entire course of the war would have been changed."

Thus spoke Secretary of War Stimson in his farewell statement on September 19, 1945.

A narrow strip of sandy land between El Alamein and Suez was denied to Rommel. As a result Palestine was saved and Hitler was prevented from moving towards a junction with the Japanese in India. If that had happened the Axis might have won a stalemate or prolonged the war for several years.

I was in Cairo the day Rommel smashed the British tanks. At the press conference that evening every face looked black. "This is it," an English journalist said. But Marshall beat Rommel to it.

I arrived in New York by Clipper on August 5. The battle for Egypt still raged. India was seething. Gandhi and Nehru were about to proclaim a nation-wide civil disobedience movement. They did so on August 8. The British promptly arrested them. On August 5, therefore, all eyes were on India. A large group of reporters met me at LaGuardia field for my views on the Indian crisis. *The New York Times* next morning printed a three-column photograph of me "At Home with Gandhi" together with three-fourths of a column of text. The *New York Herald Tribune* devoted the same amount of space to my comments. The photograph and part of my statement were reprinted throughout the United States. If I had not frivolously stopped in Palestine and arrived home ten days earlier, before Indian events were in focus, the papers would have announced the arrival of the clipper and said: "Among those on board was Louis Fischer."

Part Two

Journey through War to Peace

13. *Roosevelt, Gandhi, and Chiang Kai-shek*

ALARMED by the situation in India, Generalissimo Chiang Kai-shek sent President Roosevelt a fifteen-hundred-word, secret, coded cable on July 25, 1942. Roosevelt received it on July 29 and replied on August 8, in approximately three hundred and fifty words. Chiang came back on August 11 with a shorter message which Roosevelt answered the next day.

These cables, which show how two heads of state correspond with one another, have never before been published nor was their existence known to more than a few high officials of the American and Chinese governments.

Chiang began by saying that "the Indian situation has reached an extremely intense and critical stage. Its development in fact constitutes the most important factor in determining the outcome of the United Nations war, and especially the war in the East." He wanted Roosevelt to act. "Your country," he wrote, "is the leader in this war of right against might and Your Excellency's views have always received serious attention in Britain. Furthermore, for a long time the Indian people have been expecting the United States to come out and take a stand on the side of Justice and Equality."

Chiang feared trouble in India. He knew that Gandhi and Nehru intended to launch an India-wide passive resistance campaign. He accordingly told President Roosevelt that "the only way to make them reconsider their course of action is for the United Nations and especially the United States, which they admire, to come forth as a third party and to offer them sympathy and consolation. This will help them regain their sense of proportion and strengthen their faith that there is justice in the world. Once the situation is eased it can be stabilized and the Indian people, grateful to the United Nations for what they have done, will willingly participate in the war. Otherwise the Indian people, in despair, will have the same feeling towards other members of the United Nations as towards Britain and when this comes to pass it will be the world's greatest tragedy in which Britain is not the only loser."

"So far as Britain is concerned," Chiang continued, "she is a great country and in recent years she has been pursuing an enlightened policy towards her colonial possessions. On the other hand, India is a weak country. With an unprecedented extensive war in progress, naturally things cannot be handled in the ordinary manner."

Chiang Kai-shek warned Roosevelt that British efforts to cope with the crisis would be a two-edged sword. "Even if such measures should prove effective in curbing the non-violence movement," he said, "the spiritual loss and blow to the United Nations will far exceed any reverse in the field. Such a situation will be particularly detrimental to Britain's interests."

"The wisest and most enlightened policy for Britain to pursue," Chiang counseled, "would be to restore to India her complete freedom. . . . The war aims of the United Nations," he stated, "and our common interests make it impossible for me to remain silent. An ancient Chinese proverb says: 'Good medicine, though bitter, cures one's illness; words of sincere advice, though unpleasant, guide one's conduct.' I sincerely hope that Britain will magnanimously and resolutely accept my words of disinterested advice however unpleasant they may be. . . ."

"I shall persist in my views," Chiang concluded. "My only feeling is that the United Nations should lose no time in adopting a correct policy towards the Indian situation and in striving for its realization so that our entire war situation will not suffer a major setback. I ardently hope Your Excellency will favor me with your sound judgment."

Roosevelt's reply began as follows: "I have been giving, as you will of course realize, the utmost consideration and thought to your message regarding the Indian situation. . . ." The President fully shared Chiang's opinion "that for the sake of common victory, the Indian situation should be stabilized and the participation of the Indian people should be secured in the joint effort."

But then came the *but*. "I know, however," President Roosevelt cabled the Generalissimo, "that you will understand the difficulty which is presented to me in your suggestion that this Government should advise both the British government and the people of India 'to seek a reasonable and satisfactory solution.' The British government believes," said the President, that the Cripps proposals already offered India a fair adjustment. "Furthermore," he continued, "the British government feels that suggestions coming at this moment from other members of the United Nations would undermine the authority of the only existing government in India and would tend to create the very crisis which it is your hope and my hope may yet be averted."

Therefore, concluded Mr. Roosevelt, "Under present circumstances, I feel that it would be wiser for you and for myself to refrain from taking action of the kind which you had in mind for the time being."

The day after the President's coded cable left Washington, Gandhi, Nehru, Maulana Abul Kalam Azad, the President of the Congress party, and thousands of their followers were arrested and imprisoned. Subsequently, Sir Maurice Gwyer, the British Lord Chief Justice of India, ruled in a published decision that the Indian nationalists had been jailed illegally under a statute that had no validity. Thereupon, on September 28, 1943, the Viceroy issued a new ordinance validating the arrests of August, 1942.

The arrests aroused India-wide indignation, and the civil disobedience campaign spread fast. Moreover, it immediately took violent forms.

Two days after the arrests, Chiang Kai-shek wired Roosevelt saying: "I feel certain you are concerned, as I am, at the news of the arrest of the Working Committee of the Indian Congress, including Gandhi and Nehru." Despite Roosevelt's hesitation to intervene in the India situation, Chiang went on to repeat his request that Roosevelt do something. "At all costs," he stated, "the United Nations should demonstrate to the world by their actions the sincerity of their professed principles of ensuring freedom and justice for men of all races. I earnestly appeal to you as the inspired author of the Atlantic Charter to take [effective?] measures which undoubtedly have already occurred to you to solve the pressing problem now facing India and the world. . . . Your policy will serve as a guide," Chiang concluded almost menacingly, "to all of us who have resisted for so long and so bitterly the brute force of the aggressors. Trusting you will favor me with an early reply . . ."

Things now moved fast. Roosevelt replied the day after Chiang dispatched his message from Chungking.

"It is scarcely necessary," Mr. Roosevelt stated, "to reiterate the deep interest of this Government, both under its long-standing policy and especially under the provisions of the Atlantic Charter, in independence for those who aspire to independence. This policy has been stated and reiterated over a long period and up to this hour by the official spokesmen of the American government. It has been put into practical application in such cases as that of the Philippines. . . ."

"It is clear," the President noted, "that despite all efforts on your part and on my part, without becoming actual parties to the internal controversy existing between the British government and Mr. Gandhi speaking for himself and his followers, to aid in bringing about an amicable adjustment of this serious disagreement and controversy, it has thus far been impossible to do so. . . ."

"We need India's help in this," Mr. Roosevelt told the Generalissimo, "and I wish Mr. Gandhi could see more clearly the need for this immediate help, and also that he understand that the worst thing that could happen to the people of India would be victory by the Axis powers.

"I told the Pacific Council today, including Mr. Soong [Dr. T. V. Soong, China's Foreign Minister], that I think your position and mine should be to make it clear to the British government and to Mr. Gandhi and his followers that we have not yet the moral right to force ourselves upon the British or the Congress party but that we should make it clear to both sides that you and I stand in the position of friends who will gladly help if they are called by both sides."

President Roosevelt summed up as follows: "I think that you and I can best serve the people of India at this stage by making no open or public appeal or announcement but by letting the simple fact be known that we stand ready as friends to heed any appeal for help if that appeal comes from both sides."

Roosevelt knew in advance that the British government would never appeal to him or to anyone else for help. So the two sides would never appeal. Roosevelt, therefore, was rejecting Chiang Kai-shek's urgent call to mediate in India. Roosevelt was considering Britain's sensibilities. He knew the Indian difficulty would delay victory. But he conformed to the traditional niceties of diplomatic practice; he would intervene only if asked to do so by both parties. In other words, he would not intervene.

President Roosevelt was recognizing the private property right of imperialist powers to their colonies. A fire raged in the colony. It might endanger others outside. But the owner of the colony refused to admit the firemen, and the firemen politely retreated.

When the imperial master is adamant, and United Nations remain aloof, what recourse other than force remains to colonies yearning for independence? The peoples of India and of Asia had no knowledge of the Roosevelt-Chiang correspondence in July-August, 1942.

But they knew that no big power was ready to help the freedom-wanting Asiatic races. That is tucked away in their memories.

When politics is guided by the conveniences of the present it usually stores up trouble for the future. Failure to meet the issues of 1942 aggravated the problems of 1945 and 1946.

Sumner Welles, who as Under-Secretary of State in 1942 knew Roosevelt's views on the subject, revealed in the *New York Herald Tribune* of August 8, 1945, that "President Roosevelt believed that Indian self-government could greatly advance ordered progress in the Far East. . . . he was convinced that only through such a free solution, and the classic process of trial and error, could the peoples of India eventually enjoy that form of self-government best adapted to their individual needs and prejudices."

Churchill demurred. "President Roosevelt's friendly suggestions to that effect, made as they were during a most crucial period of the war, were not only unavailing, but were even bitterly resented by the British Prime Minister," writes Mr. Welles.

It was not easy to change Churchill. Roosevelt tried several times to discuss India with Churchill, but he never got very far. He merely succeeded in arousing Churchill's poorly-disguised anger.

Prime Minister Neville Chamberlain was an appeaser chiefly because he was afraid that as a result of the social changes inevitable in a war, his England, the England of money, privilege, and caste, would die. But Churchill was sure that England could fight a war and win it and remain the old England. Churchill's old England included India, and to ask him to give up India was tantamount to asking him to give up the thing for which he was fighting the war.

But for the United States, the most powerful of the United Nations, to defer to Churchill and defer action on India was like postponing the explosion of a delayed-action bomb without rendering it harmless. It meant that the whole grievous problem of postwar imperialism would be in the laps of the peacemakers when the war ended. Given the necessary mood in England, it would have been much easier to deal with this issue during the hostilities, when enlightened public opinion in America and other countries would have supported an effort to accelerate victory and simultaneously rid the earth of the cancer of colonial domination.

The contrary viewpoint was put succinctly by the chief of a United States legation in a handwritten letter dated September 12, 1942. "I admit," the Minister wrote me, "that I have a one-track mind that relegates everything to considerations of the present and those considerations relate exclusively to how we can kill the greatest number of our enemies and destroy the greatest amount of their equipment in the shortest space of time, so I have no time to think of the past or of the future and no patience to hold the hands of those whose values may be constructive in the long run but for the moment seem to retard the war effort. Whether this limited view of mine applies to Gandhi and his works I wouldn't know but I know we can't do everything so I like to feel that we concentrate only on what use of force will bring us victory the quickest and then we can use the few brains we have afterwards to undo the evil of the past and create the good of the future. Does this disgust you?"

It did not disgust me: it appalled me. For it was the philosophy of a big school of thought in Washington whose principal was Harry Hopkins and whose line was formulated by an observer as "First get that s.o.b. Hitler." First win the war; never mind about the peace. The horror is that the peace did not wait. By not making the peace we made it nevertheless. Others made it despite us.

Today's troubles are due to our reluctance to grasp the nettle in wartime when our power and influence were greatest.

In an interview I had with Wendell Willkie on August 30, 1944, just one week before he entered the hospital from which he was carried to his grave, he said to me: "We started losing the peace in the spring of 1943. When I returned from my trip around the world in 1942 I saw the President and urged him to fly to Moscow to see Stalin. I told him that Stalin wouldn't leave Russia but that he, the President of the United States, would lose no prestige by going all the way to Stalin. 'We are strong,' I said to the President, 'and the strong can afford to do such things.' There was time then to change conditions before Russia became powerful and therefore cynical about the peace. The powerful are often cynical."

Willkie looked out of the window for a moment; the busy New York harbor lay full in view. Then he turned to me again and continued where he had left off: "I even had Mike [Gardner] Cowles, who went with me on the trip and who was working for the Government, prepare a memorandum outlining the objectives of such a visit by the President to the Kremlin. I wanted a written memorandum because when I got back from England in 1941 I made a similar suggestion to the President, that he go over to see Churchill and decide on the shape of the peace. At that time, something could still have

been done about India, China, and many other areas. But now . . ."
Willkie stopped suddenly. The peace was being lost because earlier
opportunities had been muffed.

It is wrong for a nation to use its power to aggrandize at the expense of others. It is good when a nation uses its power to foster a
good peace based on freedom and the principles of decent human
conduct.

Since President Roosevelt, as Sumner Welles states, "believed that
Indian self-government could greatly advance ordered progress in
the Far East," he should have insisted that the Indian problem be
solved. If the liquidation of the British Empire had been the first foundation stone of peace it would have been easier to stem Russian imperialism and to inhibit trends toward American imperialism.

Sitting three feet from Mr. Churchill, his wrath was embarrassing.
The wrath of the future will be greater.

Churchill rebuffed Chiang Kai-shek as well as Roosevelt. The Generalissimo appealed directly to the British government to make a
move in India. The Churchill government replied that if China continued to interfere in Indian affairs the Sino-British treaty of alliance
would be endangered. "If Amery [Leopold S. Amery, British Secretary of State for India] had said that to my envoy, and if mine were
a nation of four hundred million instead of fifteen," Manuel Quezon,
President of the Philippines, said to me in the Shoreham Hotel in
Washington, D. C., in September, 1942, "I would have replied: 'All
right, the alliance has lost all value to me.' And I would have negotiated with the Japs."

Quezon read aloud to me the cables he had sent to Gandhi and
Nehru on August 7 urging them not to do anything which might
jeopardize the United Nations victory. Quezon had shown those
cables to President Roosevelt who approved. The cables were never
delivered. On September 18, Quezon received a letter from Lord
Halifax, British ambassador in Washington, informing him that Viceroy Linlithgow would not permit delivery.

At a meeting of the Pacific Council, held in the White House in
September, 1942, Quezon brought up the question of India, and presented arguments for American mediation. President Roosevelt, who
presided, said he knew very little about India but most Americans
were in favor of Indian independence and it would be desirable for
the British and Indians to get together and negotiate. Lord Halifax,
who attended, stated that order had to be reestablished first and the

British would reestablish it. Quezon then turned to Dr. Soong, the Chinese ambassador, and requested his opinion. Soong declared that India was "a test of Anglo-American sincerity."

The British policy was to reestablish order and nothing else; Halifax told me so on August 28. He said: "If I were the Viceroy of India, and I am glad I am not, I would certainly not negotiate now with Congress. The millions in India," he declared, "are ignorant, illiterate sheep and if you want to govern this mob you have to show them that you can govern."

It is because of this psychology that Churchill, and Halifax, rebuffed Roosevelt on India, and Roosevelt dropped the case.

Mahatma Gandhi had given me a personal letter to give to President Roosevelt. The letter was important and if the President had acted on it much trouble might have been avoided in India. I wanted to get it into the President's hands as quickly as possible so I gave it to General Gruber, of the United States Armed Forces in India, who was flying straight to Washington by special priority and who told me he would be seeing the President. The letter, dated Sevagram, July 1, 1942, read as follows:

Dear Friend,

I twice missed coming to your great country. I have the privilege of having numerous friends there both known and unknown to me. Many of my countrymen have received and are still receiving higher education in America. I know too that several have taken shelter there. I have profited greatly by the writings of Thoreau and Emerson. I say this to tell you how much I am connected with your country. Of Great Britain I need say nothing beyond mentioning that in spite of my intense dislike of British rule, I have numerous British friends in England whom I love as dearly as my own people. I had my legal education there. I have therefore nothing but good wishes for your country and Great Britain. You will therefore accept my word that my present proposal that the British should unreservedly and without reference to the wishes of the people of India immediately withdraw their rule, is prompted by the friendliest intentions. I would like to turn into good will the ill will which, whatever may be said to the contrary, exists in India towards Great Britain, and thus enable the millions of India to play their part in the present war.

My personal position is clear. I hate all war. If, therefore, I could persuade my countrymen, they would make a most effective and decisive contribution in favor of an honorable peace. But I know that all of us have not a living faith in non-violence. Under foreign rule, however, we can make no effective contribution of any kind in this war, except as helots.

The policy of the Indian National Congress, largely guided by me, has been one of non-embarrassment to Britain, consistently with the honorable working of the Congress, admittedly the largest political organization of the longest standing in India. The British policy as exposed by the Cripps mission and rejected by almost all parties has opened our eyes and has driven me to the proposal I have made. I hold that the full acceptance of my proposal and that alone can put the Allied cause on an unassailable basis. I venture to think that the Allied declaration that the Allies are fighting to make the world safe for the freedom of the individual and for democracy sounds hollow so long as India, and for that matter Africa, are exploited by Great Britain, and America has the Negro problem in her own home. But in order to avoid all complications in my proposal I have confined myself to India. If India becomes free the rest must follow, if it does not happen simultaneously.

In order to make my proposal foolproof I have suggested that if the Allies think it necessary they may keep their troops, at their own expense, in India, not for keeping internal order but for preventing Japanese aggression and defending China. So far as India is concerned, she must become free even as America and Great Britain are. The Allied troops will remain in India during the war under treaty with the free Indian government that may be formed by the people of India without any outside interference, direct or indirect.

It is on behalf of this proposal that I write this to enlist your active sympathy.

I hope that it will commend itself to you.

Mr. Louis Fischer is carrying this letter to you.

If there is any obscurity in my letter, you have but to send me word and I shall try to clear it.

I hope finally that you will not resent this letter as an intrusion but take it as an approach from a friend and well-wisher of the Allies.

I remain,

Yours sincerely,
(*Signed*)   M. K. Gandhi.

President Franklin D. Roosevelt.

On arriving at Miami from India I telegraphed President Roosevelt asking whether I could come see him. Two days later, I received a telegram signed "M. M. McIntyre, Secretary to the President" which said that "due to extreme pressure here we have arranged for Secretary Hull to see you."

In a few days I received a letter from the President dated August 11, 1942. It read:

Dear Mr. Fischer,

I am trying to keep in very close touch with the situation. I get the latest news from several sources every day.

Very sincerely yours,
(*Signed*)   Franklin D. Roosevelt.

I was sorry not to be able to see the President and I thought that if I had kept Gandhi's letter instead of sending it by General Gruber my chances would have been better.

On August 12, a person close to Roosevelt invited me and said: "Franklin asked me to see you and to tell him what you said."

When I returned to New York from India, Mrs. Clare Boothe Luce telephoned and inquired whether I had talked to Wendell Willkie. I said no, and she arranged the interview. I went to his office at 15 Broad Street. He did not get up when I entered and kept his feet on his desk. He said he was tired. Mr. J. J. Singh, President of the India League of America, told me Willkie had received him in the same way. I liked it. I had an impression of sincerity. He was tired and gave one a sense of gray pallor although his hair was not gray at all.

Willkie said he shared my views on India. He thought he should be on record about India for that future day when things would be different and when we would use our war aims as practical peace weapons. He said he had wished to go to India on his "One World" trip, and had expressed that wish to President Roosevelt but the President held that India was no place for an American to go to now and Willkie ought therefore restrict his travels to the Near East, Russia, and China.

An unofficial adviser of the President, whom I used to visit at irregular intervals in Washington, sent word to me through a mutual friend after my return from India that he did not want me to call.

It was American policy not to ruffle the British on India. This is convenient. It is often convenient to avoid an issue. But it can be costly.

I kept an appointment with Secretary of State Cordell Hull at 12:15 P.M. on August 27, 1942. He asked me about India and then he made this comment: "The difficulty is that when the other party is immovable we cannot interfere. It is just as if some foreign country tried to tell us how to implement the Monroe Doctrine."

I said if England were carrying part of the burden of defending a Latin American nation against aggression as we were in India and if that nation were regarded by a whole continent as the test of Allied sincerity, as India was, England would have a right to a voice in the matter.

Mr. Hull declared he had always taken a favorable attitude towards independence movements and the recognition of new governments. He said: "For Christ's sake, when I was a young fellow I raised a regiment to fight for Cuban independence. In 1933, against many odds, I championed recognition for Soviet Russia. We have introduced the Good Neighbor policy in Latin America. I have favored equal rights for China. . . . But on the question of India, while the President is missing no opportunities, we cannot do much if the British are immovable. The other fellow may dig in his toes and say 'Here I stand even if everything else goes to pieces.' " He repeated this in several versions.

At 12:40, Mr. Hull's secretary came in and asked whether he would have his lunch now. Soon the secretary brought in a tray with a plate of cold roast beef, a salad, a glass of tomato juice, a glass of milk, a glass of water, and a cup of tea. When he had finished these, Hull said: "Now I must leave. I am giving a lunch today for Prime Minister Fraser of New Zealand."

Nations fight a war against a common enemy. They pool their armies, their arms, their supplies. Their sons die on the battlefield together. But when it comes to making the peace they go their separate ways, they are immovable, and they let no one trespass on their sovereignty. Unless this stops, all talk of international organization for peace is pure poppycock.

Britain is sovereign in India because she has the power to be so. If the Indians had the power to drive the British out they would be sovereign. Russia took the Baltic states and eastern Poland and included them under her sovereignty because she was stronger and brooked no outside interference. This is might without law.

In international politics, humanity is still in the Middle Ages stage when brigands ruled the highways and exacted tribute from the weak.

A world organization for peace is crippled when it is based on a map carved by strong-arm lawlessness and when it is dominated by the governments which perpetrated that lawlessness.

How, while fighting Fascism, which is power without principle or law, did the United Nations make a peace that embodies unprincipled and lawless power?

Where is America, where is the world, going?

Must there be another war, an atomic war?

14. *The Search for Security*

INTERNATIONAL politics is shaped by the relations between the strongest nation and the next to the strongest nation. Throughout the Napoleonic era, Europe revolved around the axis of Anglo-French hostility. In the first four decades of the twentieth century, except for the years between 1919 and 1935 when Germany was weak, Anglo-German rivalry provided the key to Europe's politics. Today, Russia is actually or potentially the strongest power and England the second strongest power in Europe. Anglo-Russian relations are consequently the pivot of European affairs.

For several centuries, Europe with its overseas empires possessed most of the power of the world. Europe's foreign affairs were accordingly synonymous with world politics.

Europe is no longer the chief powerhouse of the planet. Vast power centers have grown up in the United States and in the Soviet Union, a large part of which lies outside of Europe. Therefore, world politics now reflects the relations between the strongest world power, America, and the next to the strongest world power, Russia.

In Europe, Russian power faces British power. In the world, Russian power faces American power. This creates a community of interest between the United States and Great Britain but does not preclude occasional differences on important issues.

The Big Three nations won a war together. Despite social, political, and economic divergences, they helped save one another. Russia and America are far apart geographically; they are not commercial rivals. Why the friction and tension?

German power threatened England and, if England had succumbed, it would have threatened the United States. Later, German power attacked Russia. This united the Big Three.

German power is destroyed. Japanese power is ended. Italian power is gone. What could now unite the Big Three?

Could not fear of another war unite them? A major war could only be fought by the three big powers. If they united, war would be impossible.

This commonsense attitude collides with the essential character of nation states. It is in the nature of national power to vie with national power. They compete even when they collaborate. They competed throughout the second world war.

Peace depends on whether the nations can, by an effort of will, submerge their inherent competitiveness and thereby avoid destruction in the First Atomic War. The fate of humanity will be determined by the outcome of a race between the urge to suicide and the instinct of self-preservation.

How can the competitiveness of nations be curbed?

Some would eliminate competition by means of treaties and alliances among the Big Three or Big Five and, in addition, by an international body like the United Nations. Under such arrangements, nations agree when they wish to agree, and at other times they are free to disagree and to clash.

Since this is unsatisfactory, an increasing number of persons therefore maintain that nation-state competition—and war—can be eliminated only as nations give up their sovereignty and submit to a higher, international government which will compel agreement.

The states of the United States do not think of going to war with one another; they cannot go to war; the Federal government would stop them. If there were a Federal government of the world there would be no war.

The states of the United States give up some of their sovereignty to Washington, D. C., and receive a worthwhile return. They make some laws for themselves and accept some laws made outside of themselves with their participation. That is how a world government would function. That is the road to peace.

We will get world government. The only question is whether we will get it by voluntary action in advance of a war or whether mankind will first wage an atomic war out of which will emerge one victorious power—it could only be the United States or Russia—that will impose itself as the world government.

Man's choice is world government by will power or world government by war power.

The ancients had their city-states. In the age of ox-cart and the horse, the county was the unit of government. In the age of steam and electricity, the nation was an acceptable unit. In the age of airplane and atom, the world is the unit.

Nevertheless, the war years abounded in proposals to divide the world into old-fashioned orbits, spheres of influence, empires, and alliances all designed to perpetuate nationalism.

In 1943, an avalanche of alliance proposals descended on us. Governor Thomas E. Dewey of New York and Clare Boothe Luce urged an Anglo-American alliance. Earl Browder, then leader of the American Communists, advocated an Anglo-Russian-American alliance. Walter Lippmann and others prescribed an Anglo-Russian-American-Chinese alliance as the perfect instrument for the maintenance of peace after victory.

"These suggestions are harmful," I wrote in an article, "for alliances would not help the world or the United States to stay out of war." But many large-circulation magazines tend to follow the vogue of the moment; they hesitate to get ahead of the times. Today, alliances are recognized as symptoms of a crumbling peace. In 1943 and 1944, alliances were very much in style, and obviously therefore an attack on alliances and a plea for internationalism had to be kept from the broad public. My article was finally printed in the Spring, 1944, issue of the *Virginia Quarterly Review*.

I had no sooner studied the Dumbarton Oaks proposals for a United Nations charter than I exposed their inadequacy in a *Nation* article in September, 1944; I especially denounced the veto provision which enables any one of the five major powers to prevent the UN from acting against an aggressor even when it itself is the aggressor. Later, I published my objections to the Big Power veto in the San Francisco Charter, and suggested amendments. For this attitude I was criticized by Norman Cousins in an editorial in *The Saturday Review of Literature* and held up to contempt as a "perfectionist." Subsequently, the atomic bomb fell on the world, and Norman Cousins wrote a long statement in *The Saturday Review* on the defects of the San Francisco Charter. Thereupon, I sent him the following letter:

Dear Norman,
   Welcome to the "Perfectionists."
                              Cordially,
                                 Louis.

He replied:

Dear Louis,
   What are the dues?
                              Cordially,
                                 Norman.

I replied:

Dear Norman,
The dues to the "Perfectionists" are one "premature" idea per month.
Cordially,
Louis.

Thoughts that are three or six months "premature" are taboo to numerous American editors. They like to "keep abreast of events," which means that they lag behind events and their readers are therefore often caught unprepared. Especially during the war, almost the only places where one could tell the uncensored truth about world problems was on the lecture platform and in books. Elsewhere, the public was usually fed what John Foster Dulles called "a war diet of soothing syrup."

At a small lunch in Charleston, West Virginia, in 1944, I was asked my opinion about a New York columnist who writes on everything. I said: "He doesn't know much. He tickles the brain instead of feeding it."

"Oh, Mr. Fischer," the questioner rejoined, "don't say that. He makes me feel so good."

This was the purpose of much wartime writing and editing. People were making enormous sacrifices for victory and they preferred solace and the comfort of thinking that all was right with the world. Any somber color that corresponded to the facts was unwelcome. Millions of American stomachs accustomed to "soothing syrup" are still incapable of digesting more substantial and beneficial nourishment.

Re-reading wartime American "literature" on peace problems is a distressing experience. It teaches one that what "goes" in the public prints in any given period may have no relation to developments already shaping the course of world affairs. This applies in particular to the alliances in vogue in 1943 and 1944.

I based my rejection of alliances on history and on facts in the daily newspapers. "The anti-Axis 'Big Four,'" I asserted in my *Virginia Quarterly* article, "are now taking up positions from which to engage in post-war rivalries. That is the dark shape of the peace to come. It threatens to perpetuate the anarchy of the pre-1939 world. . . .

"Moreover, countries are fickle. In the first world war, Italy, ally of Kaiser Germany, betrayed Germany and switched to our side. Japan was also on our side. In this war, Italy and Japan have been our enemies.

"Russia and Japan fought a war in 1904–5. They were allies in war from 1914 to 1917. They fought a war between 1918 and 1922. They fought pitched battles in 1938 and 1939. Today they maintain friendly relations, though the war partners of each are at war with one another. . . .

"Great Britain and France bled together as brothers on a score of battlefields while fighting Germany between 1914 and 1918. Yet within a few years, British policy became more anti-French than anti-German. . . .

"Alliances have been weighed in the balance of power and found wanting. History shows that every balance-of-power has inspired a counterbalance-of-power and ultimately a clash. In 1918, France and Britain were victorious and Germany was in a state of collapse. But the rivalries of Europe plus the emergence of the airplane as a decisive weapon of war gave Nazi Germany her chance to fight. In like manner, some new technical device or chemical substance may again alter the balance of war-making power, and then fears or hopes or jealousies can split an invincible-looking alliance until it becomes so weak as to encourage a nation or group of nations to take the war-path.

"What is needed," I wrote, "is not an alliance to guard over the *status quo* but an international body to cure the causes of war."

The portents of post-war friction among the Big Three were written on the pages of newspapers for all who can read; but political illiterates fill the earth. The sound of war and the buzz of wishful "thought" drowned out the rumblings of coming troubles. Field Marshal Jan Christian Smuts, Prime Minister of South Africa, spoke up as early as November 25, 1943, in a statement in the House of Commons in London which he himself called "explosive." His remarks were off-the-record, but they were so important that they became the subject of much conversation, and distortion, and the entire address was accordingly published by the British government.

Smuts declared that after the war the world would be dominated by a trinity. In that trinity, however, Great Britain will be "poor" and "crippled here in Europe," whereas Russia is the "colossus of Europe," and America has "wealth and resources and potentialities of power beyond measure." This inequality troubled Smuts. "I should like to have that trinity a trinity of equals," he asserted; "I should like to see all three of them equal in power and influence in every respect. I should not like to see an unequal partnership."

Smuts' desire for equality within the trinity is, literally, a desire for balance of power. But how can a nation which is weaker and unequal achieve equality with the other two members of the trinity? Obviously, either at the expense of the other two members of the trinity —which is difficult—or at the expense of small states and colonies. This is exactly what Smuts advocated. In his speech in London, Smuts outlined two courses: first, Great Britain, he said, must bind the Empire more closely to herself; second, England must create "a great European state" comprising the small nations of western Europe.

Smuts has here answered those innocents who argue that elephants and squirrels cannot make the peace; big powers and small powers cannot sit together to draft the peace treaty; you have to leave it to the elephants. The difficulty is that not all elephants are equal. Smuts showed that one elephant, England, was afraid of being taken for a squirrel and therefore wanted to make sure that it would be as strong as the other two elephants. Harmony among elephants is just as elusive as harmony between elephants and squirrels. Certainly, elephantine attempts to dominate the squirrels—in spheres of influence—produce no love between the elephants and the squirrels and no harmony among the elephants.

Britain's spheres-of-influence policy was frankly enunciated by Foreign Secretary Anthony Eden in the House of Commons on September 28, 1944. "It will give us more authority with the other great powers," he said, "if we speak for the Commonwealth and for our near neighbors in western Europe. That seems to me the right concept of the structure we should try to build, and that is just the task on which we are now, in point of fact, engaged." Eden's motivation is revealing: "It will give us more authority with the other great powers . . ." This is a recognition of the rivalry within the trinity.

Rivalry flourished behind the word-facade of unity. But any attempt to penetrate back of the facade was condemned as "Red-baiting," "Tory-baiting," or plain "pessimism." It is pessimism, but it was true. It was creative pessimism. Problems are not solved by ignoring them. The suppression and distortion of facts are a common totalitarian practice which democracies adopt at their peril.

In every lecture I delivered after December, 1943, when I received the full text of Marshal Smuts' speech from the British information service in New York, I quoted him at length and pointed to the emerging Eastern bloc under Soviet influence and the plan of a Western bloc under British influence.

I oppose alliances and spheres of influence because they are neither moral nor practical. They subjugate weak nations. They cannot prevent war. They are part of the feverish, hopeless quest for security. But there is no national security. There is only security—security for all or for no one. This was perfectly clear before Hiroshima Day (August 6, 1945). It is completely undeniable now.

Russia does not need Poland nor the Balkans nor Port Arthur for security any more than the United States needs the Philippines or Okinawa or Saipan for security any more than England needs India or Singapore for security.

American possession of Okinawa might under some circumstances prevent certain types of attack by a resurgent, militaristic Japan if she ever is resurgent and militaristic. But ten years from now America may also be exposed to atomic attack from Argentina, Turkey, Spain, Russia, France, from anywhere. What security can the United States have against such assaults? The U. S. authorities might seize or lease bases near every nation that could possibly strike at American soil. They would soon be holding territory all over the world and arousing resentment and hostility all over the world without, however, increasing American security. For in the air-atomic age an attack might come suddenly from any nook of the planet. To be safe in the new atom-fission era the United States would have to control not only Pacific islands but all the nations of the earth. This would be tantamount to world domination by America for the sake of American security. World government by consent is preferable.

Armies, navies, air forces, and bases may still have their uses in conquering a foreign country after it attacks or in conquering a foreign country which has not attacked. But no military arm, however powerful, could prevent an attack by radio-directed robot planes hurtling from thousands of miles away with atomic charges in their warheads.

Professor Henry DeWolf Smyth, Chairman of the Department of Physics at Princeton, who wrote the official history of the making of the atomic bomb, said on March 13, 1946: "Scientists now estimate that one atomic bomb dropped on New York City will kill from three hundred thousand to one million persons within a few seconds."

Professor J. Robert Oppenheimer, who directed the work at Los Alamos, New Mexico, where the first atomic bomb was experimentally detonated, told a Senate committee that forty million Americans might be killed in the first atomic air raid.

Brigadier General Thomas F. Farrell, who assembled the first bomb used at Los Alamos as well as the two dropped on Japan and who therefore knows how destructive even those crude, small bombs were, stated on October 19, 1945: "Uncontrolled, the atomic bomb could be developed to a point where the entire population of the world could eventually be wiped out."

And fools talk of security.

There is no safety in territory when winged bombs and airplanes erase distance at supersonic speed. Where then is Russia's security? Where is America's security?

The second world war resulted from the desire of some nations to keep themselves out of war instead of keeping the world out of war. The goal of each appeasing nation prior to 1941 was to stay out and guard its own peace and security as long as possible. That paved the way to war. Hitler, Hirohito, and Mussolini were encouraged to believe that they could strike down their victims one by one. They almost succeeded. No one nation can, by taking measures, add to its individual security against atomic-air attack. It can only add to its power to retaliate after the attack. Nations that are strong militarily will enjoy a single advantage: in the process of being destroyed they will also destroy others. But no one can win an atomic war. Who won the San Francisco earthquake?

Far from making war less likely, the atomic bomb, despite its deadliness, will make war more likely. Atomic armaments will serve as the greatest encouragement to aggressors. Hitler thought he could win by striking quickly with his Panzers and planes; in the same way, a new aggressor, weaker than the country it hopes to defeat, will nevertheless plan on achieving success by accumulating a large supply of atomic projectiles and launching them unexpectedly in one crippling blow. If there is ever an atomic war it will start with a super-Pearl Harbor aimed not merely at sinking half a navy but at killing half a nation. An atomic aggressor will gamble on so maiming his victim in the first assault as to prevent effective retaliation. The initiative will be a tremendous advantage in such a conflict, and, given sufficiently destructive bombs in a few years, it could be decisive.

The atomic bombs which obliterated Japan's cities were "firecrackers compared to what will be developed in ten or twenty years," three University of Chicago atomic physicists said on November 6, 1945. Since the human imagination is limited anyway and further limited by survival optimism, we are probably underestimating rather than overestimating atomic bombs.

The atom bomb has introduced the age of total insecurity. Mankind's choice today is universal insecurity or universal peace.

What would remain, then, of the national security of the United States or of Russia in 1956 or 1960? The *cordon sanitaire* which Moscow is erecting in eastern and central Europe could not stop British or American robot plane attacks on the Soviet Union. Russia's expansion in Europe and Asia will merely make other nations nervous and suspicious and thus increase Russia's insecurity. Similarly, the extension of American or British domination would irk Russia and intensify the general tension.

If the big powers want security they had better keep hands off small nations and weak colonies. The relations between Russia and England and between Russia and America are determined less by their relations to one another than by their relations to the weak countries of the planet.

Hitler did not attack Great Britain in 1939. He attacked Poland. That started the second world war. The major non-aggressors tolerated some acts of Nazi-Fascist aggression and facilitated others. Finally, the moment came when England said: Thus far and no farther; cross this line and there will be war. Hitler crossed it into Poland. The result was the destruction of Germany.

The most serious menace to peace is expansion by the big powers until one of them reaches a line which the other considers its line of defense.

At the end of 1945, Russia had effective control of half of Europe and Manchuria and northern Iran. Yet on February 7, 1946, Lazar Kaganovitch, a member of the supreme Politbureau in Moscow, declared: "Our country continues to be within a capitalist encirclement. Therefore there is no place for complacency. We must not relax. . . ." Russia accordingly demanded Turkish territory and tried to dominate the Iranian government in Teheran. Having annexed new territories the Bolsheviks must make those new territories secure by annexing more territory, and then more territory to make that secure. Where does it end? And is it not inevitable that such self-inseminating aggrandizement alarm other nations who will take countermeasures?

In the modern age, the pursuit of national security leads to insecurity, and continued long enough, it leads to war.

The more weak states the big nations swallow the closer the big nations come to one another. In the end, their spheres will touch one another with no buffers between. What reason is there to suppose that the rivalry which spurs them to establish their spheres of influence will cease when they face one another across the narrow barrier that separates their completed and consolidated spheres? None.

The key to peace in the atomic age is Big Three respect for small countries and independence for colonies. This would stop Big Three competition by making unavailable the prizes and loot for which they now compete. Then we could outlaw the atomic bomb and have world government and peace. National sovereignty is important only as a means of suppressing somebody else's national sovereignty. But if no nation's sovereignty can be interfered with, no nation will need sovereignty. The end of national sovereignty means international government.

The State of New York cannot encroach on the sovereignty of Connecticut. That is why they do not object to membership in a union. The union government can, of course, encroach on the sovereignty of each state, and adjustments in this field proceed throughout decades. But no state any longer tries to secede from the union on account of these adjustments.

Sovereignty makes insecurity.

Secretary of State Byrnes said at the *New York Herald Tribune* Forum on October 31, 1945: "Far from opposing, we have sympathized with, for example, the effort of the Soviet Union to draw into closer and more friendly association with her central and eastern European neighbors. We are fully aware of her special security interests in those countries." This was the Secretary's recognition of Russia's sphere of influence in half of Europe. But it makes no sense. Against whom is Russia seeking security? Against America and England. So the American Secretary of State urges Russia to achieve security against America. Is he thereby admitting the existence of an American threat to Russia? Or a British threat? Britain would not fight Russia without American assistance. Or a German threat? Germany is no threat to Russia now and never will be if England and America want Russia to have security. Germany can only be restored by American and British help with a view to using her against Russia, and if Mr. Byrnes is so solicitous about Russian safety he will not restore Germany for that purpose.

Mr. Byrnes' words, therefore, carried no conviction, and his speech, in fact, contained other passages about the maintenance of democracy in eastern Europe which reflected the well-known desire of the United States and Great Britain to loosen Russia's hold on her sphere of influence. Diplomats' phrases often mean exactly the opposite of what they appear to mean. A diplomat carries water on both shoulders and often arrives at his destination with two empty buckets.

How can an East European country be free when it is required to have a government friendly to Russia? Suppose its citizens choose a government which Moscow considers unfriendly? Moscow presumably could veto the election and insist on another government. Suppose the country has a foreign minister whom Russia regards as unfriendly. He must, I assume, resign. Suppose the country enacts a tariff, or a law, which the Kremlin regards as unfriendly? It would have to be rescinded. What becomes of that country's independence? How can it be a democracy? Russia would be interfering in its affairs and dictating its life. Compulsory friendship is subjugation. The idea of imposed friendship is a fantastic modern invention to cloak imperialism. Persons who support this proposal are champions of the rights of big bullies.

Cordons sanitaires, spheres of influence, and empires, belong to the pre-atomic age. Security is a pre-atomic idea. Humanity, however, will pay billions of dollars and maybe millions of lives to pursue unattainable safety. It would be cheaper in money, and spare all the lives, if nations became states in a union.

I know the problems this raises. But the alternative is the first atomic war which may wipe out five hundred million human beings.

The central problem of world organization is the relationship between Russia and the rest of the world.

15. What Are Russia's Motives?

FOREIGN policy reflects domestic policy and domestic conditions. But for most persons the Soviet Union is an intellectually inaccessible area, "a riddle wrapped in mystery inside an enigma," as Churchill said in 1939. When it comes to interpreting Soviet foreign policy, therefore, the voice and pen commentators try to substitute "logic" for the facts they do not possess or do not want to face. "Russia," they say, "is a big country; she obviously does not want any more territory." They forget that Russia, big enough already, annexed Baltic, Finnish, Polish, and Balkan territory in 1939 and 1940; Czechoslovak, German, and Japanese territory in 1945; and demanded Turkish territory and Mediterranean bases in 1945. "Russia," they say, "is now concentrating on post-war reconstruction and is not interested in foreign expansion." They forget that foreign territories might be a lucrative source of materials and machines for Russian reconstruction.

Motive Number One of Soviet foreign policy is Russian nationalism, Ukrainian nationalism, and Slavism. The Soviet Union used to be the land of internationalism. Bolshevism taught that what counted was the individual's economic and social position, not the shape of his head nor the shade of his skin nor the place of his birth, none of which we choose in our pre-natal states. Soviet doctrine emphasized that an Ukrainian workingman, for instance, was closer to an Italian workingman or a Chinese workingman than to an Ukrainian capitalist. Such education was calculated to make the Ukrainian workingman an internationalist rather than an Ukrainian nationalist. I have much more in common with a Spanish anti-Fascist or an Indian social reformer than with an American pro-Fascist.

When Russia's domestic policy was internationalist her foreign policy was internationalist, and Litvinov pleaded for collective security.

Race supremacy or national superiority had no place in Soviet ideology—until 1935. Then a new trend, Russian nationalism, appeared. I traced its development in my book, *Men and Politics*, which

183

was published in 1941. Since then, the Soviet government, with characteristic pendulumism and energy, has fostered not only Russian nationalism but also Ukrainian nationalism as well as the concept of Slavism. This emphasis on blood ties conflicts with the fundamental tenets of Communism, Socialism, and Bolshevism, and with earlier Leninist practice in the Soviet Union. It is a reactionary step.

Stalin spoke a toast at a dinner in the Kremlin on May 24, 1945. "I drink first of all," he said, "to the health of the Russian people because it is the most outstanding nation of all the nations that constitute the Soviet Union. I raise a toast to the health of the Russian people because in this war it has earned general recognition as the leading power in the Soviet Union among all the nations of our country." Mr. W. H. Lawrence who was *The New York Times* correspondent in Moscow, wrote in the *Times* recently that this statement was "a gesture that disturbed the Jews."

Such a toast would have been impossible ten or even eight years earlier. It would have been considered shockingly anti-Bolshevik to exalt one nation as the "leading" nation in the Soviet Union. All nationalities were equal; none led and none followed. When one leads the others are subordinate.

"Russia" is a term of convenience. "Russia" is not Russia but the Soviet Union. Russians are only fifty-four per cent of the inhabitants of the Soviet Union. The remaining inhabitants belong to the Kalmucks, Buryats, Turkomans, Georgians, Armenians, Tartars, Ossetians, and scores of other nationalities—in fact, more than one hundred and twenty. Bolshevism boasted that it did not differentiate between them. Race did not elevate. No nationality has a position of special distinction.

Now the Russian nation has the leading position in the Soviet Union.

"In attacking the Soviet Union," Foreign Minister Molotov said on November 6, 1945, "Hitlerite Germany aimed not only at seizing our territory. Hitlerism had declared its aim of the extermination of the Russian people and the Slavs in general." If he had spoken under similar circumstances a decade earlier Molotov would have stated that the foreign enemy wished to crush the Bolshevik revolution and Socialism. In 1945, it was Hitler warring on Slavs and Russians.

This is the major transformation of the Bolshevik revolution. It changes the whole nature of the Soviet regime. There is natural progression from Russian nationalism to Slavism to imperialism.

In their former internationalism, the Bolsheviks were poles apart from the Nazis who put race above class, who, indeed, nursed the feeling of race so as to create a nationalist frenzy which would end the war of classes. Nationalist frenzy then provided the fuel for Hitler's engine of aggression. Hitler began by objecting to the Versailles amputations of German territory. Then he wanted Austrian and Czechoslovak territory which had not belonged to Germany but which, he claimed, was inhabited by Germans. From there he went on to conquer territory which was not inhabited by Germans.

Dynamic nationalism needs food, and the food of nationalism is territory.

What impelled Stalin to cultivate Slavism and Russian and Ukrainian nationalism? The Soviet regime had always fought Russian and Ukrainian nationalisms. Several bloody purges of Ukrainian nationalists, some of them Communists, to which the Soviet press alluded in the twenties and thirties, testify to the vigor and persistence of nationalist sentiment among the twenty-eight million Soviet Ukrainians. Economic difficulties and the Ukrainian famine of 1932-33 were laid at the door of the Moscovites and served to nourish the sentiment. Unable to crush Ukrainian nationalism, Stalin befriended it. He would lead the Ukrainian nation into a golden era. No longer would there be Ukrainians in Poland, Czechoslovakia, and Rumania. He would unite them all under the Soviet flag. This alone can explain Stalin's annexation of the Czechoslovak area of Carpatho-Russ or Carpatho-Ukraine inhabited, according to official Soviet sources, by seven hundred and twenty-five thousand persons of whom sixty-five per cent are Ukrainians. It had never belonged to Tsarist Russia. Czechoslovakia certainly never harbored any hostility or aggressive intentions against Soviet Russia. Quite the contrary. No nation could invade Russia across the Carpathian Mountains. Yet as early as 1943, Moscow raised the Carpatho-Russ question. When I talked with President Benes of Czechoslovakia on May 17, 1943, during his stay in the Blair House in Washington, D. C., he told me he thought he had succeeded in dissuading the Soviets from taking the small, backward region in the Carpathians. He underestimated Stalin. Russia annexed Carpatho-Ukraine on June 29, 1945.

To the Ukrainians, Stalin gave pieces of Poland, Czechoslovakia, and Rumania, and hoped thus to win their loyalty. To the Great Russians, he gave the Baltic states, a bit of Finland, and the vista of a mighty Russia. To the Azerbaijans in the Caucasus he would give the neighboring area of Azerbaijan in Iran. For the Armenians he would ask nearby Turkish provinces.

Russian expansion is not limited to regions in which Slavs predominate. But Soviet policy directs special attention to the Slav parts of Europe. When the Soviet Union was internationalist its slogan was "Workers of the World, Unite." Now it also seeks to unite the Slavs. During the second world war, several Slav congresses met in Moscow attended by delegates from many foreign countries. But no international proletarian congress or workers' congress or trade union congress took place in Moscow in all the years of the war. The Slav congresses stressed the bond between Russia and the Slav countries of eastern Europe and thus foreshadowed the formation of the Soviets' Eastern bloc which has disturbed Russia's relations with Great Britain, France, and the United States. But in the accomplishment of his purpose, Stalin never hesitates to irritate, and if need be destroy, ally or enemy.

The Soviet authorities were catering to nationalist tendencies that had survived the Revolution in some persons, reviving nationalist feelings that had lain dormant in others throughout the Revolution, and planting them in the minds and breasts of the new Soviet generation, now the bulk of the population of the Soviet Union, which had never known nationalism and which had been brought up in internationalism.

Nationalist passion diverts attention from the non-gratification of material needs.

During successive Five Year Plan periods, the Soviets built many new cities and vast industrial enterprises whose output helped defeat the Nazis. An industrial base for further progress has been established in the shape of a machine tool industry, a gigantic electric power network, new iron and steel works, an aluminum industry, the improvement of transportation, the discovery and exploitation of far-flung metal and mineral resources, and the training of many thousands of male and female technicians. Moreover, agriculture has been collectivized, and the collectives represent the first advance in the form of agrarian organization since the serfs of Europe became peasants.

But all these tremendous historic changes have not yet yielded material dividends to the Soviet individual. The standard of living of the masses continues to be low even by East European standards. The return to the Soviet citizen is not commensurate with his exertion.

The discrepancy between the value of his labor and his wages represents the cost of the new industries, the armaments, and the immense government office-holding class. Somebody has to pay. The people pay. The people suffer.

Yes, but the nation is benefiting, Soviet propaganda argued. It sought to cultivate pride in the nation. Pride in the Bolshevik revolution and the Soviet system were apparently not regarded by the Kremlin as sufficient incentive or as having sufficient emotional appeal to compensate for numerous daily privations. Assuming that revolutionary ardor had cooled, a new incentive was offered: nationalism. Once offered it had to be fed. This is the first impulse behind Soviet expansion.

With the war won, Moscow now faces the unprecedented task of restoring the country's economy and rebuilding its ruins. At its deepest penetration into Russia, the German Army held territory three times the area of Germany. This was the richest and most highly-developed part of the Soviet Union. What was not pulverized as million-headed German and Soviet armies moved to and fro in the course of the fighting, the Nazis destroyed deliberately. It is a heartbreaking job to rebuild that which was built so recently at such expense. Again the Soviet citizen is called upon to pay in reduced food, clothing, and shelter, and in increased, intensified work.

Outsiders have little appreciation of the strain under which Russia has lived since 1916. There have been few normal months, and for some, few normal minutes in those many years. Life for all but a select minority has been full of incessant pressure and uninterrupted sacrifice, full of short rations and long queues. Now, after that weary era, and after the blood-letting war, the Soviet peoples must take up the burden once more and put the country's economy back on its feet. Naturally, the Soviet government wishes to shorten the period of reconstruction and cut its price to the Soviet population. How? By dovetailing the economy of central and eastern Europe and of Manchuria with the economy of Russia so that their industrial, raw material, and human resources serve Russian needs. Hence Moscow's efforts to obtain control of Austrian and Rumanian oil, of Hungarian industries and agriculture, of Czechoslovak factories, of Yugoslav mines, and, in general, of the economic life of the one hundred and fifty million people who inhabit the Soviet sphere of influence in Europe. This is *Motive Number Two* of Soviet foreign policy.

Motive Number Three is opportunity. Nations act because they can oftener than because they must. The defeat of Germany and Italy and the weakness of France have created a vast power vacuum in Asia, notably in China. Now international politics, like nature, abhors a vacuum. So each of the Big Three either wishes to occupy as much of the vacuum as possible, or, at least, to prevent the other two from occupying the vacuum. This is the source of the friction among the Big Three. Admonitions will not eliminate it. A prize richer than any that has tempted nations for decades lies waiting in the arena of international affairs. Small wonder the competition is great.

The disappearance of the three vanquished great powers opens up unusual possibilities of expansion for the three victorious great powers. The exhaustion and helplessness of the weak states increases the suction towards aggrandizement and domination.

Originally, the Russians and their foreign champions, as well as a considerable number of Americans and Englishmen who believed in a balance-of-power peace, hoped that the spoils of the second world war would be distributed amicably among the Big Three with each holding an undisputed sphere of influence. This loot-sharing, they hoped, would then become the foundation of a post-war settlement which the Big Three would be interested in sustaining.

Events took a different turn. Stalin looked out into Europe and saw nobody who could stop him. So he gathered up an armful of small countries. Now Britain, France, and America feel that Russia has seized the lion's share of the European vacuum and filled it with her puppets. Similarly, Russia seems to feel that America has seized too much of the Asiatic vacuum. Nevertheless, America wonders about Russian designs in China and in the Pacific land and sea areas. It is difficult to maintain an equilibrium in a vacuum. Since balanced power is impossible each nation strives for maximum power.

The Big Three, to be sure, will continue their efforts to adjust and accommodate their rivalries. They do not want war. They will bargain and compromise. This is a precarious base for world peace.

England, the weakest of the Big Three, is trying to hold her own. She is under Russian attack. America and Russia are competing for positions in Asia.

Opportunity knocked at the Kremlin gate, the opportunity to extend Russia's power. The temptation was too great to resist.

Russia is acting no worse than other nations have in the past; no worse, and no better. Lenin, the internationalist, gave Poland more

territory in 1921 than the Poles had asked. He willingly recognized
the independence of Finland and the three Baltic states. He gave
Afghanistan some bits of land. He relinquished Russian rights and
properties in China. He returned to Iran oil and other concessions
extorted from her by the Tsars. He befriended Turkey. He had no
interest in promoting Pan-Slavism. He was making a revolution, not
building an empire. But Lenin is a shrinking mummy and a receding
memory in Russia.

To measure one must have a fixed standard of measurement. Linear,
area, weight, and temperature standards are fixed by scientists. Each
person fixes his own ethical, moral, and political standards. He does
so according to his religious or philosophical inclinations. His fixed
point of virtue may be God or a set of principles. But if his fixed
point of virtue is a man or a government his measurements, in other
words his judgments of events and ideas, will be distorted, for men
and governments always deviate from their underlying principles and
philosophies. No political instrument, no human being, is immutable
or infallible. Now when a Communist says, the Soviet government
is always right, or, Stalin is always right, and measures everything
and everybody accordingly, he cannot see or think straight, he cannot
measure; no country, or government, or leader but makes serious
blunders. The proof is writ large in each morning's newspaper.

When Argentina was admitted into the United Nations in 1945,
the Soviet government and its supporters abroad denounced the move;
there must be no relations with Fascist regimes, they argued. But
when the Soviet government recognized the Peron dictatorship in
June, 1946, and entered into diplomatic and trade relations with it
no Communists denounced the Kremlin. They lack a fixed standard
of measurement. This is opportunism. This means that what the
Soviet government does is good even though it be a pact with Hitler,
or a pact with Peron, or militarism, or terror. With such a standard
of measurement, judgments are likely to be worthless.

16. *What Has Happened to the Revolution?*

A REVOLUTION rejects yesterday and, unmindful of the costs today, rushes on towards tomorrow. Revolution is a new beginning. Repudiation of the past is the essence of revolution. The Bolshevik revolution was an attack on the black heritage of Tsarism. That was its justification, its inspiration, its function.

The Bolshevik revolution has been a struggle between Karl Marx and Peter the Great, between the Communist future and Russia's past. The new met resistance from the old. At times, Marx prevailed. Now Peter is the victor and Marx his prisoner. On the crucial question, Peter and Marx agreed: both stood for dictatorship. In recent years both have been growing together into one Janus-like creature with two unlike faces. Some look and see Marx. Others look and see Peter. This confuses.

Soviet Russia is neither pure Marx nor pure Peter. The combination of both has produced something completely different and unprecedented yet clearly defined.

Unfortunately, world public opinion has usually lagged years, on occasions as many as ten years, behind events in the Soviet Union. About 1929, foreign correspondents in Moscow, among them myself, began reporting that Russia was building industries and becoming strong. That was pooh-poohed as propaganda. Propaganda is sometimes a truth told too early before you are ready for it. When the correspondents wrote, ten years too early, that Russia was growing strong it was called propaganda. When former Ambassador Joseph E. Davies, in his *Mission to Moscow*, wrote it ten years too late he became a best seller.

Now, too, most persons lag eight or ten years behind tremendous events inside the Soviet Union which alter the very nature of the regime.

Governments, leaders, and parties often change. Napoleon started his career as a revolutionary military hero. He became an emperor. Mussolini was a Socialist, a left-wing Socialist. Later, he turned nationalist and, by so doing, took a long step towards becoming a Fascist. Pilots of the ships of state frequently toss their principles overboard to make room for other freight. They may continue, however, to pay lip service to the principles.

The truth about a country is not in its official apologies. Karl Marx once noted that whereas a housewife puts no trust in the shopkeeper's praise and examines the chicken herself, historians and journalists accept a government at its word. Marx's advice to the modern journalist would have been to take government chickens with a grain of salt.

Russia's leaders and most of her territory are inaccessible to outsiders. Yet the impression of mystery is due not to ignorance but to unpredictability. It is not that we do not know what Russia is but rather that we do not know what Russia will do. This is the source of the enigma. Every dictatorship is enigmatic because no public opinion checks the dictator and no free press exposes him.

Russia is not a mystery. All the necessary facts for an honest interpretation can be found in Soviet publications which are illuminating as much in what they do not say as in what they say and the way they say it. The Soviet government can also be judged by its numerous deeds.

The basic facts on Soviet Russia are available and easy to grasp.

In Russia the Government owns all capital. No Soviet citizen can buy or sell or own land. The Government owns all the land. No Soviet farmer owns a horse or an ox or a plow or a truck or a tractor. Those are means of production, or capital, and therefore belong to the State. The Soviet government owns and operates all the factories of the countries, all railroads, all oilfields, mines, public utilities, newspapers, printing presses, wholesale and retail stores, all beauty parlors, barber shops, cafés and restaurants, all airplanes, all means of transportation: in a word, everything that earns wealth.

An individual may own a watch, a suit of clothes or several suits of clothes, a library, a home, a summer bungalow, or even an automobile, although Russia is so poor that probably no more than two hundred persons own private cars. But let a person who owns an automobile use it as a taxi; that is, use it to earn money, and it becomes capital, and it is illegal for an individual to own capital. A citizen may hold wealth or personal property for his or his family's enjoyment. But he must not use it as capital.

The Soviet state is the only capitalist in Russia. Russia is today more collectivized than ever and, superficial fly-by-weekend foreign

observers notwithstanding, no trend away from Government ownership of capital is discernible.

Critics of private capitalism correctly ascribe many ills to it. But
it does not follow that new ills may not be born where private capitalism has died.

One source of Soviet ills is its work incentives. The Bolsheviks try
to invoke intangible incentives like service to the nation and sacrifice
for a cause, and these undoubtedly play a role. They try to stimulate
civilian effort by medals, publicity, and awards. But the chief incentives in Russia are three, and they are all practical: Pay, Privilege,
and Power.

The Soviet government always permitted varied compensation for
varied quantities and qualities of labor. Greater ability, more training,
and special talents are rewarded. In recent years, however, the discrepancy between highest-paid and lowest-paid has become very wide.
A completely pro-Soviet report of a C.I.O. delegation's trip to Russia in 1946, published in the American press on March 18, 1946, told
of "workers' monthly pay ranging from three hundred to three thousand rubles" in a typical factory.

More and more, the emphasis is on the money incentive. With insignificant exceptions, industrial workers and farmers are paid on a
piecework basis. Plant managers and mine directors are granted bo-
nuses for every per cent of increase in the output of their State-
owned enterprises. During the war, a Soviet paratrooper got an extra
month's pay for every combat jump he made. The family of a high
army officer receives a tremendous government allowance in case of
his death. Thus, on February 27, 1942, the family of Major General
Levashev, and on March 12, 1942, the family of Vice-Commissar
Kartushev—these are illustrations taken at random from the Soviet
daily newspapers—were each granted a lump sum of twenty thousand rubles (which compares with the five hundred rubles an average
factory workingman earns per month) and, in addition, a monthly
pension of five hundred rubles for the wife and three hundred rubles
for each child of the deceased. "Stalin Premiums" of from one hundred thousand to two hundred thousand rubles were granted to a
number of scientists, according to the *Pravda* of April 11, 1942, and
premiums of from fifty thousand to one hundred thousand rubles
were given to a number of artists and authors, according to the *Pravda*
of the next day.

Sharp inequalities of monetary reward are sharpened still further by special emoluments such as good homes and apartments, summer villas, access to better hospitals, free travel on trains, and the use of limousines and cars which the State gives to privileged persons. In a country where comforts and luxuries are rare, great importance attaches to the possession of an apartment or the availability of an automobile or the ability to get treatment in a good, uncrowded dispensary.

The contrasts between rich and poor in Soviet Russia are more glaring than in capitalist countries. Stalin earns a modest salary and probably never touches money. Yet anything material a man may desire is accessible to him. Stalin lives at least as well as Roosevelt did. A Soviet workingman, on the other hand, has far fewer worldly benefits than an American worker.

The inequalities in Soviet living standards are not an accident. They are designed. In the middle of the nineteen-twenties, Soviet writers began ridiculing equality as a bourgeois prejudice and a democratic folly. Since then inequality of status and living conditions has been consciously cultivated by the Government. The purpose is not merely to increase industrial and agricultural output; it is to form an élite, a privileged class. That class now exists in Soviet Russia.

Stalin deliberately created Russia's new aristocracy because of the country's low living standard and the difficulties encountered in raising it. When everybody can be satisfied, a regime need not take special pains to satisfy a thin upper crust. But where the benefits available are insufficient to give contentment to the mass of people, a dictatorship must have a loyal élite. In Russia this élite consists of the military officers, the key men of the secret police, the industrial managers, a relatively small number of skilled, highly-paid workers, engineers, and scientists, a top layer of state and party officials, and the artists and writers who supply the circuses and propaganda. Altogether this aristocracy might number four million persons plus their dependents. They live well even by European standards and infinitely better than the average Soviet citizen.

A nation's standard of living is a complicated combination of many factors. Food, clothing, and shelter constitute the primary factor. A steady job is another. Soviet citizens who are physically fit, mentally normal, and politically conformist have the assurance that they will not be unemployed. This is a great boon.

I used to think that Soviet full employment, which began about 1931, was the result of Socialism and the non-profit system. I am not so sure today. Republican Germany had full employment between 1922 and 1924. Nazi Germany had full employment in the thirties. The United States, England, and Nazi Germany had full employment throughout most of the second world war.

The full employment periods of Soviet Russia, Germany, and the belligerent nations all had these things in common: increased production for export or for the expansion of heavy industry or for war, and scarcity of consumers' goods. The result of both these circumstances was inflation.

When the mark was stabilized in 1924, full employment ended; Germany began having some unemployed. Between 1924 and 1928, the ruble was stable; Russia had unemployment; the Government maintained unemployment exchanges. In 1928, the first Five Year Plan inaugurated an era of buoyant industrial building. The value of the ruble dropped, and by 1931, inflation was in full swing. Food and other consumers' commodities grew very scarce. Full employment appeared.

I am not suggesting that full employment is attainable only in times of scarcity and inflation. But so far, full employment has everywhere coincided with these phenomena.

Full employment comes inevitably when there is a market for everything that is made. Full employment is the Siamese twin of full distribution. Theoretically, there would always be full distribution under Socialism. But to date, distribution has been full—in Republican Germany, in Soviet Russia after 1931, and in countries at war—only when there was not enough to go around. The question is: Would distribution be full in a condition of plenty? Soviet performance gives no answer. For at no time since the Revolution has the Soviet Union been blessed with plenty of food, clothing, and shelter. The Bolshevik revolution has been conducted in a condition of unrelieved scarcity of material things.

How is it then that the Russians fought so well during the war? Does that not prove that they were contented?

The British fought valiantly and resisted beautifully under Winston Churchill. Then they threw him out of office. The Soviet citizen no more fought for Stalin than the British did for Churchill or the Americans for Roosevelt. War is not a political election. The Indian Army did not cover itself with glory in battle because it loved British imperialism.

Intricate philosophical, emotional, and practical stimuli commingle to condition men to fight and die in war. Next to the International Brigade, in which I was the first American to enlist, the best troops in the Spanish civil war were Franco's Moors. Soviet tank drivers helping the Loyalists used to tell me that when they came back to their garages they would find encrusted in the caterpillar treads of their machines the flesh of Moroccan soldiers who had refused to yield ground even in the face of overwhelming, unaccustomed mechanical power. Yet the Moors did not know what the war was about. This is an extreme case of divorce between valor and motive. The point is merely that bravery in combat does not necessarily warrant an assumption of the soldier's approval of the war or of those who sent him to war.

An army is usually as good as its officers, and the Red Army field officers were good. Moreover, the Russians have always fought well against an invader. They fought against Napoleon and stopped him. The Russian Army then, as now, was peasant in its bulk, and the Russian peasants of the second decade of the nineteenth century were serfs. Yet they let themselves be killed in the legions of a despotic Tsar. The Russians also fought well in the first world war; although hopelessly under-equipped (often a man had to wait until his comrade fell before he could acquire a rifle), they held the Kaiser's eastern front army far from Moscow, Petrograd, the Volga, and the Caucasus.

The Red soldiers knew what foreign occupation had meant in 1918, 1919, and 1920. Many of them also saw the effects of brutal Nazi atrocities on persons, towns, and villages. The Soviet people did not wish to be ruled by a foreign conqueror. Many individuals, officers in particular, had benefited from the Revolution. Enormously-expanded educational facilities, enormously-expanded employment facilities, a nationwide health service, pensions, annual vacations, and other social amenities strengthened the loyalty of Soviet citizens towards the State. The absence of racial discrimination and the cultural freedom granted to national minorities likewise reinforced the individual's attachment to his government. Despite oppression, strain, and sacrifice, the vast majority supported their country in war.

Some Red Army soldiers deserted and preferred to stay abroad for the rest of their lives. Some Red Army commanders deserted and fought for the Nazis. There is no instance, as far as I know, of an American general, or British or German or French, or in fact any European general or high army officer who was prepared to fight against his own country. But Major General Andrei A. Vlassov, who distinguished himself in the defense of Moscow in 1941, received the Order of the Red Banner on January 2, 1942, was mentioned as an outstanding Soviet general by the Moscow *Pravda* of January 6, 1942, and was captured by or deserted to the Nazis in 1942, did become a Hitler puppet and raised an army among Russian prisoners of war in Germany to fight the Red Army. Vlassov, and a few like him, however, were the black exceptions; on the whole, the Red Army battled loyally and well for the homeland. Most civilians were likewise loyal.

A dictatorship uses its secret police and other weapons of terror to enforce obedience. Then it uses its monopoly of propaganda and education to win acquiescence. It often succeeds. The mind of the little individual is helpless against the state even in a democracy where he has access to justice and can listen to the other side of the argument. In a dictatorship only a few stalwart souls can resist the official assaults on their independence of thought, indeed on their very capacity to think. Democratic observers mislead themselves by drawing big conclusions from the support which the citizens of a dictatorship give to their masters. The dictators themselves are never misled by this support. If they were they would scrap their GPUs and Gestapos, their concentration camps, their one-party elections, their censorship of everything that is said, sung, painted, photographed, and written within the country, their purges, their shrill, incessant official agitation which is aimed to capture or at least to paralyze the minds of the population, their Chinese Wall of secrecy separating people from leaders, and the elaborate precautions for their own personal safety.

It is often said that the Soviet government is suspicious of foreigners. This is a partial truth. The real truth is that the Soviet government is suspicious of its own citizens, even of its highest officials. Why else would it prohibit foreign newspapers from entering the country? In the twenties, German and British capitalist newspapers were sold in stores in Moscow and in many places throughout the country. I regularly bought the Berlin *Tageblatt*, a bourgeois daily, at railway stations in the Ukraine and the Caucasus. But this was stopped years ago. In the few special libraries which carry foreign papers, only chosen persons can have access to them. No one can buy or borrow a book by Trotzky, or Bukharin, or anyone who has ever taken issue with Stalin. Why are so few Soviet writers, scientists, and industrialists permitted to travel abroad except on official missions, and then with peculiar precautions? Why does the Soviet government prohibit emigration or, for that matter, immigration of refugees? Why are only very few, select persons allowed to meet foreigners in Russia? Is the Kremlin afraid foreigners will corrupt its subjects? Has it so little trust in them? Why wouldn't it expect its subjects to convert the foreigners?

On June 6, 1945, Commander King-Hall, member of the British Parliament, asked his Government how many broadcasts a week are sent in the English language from Russia to Britain; and how many in the Russian language from Britain to Russia. Mr. Lloyd replied for the British Ministry of Information and stated in the House of Commons that: "There are fifty-three broadcasts a week in English from the Soviet Union. There are no BBC broadcasts in Russian to the Soviet Union."

The BBC broadcasts in all languages to all countries. It did not send to Russia because the Kremlin did not want Soviet citizens to hear the foreign radio. With the exception of high military and political leaders, individuals in Russia are not permitted to have strong sets that can receive non-Soviet stations, and Soviet stations refuse to rebroadcast the BBC. The British people can hear fifty-three Soviet broadcasts. Stalin does not trust his people to listen to any British broadcasts.

The Russian dictatorship soft-pedals as much as possible all evidence that foreign governments are friendly to the Soviet Union. This is one reason why it never stressed American and British wartime Lend-Lease. For if foreign governments are friendly why not allow more contact with foreign countries? Why the strain, tension, and suspicion in Russia?

A dictatorship is a nervous form of government. It is nervous even though modern governments are too powerful to be overthrown by people's revolution in normal peacetime. A dictator has no fear of the people unless there is a rival set of leaders who wish to dethrone him. That is why Stalin's chief obsession has been the problem of leadership. He rose to monolithic supremacy by getting rid of rivals, and he has continued through the years to purge possible or potential rivals who might displace or obstruct him. At the same time, he has sought to perfect devices for winning the adherence and devotion of his subordinates.

In a country like Russia, where life has been very hard for decades and is likely to remain so for years, a satisfied aristocracy of the managers, the military, the secret police, and servile intellectuals bound to the Government by favors received and promises of further benefits is a great comfort and asset to the never-confident supreme ruler.

Nothing makes one so insensitive to popular hardships as a safe distance from them. Privileges and luxuries enjoyed by the Soviet upper caste serve the double purpose of separating it from the masses and attaching it to the social system.

High living standards conduce to democracy; low living standards have, throughout the ages, conduced to oligarchy, aristocracy, and dictatorship. Latin America, Asia, and Europe are full of examples today. Russia is an example.

How the new Russian aristocracy was born can be seen through the emergence of the military caste. Every army must have officers and the Red Army always had its officers. The chasm between officers and men in the Red Army was narrow, narrower probably than in any armed force in the world—until 1935. Then a far-reaching change began.

A Red Army officer's rank used to be indicated by his function; he was battalion commander or regimental commander, and so forth. But in September, 1935, Red Army officers were given titles: lieutenant, captain, major, and colonel but, significantly, not general. This seems innocent enough. The day this innovation was announced I had a long argument about it with Sergei Tretiakov, Soviet author of *Roar China, Chinese Testament*, and other revolutionary books and a frequent contributor to Soviet publications. Tretiakov defended the change though he could not explain it. The official announcement was bald; no reason was given. Obedient Soviet citizen however (even though he was later shot in the purge), Tretiakov automatically accepted what he did not understand. The best justification he could offer for officers' titles was that all foreign armies had them.

"But this was true from 1918 to date," I replied as we walked up and down on the broad pavement of the Hotel Metropole in Moscow. "Why now? Why suddenly imitate capitalist countries?"

Officers' titles, I submitted, and especially the title of colonel, had a special connotation in Russia. They connoted Tsarism, the old monarchist Russia, and the power of the pre-Revolutionary officer to be the ordinary soldier's lord and master.

"That will never happen in the Red Army," Tretiakov stated emphatically.

He did not realize how far a small beginning can lead.

On May 7, 1940, the Soviet authorities introduced the titles of general and admiral. Stalin is a master of dosage; he executes policy in installments. In 1935, titles up to the rank of colonel. Then he allowed time for public distaste to dissipate. In 1940, titles for generals and admirals.

On July 21, 1940, a decree provided for brilliant field uniforms for generals, with gold buttons, silver and gold braid, and shoulderstraps.

On August 10, 1940, Navy Commissar Nikolai Kuznetsov, whom I had known well in 1936 in Spain as a simple, democratic, informal fellow, decreed that sailors must no longer address themselves to higher officers of the fleet but instead speak to their immediate low-rank superiors. The traditional comradely approach and equality of the Red Fleet disappeared. On duty and off parade a new stiffness separated officers from men.

Democratic, voluntary discipline was now gone.

On October 12, 1940, Defense Commissar Timoshenko issued a "New Disciplinary Statute of the Red Army." Interestingly enough, this statute was not published by the *Pravda* or *Izvestia*, Moscow's leading dailies. But four days later, in the *Pravda*, Lieutenant General Kurdiumov commented on it. "The statute," he declared, "demands unquestioned obedience from subordinates to their commanders. The commander's order is law to his subordinates. . . . No difficulties, hardships, or misfortunes can serve as a reason for not carrying out a commander's order. The commander must not hesitate to adopt the sternest measures, and even the use of armed weapons, in dealing with malicious violations of discipline. . . . Moreover, in seeking to overcome such violations through the use of extreme measures, the commander carries no responsibility for the results." Red Army commanders may enforce discipline by corporal punishment and even by the shooting of soldiers.

"The commander has no right to be liberal," General Kurdiumov continues in the *Pravda* of October 16, 1940, "or to benevolently ignore violations of army rules. . . . A false democracy in relation to subordinates has to be uprooted in the most energetic fashion."

This "false democracy" had always been regarded as the true democracy; the Bolsheviks and their foreign admirers, including myself, had for years boasted of it as one of the outstanding achievements of their revolution. So it was. But the Revolution succumbed to the Tsarist past.

On January 7, 1943, embroidered gold and silver epaulets were made part of Soviet officers' uniforms. The *Red Star*, Red Army daily, said in that connection: "We, the legitimate heirs of Russian military glory, take from the arsenal of our fathers and grandfathers everything best which enhanced martial spirit and strengthened discipline."

Stalin ridiculed "Russia's military glory" in a speech in February, 1931. "The history of old Russia," he recalled, "shows that our country was uninterruptedly beaten for its backwardness. We were beaten by the Mongol Khans; we were beaten by the Turkish beys; we were beaten by the Swedish feudatories; we were beaten by the Polish and Lithuanian landlords; we were beaten by the English and French capitalists; we were beaten by the Japanese barons."

Twelve years later, however, Tsarist Russia's defeats and helplessness became "glory." History is a handmaiden in the hands of the dictator.

On June 6, 1943, Cyrus L. Sulzberger reported from Moscow to *The New York Times* that: "Officers now are not supposed to carry parcels or baggage except in the vicinity of railroad stations. Ordinarily they are expected at most to carry a small, neat package in the left hand." In Kipling's India too, officers refrained from demeaning themselves by bearing bundles.

"Junior officers," Sulzberger continues, "are not permitted to sit down in public conveyances while senior officers are standing and must receive permission from their superiors to sit. . . . Finally, a regulation standard orderly system has been introduced for all officers from the rank of platoon commander upward. It was officially explained that Peter the Great had first recognized the importance of orderlies whose main duty was caring for officers' personal affairs, food, and clothing. . . ."

Then this policy bears a first crop of ugly fruit: on July 24, 1943, a Government decree states that heroism on the field of battle will not be a primary quality justifying promotion from the ranks. Promotions will henceforth be given to graduates of special military schools.

In 1943, the Soviet government established Suvorov schools, named after Count Suvorov, a Tsarist field marshal who lived from 1729 to 1800, where boys would begin their life careers as army leaders. They "have been organized," wrote Ralph Parker in *The New York Times* of November 7, 1943, "on the model of the Tsarist cadet schools. . . . They will be attended principally by children of officers killed during the war. . . ." Children of officers killed, not children of soldiers killed. This is how a caste is perpetuated. On November 7, 1945, for the first time in Soviet history, these Suvorov boys, average age twelve, paraded with the army through the Red Square.

Maurice Hindus, having visited a Suvorov school near the town of Kalinin, reported to the *Herald Tribune* of May 16, 1943: "Dancing, ballroom as well as folk dancing, is as much a part of their school life as sports." Ralph Parker's article states, similarly, that *Red Fleet*, the Soviet Navy daily, recently "advised future naval officers to take dancing lessons. . . . They would be the future representatives of the best stratum of the Soviet intelligentsia and therefore should know how to conduct themselves in society." In what "society"?

"Soviet officers, as *Red Star* wrote recently," Parker proceeds, "find a good deal in the old traditions of Russian officers that is making clear to them the origin and development of Russian military strength. Under Peter . . . the Russians are now being reminded, grew up a comprehension of the officer's 'true honor.' Peter's influence in contemporary Russia is probably greater than that of any Russian of the past except Lenin." So Communist Russia is getting its comprehension of "true honor" from Peter the Great who reigned from 1694 to 1775 and killed hundreds of thousands of serfs in the construction of his cities and palaces.

On September 16, 1945, Brooks Atkinson telegraphed *The New York Times* from Moscow that "Red Army clubs would be for the exclusive use of officers. All members of the army previously had been entitled to use club privileges." These Red Army clubs, many of them beautifully built and furnished, exist in numerous Soviet cities and were formerly accessible to officers and men. But Red Army men, clad in shoddy uniforms, poorly shod, poorly fed, are the inferior "proletariat." They no longer belong.

Says *Red Star:* "The Party and the Government are doing their best to continue improving the standard of living of generals and other officers."

In describing the hall where the Moscow partners in the American-Soviet chess match were taking part, *Izvestia* of June 2, 1945, wrote: "Among the spectators were many officers." Privates were not mentioned. Ten years earlier this would have been inconceivable in a

Soviet publication. It would have been considered anti-Bolshevik. It is.

Major General John R. Deane, who was in Russia for two years during the war as Chief of the United States Military Mission, told a New York audience early in November, 1945, shortly after his return from Moscow: "The line of demarcation between officers and enlisted men, indeed the distinction between all ranks [in the Red Army], is probably more marked than in any other army in the world."

Soviet engineers, Party chiefs, high Government officials, and factory directors likewise live far above the economic level of the ordinary citizen. In *Life*, John Hersey described a visit to Nikolai Puzirev, the manager of the Putilov steel plant in Leningrad. Puzirev lived in a four-room apartment, and that in a crowded city where many families of four were crowded into one room. He had a limousine for his personal use, a personal chauffeur, a private Douglas DC-3 transport plane, a yacht, a country house, two servants, ample supplies of food and alcohol, and the best reserved seats in the theater and opera.

I lived for a week in the Putilov factory in 1932, and went back to it for regular summer visits until 1936 so as to study changes that took place there. I knew its directors, engineers, Party officials, and workers. The luxury life of Mr. Puzirev in 1944, during the terrible Russo-Nazi war, had no equal even in peacetime.

Capitalism fosters lavish living by the side of poverty. In Russia, the crass and growing inequality between upper and lower strata is all the more incongruous because those above are supposed to be the comrades and servants of those below. Equality may be impossible or undesirable. But when a regime born of Bolshevism encourages ever-sharper distinctions between rich and poor the Revolution would seem to be losing its essence.

However, the broad gap between top and bottom economic levels in the Soviet Union is as nothing compared with the gulf that divides the politically-omnipotent dictator from the politically-powerless individual. In no country in the world is government authority so concentrated as in Bolshevik Russia.

A despotism may be benevolent. It may be for and of the people. Only a democracy is by the people. And Socialism has no meaning if it does not mean the active participation of the people in the direction of the state. Lenin said: "Every cook must be able to run the government." Every cook, every miner, every cab driver, every peasant did experience the elation of the Bolshevik revolution because he felt it was his Government and he would help manage it. The soviets, local committees or councils with administrative functions, were conceived as the instruments of mass membership in the State. It was the soviets, more than anything else, more than the elimination of landlords, which created the widespread popular enthusiasm for the Revolution. By instinct the people knew that their greatest gain was not what the Government gave them but rather their control of the Government so it could not withdraw its gifts.

In 1923, I visited a small town near Moscow and spent some time at the home of an old local judge. I asked his wife, who was not sympathetic to the Bolsheviks, what difference the Revolution had made.

"The people talk more," she said contemptuously.

This was the chief achievement. The people talked about their problems because they thought their views counted.

The Revolution's original élan was of course a composite emotion. Destruction of the past accounted for it. Hope made it stronger. Chiefly, I think, it came from a sensation of the individual's integration with the community so that he lived through the community and was lifted above himself.

Within a few years of 1917, however, the soviets fell under the complete domination of the Communists in them, and these acted on instructions from provincial capitals and from Moscow. Today, the soviets are the Kremlin's rubber stamps and have ceased to be a reality in the lives of the people. Elections to the soviets are humdrum performances in which the Communist slate is never opposed.

Before long, the fate of the soviets overtook the Communist party.

In the early years of the Revolution, there was wide freedom for Communists in the Communist party. At the time of the Brest-Litovsk negotiations between Kaiser Germany and the new Bolshevik regime in the beginning of 1918, the Soviet government was very weak. Dangers threatened from within and the Reichswehr was poised to invade Russia. Nevertheless, in that life-and-death crisis, a group of Communist leaders, among them Radek, Kollontai, and Osinsky, began publishing a daily paper in Moscow called *The Communist* for the purpose of defeating Lenin's policy of peace with imperial Germany.

In subsequent years, Lenin engaged in fierce polemics with Bukharin and others at Communist conferences. But after flaying Bukharin ideologically he could put his arm around him affectionately and call him *Bukhashka*. Lenin and Trotzky had quarreled often before the Revolution on matters of principle and theory. They worked in intimate collaboration after the Revolution.

Lenin argued with the Communist opposition and defeated it in debate. He had the personal qualities which enabled him to work with men who did not share all his views. Stalin could not worst Trotzky or Zinoviev in controversy. But he could arrest them.

From 1917 to 1927, the chief task of the GPU was to liquidate enemies of the Revolution. In 1927, the GPU, under Stalin's orders, began something quite unprecedented in Bolshevik history: it began to concentrate on liquidating Communists. When, in January, 1928, GPU agents carried Trotzky down the stairs from his Moscow apartment—he refused to walk—nobody had accused him of anything more than doctrinal and political differences with the Stalin-bossed Communist party. It was an unheard-of procedure for the organ of Government compulsion to intervene in a Party dispute. Since then it has been common practice. It makes discussions within the Communist party superfluous. The revolver of the GPU agent is the decisive ideological argument in Stalin's Russia.

Communist oppositionists like Trotzky, Kamenev, and Zinoviev were once permitted publicly to express their views. They could publish books and articles attacking Soviet leaders and policies. On the eve of Communist party congresses and conferences, the Moscow *Pravda*, organ of the Party, printed a special "Discussion Page" where the dissidents could have their say. Now, no Party member dares proclaim himself an oppositionist and ask for the right to criticize the politics of the Government.

The Communist party has several million members and could have more, for it is the Soviet bandwagon, but membership is restricted. The rank and file, however, are passive cogs in a big machine. Nor does Stalin like to report to the Party or consult it. From 1918 to 1925, despite war and turmoil, the Party convened in national congress once a year. Then Stalin became dictator. The Fifteenth Party Congress met in 1927 after a two-year interval. The Sixteenth met in 1930; the Seventeenth in 1934; the Eighteenth in 1939.

The purges destroyed the spirit and prestige of the Soviet Communist party. Since the highest Communists could be "Fascists" and "agents of foreign powers," people thought, how could you tell whether the unpurged were not equally contaminated? As a matter of fact, several of those who conducted the purge one year were on trial a year later and sentenced to death.

The Communist party has become an automatic weapon of the dictator.

The Soviet trade unions also used to have free discussions. Annual and much-publicized conventions were held by the Miners' Federation, the Textile Workers, and so forth, and by the all-inclusive Trade Union Congress. The last convention of the Soviet trade unions took place in 1932.

Every year, in January, the trade union members of a factory or office met with the management and publicly deliberated on a collective bargaining agreement which ran till the next January when it was renegotiated. In 1931, hiring of labor became the exclusive right of management. In January, 1933, few collective bargaining agreements were renewed; in January, 1934, still fewer; in January, 1935, very few; in January, 1936, none. Since the beginning of 1936, there has been no collective bargaining in Soviet Russia. The bureaucracy of the trade unions exists to carry out Government tasks. The bureaucracy can also play a role in foreign trade-union movements.

The suppression of freedom for Communists, for trade unions, and for friends of the Soviet regime has nothing to do with foreign dangers. When the Soviet government was a puny fledgling in 1918 there was more freedom than when the Soviet Union became a mighty power.

It has become habitual for ignorant apologists to say that in the purges and trials of 1935 to 1938, Stalin killed the "Fifth Column." This, it is said, explains why Russia had no saboteurs during the war. Well, having exterminated the enemies of the regime at home why are civil liberties still denied the population? Why does not the ubiquitous, omnipotent secret police close up shop?

No, the crushing of the independence of the soviets, the Communist party, the trade unions, and of all mass organizations, as well as of all individuals, is the result of dictatorship. (A similar process took place in Fascist Italy and Nazi Germany.)

The Soviet political system used to be a broad-based pyramid. The broadest, lowest level of the pyramid was the soviets; above it were the trade unions; then, narrower still, the Party; then the Party leadership; and then the point of the pyramid, the leader. Gradually, Stalin turned this pyramid over and stood it on its point. All the political authority which formerly resided in the broader layers flowed out of them and down into the point, to the dictator. When the soviets, the unions, the Party, and the Party leadership lost their authority they lost their vitality, their zest, and their faith. They became frightened robots.

It is significant that Stalin's Russia has developed no great orators. The Communist party had renowned orators. But they are dead, and the country has no need of new ones. There are no political debates in the country. All political arguments are pre-cooked by the hacks in the Party kitchen and handed out to speakers. No one deviates because deviation may be dangerous.

Soviet citizens who are intellectually and politically equipped to do so bear many "social loads." They liquidate illiteracy, organize Asiatic women to drop the veil, get youngsters to join the Pioneers (Boy and Girl Scouts), speak on various topics at factory and other meetings, lead excursions to historic and archaeological sites, etcetera. But Communists have admitted to me in the quiet privacy of my Moscow apartment that the excitement of Soviet political activity is nil because everyone realizes that he is merely reacting to distant button-pushing, and mouthing slogans or rehashing *Pravda* editorials without expressing his own opinions or his own personality.

The Soviet people, to be sure, have other thrills, the thrill of the Stalingrad victory, of the heroic civilian resistance of Leningrad, of the triumph over Hitler. These are, so to speak, biological sensations, a thrill to soil, rivers, and cities, rather than to social goals and political purposes. This is the clue to what has happened to the Bolshevik revolution. It became national because it was not permitted to remain political; politics was not for the mass. It began to appeal more to primitive emotions and less to the ideal of a new society. Tsars and Tsarist generals crowded reformers, revolutionists, and sociologists off the stage. Peter the Great eclipsed Karl Marx. Stalin found it easier to evoke Petrian intestinal responses to the Russian fatherland than Marxian mental responses to a new international social system.

Unable to give the Soviet people enough food, clothing, and shelter, unwilling to give them any voice in government, Stalin gave them nationalism and, to those who wanted it, religion. To a small minority whose devotion he wished to purchase he gave the opiate of material luxuries and social privileges.

The economic forms of Soviet state ownership remain. Compulsion remains. It is compulsion from above, from outside the individual.

The common man is a means to an end. The end is the powerful state.

The body is the body of Socialism. But the soul is gone because freedom and internationalism are gone.

Socialism without democracy is state dictatorship. Socialism in one nation without internationalism is National Socialism. That is not Hitlerism. Every country develops its own brand of National Socialism.

Russia is caught in the contradictions of Socialism in one country. Stalin has tried to escape from this dilemma. He tried to introduce democracy by drafting the 1936 Constitution. But the attempt failed because he was not ready to curb the dictatorship and scrap the secret police. Every year since Stalin became dictator there has been less democracy. Stalin probably thinks he is introducing internationalism by extending the borders of the Soviet Union and absorbing more countries into the Soviet zone of influence. But the subjugation of small countries, insistence on the veto in the UN, and the policy of Big Three domination is not internationalism, it is super-nationalism, it is imperialism.

Internationalism and democracy cannot thrive under a nationalistic dictatorship. Socialism, therefore, cannot thrive under Stalin. Russia's Socialism is a name and a shell. Life has gone from it. Life was crushed out of it by the weight of its victims who languish in concentration camps or were shot in the terror.

17. *Laskiology*

HAROLD J. LASKI, British Labor leader and publicist, has got
stuck in the molasses of Marxist materialism. He is therefore
incapable of understanding Russia. To Laski, the elimination of the
private businessman and of the private market suffices to usher in the
Socialist millennium. This is a tragic error. There can be no Socialism
without personal freedom. Economic freedom from capitalist exploitation still leaves room for economic serfdom and political subjugation by the state.

Laski thinks government ownership of the tools of production and
state economic planning give Russia immunity to evil. But state ownership combined with terror is not virtuous.

Laski forgets man. In applauding the regimentation of Soviet machines he overlooks the regimentation of Soviet man.

Laski is the most intelligent of those intellectual rejectors of capitalism who are ready to embrace anything which destroys capitalism.
"It is significant," said Laski at *The Nation* dinner in New York on
December 3, 1945, "that only in the new world of Russia has the businessman ceased to count." That is correct but that is not all. Many
other men have ceased to count, because one man, the dictator,
counts for everything.

Laski, emaciated and wasp-tongued, calls himself "an inoffensive
scholar." He wields a deft pen which is the envy of writers who only
reveal their inadequacies when they try to imitate him. He formu-
lates programs with felicity and demolishes opponents with facility.
I have heard him deliver a finely-chiseled intellectual lecture to the
Fabian Society and I have also heard him delight an election-campaign
Labor audience with salty diatribe. But there are at least two Harold
J. Laskis and they are no friends. The perceiving Laski sees what is;
the believing Laski, in scintillating debate, persuades the perceiving
Laski that what he sees isn't so.

In 1943, Laski published a powerful book entitled *Reflections on
the Revolution of Our Time*. It includes many pages devoted to the
horrors of the Soviet dictatorship and the Stalin terror. In 1944, Laski

wrote another book entitled *Faith, Reason and Civilization,* in which he proclaimed "the Russian idea" as the world's saving faith destined to replace Christianity.

I reviewed *Faith, Reason and Civilization* in the August, 1944, issue of *Common Sense.* The review was called: "Laski Should Know Better." The editors mailed a copy to Laski in England and asked him to rebut. He sent back a letter saying: "In this case, my friendship for Louis Fischer would make me humbly accept the application of his whip without repining."

I prize my friendship with Harold Laski and feel sure it will not be affected by sincere criticism of his politics.

"Professor Laski has made the most basic error of his career as a social thinker," I wrote in my review of the book. "He urges the world to adopt Russia's new values when in fact Russia has been dropping those values and adopting more and more of the old values of the bourgeois world."

"The victory of Christianity over paganism," Laski stated in his new book, "meant a revitalization of the human mind. . . . I do not think anyone can examine with care our contemporary situation without being constantly reminded that we again require some faith that will revitalize the human mind." I agree. But because a new faith is so important, one must choose carefully. Laski himself cautions that the new faith should not be nationalistic. "The new passion for nationalism," he declares, "may easily take us down the road which leads to wholesale disaster." This is one of my chief objections to the new "Russian idea," which harnesses political dictatorship, economic statism, and Russian nationalism in a prancing troika.

Laski compares the theory of Communism with the realities of the Christian world; the theory of Communism wins. He should also have compared the theory of Communism with the realities of the Russian world.

"Laski," I wrote, "sends us to Soviet Russia for the new faith, but Stalin, who is somewhat better informed on Russia than our good British Laborite friend, made up his mind years ago that he would fetch himself a new faith out of Russia's middle ages and out of the Tsarist past. So the new heroes of the Soviet Union are Alexander Nevsky, a medieval Russian knight and priest; Suvorov, a marauding general of the eighteenth century; Kutuzov, a Tsarist prince, whose military victory over Napoleon kept the French revolution out of

Russia and blocked Russia's progress for a century; and other equally ancient, moth-eaten figures whom Lenin and the old Bolsheviks reviled and rejected."

Russia has a revolutionary past. But Stalin is going back to her reactionary past for inspiration. The highest military decoration in the Soviet Union is the Suvorov Medal. The second highest is the Kutuzov Medal. The third is the Bodgan Khmelnitzki Medal decreed on October 10, 1943. Khmelnitzki was an Ukrainian leader, trained in a Jesuit school in Galicia, who lived at the end of the seventeenth century, fought the Poles, killed Jews, and—this is emphasized by Soviet journals—fostered the union of the then independent Ukraine with Tsarist Moscovy.

"The literature coming out of Russia is Pan-Slav and nationalistic," I continued in my analysis of Laski's book. "That is Stalin's new faith. Moreover, Laski, with all his wishful thinking, has too penetrating an eye not to see that the revival of the church in Russia— under the aegis of the Soviet state—is more than a move to win support among Greek Orthodox residents of the Balkans or a sop to religious groups inside Soviet Russia. It points to a deep crisis of faith within Russia; the Revolutionary flame, under Stalin's care, became cold and ceased to warm the Soviet heart."

Actually, the world's crisis of faith finds Russia in the midst of a worse crisis of faith. Laski can propose Russia as the new "myth" or the new "idea" in place of Christianity because most of those who read him do not know Russia, and it is always easier to clothe the unknown in religious attributes. But the Russians know Russia; for them, therefore, Stalin conjures up a synthetic "faith" out of the musty past.

"Laski," I complained in my *Common Sense* review, "never once mentions this Stalin quest for a new faith to replace 'the Russian idea.'"

"Laski," I wrote, "recognizes only one possible argument against his thesis: that is its cost. He admits that the Stalin government has 'committed fantastic cruelties.' But he believes that the executions, concentration camps, purges, and trials were necessary for the victory of the Revolution. This is a cardinal blunder, and I must say that it makes me doubt Laski's grasp of Soviet history. My quarrel is not so much with the early terror to establish the Revolution. My quarrel is with the Stalin terror to entrench the present Russian counterrevolution. The reason for the purges should be clear by now: Stalin liquidated the Revolutionists in order then to liquidate the Revolution."

Laski wrote during the war and under the psychological impact of the great Stalingrad victory. "The spectacle of Russian heroism in the two years of the struggle against Hitlerism has convinced the common man, all over the world, that there is a magic in the Revolution of 1917 somehow adaptable to his own concerns." But elsewhere in *Faith, Reason and Civilization* Laski indicts himself when he says: "We stand in grave peril of men who mistake courage for ideas."

Courage at Stalingrad? Yes, mountains of it. As much as at Dunkerque, as much as at El Alamein, at Tarawa, at Iwo Jima, in Warsaw, and in the streets of London and Coventry. The Nazis and Japanese also fought fanatically. I do not therefore accept the Nazi way of life or the Japanese faith. Modern man is lost if he takes his ideas from the battlefield. And which battlefield? Britain and America won the war too.

The victory at Stalingrad was achieved because, at a point where Germany's lines of supply were longest and Russia's manpower reserves closest, Stalin was ready to pay the price in lives required to hold the city. It was perhaps the decisive battle of the second world war. Stalin's determination and the Red Army's bravery deserve all the tributes which poets and historians will shower upon them. But Stalingrad was a power phenomenon. It no more attests to the superiority of the "Russian idea" than the magnificent performance of British and American fliers, submarine crews, paratroopers, general staffs, scientists, and industries are proof of the superiority of an Anglo-Saxon idea. An "idea" is more likely to be found in a still, small voice than in the thunder of cannon and the explosion of bombs.

The abundant and moving heroism of the war, at Stalingrad and in many places, merely shows that the human animal is a better master of the art of dying than of the art of living. There is something wrong with a civilization whose finest manifestation is the manner in which men die.

Laski's trouble is that his thoughts on various subjects seem to be confined in separate compartments which are insulated against seepage. Thus, speaking of Christian history, Laski writes: "I think the outcome of persecution is to breed cruelty and arrogance in the persecutor, and hypocrisy and servility in the persecuted." This is an exact description of the state of affairs in Russia, but Laski does not recognize it.

Laski's entire misinterpretation of Russian life is born of the illusion that the Soviet revolution has created a new type of state and a new type of person.

"The Russian state," I wrote in August, 1944, in my discussion of Laski's book, "is playing power politics like many other states in history and in the present. I see nothing in Soviet foreign policy which is the distinctive child of 'the Russian idea.' Its criterion is nationalistic advantage. The Kremlin has collaborated on friendly terms with Fascists, personal dictatorships, monarchists, reactionaries, radicals, and democrats." Russia's state-owned economy has not been a bar to imperialism.

Similarly, Russia's state-owned economy has not bred a new Socialist individual or a new Socialist morality. Laski believes that the Soviets offer "a sense of individual fulfillment now wholly unattainable within the confines of any alternative social system." The Russian revolution, he adds, has insisted on the common man's "inherent dignity as a person." In Bolshevik Russia, he asserts, "more men and women have had more opportunity of self-fulfillment than anywhere else in the world."

How, I ask Laski, can there be dignity with fear? How can there be self-fulfillment without liberty? There is enormous professional self-fulfillment in Russia. People from the so-called "lower classes," members of the once-persecuted national minorities, and women have received from the Bolshevik revolution new and rich opportunities. The expanding economy of Russia has opened endless possibilities of employment and educational advancement. Ultimately, too, the Russian standard of living will be raised above its present low level.

I can understand Soviet citizens and foreigners who are carried away by these circumstances, because for many years I was. The statistics of rising Soviet production and the progress of Soviet industrial construction inspired my enthusiasm. Added schooling facilities and the increased circulation of books and newspapers moved me to praise. The Soviet policies towards national minorities, women, children, colonial countries, imperialism, collective security, and towards Fascism when that black movement emerged, made me a stalwart champion of the Soviet Union. I have a long record as a friend of the Soviet regime.

Why did I change my attitude towards the Soviet Union?

I changed because Russia changed. There were no personal, private, or professional reasons for my dissent. I was reacting against new policies and new conditions in Stalin's Russia. I was reacting against nationalism, the inhuman purges, the mounting inequality, the new aristocracy, the growing cynicism (the Soviet-Nazi pact was only one of its products), and the personal dictatorship with all its concomitant evils.

My opposition to the present Soviet government is a response to its nationalistic, imperialistic, undemocratic policies. Especially do I decry the new Russian nationalism. Moscow's internationalism was, for me, its greatest attraction. In the fourteen years I lived in the Soviet Union, I was never interested in the country as a collection of earth, rivers, stones, and trees. I was interested in Russia as the place where tremendous changes were taking place which might benefit that nation and other nations. Most of all, I was interested in the development of Soviet internationalism, for I regard nationalism as a supreme evil, the great curse of mankind, and a chief cause of wars. Moscow's adoption of nationalism is one of the great personal tragedies of my life. I had invested much hope in the Soviet Union because of its internationalism, because of its anti-imperialism, because of its espousal of ultimate democratic ends.

Shall I, when I disapprove, remain silent? Intolerance of criticism is the thin edge of totalitarianism. Criticism is democracy. Democrats who urge a moratorium on criticism of the Soviet government are serving the cause of dictatorship. In an age when governments everywhere make so many mistakes and bring so many human woes, the call for a moratorium on criticism of any government is harmful. Would those who suggest it cease their attacks on governments other than the Soviet? For some, criticism of Bevin, Truman, de Gaulle, the Pope, Chiang Kai-shek is perfectly legitimate. Criticism of Stalin is "Red-baiting." In Russia there is no criticism of Stalin. The foreign totalitarians who like that would outlaw criticism of Stalin outside of Russia too. The best way to get rid of criticism is not to suppress it but to remove or improve the circumstances which justify it.

One reason for my resignation as contributing editor of *The Nation* was its practice of not saying anything about Russia when it could not say something favorable. The effect was silence about many developments in the world's most challenging country.

The suppression of facts does not make for true friendship among nations. Friendship purchased with lies is a brittle affair and will crack at the first stress.

I do not expect perfection of any government. One's relation to a social system or a government is determined by the ratio between good and bad. If the good, both existing and potential, outweighs the bad, one favors it. If the bad far outweighs the good and bids fair to poison the good, one rejects it.

A major difficulty in picturing Soviet conditions to people who live in democracies is that they are often incapable of realizing how bad a dictatorship can be. Certain reactionary Americans, for instance, charge that Franklin D. Roosevelt was a dictator and that the New Deal was totalitarian. To anyone who has lived in a dictatorship this is not merely completely ludicrous; it means that the accusers simply do not understand what dictatorship is. Similarly, it has been said that Chiang Kai-shek is a dictator. I myself have criticized him for his retrogressive politics. But some time ago a group of Chinese professors in the town of Kunming drafted a letter which they sent to Chiang Kai-shek and to the Chinese Communist leader, Mao Tse-tung. They also mailed it to friends abroad and one of them had it printed in the *New York Herald Tribune* of December 18, 1945. The letter stated that "it is imperative to terminate the one-party dictatorship." Moreover, they wrote: "Concentration of power in the hands of a single person should be terminated. . . ." Anybody acquainted with conditions in Russia knows that such a thing would be inconceivable there. No professors, no persons, unless they wished to commit suicide, would put such words on a piece of paper or think of sending them to Stalin or dare to mail them abroad.

I always hated the secret police terror in Soviet Russia but, first, I hoped it would abate, and second, I measured it against social and economic achievements. After a while I began to see that the terror became increasingly ruthless year by year; after devouring its enemies the Revolution commenced to devour its creators and offspring. I also began to see that many of the benefits of Bolshevism lost their real value through the absence of personal freedom.

For instance, the Soviets grant freedom to national minorities. Technically, the republics of the national minorities, the Georgian, the Ukrainian, and the other constituent republics of the Soviet Union federation, have a right to secede if they wish. In fact, they would not be permitted to do so. Technically, they have political and economic autonomy; actually, their Communists, who dominate them, take their orders from Moscow. Since 1941, in fact, Moscow has suppressed several national republics and deprived their peoples of autonomy. This was done without official announcement (it only became known when the list of electoral districts appeared). It was done in violation of the Soviet Constitution. But in cultural matters, Moscow lets the minorities develop their national tastes and desires, except that lately there has been more emphasis on the teaching of Russian history and the Russian language, except, too, that in recent years, according to Soviet publications, Moscow has tried to repress the growing nationalism of some minorities, notably of the Tatars and of other non-Slavs.

Racial discrimination against minorities is uncivilized and indecent. Yet cultural freedom for ethnic groups coexists in Russia with complete lack of freedom for individuals. The Armenian race in the Soviet Union has freedom. But no Soviet Armenian has personal freedom. Nor has an Uzbek, Ukrainian, or Tadjik. In that they are all equal.

The Uzbek is not persecuted by the Ukrainian or the Russian. But he can be arrested by the secret police without explanation and exiled without trial. He cannot vote for an anti-Communist, as an American can vote for an anti-capitalist. He cannot criticize the politics of the Government or its leaders without incurring serious personal consequences. He conforms and obeys; even when he disagrees he will know the wisdom of proclaiming his agreement.

The Soviet regime is civilized in relation to all races and uncivilized in relation to all persons.

The Soviet government has a very modern attitude towards science. It fosters scientific research with huge subventions and many material facilities. Scientists belong to the Soviet aristocracy. But though science is free, the scientist is not. He cannot correspond freely with foreign scientists. That must be supervised by the GPU. Few Russian scientists go to international congresses; they cannot travel abroad when they need to. The Soviet physicist, biologist, mathematician, philosopher, and historian must be careful not to arrive at a theoretical conclusion which seems to conflict with the current interpretation of Marxism and of materialism, for he knows that many of his colleagues have been denounced and punished as counter-revolutionaries because they made the mistake of reaching non-conformist views. Many Soviet scientists have been victims of the purge.

Julian Huxley, Professor Laski's friend, and a prominent British scientist, visited Russia in 1945, and wrote in *Nature:* "In some branches of Russian science, a certain spirit of scientific nationalism is to be observed." Those who demur are dismissed.

Professor Peter Kapitsa is one of the world's great physicists.

In 1922, when there was still a little emigration out of Russia, Kapitsa left Russia and went to Cambridge University in England. In 1926, Lord Rutherford, the famous British scientist, especially equipped a laboratory at Cambridge where Kapitsa could work on his ideas about magnetic fields and kindred subjects. In 1935, Kapitsa went on a visit to Russia. The Soviet government kept him there against his will and despite the protests of the British government, of Lord Rutherford, and of others. Thereupon the Soviet embassy in London issued a statement saying that in view of the extraordinary development of science in the Soviet Union and the insufficient supply of scientists, Russia must utilize those who had worked abroad. It added that Professor Kapitsa was comfortably situated and well remunerated. This is undoubtedly true. But Kapitsa, who may be able to free the atom, is not free.

In recent months, astute Soviet apologists in America and England have tried to persuade the public that a subtle difference exists between the Western and Soviet concepts of democracy, and that the Soviet citizen has freedom, though it is a different kind of freedom. Not many Soviet citizens would swallow this nonsense. There are two kinds of Soviet citizens: one knows that he is not free and is irked by it; the other knows and does not care because his need and taste for freedom have atrophied.

Those who were sixteen years of age or older in 1927 remember the open discussions within the Communist party. Many workers remember that they had collective bargaining and have it no longer. Everybody in an apartment house knows when the GPU comes to an apartment at three in the morning and takes away one or more members of the family. When Arbat Street is cleared at a certain hour of the day pedestrians know that Stalin's car is about to pass and they wonder why it would hurt if they stood by and watched. When GPU men visited all apartments along the route which Stalin would take in following his wife's bier people realized they were not trusted.

If Soviet citizens thought they were free they would not whisper so much. They would not twist their necks so much to see whether they were being overheard. They would not break off contact with an old friend because his relative had been arrested. Soviet citizens adapt themselves to the police state and after a while it is all so automatic they sometimes do not feel that they are doing it.

Soviet newspapers report strikes in democratic countries; Soviet workingmen know they cannot strike, though they would sometimes want to. The proof is that when the Stakhanov speed-up movement began in 1935 and brought about a rise in the amount of work required from a miner or factory hand, some Stakhanovites were killed or beaten up; the Soviet press reported these incidents and also reported the punishments.

Soviet citizens know that their votes in a one-party election do not count. Those who are naive—our maid, for instance—asked what sense there was in her casting a ballot showing only one candidate. Most people in Russia no longer ask questions; they do as they are expected.

The inhabitants of the Soviet Union are not stupid even though they are powerless. They know they live under a dictatorship.

One of the most revealing phenomena in Soviet life is the public attitude towards arrests by the secret police. When a person is arrested, the general reaction is not that he is guilty but that he was unlucky. Most Soviet citizens are close enough to persons who have fallen within the GPU net to know how often arrests are part of wholesale purges and have nothing to do with individual misdemeanors; arrests may result from denunciations to gratify personal grudges, or from ancient "sins" like lifelong friendship with a person accused of an anti-Government act.

Alexander Afinogenov was a very successful and able young Soviet playwright whose plays were performed by the Moscow Art Theater and other excellent theaters. Like many other artists and writers, he frequented the home of Genrich Yagoda, chief of the GPU, who fancied himself as a patron of the arts. In fact, the Afinogenovs were favorites of Yagoda and received a big apartment in a fine new Moscow apartment house inhabited by GPU officials. Then Yagoda was arrested, tried, and sentenced to death for having been a traitor during the years in which he was arresting, trying, and shooting other Soviet leaders for being traitors. When Yagoda was arrested, Afinogenov lost his apartment and was expelled from the Communist party. Thereupon, all the little critics fell upon him and said his plays were never any good; the theaters stopped performing them. At literary meetings he was attacked for "counter-revolutionary inclinations" and "anti-Bolshevik views." All this seemed to be the usual prelude to arrest, but suddenly Afinogenov was rehabilitated, readmitted to the party, and praised again by the little critics who had barked at him. Most people assumed that his restoration was due to the personal intervention of Stalin. In the twenties, Afinogenov had written a play on the hypocrisy of Soviet life which he called "The Lie." One day he received a summons to Stalin's office. The manuscript had been sent to Stalin to read. Stalin told Afinogenov the play was good but should not be put on the stage. He urged Afinogenov to withdraw it, which Afinogenov of course did.

After Afinogenov's political rehabilitation, he called for my wife Markoosha and me to drive us out in his private Ford car to his country bungalow. I sat with him in front, and at one point in our conversation, I said: "Shura, you know that all the terrible accusations leveled against you were untrue. Won't that mean that when you read similar accusations against others you will know that they are very likely untrue?"

He turned his face to me and smiled. He agreed.

(Afinogenov was killed by a German bomb dropped on Moscow during the war.)

What did Laski say? Persecution breeds "hypocrisy and servility in the persecuted." It also breeds cynicism in the persecuted and in those who hear of the persecutions. The Soviet citizen does not connect punishment with guilt. He connects it with some political design of the persecutors. The effect of the Bolshevik revolution had been to increase fear of the law but not respect of the law. There is no respect for the law because there is really no law in the Soviet Union; the dictatorship is a law unto itself; it makes and unmakes and modifies laws with a cynical disregard of earlier enactments which shows its own disrespect for the law. Fear of the law in Russia is fear of those who are the law. Law exists only when the Government obeys it and is therefore entitled to expect compliance by citizens.

Article 121 of the 1936 "Stalin Constitution" says: "Citizens of the Soviet Union have the right to education. This right is ensured by universal, compulsory elementary education; by free-of-charge education, including higher education; by a system of Government stipends for the overwhelming majority of the students in universities. . . ."

Fine. But on October 2, 1940, the Soviet government, by a decree of the Council of People's Commissars, the Soviet Cabinet, abolished free-of-charge education in the upper grades of high schools, in colleges, universities, and higher technical schools. At the same time the stipends and scholarships were discontinued.

The Constitution was not amended. The people were not consulted. The Government simply ignored and overrode the Constitution. No one uttered a word in protest. Who would have dared? Who would have printed it, the Government press?

This unconstitutional act of the Soviet government made it harder for worker and peasant children to study in high schools and colleges and left more vacancies for the sons and daughters of the rich. Stalin was preparing a new generation of the élite.

On the very day of the annulment of Article 121 of the Constitution, the Soviet government ordered the establishment of factory and railroad technical schools of high school grade to receive some six hundred thousand pupils who, because of the new tuition decree, could no longer afford to attend high school and college.

Thus the sons and daughters of the élite were started on their careers as future engineers, professors, industrialists, scientists, and so forth, while the sons and daughters of workers and peasants were started on their careers as mechanics, skilled artisans, tractor drivers, and railwaymen.

In February, 1944, after this arbitrary shelving of the Constitution had given the young aristocrats the inside track in the universities and made the young non-aristocrats see their future in terms of second-rank jobs in industry and agriculture, the dictatorship suddenly and again without explanation restored Article 121, abolished paid tuition in colleges, and renewed the scholarships.

Here one sees how the Government observes the Supreme Law, how the dictatorship regards education, and how the leaders treat the people. The leaders are cynical. The people learn to wear an armor of cynicism and indifference: why worry if you cannot possibly influence the course of events?

At a reception in Mexico City, Constantine Oumansky, the Soviet ambassador, old friend of my Moscow days who was killed in a sad airplane accident, dilated on the expansion of Soviet educational facilities.

"Yes," said a lady. "May I ask Your Excellency of what use this wonderful education is if there is no freedom of speech in your country?"

"Madame," replied Oumansky, according to an article by Emily Barret Blanchard, an ear-witness, in *The Saturday Evening Post* of December 23, 1944, "I consider that a reactionary question, and I refuse to answer it."

Nowadays, anybody you don't like is a "reactionary," in fact he is usually a "Fascist." But the diplomat's evasion notwithstanding, the lady's question is *the* question. Literacy is tremendously important. But thought—and art—are the product of liberty more than of literacy. Despite the provision on the paper of the 1936 Constitution, Soviet citizens enjoy no freedom of speech, or press, or assembly— except what freedom the Government wants them to have and for the purposes the Government wants them to have it.

On December 6, 1936, the new Soviet Constitution was solemnly signed in the Kremlin by thirty Soviet leaders, among them Stalin, Molotov, Voroshilov, and Litvinov. By 1939, fifteen of the thirty had been purged without trial. Most of the fifteen were shot. The fifteen included Marshal Bluecher, Commander-in-Chief of the Far Eastern Red Army; Kossior, a member of the supreme Politbureau; Rudzutak, deputy member of the Politbureau; Postyshev, the Communist party leader of the Ukraine; Yezhov, head of the GPU, who succeeded Yagoda; Lyubchenko, Prime Minister of the Ukraine; and Eiche, the Communist party chief in western Siberia. That is how Stalin treated Russia's founding fathers. There was never any announcement that they were purged or why. They simply disappeared and have not reappeared.

The prolonged existence of a harsh, all-pervading dictatorship discourages critical faculties, for they are dangerous; it discourages political courage, for it is a death warrant; it discourages thinking, for only a handful of men at the peak of the pyramid need it. All the others repeat, echo, and mimic. Russian education is geared to doing, not to thinking.

It was anticipated by the fathers of Bolshevism that under Socialism the state would wither away. Instead, Socialism in Russia has withered away, and interest in politics has withered away, and concern for justice, ethics, and thought has withered away.

This is the Russia where Laski asks us to find our new faith.

Harold J. Laski and those who agree with him on Russia must face this problem: a considerable percentage of the new Soviet generation, which includes, say, all those thirty years of age or younger, are completely materialistic. Since their parents lived near pigsties and were illiterate, while they can become teachers, army officers, etcetera, and be certain of an education for their children, the Soviet regime is considered a good regime. And liberty? "Liberty?" they reply. "What is liberty? Have you got liberty in capitalist countries? Next year we will have another tractor for the collective and more leather for shoes." I have had many such conversations in Soviet Russia.

"Morality," says a character in a 1931 Soviet novel called *Unknown Artist*, by V. Kaverin, "morality? I have no time to think of the word. I am busy. I am building Socialism. But if I had to choose between morality and a pair of trousers, I would choose the trousers." Very early, the artist sensed the emerging Soviet trend. Much later than Kaverin I understood that dictatorship kills idealism.

The effect of Soviet life is to center attention on physical goods. Those goods are scarce and were always scarce for most Russians. Their acquisition, and the prospect of more comfortable living with greater possibilities of professional advancement, loom as the central goal for all human endeavor. If a dictatorship promises to achieve this purpose, the dictatorship is beyond reproach, even though its methods are immoral, undemocratic, and destructive of cultural and ethical values.

This is the dominant spirit in Russia today.

It may be argued that a marked improvement in the Russian living standard will bring a change. But that improvement is years distant. Meantime the suppression of civil liberties, mass killings, huge concentration camps, monotonous totalitarian propaganda, and other unscrupulous dictatorial measures—all in the name of more groceries, more schools, more books, more babies, and more guns—have been built up into a great philosophy which even the liberals and sociologists of the West cannot resist. Meanwhile, too, the Soviet people themselves are being convinced by the dictatorship that, first, they have all the freedoms, second, these freedoms are unimportant compared with the material things to come, and third, the capitalist countries have no freedom either. Just as the capacity to use liberty is learned in the exercise of liberty, so the prolonged disuse of liberty tends to atrophy the desire to enjoy it. Except for a few months in 1917, Russia never had civil liberties, and most Soviet citizens therefore do not know how pleasant they are.

Many Soviet citizens lack the mental equipment with which to understand freedom. Thus, in Pearl S. Buck's *Talks about Russia with Masha Scott*, Mrs. Scott, a former Soviet factory worker and now married to John Scott, American author and son of Scott Nearing, tells Pearl Buck: "I would like to say that I do not agree that your way is so good to teach people. For example, we would not find in our country [in Russia] two completely different points of view in our press, that is, one man says this is true and another says it is not true. How can the people know which is the truth?"

Masha Scott and her generation, the new Soviet generation, have learned to depend on somebody to tell the people which is the truth. The Soviet government tells them.

My older son George was a captain in the American Army at twenty-one. For a year during the war he was stationed at the United States Shuttle Air Base in Poltava, Soviet Ukraine. He was raised in Russia while I worked there as a foreign correspondent, and speaks an excellent Russian. In the autumn of 1944, the American boys who operated the base cast their ballots in the Presidential election. Before doing so there was naturally much discussion among them on the relative merits of the candidates. The Soviet military who were at the base with the Americans noticed this unusual political activity and asked what it was all about.

"Every four years," George explained, "we elect a President. This year the Democratic candidate is Roosevelt, who is now in office, and the Republican candidate is Dewey, and each one of us will vote either for Roosevelt or for Dewey."

"I don't understand," a Red Army lieutenant said. "You mean that Roosevelt is a Democrat and he has been President for several years, and there are still Republicans in the American Army?"

Stalin would have got rid of them.

Has Laski seen a close-up photograph of the new Soviet man's intellectual makeup? Dictatorship is not merely prisons and executions. Dictatorship does something much worse than kill bodies. It kills the minds and wills of the survivors.

The justification of ruthless dictatorship on the ground that it brings jobs for all and the chance of better living conditions for the masses transcends Russia; it has become a world issue, perhaps the biggest issue facing modern man. If dictatorship is the road to plenty and security—Russia's experience has not proved that it is, but propagandists nevertheless assert it—then a billion and a half persons in Asia, Europe, Africa, and Latin America, who have suffered from poverty for decades may be induced to favor the Russian way of life and Russian expansion. If Russia is the guarantee of peace—Russia's aggressions do not prove it but it is loudly affirmed by the naive, the ignorant, and the sinister—then why not scrap democracy and adopt Stalinism everywhere?

In the next decade, a billion persons in Asia, and several hundred million in Europe too, will probably have to choose between the Russian and the American ways of life. Certain American intellectuals are telling them to choose the Russian way. Harold Laski chimed in.

The Laskis have a tremendous responsibility. Democracy survived the second world war but it may not survive the intellectual civil war that is raging in democratic countries (where, fortunately, governments let it rage) unless the truth about Soviet Russia is told in full. The strangest phase of the fight is that liberals who start a vast movement of indignant protest, as they should, against a Sacco and Vanzetti atrocity, or a Mooney case, or a Scottsboro case, or the lynching of a Negro, or the unfair treatment of a conscientious objector, or the censoring of a book or play, nevertheless champion the Russian regime where cruel executions, deportations, character assassinations, and the suppression of personal liberty and of the freedom of artists and writers are daily events. Their strange behavior is due, at least in part, to the hope that Russia's methods will solve the modern world's economic problems.

It ought to be obvious by this time that the end of the private businessman and of the private market in Russia has not brought the millennium. To dethrone the capitalist and enthrone a tyrant who holds the power of the totalitarian state machine plus all the power of all the capitalists is not progress towards decency, plenty, or peace. There must be another way.

18. *Joseph Stalin*

ONE afternoon, Markoosha brought me a surprise. Although she is working on a novel about Russia (after writing *My Lives In Russia* in 1944) she has found time to do much of my research work. In the library she unexpectedly came upon an article of mine in *Current History* of June, 1925, which I had completely forgotten. I read it with the same special interest that attaches to an old letter or diary which disinters a lost chapter of one's past.

The article contained this passage on Stalin: "Abler and stronger than Zinoviev is Stalin, Secretary of the Communist party, considered by many the central figure of the triumvirate [the Zinoviev-Kamenev-Stalin trio which ruled Russia immediately after Lenin's death in 1924]. Born Djugoshvili, trained for the ministry, five times arrested for revolutionary activity, five times exiled in Siberia and five times escaped, Stalin, naturally reticent and diffident, is the mysterious power behind the Bolshevik throne. He is a good organizer and a good debater. In rebuttal he is cruel and contemptuous, giving no quarter and recognizing no polite limits. He is typical of the whole Revolution—unsentimental, steel-willed, Jesuitical, allowing no object to bar his way to a given end, wholly unscrupulous. From the little he says much dynamic energy oozes. His office, where he sits most of the day and night, is a gigantic powerhouse; from it issues the current which electrifies the entire Party into unremitting activity. He is its Secretary and therefore its manager-in-chief.

" 'Lenin trusts Stalin. Stalin trusts no one.' This is the way they speak of Stalin in Russia. Whether it is true or not, it is indicative of the opinion men hold of him. His picture tells a tale. The furrows and wrinkles around his eyes speak of shrewdness and Oriental cunning."

The world knows a great deal more about Stalin now, for he has become the most influential man on earth, not because his country is the most powerful on earth but because he uses its power to the full.

Stalin is a man of power. He understands the rules of power. He wanted power at home and got it; he wanted power abroad and has taken steps to get it.

"Stalin" is the pseudonym of Joseph Vissaryonovitch Djugoshvili, born in 1879 to a poor cobbler who drank and a religious mother who sent him to a seminary from which he was expelled.

"Stalin" means steel. Steel may be straight and firm. It can also be twisted into delicate springs and winding screws. Stalin is tough and hard, malleable and adjustable. He is quick on the trigger and endlessly patient. He can watch and wait while others grow nervous and act and lose. He is thorough, pedestrian, and prosaic. He rewards those who submit to him but never forgives anybody who has crossed him. His memory is long.

Soviet leaders do not publish their memoirs. We judge Stalin by his speeches and articles but mainly by what Russia is, for since about 1926 he has been molding the Soviet Union in his image. To know Soviet Russia is to know something about Stalin, and to know Stalin is to know something about Soviet Russia.

Shortly after the United Nations victory in Europe, General Dwight D. Eisenhower gave a dinner at Frankfurt to Soviet Marshal Zhukov, hero of Moscow, conqueror of Berlin, commander of the Red Army. The following conversation took place between the two military leaders. It was printed in the *New York Herald Tribune* of June 18, 1945, and in the official publication of the United States Army in Germany.

Zhukov: "We've got some of those German synthetic oil plants that we captured over in our territory. We have repaired them but we haven't been able to get them running yet. I understand you've got some running over on your side. Could some of my experts come over and see how you got yours working?"

Eisenhower: "Sure, send 'em over. We'll show 'em how to do it."

Zhukov: (in a surprised tone) "You mean you don't have to ask your Government?"

Eisenhower: "Of course not. Send 'em on over."

Zhukov was surprised because he would never have dared to do such a thing without getting the permission of the secret police or of Stalin. Even the very highest Soviet officers have no independent authority to make decisions; they take orders. This is the Soviet system as Stalin has shaped it.

That is something we know about Russia and Stalin.

The Reader's Digest of October, 1944, published *My Talk with*

Joseph Stalin by Eric A. Johnston, President of the United States Chamber of Commerce. Mr. Johnston told me that the conversation as quoted in the article was taken verbatim from the Russian text supplied him by Stalin's office.

Eric Johnston was going on a trip into Siberia. He said to Stalin: "I would like to ask permission to take four [American] correspondents with me to the Urals."

"Why not?" said Stalin.

"Does that mean that I can take them?"

"Of course it does."

"Well, thank you, Marshal Stalin," Johnston said. "But I don't know whether Mr. Molotov will approve. You see, his office [the Foreign Office] has not yet granted my request."

"Molotov," Johnston writes, "who had been looking at me, shifted his eyes to Stalin and said quickly and firmly: 'I always approve of Marshal Stalin's decisions.'

"The Marshal cocked his head on one side. A broad grin animated his face. 'Mr. Johnston, you really didn't expect Mr. Molotov to disagree with me, did you?' "

That shows Stalin the person, Stalin the dictator, and Russia.

Frederick Kuh of the United Press and I interviewed Marshal Voroshilov, then Commissar of Defense and probably Number Three Soviet leader, in Moscow. Kuh's dispatch had to be censored before it was telegraphed abroad. Voroshilov did not dare to censor it himself. He took it to Stalin.

At first, the dictator forbids his subordinates to make important decisions. After a while they do not want to. It is safer and easier not to. The commonest characteristic of Soviet officials is the desire to pass responsibility to a superior. The Soviet embassy in Tokyo once asked Moscow by wire whether it should give a social tea. Soviet delegates are always delaying international conferences because they must wait for instructions from the Kremlin before they can vote or answer a question. Just as Mr. Molotov must have felt very small when Stalin humiliated him in Eric Johnston's presence, so all Soviet officials feel small and then become small. No one is more pleased than Stalin.

As a result of this policy, Stalin becomes associated in the mind of the nation with every Soviet success. During the first months of the Soviet-Nazi war when the Red Army retreated constantly, Stalin's name practically disappeared from the press and the radio. Stalin is an excellent though elementary psychologist; he did not want the public to think of him while it was thinking of defeat. The moment the Red Army began making a better showing, Stalin's name reappeared, and the victories were attributed to him.

The legend built around Stalin by assiduous propagandists makes him the greatest general of all time. I do not know whether this is true; neither does anyone outside a tiny inner circle. Nobody in that group talks for publication. Moscow is not Washington nor London nor Paris where everything becomes known sooner or later. Who can tell whether Stalin drafted the strategic plans or merely approved the plans drawn up by a general or staff of generals?

Lord Moran, Churchill's personal physician, said: "It is not easy to get into Stalin's mind." Churchill told him that. Churchill could carry the expansive Roosevelt along with him, but the self-made man from the Caucasus Mountains maintained his stolid taciturnity in the presence of England's most articulate word-lover.

Stalin has reduced spontaneity to zero. His acts, words, gestures, silences, and absences fit a carefully-woven design. When he smiled broadly at the signing of the Soviet-Nazi pact, the smile was political; it was a message to Hitler.

Stalin did not want Churchill to get into his mind.

Until 1936, top-rank Bolsheviks invariably referred to Stalin as *Khozyain* or "boss." Suddenly, at a signal, they started calling him *Starik* or "old man," which is more affectionate. In a dictatorship, all things, even nicknames, are regulated and calculated.

The Soviet propaganda machine has tried to pile-drive Stalin into the hearts of the people.

In 1945, a petition of reverence and glorification was presented to Stalin after it had been personally signed by 2,547,360 residents of the White Russian Soviet Republic. On November 18, 1945, Joseph Barnes reported from Moscow to the *New York Herald Tribune* that "The twenty-fifth anniversary of the establishment of the Kazakh Soviet Socialist Republic was celebrated here today with the publication this morning of a letter to Generalissimo Stalin signed by more than 2,500,000 Kazakh citizens." The Kazakh republic is an immense, sparsely-settled area in Central Asia with an average population of four persons per square kilometer. Stalin knows how much time, energy, and money had to be expended, in a war-weary country, by harassed officials to get up these petitions which are becoming a common phenomenon in Russia.

(On April 6, 1946, Generalissimo Franco was presented with fifty bound volumes containing 700,000 signatures of Spaniards confirming their allegiance to him. Labor Minister Giron, who made the presentation, said to Franco: "You are the only Spaniard we always are ready to follow against everything and everybody.")

Engineered approbation by the populace never fools the engineers. It is designed to fool the populace—and the naive foreigner. Endless repetition has tremendous force.

"Our dear father, friend, and teacher, our pride, our glory—the great Stalin," the Moscow daily *Trud* wrote on January 26, 1939, in a typical utterance which one can find in practically any edition of any Soviet publication. The Moscow magazine *Bolshevik* of July, 1945, in an authoritative article on Soviet history, philosophy, and jurisprudence, calls Stalin "The greatest scientist of the age." Every day, the unctuous adulation of Stalin, possessor of a million traits of genius from whom all blessings flow, reaches new heights and occupies more space in Soviet newspapers and magazines.

The "Fuehrer" principle of the Big Man dictator, which the Bolsheviks adopted before Hitler, was an abomination to me when it first manifested itself many years ago. Although the Soviet Foreign Commissariat did not like foreign correspondents in Moscow to attack Stalin, I wrote from Moscow to *The Nation* of August 13, 1930, reviling "the orgy of personal glorification of Stalin which has been permitted to sweep the country. . . . He has become the object of thickly smeared praise, fawning adulation and tasteless obeisance. . . . Lenin never permitted such antics and he was more popular than Stalin can ever hope to be. . . . It is as un-Bolshevik as it is politically unwise. If Stalin is not responsible for this performance he at least tolerates it. He could stop it by pressing a button."

He liked it. He still likes it. He has encouraged it. It has become more tasteless and more indecent with passing years. Eight cities have been named for Stalin: Stalingrad, Stalinogorsk, Stalinabad, Stalin, Stalino, Stalinir, Stalinissi, and Stalinaoul, in addition to numerous villages, factories, collective farms and schools. This Oriental near-deification probably feeds a psychological hunger in Stalin to be a "father." But it is also a calculated means whereby the dictator seeks to make the people obey and love him. Perhaps Stalin felt that a suffering nation, deprived of religion, would be more attached to its government, naturally regarded as the cause of its suffering, if a "father" was at the head of the government. I never saw any evidence that Soviet citizens loved their aloof parent in the walled Kremlin. Lenin was known affectionately as "Ilitch." Marshal Klementi E. Voroshilov, former Commissar of Defense, is adored by the common man and children who call him "Klim." (Voroshilovsk, a city named after him, was recently changed back to its original name of Stavropol.) But Stalin, despite every effort, remains *Stalin*, steel. He is admired for his immense ability, appreciated for his accomplishments, feared for his forceful methods. He is not the sort of person who is loved. He does not vibrate. His face seems to indicate that everything in him is incoming, not outgoing. Hitler magnetized millions with his hysteria. Churchill charmed England and many beyond her borders. Roosevelt's voice, grace, and warmth won him friends and successes. But Stalin has little magnetism, charm, grace, or warmth. I once sat by his side for six and a quarter hours at an interview. The total impression was one of calm strength, cold determination, conscious direction, and concentration on a single objective. With these, and with his consummate political skill and superior organizational technique, he won the power which popular appeal has given other world leaders. He has kept that power these twenty years—no mean physical and political achievement. It has required daily attention to the myriad tasks which face all governments and, in addition, the weakening of institutions and the annihilation of persons who might have criticized, challenged, obstructed, or thwarted the will of the dictator.

Stalin's principle of organization resembles military strategy: he disrupts his opponent's strength while building and using his own. He applies this principle to international relations and to Soviet domestic affairs. In both these fields he displays an extraordinary talent to confuse, divide, immobilize, and paralyze opposition.

The possibility of opposing the dictator is drastically reduced by the nature of the Soviet system as Stalin has perfected it. The peasants, who are a majority in the country, live on state-controlled collectives which are not permitted to organize into groups; the Government owns the land, machinery, and farm equipment of the collectives and is their chief customer. The peasants, therefore, have neither political unity nor economic power. The workingmen, similarly, are employed by the Government; they cannot strike; trade unions, in the sense of bodies which make demands on employers, do not exist. Nor have the several million Government officials and Government-employed industrial managers any means of opposing or checking the dictator's omnipotence. Without these bureaucrats, to be sure, nothing moves. But he who does not work in Russia does not eat, and he who objects is arrested. The bureaucrat highlights the paradox of Soviet security: he can always have a job and he can always go to jail. Any official, from Molotov down, can be purged without redress. The bureaucracy is an indispensable motor, but it gets its current from the dictator. The Communist party is also incapable of independent action against Stalin. Once the fountain of all political authority in the Soviet Union, the purges deprived the Party of its leaders and filled the survivors with fear. There is no political activity outside the Communist party and in it there is silence. Nor is a single individual free to protest or oppose, for freedom is illusory when a person is free only because the secret police has not decided to arrest him.

In Stalin's Russia, accordingly, there is no medium for the expression of opposition. The power which might have belonged to the press, Party, trade unions, farm unions, and Government offices has passed to the dictator. These institutions therefore could not be used to channel or voice popular discontent if it existed. The people might conceivably riot or practise non-violent non-cooperation as in India. But except in case of the highly improbable disorganization of police authority at the top, such manifestations are precluded. The GPU has trained the Soviet people in humble obedience and drained them of self-confidence.

A national republic, say Georgia in the Caucasus, might rebel against the Moscow dictatorship if its local officials sympathized with the insurrection. But the governments of all national republics which comprise the Soviet Union are honeycombed with Russians and Communists who take their orders from the Kremlin. No uprising could succeed without the aid of the Red Army.

The Red Army and the secret police are thus the only two institutions which might question Stalin's power. The way Stalin handles them shows his genius and the reasons for his supremacy.

The Soviet secret police or NKVD (People's Commissariat of Internal Affairs), which the people still call the GPU, has agents in all cities and villages, in all factories and offices. Some of the finest buildings in Russia, usually in the center of town, house the GPU's combination headquarters-prison. It is not in the nature of the GPU to hide its might under a bushel. Its acts are secret but not the fact that it acts.

The GPU also conducts numerous economic enterprises. I have seen it constructing canals and railroads with slave labor; it has been commended officially for this activity. The GPU, moreover, maintains its own armed units which guard the frontier, communications, and important buildings.

I have met many GPU officials. Some were men and some were women. Some were in uniform and some were in civilian clothes. Some were in the Soviet Union and some were in Soviet embassies abroad watching their own and foreign diplomats. Some were idealists convinced that their jobs were necessary though unpleasant. Some liked the luxuries and the power which their positions gave them. All were distinguished by hard work, secretiveness, and fear, for no punishment meted out by the GPU is as fierce as that which it metes out to its own members who falter or blunder. All are bound together by a strong *esprit de corps,* a pride in their assignment, a sense of "art for art's sake." The GPU is like an ancient fraternal order united by a common vow of silence, a common dedication to a paramount function, a common enjoyment of special status and privilege, and a common apprehension of failure.

The GPU is Stalin's spiritual child.

For some years, the GPU seemed to assume that its numbers, armed strength, multiplicity of key tasks, and indispensability to the dictator made it at least partly autonomous. Its knowledge of the measures, not all of them savory, by which the dictator aggrandized his power and liquidated his victims, gave it the illusion that it was a state within a state.

In 1931, the GPU defied Stalin. I told the story at the time in *The Nation*, and wrote its sequel in *The Nation* of August 9, 1933; both articles were mailed from Moscow.

"Two years ago," I explained in *The Nation* of 1933, "Akulov was appointed Vice-President of the GPU. As such he superseded Yagoda, the active head of the organization, and became chief of the institution. Apparently, however, friction developed between Akulov and the permanent officials and before long the newcomer with a penchant for reform was sent to a rather inferior post in the Donetz coal basin."

Yagoda, for many years the master of the GPU, had sulked and refused to work with Akulov. Stalin was consequently forced to remove Akulov and restore Yagoda's supremacy. The GPU won a battle against Stalin.

But Stalin is not easily defeated. Characteristically, he waited, and then tried again. This second time he did not put Akulov in the GPU. He put him outside of it and over it.

"Akulov," I wrote in *The Nation*, "an old Bolshevik and former associate of Lenin, has been appointed Attorney General of the Soviet Union. This is a new office. . . . The most surprising of Akulov's functions is his right to watch over the activities of the GPU. One of the Attorney General's duties is 'the supervision . . . over the legality and regularity of the GPU's acts.' "

This change brought a relaxation of the Bolshevik terror. I knew Soviet citizens arrested by Yagoda who were liberated by Akulov. He could not resurrect the dead but he did release some of the living who had been falsely accused. In the latter half of 1933 and throughout 1934, the country witnessed a perceptible easing of the atmosphere. For the first time in Soviet history, the secret police could not, without consulting higher authority, arrest an important engineer or a Red Army officer.

In January, 1934, some of the judicial functions of the GPU were transferred to the Soviet courts, and the GPU was renamed Commissariat of Internal Affairs. For seven months, however, the Commissariat remained without a Commissar. This was most unusual. Stalin was resisting the appointment of Yagoda. In the end, in July, 1934, Yagoda became Commissar. Yagoda, though shorn of some powers, had won again.

The assassination of Sergei Kirov, Number Four Bolshevik and Leningrad political chief, in December, 1934, caused a short, high wave of executions and wholesale deportations which did not, nevertheless, interrupt the liberalization of the regime. The new phase culminated in the handing down of the Stalin constitution of 1936.

But while the Constitution was being drafted it was being killed by the famous Moscow trials and the recrudescence of the purge. Thousands of high Soviet officials—I named hundreds of them in *Men and Politics*—were shot or banished.

The Soviet Constitution has been more breached than honored. For some, what is on paper is. But the civil liberties written into the Stalin constitution do not exist in Soviet life. The people thought they would get those liberties and were jubilant. The jubilation reflected the yearning of the population for freedom and their consciousness of its absence. This is what may have caused the Soviet leadership to ignore the Constitution; it had been taken too seriously by the country. The GPU may have showed Stalin reports about the mood of the nation which convinced him that liberty would imperil the dictatorship. The fact is that the trials and purges and the accompanying accentuation of the terror robbed the Constitution of all reality. After the relaxation of the terror in 1934, the preparation of the Constitution in 1935, and its proclamation in 1936, the trials were a shock to me. At those trials, not only certain prominent persons were condemned to death. Democracy was condemned to death.

The 1936 and 1937 trials were skillfully staged by Genrich Yagoda as head of the secret police. But on March 2, 1938, Yagoda, a short, thin man with a Hitleresque mustache, appeared in the dock of the biggest Moscow trial. On March 13, the court sentenced him to death for treason. Stalin had finally disposed of the man who defied him.

Yagoda's successor was Yezhov, a man about five feet tall. He intensified the purge. Then Stalin purged him. Yezhov's successor was Levrenti Beria, a Georgian like Stalin, short and ruthless. I talked with him in Tiflis in 1924 when, as head of the Georgian secret police, he exterminated the Georgian Mensheviks. He owed his rise to Stalin. Under Beria, the GPU became the completely subservient and obedient "flaming sword," as Soviet writers call it, of the dictatorship. The Attorney General was forgotten.

On January 14, 1946, however, Colonel General Sergei N. Kruglyov replaced Beria. The chief of the GPU is the most powerful man in the Soviet Union next to Stalin, and a person who has exercised much power for a long time may become ambitious and dangerous. Stalin changes the guard when he thinks it is developing independent ideas.

The GPU is Stalin's faithful tool.

Stalin also experienced great difficulty with the Red Army.

Generals, general staffs, and armed forces play a political role even in democracies where there is a traditional objection to such an undemocratic invasion of people's rights and a traditional fear of "Bonapartism." Democracy presents a whole array of defenses against political meddling by the military: free elections, elected civilian officials, parliaments which allocate the money for the armed services, an uncontrolled press which can expose assaults on the constitution, and so forth. But a dictatorship would not be a dictatorship if it were certain of the free approval of a majority. Lacking affirmative public consent, a dictatorship is more dependent on the military than a democracy. This enhances the importance of the military. In Japan, the military ruled. Hitler kept a keen eye on his generals; they obeyed him and took the army into war against the better judgment of some of them; yet many were disloyal to him and finally, very late, plotted to kill him. Mussolini too had his troubles with the military. In Spain, in Argentina, and elsewhere the dictatorships rest painfully on bayonet points.

The political importance of the Red Army is enhanced by its popularity. It is a people's army, and the people like it. The Soviet dictatorship is a cold precision instrument and none of its leaders, neither Stalin, nor Molotov, nor Zhdanov, nor Andreyev, nor Malenkov, has been able to establish an emotional bond with the masses. The Red Army, on the other hand, is human. Its marshals and generals—Tukhachevsky in his time, Timoshenko, Zhukov, and others— evoke a warm response.

Stalin's difficulty with the Red Army can be seen through the fate of two persons: General Boris M. Shaposhnikov and Marshal Michael N. Tukhachevsky.

Shaposhnikov was born in 1882 and served as a colonel in the Tsar's Army. He was a professional military man and not interested in politics. He did not enter the Communist party until 1930 when his high military rank made the formality necessary. Like thousands of other Tsarist officers, he joined the Red Army in 1918 because he was a Russian nationalist patriot and wanted to defend his country against foreign intervention.

Tukhachevsky was born in 1893. He belonged to a new generation. He was a young lieutenant in the Tsar's Army and became a member of the Communist party in April, 1918, when that step required political conviction and entailed extra dangers and responsibilities. At the age of twenty-seven, Tukhachevsky commanded the Red Army in its brilliant dash across Poland to the gates of Warsaw. In Europe, he earned the reputation of a modern Napoleon. But in addition to being a military genius, Tukhachevsky was politically-minded. The many young Communist officers in the Red Army looked to him as their leader.

A rivalry developed between the non-political, Russian-nationalistic, old-guard military specialists exemplified by Shaposhnikov and the young Communist officers of the type of Tukhachevsky. Stalin sided with Shaposhnikov.

Shaposhnikov was appointed Chief of Staff of the Red Army in 1926. But pressure from the Tukhachevsky school of officers caused him to be removed and transferred to a minor command in the Volga district. Ultimately, Tukhachevsky succeeded him as Chief of Staff.

On May 11, 1937, Tukhachevsky was removed and transferred to a minor command in the Volga district. Shaposhnikov succeeded him.

On June 12, 1937, Tukhachevsky and eight of the highest generals and marshals in the Red Army were executed on the never-proved charge of conspiracy. The decree of May 11 which demoted Tukhachevsky also reintroduced political commissars into the army. The commissars were civilians who shared authority with army officers and often vetoed officers' orders. The commissars, said the *Pravda*, "are the eyes and ears of the Communist party in the army." This meant that the party and GPU felt they had to watch the army after the liquidation of Tukhachevsky and the officers who were loyal to him.

The army officers resented the presence of the commissars and had no taste for Shaposhnikov. On August 10, 1940, Shaposhnikov was relieved of his duties as Chief of Staff. On August 12, the commissars were abolished.

The commissars came in with Shaposhnikov and went out with him.

Then, on July 16, 1941, when the Red Army was retreating before the Germans and the prestige of the officers was therefore lower, the commissars were again restored. On November 3, 1941, when the Reichswehr stood before Moscow, Shaposhnikov again returned as Chief of Staff.

Stalin's manipulations, though undistinguished by brilliance and inventiveness, become impressive through their implacable persistence. In Stalin's wartime speeches and Orders of the Day, for instance, the striking thing is the elementary approach and the manner in which all his statements over the four fighting years fit a single stencil; in each review of the war he treats the same subjects in the same way. No new thought or brave analysis mars the high-school student summaries. Yet the droning repetitiveness has the relentless strength of a giant engine's flywheel. Not having great intellectual attainments Stalin has little intellectual arrogance. He never seems self-conscious about anybody saying "Oh, he has done (or said) this before." The sameness may reveal his limitations. But for his victims it appears to have had a paralyzing fascination.

Twice Stalin tried to check secret police chief Yagoda with Aku-lov. Three times Stalin brought in the commissars to create a balance against politically-minded officers in the army. He follows the same pattern over and over again.

Stalin ousted the commissars once more on October 10, 1942, and gave the military commanders unlimited authority. This documented their ascendancy. In the war situation, Stalin had to bow to the military caste he had created. He could not purge it in the midst of the battle with Germany.

But while yielding to the officers' corps, Stalin did not neglect countermeasures. He shifted generals often and endeavored especially to win the favor of the middle-rank officers. On the assumption that soldiers will be loyal to their military superiors, Stalin gave high rank to civilian heads of the Communist party like Andrei A. Zhdanov who was named Colonel General, and N. Khrushchev, Ukrainian party leader, who was named Lieutenant General. Meanwhile, he took care to keep the supreme Politbureau closed to front-line generals. But the chief of the GPU was admitted as a deputy member and received the title of Marshal though he had never fought at the front; he thereby acquired equal status with the highest fighting army commander. Stalin did not want the Red Army to outrank the GPU. Stalin himself conferred on himself the exalted, unequaled rank of Generalissimo.

Walter Kerr, keen observer of the little details which reveal big things in Russia, noted in a dispatch from Moscow to the *New York Herald Tribune* of November 18, 1942, that whereas the fourteen topmost civilian leaders of the Soviet Union were frequently mentioned in the newspapers, "the names of high officers like General Zhukov, Marshal Timoshenko, Marshal Boris M. Shaposhnikov, and Marshal S. M. Budenny are published rarely." Stalin did not want the military to be too popular or to get too much credit for victories.

Adroit political artist, Stalin was able, despite difficulties, to maintain his hold on the military throughout the war. Peace facilitates the dictator's task.

But Stalin has not been able to prevent, and there is no evidence that he wished to prevent, the rise of a cult of Russian militarism. Soviet diplomats have been corseted into gold-braid uniforms with big epaulets. Admirals and generals are taking diplomatic posts. "The profession of military commander," wrote the *Pravda* of August 30, 1940, "is the most respected in the country." The youth is encouraged and forced to go military. Co-education has been abolished in Soviet schools not because of any inadequacy in the method but because all boys begin their military training at the very inception of their school careers and, girls being what they are, there must therefore be special schools for girls. Russia's postwar Five Year Plan is officially described as a means "to develop the military and economic strength of the Soviet Union." General John R. Deane, former American Army representative in Moscow, says the peacetime establishment of the Red Army will be "about four million men, which is probably all or more than the economy of the country can stand." The maintenance of such a large army, and the expansion of the Red Navy in accordance with Stalin's published instructions, means many officers with privileges and political aspirations; it means propaganda at home to prove that foreign enemies threaten the country and that the population must accordingly bend every effort to make the nation stronger; it means that Russia will continue to live in an atmosphere of strain and tension.

In 1813, a Tsarist army entered Paris. Russian officers and soldiers in great numbers saw Europe. It opened their eyes to the backwardness, poverty, and oppression that existed at home. In 1825, Russian army officers who were inspired by the French revolution staged the famous Decembrist revolution. They wanted a constitution for Russia. The revolt failed but it never died in the memory of the people.

Now another Russian army has seen Europe, a bombed, rubbled, hungry, ragged, numbed, anguished, unhappy, directionless Europe. Yet even such a continent impressed the Red soldier and commander as more comfortable, more advanced, and freer than his native land. The Kremlin watched and was somewhat worried. The *Pravda* one day in September, 1944, published six columns from the pen of Leonid Sobolev, war correspondent with the Red Army in Bucharest, wherein he urged the Russian soldier not to be dazzled by "a lot of tawdry brilliance." Konstantin Simonov, Soviet novelist, took up the same subject in the army newspaper *Red Star* in October, 1945, and asked the soldier to remember that sacrifice for his country is more creative than indulgence in a luxurious private life. But lest this appeal fall on deaf ears, Simonov added the assurance of a brighter material future for the citizens of the Soviet Union.

The Red Army, its eyes opened by European conditions, is likely to press for national economic improvements. In Russia's straitened postwar conditions, however, higher standards of living can only be attained at the expense of the industries and funds needed to equip the Red Army. This is another problem in political navigation for the masterly hand of pilot Stalin.

Suppose Stalin dies? The question has been debated everywhere in the democratic world. Rarely has so much thought, and in some circles so much hope, been invested in the demise of a single human being. Will the Red Army take power after Stalin? Will it name his successor? The answers are in the negative.

No man's deeds die with him. He leaves a legacy, and in Stalin's case it is a big one. Twenty years of his rule cannot be sloughed off quickly if at all, especially since what he did has become rooted in geography, psychology, and institutions. Stalin remade the map. That remains. He remade minds. That is not easily changed. He crushed private capitalism and substituted the state; few if any leaders would risk inviting chaos by reversing this situation.

The Soviet system is not likely to undergo many important changes when Stalin passes. Violent political battles raged in Russia after Lenin's death. They lasted long and involved all front-rank Bolsheviks. But the safety and stability of the regime were never imperiled. That after-Lenin controversy was a Communist party controversy. It precipitated a countrywide public debate. Leaders and members argued the issues in the open. Today the Party has been reduced to a passive agent of the Kremlin. Its spirit is dead.

Stalin's death will not create a political disturbance beyond the narrowest leader group that surrounds him. His successor—assuming, as I do, that he will name one—could only be vetoed by the GPU, not by the army.

The GPU is much smaller than the Red Army and has less physical force. Yet it has more political power. Stalin and his GPU can always outmaneuver the Red Army just as Hitler and Himmler could worst the Reichswehr in any political struggle. This is why it was possible for Stalin to execute Tukhachevsky and the leading generals of the Red Army. That tremendous event, perhaps the most momentous political act in a decade of Soviet history, actually required nothing more than simultaneous unheralded nocturnal visits by GPU men to the apartments of the nine marked marshals and generals. If the generals had been plotting a revolt they might have been quartered with their troops and offered resistance to arrest. But they were probably found at home in their pyjamas. One of them, General Gamarnik, a hero of the Bolshevik civil war and director of political education in the army, was officially reported to have committed suicide when the secret police called for him. Each of the others knew that the alternative was a shot in the mouth from his own revolver or a shot in the back of the neck from a GPU revolver and presumably chose the latter because it is better to die later.

This illustrates the advantage which a dictator enjoys over the army. Unless an army group is planning a *coup d'état* it can only exert pressure on the dictatorship, and such pressure would be the signal for a night-swoop by the GPU.

For Red Army dissidents the choice is armed insurrection or silent submission. A palace revolution against Stalin or his successor might be undertaken by a small band of officers, or one officer might try assassinating the dictator. Stalin is carefully watched, and even a Red Army general must check his sidearm before entering Stalin's presence; individual acts of terror are therefore unlikely though not impossible. But assassins or a conspiratorial committee would realize that they were taking grave risks upon themselves, their families, friends, co-workers, and acquaintances without, however, ensuring the success of their venture. A successful uprising would require a nation-wide organization. It would require consultations with commanders of garrisons outside Moscow and with regional military chiefs.

A general might discuss a conspiracy with a friend in the army. They might discuss it with a third military man. But if they took the matter to a fourth or a fifth person he would be very likely to say to himself: "Are they testing me? Are they trying to find out for the GPU how loyal I am? If I don't report them they may report me." He, accordingly, would inform on them in the interest of his own safety. Moreover, every office and regiment has men in it who work for the secret police and who would covet the credit of exposing a plot against the authorities. In this way, the GPU holds the key to power in Russia. An army insurrection in the Soviet Union would be a gigantic gamble. Only light-minded adventurers or high-minded idealists would try, and they would almost certainly fail.

The power which the GPU holds over the Red Army has always been a source of irritation between them. Hostility is enhanced by the overlapping of some of their functions. The GPU has a foreign espionage service and so have the military. The GPU stands guard over Soviet frontiers and the Red Army is encamped not far behind.

Even in the best-coordinated governments, jurisdictional disputes occur. What has especially intensified army feeling against the GPU is that it maintains spies in the army and can again arrest army officers.

It would be folly to prophesy whether a less skilful dictator than Stalin will have trouble curbing the GPU or the army. A secret police can always attempt to make itself indispensable by "discovering" plots and domestic enemies. An army can try to bolster its political power at home by preparing for adventures abroad.

Because the Red Army is anti-GPU for institutional reasons, hopes have been reposed in it to make Russia more democratic; any triumph over the GPU would be a triumph over its terror methods and its unlimited right to invade personal life. So far, there are no signs that the Red Army or anybody else has effected an increase in Soviet political democracy. I scour the Soviet press for such a sign and would be happy to record it. The wonderful Soviet people, and the world, would be safer with more democracy in Russia.

The prospects of Soviet democracy after Stalin's death are dimmed by the official attitude that Russia is a democracy. In the early years of the Bolshevik revolution, democracy was offered as a goal. Now, with the country enjoying less liberty than it had then, the Government says democracy already exists. If the absence of freedom is officially called freedom how can a movement for freedom be tolerated? It would be branded an assault on freedom.

The Moscow *New Times* of January, 1946, contended that Rumania and Bulgaria must be protected from the "abstract standards of Western democracy" which evil Messrs. Byrnes and Bevin were just then trying to inflict on those two Balkan countries reveling in their Moscow-imposed concrete (steel) "democracy." The standards of Western democracy are imperfect, but they are abstract only to those who do not enjoy them. What is good in those standards is very good. Stalin, however, seeks to protect Rumania and Bulgaria, as to date he has protected Russia, from the abomination of free elections, free assembly, free trade unions, free courts, free speech, and free press. Stalin stands for state power without abridgment.

What does a state give the individual to whom it denies political rights and whom it cannot supply with material goods? Stalin has faced this problem. He offered the Soviet citizen nationalism. He pinned medals on his chest. He gave him an icon lest he become an iconoclast. He strengthened the family albeit by such dubious means as encouraging more babies and making divorce less accessible to the poor. He stressed and exaggerated the social achievements of the regime and contrasted them with the horrors endured by the "capitalist slaves" of Western bourgeois countries. He gave him circuses in the shape of festivals, carnivals, aviation shows, trans-Siberian flights which are played up in the press—day after day newspapers devoted more than half their total space to one such feat—until the readers think that no other country ever saw a trans-continental hop, parades, and other sensations.

The technique of diversion has been employed by all dictatorships; Stalin has developed it to a fine art.

Sometimes, foreign successes—diplomatic or military—serve as diversions from the hard life. The Nazis, Italian Fascists, and Japanese militarists needed foreign victories to bolster domestic control. They hailed war as a virtue. "Only war raises all demonstrations of human energy to the highest pitch and places the stamp of nobility on nations which can meet it openly," wrote the ignoble Mussolini in 1934. Stalin has never uttered such nonsense nor have the Bolsheviks preached it.

Philosophers attribute the aggressive tendencies of some nations to their philosophers. Psychologists explain such tendencies by national trauma or psychoses or primitive experiences. But whatever their roots, recent history shows that these tendencies do not explode into wars unless dictatorships are in power. Soviet Russia has committed aggression without philosophers.

Dictatorship brought on the second world war with the help of the appeasing democracies. Appeasement is an abdication of strength resulting from an abdication of intelligence. With all its material strength, democracy since the first days of Hitler has been in retreat before totalitarian attack.

In relation to Hitler, Mussolini, and Hirohito, the democratic retreat was chiefly physical; they advanced, we retreated. We thereby reinforced them at home and increased their contempt for us until they believed they could conquer the earth.

In relation to Stalin, the retreat of the Western powers is not only physical; it is spiritual as well. We not only yield to him; we glorify him. This is one of the most startling social phenomena of our time.

Son of Asia, Stalin has cast a spell over his native continent and a shadow over Europe. His influence, via friends of Russia and of Communism, reaches into every corner of the Americas. Nobody with the possible exception of the Pope (hence, in part, the hostility between them) affects the lives of so many people.

Stalin's international influence stems from his abilities, from the power and accomplishments of his country, and from the intellectual bankruptcy and political anarchy of the Western world. Capitalism lacks faith in itself. Because of its imperfections, capitalism cannot hold its intellectuals. Democracy is unsure and insecure. This inner moral weakness of the West has not eluded the shrewd eye of Stalin; it guides his foreign policy.

19. *Roosevelt, Churchill, and Stalin Make the Peace*

THE WAR leaders were the peacemakers. They forged the peace while fighting the war.

The real peace conferences were held in Teheran in December, 1943, in the Crimea in February, 1945, and, to a less extent, in Potsdam in July-August, 1945. All the other meetings during and after the war, including San Francisco, were elaborations of the main peace lines laid down by Roosevelt, Churchill, and Stalin at Teheran and Yalta.

The usual order is to win a war and then write the peace. Roosevelt and Churchill would have followed this procedure. Secretary Hull told Congress on November 18, 1943, that the American government wanted all boundary questions left in abeyance until the termination of hostilities. But this had disadvantages for Russia. A peace is shaped not by the countries that have contributed most to victory but by the countries that have most strength left after victory. Stalin knew that the Soviet Union would be weakened by the casualties and destruction of the war. He felt, too, that Russia could impose her will on her allies while she was indispensable to victory but might lose this leverage when hostilities ceased.

Imagine a partnership of three which must under no conditions be dissolved. Then if one partner asks for something and refuses to desist the others give it to him. This was the basis of Stalin's strategy at Teheran and Yalta.

But England and America were partners too. Why couldn't they insist?

Stalin understood that America and England would not quit the war. They would not come to terms with Hitler or Japan. Roosevelt and Churchill, however, did not have the same trust in Stalin. This was Stalin's greatest asset in the making of the peace.

The Soviet-Nazi pact of August, 1939, placed a permanent imprint on world diplomacy. It signified that anti-Nazi Russia, champion of collective security against aggressors, could sign a treaty of friendship and neutrality with Nazi Germany, the great aggressor. The fear that Moscow might repeat this performance constantly obsessed Roosevelt and Churchill.

At Casablanca in January, 1943, Roosevelt and Churchill issued their famous "Unconditional Surrender" statement. The United States and Great Britain, they announced, would sign no peace with the enemy until he was completely defeated. That was eighteen months before the cross-Channel invasion of Normandy. The American Army merely had a hold on North Africa. The unconditional surrender pronouncement could have no immediate effect on Hitler's policy and ultimately it could only strengthen Hitler and the German will to resist. The declaration was not meant for Germany. Nor was it needed to bolster American morale; once in the war the Americans would see it through. The Roosevelt-Churchill "Unconditional Surrender" statement was meant as a hint to Stalin to adopt the same unconditional surrender formula. But it would have been stupid for him to do so. What Roosevelt and Churchill affirmed at Casablanca revealed their uncertainty about Russia's intentions and showed Stalin that he could trade on it.

Stalin talked and acted quite the reverse of unconditional surrender. He made an undisguised appeal to the German Army and the German people on May 1, 1942. "The Germany Army," he said, "is called on to shed its own and other people's blood and maim itself and others not so much in the interests of Germany but to enrich German bankers and plutocrats. . . . For the German people it is growing ever clearer that the only outlet from the position in which they now find themselves is the freeing of Germany from the freebooting clique of Hitler and Goering. . . . We have no aim of seizing foreign territory or conquering foreign peoples. Our aim is clear and honorable. We want to free our Soviet land from the German Fascist beasts."

Stalin was even more direct in a speech on November 7, 1942. "It is not our aim to destroy Germany," he said. "It is not our aim to destroy all military force in Germany, for every literate person will understand that this is not only impossible in regard to Germany, as it is in regard to Russia, but it is also inadvisable from the point of view of the future. . . ."

This was a plain bid to the German Army leaders to overthrow Hitler and make peace with Russia.

Churchill had been in Moscow and explained to Stalin that the British were in no position to land in western Europe and start a second front there. The clamor for a second front nevertheless continued unabated; both Russians and pro-Russians abroad ceaselessly demanded it. Nothing could have been more natural for Russia, bleeding profusely, than to want relief by the deflection of some Nazi forces to another fighting area. But in view of the fact that Stalin was provided with complete information on the Western allies' plans and strength, the agitation for a second front was in the nature of a reminder that Russia felt unhappy about her allies and wanted more from them. It suggested that Russia might seek relief in a separate peace with Germany.

In the summer of 1943, the nervousness in London and Washington over Stalin's intentions rose to maximum intensity. For on July 12, 1943, the "National Committee for a Free Germany" was organized under Soviet auspices in Moscow. It consisted of German Communists long resident in Russia and of Nazi prisoners of war, some of them high officers, some noblemen, whom the Soviet government had released for this purpose. The Committee drafted a manifesto on July 21 which was dropped in millions of copies by Red Army airplanes over the German lines and then printed in the Moscow *Pravda* of August 1, thus making it official.

The manifesto called for the establishment of "a genuine national German government" in place of the Hitler regime. "This Government will immediately cease military operations, will recall the German troops to the Reich's frontiers, and embark on peace negotiations, renouncing all conquests. In this manner it will attain peace and once again place Germany on an equal footing with other nations."

"Peace negotiations"; "Germany on an equal footing with other nations"; that is not Unconditional Surrender.

All this might be viewed as a legitimate Soviet attempt to cause a rift between the Reich's Army and Hitler. But it was not so interpreted by Roosevelt and Churchill. From Quebec where he was conferring with the President, Winston Churchill delivered a speech on August 31, 1943, which, though full of deference to Stalin and Russia, was rather bitter about Soviet and foreign Communist demands for a second front. "We once had a fine front in France," Churchill recalled, "but it was torn to pieces by the concentrated might of Hitler, and it is easier to have a front pulled down than it is to build it up again." This was a frontal attack on Stalin's policy during the Soviet-Nazi pact period when a different Russian attitude might, so Churchill implied, have saved France. It was thanks to Russia's understanding with Germany, Churchill was saying, that Hitler could throw his "concentrated" strength against France.

Churchill was venting his irritation with Russia. An even more startling statement came from the pen of Harry Hopkins that summer. Writing in the *American Magazine*, Roosevelt's intimate political adviser said: "If we lose her [Russia] I do not believe for a moment that we will lose the war. . . ." The Red Army had taken Stalingrad and pushed the Germans back elsewhere. It was no longer a question of Russia's succumbing to Hitler's blows. We could "lose" Russia only by a separate Russian peace with Germany.

Secretary of State Cordell Hull explained to me in his office in the State Department on January 19, 1944, why he went to Moscow for the first Conference of Foreign Ministers the previous autumn. "I wanted to get to the bottom of the many stories of a separate peace between Russia and Germany that had been heard in Washington, London, and Chungking," he began. "We were in the dark on that. . . ."

The American and British governments were worried about Stalin's loyalty to the Big Three coalition. This carefully-concealed sentiment dominated American and British diplomacy at Teheran in December, 1943. It created a perfect situation for Stalin. Behind each request he made for Polish territory or for other advantages was the unspoken threat that in case of rebuff he had an alternative: an agreement with a Hitler-less Germany.

The Teheran conference was a total Stalin victory and "Teheran" therefore became the slogan and program of foreign Communists, especially of the Browder-led American Communist party. But the Kremlin soon decided, apparently, that the conference had killed too many doubts about Russia's future course. Stalin never likes anybody to be sure about what he will do. On January 17, 1944, accordingly, the *Pravda* published a strange story from its "own correspondent" in Cairo (where, as subsequently revealed, it had no correspondent) to the effect that "two leading British personalities" had been negotiating with Nazi Foreign Minister von Ribbentrop for a separate peace with Germany. The *Pravda's* "own correspondent" in Cairo stated that he got his information from "Greek and Yugoslav" sources; the Ribbentrop talks, he alleged, took place in the "Iberian peninsula."

The story had all the earmarks of an invention, and the *Pravda* does not normally publish such vague, questionable tales. It was a tale with a purpose. The American and British papers gave it great first-page prominence. The news was not the rumor but the fact that *Pravda* had printed it.

I was in Washington the day the *Pravda* sensation appeared in America. I had tea alone with Lord Halifax, the British ambassador. The first thing he said was: "Tell me, what are the Russians up to? Why do they accuse the British government of wanting a separate peace with Germany?" The same question was in the minds of Secretary Hull, Under-Secretary Stettinius, Assistant Secretary Adolf A. Berle, and other American and foreign diplomats I saw those days. They were all perplexed and disturbed.

In my view, the purpose of the *Pravda* story was to produce just that state of disturbed perplexity. "Maybe Moscow's charge that we are negotiating with Germany is only an excuse to justify Soviet negotiations with Germany," the diplomats reasoned. The post-Teheran feeling of Russia's loyalty to the coalition left them. They fretted. Russia had to be courted again. Russia must not be thwarted. In this atmosphere, Stalin could consolidate concessions already wrenched from Roosevelt and Churchill and ask for more. It also helped him to get more Lend-Lease material.

As soon as Russia started winning battles in 1943, the possibility of a separate Soviet-German peace loomed; Stalin could consequently dictate terms to England and America at Teheran. Still later, the Red Army moved into eastern and central Europe, and the Kremlin began imposing itself on small countries. That inaugurated a new phase in the relations within the Big Three. To curb unilateralism and more Soviet expansion, the United States and Great Britain again saw themselves compelled to compromise with the Soviet government by yielding to most of Russia's wishes at Yalta.

During the war democratic governments felt a special need to guard against popular moods of depression. The public wanted to believe that all was best in the best of worlds, and political leaders wanted them to believe it. Each conference was therefore proclaimed as an important milestone on the road to victory and the postwar paradise. Roosevelt and Churchill could not leave Teheran or Yalta without a resounding announcement of agreement and progress. Stalin made them pay for his signature.

But was there an alternative? Could Roosevelt and Churchill have risked alienating Russia and driving her into a separate peace with Germany? That would have meant the prolongation of the war and a horrible rise in American and British, as well as other, casualties.

Despite Harry Hopkins' optimism, the Western allies might have lost the war if we had lost Russia. To refuse to give Stalin what he asked, in Poland for instance, might have induced him to get it by an understanding with Germany. He had done it in 1939, and he might have felt that conditions were more favorable now than they were then.

It was a terrible responsibility indeed. Whenever I discussed this central issue of the wartime peacemaking with Allied officials their ultimate retreat was in the question "And suppose Russia quits the war?" Once I talked with Secretary Hull about Russia's designs on Poland and the Baltic states. "If you want to take that up in Moscow," he said, "you had better take the American Army and Navy with you." Stalin, in other words, would only be deterred by the use of instruments and methods which the United States and the British could not employ.

The private citizen can criticize. But suppose he knew that the policy he advocates might cost the lives of a hundred thousand boys? Roosevelt, Hopkins, and Churchill courted Stalin with concessions because they thought the outcome of the war was at stake. It probably was not. A Russian separate peace with Germany was very unlikely. In fact, it seems impossible. How could it have come about? Any serious German offer of peace would have proved to Stalin that Germany was on her last legs and that he would therefore be foolish to accept. Equally, any peace offer from Moscow would have been read in Berlin as a confession of serious weakness and would have induced Germany to redouble her efforts to crush Russia.

A second Stalin-Hitler pact presented insuperable obstacles and so, as the history of 1944 and 1945 in Germany shows, did the overthrow of Hitler. The Moscow Free German Committee and all of Stalin's gestures to the German Army were not to be taken seriously; Hitler stayed at the helm to his last suicidal day.

Moreover, during the war, Moscow developed grand expansionist ambitions at the cost of Germany and Europe. Those ambitions could not have been satisfied by a separate German-Russian peace. Such a peace would have been a compromise and therefore a limitation on Soviet designs. Russia's empire is bigger now than it could ever have been after a separate peace. This consideration, too, would have dissuaded Stalin from concluding a separate peace.

There was only a short period, perhaps a few months in 1943, when Hitler might have begun to doubt his ability to smash Russia and before Stalin was convinced that he could expel the Germans from his country, during which a separate Russo-German peace might have been concluded. But Hitler's intransigence and "intuition" were one big obstacle; Stalin's experience with Hitler another.

The future is a fog. Like an airplane pilot, a statesman flies on estimates. He moves toward the future on instruments and the instruments are his knowledge, his judgment, his instincts, his study of opposite numbers. The chances of a separate Russo-German peace were so small, and the Anglo-American cards were so strong (Lend-Lease, growing military power, etcetera) that the least one can say is that Roosevelt and Churchill did not have to surrender as abjectly to Stalin as they did in Teheran and Yalta. There was even less reason for the surrender at Potsdam in August, 1945, when Germany had fallen and Japan was about to reel under two American atomic bombs. The American and British negotiators displayed less skill than Stalin.

President Roosevelt, Secretary Hull, and Under-Secretary Sumner Welles vehemently opposed Russia's annexation of the Baltic countries. Roosevelt objected to Stalin's wartime Polish solution. Yet at Teheran and Yalta, Roosevelt and Churchill acceded to Stalin's wishes. They obviously acted under a powerful compulsion: it was the desire to placate Stalin lest he sign a separate peace.

As a result, the decisions of the wartime peace conferences—and today's peace stems from them—were based not on justice or what was considered best for a happy postwar world, but rather on a hurried, emergency give-and-take in which the Western powers gave more than they took and the Bolsheviks took. Nobody asked: Is this good? They asked: Is this unavoidable?

Stalin's plans, as always, followed a simple recurring pattern: the annexation of eastern Poland would give Russia a common frontier with Czechoslovakia. The annexation of the Baltic states and East Prussia would give Russia a common frontier with Germany. The annexation of Carpatho-Russ (Ruthenia) would give Russia a common frontier with Hungary. The annexation of Iranian Azerbaijan or its absorption under a disguise would lengthen Russia's common frontier with Turkey.

Before the second world war, the Soviet Union did not have a common frontier with Czechoslovakia, or Germany, or Hungary, or Norway. Now she has and she therefore has more influence over them.

Russian occupation of half of Germany, Austria, and Hungary

was calculated to enhance Soviet power throughout all of Europe. Russian occupation of Rumania, Bulgaria, and the supremacy of Comrade Tito in Yugoslavia threw the shadow of Russia over Italy, Greece, Turkey, and the Mediterranean.

Nor did Moscow neglect China, and other Asiatic countries.

Just as Britain's position in India is linked with events in Indonesia, Palestine, Greece, and Italy, so Russia's motives in Finland are clarified by Russia's acts in Iran; the Curzon Line runs to Berlin; Rumania is a station on the road to the Dardanelles.

Stalin dreamt of a big Russian empire that would fill out the vacuum created by the disappearance of German and Japanese power and by the postwar weakness of France and England.

In the Stalinist era, Soviet propaganda has exalted Ivan the Terrible, Peter the Great, Catherine the Great, and any Tsar or general who, whatever his despotic sins and cruel crimes against the Russian people, helped extend the territory of the realm. They are specifically exalted in Soviet publications for this reason. Stalin is in the old Russian tradition.

Soviet Russia thus became the central problem of wartime and peacetime peacemaking. To deny or to ignore this circumstance is to lose the key to world events.

During the war, Moscow was ready to recognize British and American imperialism in order thus to facilitate Russian imperialism. Moscow wanted a three-way sharing of the spoils of war and a three-way partition of the world. In the circumstances, foreign Communists grew tolerant of imperialism; in fact, after Teheran they said there was no imperialism. After the war, however, Russian imperialism took a more hostile attitude towards England and America.

Before adopting a single decision the Big Three conferences at Teheran and Yalta established a decisive principle: that three men, speaking for three powers, could determine the fate of weak Allied countries like Poland which were not even present. More than twenty nations fought the Axis. Three shaped the peace. This is United Nations arithmetic. Try as they did, rebel as they did, the governments of the smaller states were unable to liberate the postwar process of peacemaking from the Big Three's wartime grip.

The Big Three contributed most to victory. That gives them no monopoly of wisdom or decency. But a monopoly of decision gives free rein to their selfishness and unlimited scope to crude power bargains. Priority to the strong is a denial of democracy and justice. In every democracy the problem is to check the power of the few with the votes of the many, to balance the diffuse political might of the electorate against concentrated economic might. The Big Three, however, permitted the numerous little ones nothing more than "consultation" and "discussion." Among the Three, moreover, one could veto two. One, therefore, could dictate to the world. This is the ultimate in nationalism and the minimum in internationalism.

The only escape from the iron rule of the Big Three is in world government with Big Three approval. That suggests the obstacles facing world government. But the issue never arose at Teheran and Yalta or Potsdam.

The second world war was not a war about a map. It was a war caused by the disease of our civilization. Back in 1943, in a little book entitled *Empire*, I wrote: "This war will either bring a new world or it will bring a new world war." The peacemakers should have sat as a concilium to diagnose the disease and prescribe a cure. But they had no time. Modern statesmen go so fast they frequently cannot stop to think where they are going. Roosevelt, Churchill, and Stalin were the three busiest men in the world and met together for five days to decide quickly the future of two billion human beings. Their first business was to win the war. With that in view they plotted military moves and with that in view they made the peace. The peace made at Teheran, Yalta, and Potsdam was not a peace to prevent a third world war; it was a peace to help win the second world war. It was a peace to keep the warmaking coalitionists happy. It was as much a military measure as allocating Lend-Lease to Russia or planning the invasion of France.

On August 14, 1941, Roosevelt and Churchill had enunciated, and on January 1, 1942, the Soviet government had signed the Atlantic Charter. No ideal octolog, the Charter might nevertheless have served as the base of a solid peace. At Teheran it became a scrap of paper. At Yalta, they burned the paper.

The first of the eight points of the Atlantic Charter states: "Their countries seek no aggrandizement, territorial or other." Point Two says: "They desire to see no territorial changes that do not accord with the freely expressed wishes of the peoples concerned."

Both these provisions were flagrantly violated by the decisions on Poland and Germany which Roosevelt, Churchill, and Stalin took at Teheran and Yalta. By undermining their own words they commenced to undermine the peace.

After the Soviet Union originally seized eastern Poland in 1939, it conducted a "plebiscite" there and of course over ninety per cent of the voters, after more than a million had been deported to Siberia and Turkestan, voted for Russia. The Soviet Congress of November 18, 1918, in the days of idealism, resolved that when any country is occupied by another and "if this nation is not accorded the right to decide the form of its existence as a state without any pressure, through a free vote while the armed forces of the affiliating state, or a stronger state, are removed completely, then such affiliation is an annexation; it is foreign rule and a crime."

Out of the mouths of a Soviet congress which met in the spirit of Lenin, Stalin's seizure of eastern Poland is condemned as a crime.

Karl Marx, who wrote authoritatively on European political problems, said in the *Neue Rheinische Zeitung* of August 19, 1848: "The creation of a democratic Poland is the first condition for the establishment of a democratic Germany. . . . It is not a question, however, of building a Poland independent on paper only, but of the building of a state on a lasting foundation, capable of genuine existence. Poland must regain at least the territory which was hers in 1772." That is more than Poland had in 1939. Do they read Marx in the Kremlin?

Russia annexed eastern Poland by agreement with Hitler in September, 1939. But on July 30, 1941, Russia and Poland signed a treaty in London whereby "the Government of the Union of Soviet Socialist Republics recognizes the Soviet-German treaties of 1939 as to territorial changes in Poland as having lost their validity." That annulled Stalin's territorial grab by the grace of Hitler. It annulled the "plebiscite" in the presence of the Red Army. It gave the territory back to Poland.

Yet at Teheran in December, 1943, after Russia had signed the Atlantic Charter, and before the Soviets had reconquered eastern Poland from Germany, Roosevelt and Churchill gave it to Russia; this was aggrandizement. They did it without consulting the population. They only consulted Stalin. Important as the fate of Poland is, this action is much more important than Poland. It established the vicious, pernicious principle that principles do not count when the Big Three get together.

After the fact, of course, all the huge propaganda machines of governments and Communist parties and naive fellow-travelers of the Communists were rolled into position and began a deafening barrage to show that Russia's seizure of Polish soil as far west as the Curzon Line was justified. It is one of the tragedies of our age that this loud noise did convince or at least confound many people in democratic countries.

The propagandists say: Poland up to the Curzon Line formerly belonged to Russia. This is not true. Eastern Galicia, a large part and the richest part of the claimed region, never belonged to Tsarist Russia.

Only a portion of the region was Tsarist. How did the Tsars get it? Lenin, founder of the Bolshevik regime, is a good witness. In *War and Revolution*, published in May, 1907, Lenin wrote about the partitioning of Poland and Courland, a province of Latvia, by Tsarist Russia, imperial Germany, and the Austro-Hungarian monarchy. "Courland and Poland," he said, "were partitioned together by the three crowned brigands. They partitioned them for a hundred years. They tore their living flesh. And the Russian brigand tore away most because he was then the strongest."

The Bolshevik Stalin bases his claim on a brigand Tsar's theft. What else could one expect after Stalinism had turned to Tsarism for inspiration?

Here is another condemnation of Stalin by Lenin: to a party conference on April 29, 1917, Lenin said: "At one time, Alexander the First and Napoleon bartered with Poland. At one time, the Tsars bartered Poland. Are we to continue the tactics of the Tsars? That would be a rejection of internationalism. That is chauvinism of the worst kind." It is Stalin's chauvinism.

The notion that a country is entitled to territory which it once owned is preposterous; it would make the world an insane asylum. England would take Virginia, Boston, and a part of France; Rome would take London; the Dutch would take New York; the French would take New Orleans; the Turks would take Egypt, Palestine, Soviet Ukraine, Bulgaria, and Rumania; Sweden would take a big chunk of Russia; Spain would take California; Italy would take Spain; Japan would take China and Indo-China; China would take Indo-China; Iran would take a piece of India; Greece would take the same piece of India; and so on endlessly into anarchy.

The propagandists say: Russia was weak in 1920 and therefore had to surrender this territory to Poland. That is not true. Again Lenin, then head of the Soviet government and always a merciless analyst of his own acts, is the best witness. He declared in Moscow, on November 20, 1920: "Especially great is the victory won by the Red Army, despite the setback at Warsaw, because it put Poland in a position where it had no strength at all to continue the war. The general condition of Poland had become so unstable that there could have been no question of her continuing the war." This statement is accurate history. So it was not a matter of a strong Poland wresting the area from a weak Russia. Lenin, in fact, willingly gave Poland more territory than she asked in the 1921 peace negotiations because he had no desire to bring the inhabitants of the Curzon Line region into Soviet Russia. Many of them were Roman Catholics and he did not want to have a Roman Catholic problem on his hands. He sought and obtained a religious frontier between Russia and Poland.

Suppose it were true that Russia was then weak and had to cede the territory to Poland. The cession might nevertheless have been an act of justice. There can never be any justice or stability in the world if a country which has lost territory when weak seeks to regain it immediately it becomes strong. What about Germany, Japan, and Italy in the years to come?

The propagandists say: The majority of inhabitants in the disputed Curzon zone are Russians or White Russians or Ukrainians. The majority of the inhabitants of Austria and the Sudetenland were German. Did we therefore applaud Hitler's annexations? Nothing justifies forceful annexation. If the majority are Russians why should Moscow not have waited for a free election conducted under international supervision after the withdrawal of the Red Army and the GPU?

The propagandists say: Eastern Poland will be better off under the Russian government than under the former rotten Polish regime. Who knows that? Who is to decide? Isn't there a new regime in Warsaw which is friendly to Moscow and, according to the same propagandists, quite an improvement on its predecessors? Why not let it rule eastern Poland?

The excuse that Poland or the Baltic countries or the Balkan nations will benefit from Russian domination or absorption is the habitual arrogance of imperialism. It is the counterpart of the British argument about "the white man's burden" in India and of Mussolini's argument that he went into Abyssinia to rid it of slavery. Hitler also contended that he would give Poland a better life. The annexation of all or some of the Latin American republics by the United States would raise their living standards, their health conditions, their education, their communications, and their political status. Should the United States therefore annex them?

All the specious excuses which the Soviet government and its foreign apologists have made for Russia's actions in Finland, Esthonia, Latvia, Lithuania, Poland, Rumania, Iran, and Turkey since 1939, were answered in advance in a Convention for the Definition of Aggression which Soviet Foreign Commissar Maxim Litvinov, the Last of the Bolshevik Mohicans, induced Afghanistan, Finland, Esthonia, Latvia, Lithuania, Iran, Poland, Rumania, Yugoslavia, Czechoslovakia, and Turkey to sign with the Soviet Union in 1933. It says: "No consideration of a political, military, economic, or any other nature, can serve as an excuse or justification of aggression." The reason is that aggression and expansion by one power create suspicion in and friction with other powers who sooner or later take countermeasures which may lead, and often have led, to wars. That is the way World War Two started.

Yet in the midst of the war that resulted from the aggressions of Hitler, Mussolini, and Hirohito, Roosevelt and Churchill at Teheran and Yalta sanctioned new aggressions by Russia.

Lenin said to a conference on December 22, 1920: "You know that a final peace has been signed with a series of countries on the western border of Russia, countries which were formerly parts of the Russian Empire and which, in accordance with the basic principles of our policy, have received from the Soviet government the unconditional recognition of their independence and their sovereignty."

The Kremlin discarded the "basic principles" of Soviet policy when it robbed that series of countries of their independence and sovereignty. I wrote a two-volume book on Soviet foreign policy, *The Soviets in World Affairs*, which was published in 1930. For years I was in constant contact with the makers of Soviet foreign policy. I studied all pertinent Soviet documents and publications. From 1920 to 1939, no Soviet spokesman and no Soviet publication ever complained about or criticized Russia's frontier with Finland or Poland or inveighed against the independence of the Baltic nations. Moscow recognized all those countries and maintained diplomatic and commercial relations with them. If the boundaries had given the Bolsheviks displeasure they could have complained as they did in the case of Bessarabia which Rumania grabbed in 1919. The Soviet government never accepted the loss of Bessarabia, and Soviet maps showed Bessarabia in stripes connoting that while Rumania ruled the province it belonged, by right, to Russia. But the Soviets took no such position towards Polish possession of the Curzon Line zone or to any part of Finland or to the Baltic states. It laid claim to them only when it had the might to seize them. Thereupon all the political lackeys began to concoct the excuses necessary to mislead soft democratic brains. And how successful they have been! The world is in its present mess not solely because of evil-doers but because so many good people are ready to appease and apologize for the evil-doers.

In an attack on Nazi aggression, which applies to Bolshevik aggression as well, Michael Kalinin, President of the Soviet Union, recalled these words of Frederick II of Prussia: "If you like a foreign province and you have enough force, take it immediately. As soon as you have done that you will always find enough lawyers who will prove that you were entitled to the occupied territory." And not only lawyers.

Most persons try to judge Soviet policy by the forms it assumes in Iran or Poland, and American policy by its expression in China and all other countries. A much better perspective of foreign policy is obtained by viewing it where it originates, at home. Then it is possible to assess the interplay of personalities, economic pressures, political interests, and, in democracies, the party struggles which together shape policy. Thus the American government's embargo on the shipment of arms to Loyalist Spain had little to do with the issues in Spain; President Roosevelt was pro-Loyalist and desired the defeat of Franco. The arms embargo was the product of Catholic pressure, British pressure, and the Administration's fear of irritating the voters who held isolationist "neutrality" opinions. Such cases are legion.

Tracing Soviet motives in Poland to their source one arrives at the spot where all the secrets of Soviet foreign policy are hidden. In annexing eastern Poland with several million Ukrainians, Moscow hoped to reinforce the loyalty of the Soviet Ukrainians. It hoped to please Russian nationalists who wanted their country to regain its Tsarist frontiers and more besides. During the war, the Kremlin stressed not the social, political, and economic achievements of the Revolution but the fact that it had saved Russia. For instance, A. S. Scherbakov, member of the supreme Politbureau, declared at a Lenin memorial meeting on January 21, 1944, that Tsarist Russia "was moving on a road which would inevitably have led it to the loss of national independence. From such shame our country was saved by the Bolshevik party." The Communists were apparently arguing with Russian nationalists who had to be given good reasons for supporting the Soviet regime. The annexation of foreign territory is the most convincing argument for a nationalist.

The Bolsheviks were always conscious of Germany's pivotal position in European affairs. To achieve maximum influence over the fate of Germany Stalin planned the following: the annexation by Russia of half of Poland in the east; compensation to Poland in the form of large blocks of German territory—Upper Silesia, Pomerania, and part of East Prussia—comprising about a fifth of prewar Germany; the domination of Poland by Russia; the annexation by Russia of a large section of East Prussia including the city of Koenigsberg; the assignment to Russia of the bulk of German reparations; the post-victory occupation of half of Germany by the Red Army (while America, England, and France would occupy the remaining half); the conquest of Berlin by Russian troops—this for prestige.

Roosevelt and Churchill gave Stalin all these things at Teheran and Yalta.

Poland's loss of Polish territory east of the Curzon Line weakened Poland. Annexation of tremendous stretches of German territory, rich in industries, saddled Poland with technical, economic, political, and military problems which she could not solve without Russian aid. These factors, plus the necessary presence of the Red Army in Poland in the course of defeating Germany, enabled Stalin to make Poland a Russian puppet state. Poland has a long frontier with Germany. Russian control of Poland is a prerequisite to Russian control of Germany. Stalin's Polish policy is part of his German policy. His German policy is part of his European policy. Who controls Germany controls Europe.

In Asia, the Yalta Conference gave Russia the southern part of Sakhalin Island and the Kurile Islands north of Japan, and control of Manchuria's railways and two Manchurian ports. Stalin had this put in writing and had it signed by Roosevelt and Churchill. It was his price for the promise to fight Japan. That is how Stalin does business with the democracies.

Neither the United States nor Great Britain was awarded any territory in Europe or Asia at the wartime peace conferences. This is not a complaint; on the contrary, it is a statement of fact. It was assumed, however, that Russia and England would have their spheres of influence in Europe. Russia and America would have their spheres in Asia. England kept her empire in Asia.

This is the peace as the Big Three handed it down. They sanctioned annexations. Then they talked principles. They sanctioned spheres of influence. Then, on that shaky foundation, they started to establish a most imperfect union, the United Nations.

President Woodrow Wilson hoped the League of Nations would correct the evils of the Paris peace treaties which ended World War One. President Franklin Roosevelt trusted in the United Nations.

In 1944, at Dumbarton Oaks, American, British, Russian, and Chinese delegates drafted most of what later came to be known as the San Francisco Charter. But they could not agree on one subject: the veto.

The decision was therefore left to the Big Three at Yalta. The Roosevelt-Churchill-Stalin ruling now stands as the essential feature of the Charter. The ruling makes the UN an ineffective instrument for preventing aggression and maintaining peace.

In the UN, the Assembly, where all member-nations are represented, cannot take any action against an aggressor. Only the Security Council of eleven member-nations can commit the UN to act against a peace-breaker. And in that council, according to the Yalta ruling and according to the corresponding text of the San Francisco Charter, any one of the Big Five—the United States, the Soviet Union, Britain, France, or China—can block action against the aggressor even if it is the aggressor. This is what is meant by the Big Power veto.

So how can the UN be effective in preventing aggression and war?

Stalin insisted on the veto at Yalta; Soviet statesmen continue to defend it against critics. Roosevelt felt that without the veto the San Francisco Charter might have been defeated in the U. S. Senate by a group of conservative nationalists. China opposed the veto publicly. The British were lukewarm to it.

Prime Minister Peter Fraser of New Zealand calls the veto "a blot on the Charter." A very big, black blot.

Under the veto, one nation can kill an amendment to the UN Charter.

That is the peace made in war.

Russia lost the first world war, and, because the then victorious Allies disliked the Bolsheviks, she was excluded from the peace conferences. The peace of 1919 was at the expense of Germany, Bulgaria, Turkey, and, chiefly, the Austro-Hungarian Empire. Now, Russia has not merely won World War Two. She has also won World War One, for she today controls what was the Austro-Hungarian Empire, Bulgaria, and half of Germany—but not Turkey.

Great Britain won the first world war militarily and politically. Her rival Germany was defeated; Russia was sunk in revolution; Turkey was shorn; Japan and America did not yet challenge her predominance; her economic might was undiminished. Great Britain won the second world war too, but not politically. She is being pushed around by Russia; her finances are low; her cities and industries need rebuilding; her Empire is going. The war exertion left her too weak to save her supremacy against Russia and America.

America won both wars. America fought the first world war to prevent the victory of Germany over England and France. The purpose achieved, America went home. It wanted no dividends, no responsibilities, no headaches, no dislocation of a pleasant life. America fought the second world war to prevent the victory of Germany over England and France and of Japan over all China. The purpose achieved, America could not go home.

Part Three

Double Rejection

20. *Double Rejection*

WHEN I talked with Englishmen in India and criticized British imperialism, they said: "But what about the treatment Americans mete out to Negroes?"

"I attack British imperialism," I replied, "and I attack the anti-Negro discrimination of American whites as well."

I am a double rejector.

I loathe Polish landlords, and I loathe Polish puppets. I object to atrocities by Germans, and I object to atrocities against Germans. I object to atrocities.

If you reject one evil and accept an equal and opposite evil you surrender principle and abandon the fight for what is good. The lesser evil may be a very great evil. It is better to accept neither evil and, instead, champion a third alternative which improves mankind.

The doctrine of the lesser evil threatens our whole culture; it also influences practical politics.

Churchill assails Russian expansion and advocates an Anglo-American alliance. Stalin assails Churchill. But Nehru preaches world order and Indian freedom within that framework. As between Churchill and Stalin I prefer neither; I prefer Nehru.

One person condemns Russian acts in Rumania, Poland, and Iran. "Yes," says the defender of Russia, "but what about the British in India and Indonesia?"

I reject both Russian and British imperialism.

"What is wrong about Russia wanting the Kurile Islands and Port Arthur?" runs another typical conversation. "Aren't Americans annexing Okinawa and other Pacific islands?"

Both are bad. Both are foolish. There is no defense in islands or bases or territory.

Either imperialism is a fine thing or an ugly thing. If it is fine for England it is fine for Russia, America, France, and Holland. If it is ugly, then even your own nation's imperialism is ugly. When you inveigh against the shortcomings of a country you dislike and praise the same shortcomings in a country you favor you are acting like a bigot and a nationalistic jingo.

Kendall Foss, in the *New York Post*, quotes an old lady he met in Berlin. "The Russians are not human," she said. "They have no regard for life or property. They seize our people on the street and the victims are never heard of again. Opposite my sister's house in the Russian sector their police have built a prison. She sees well-dressed men and women dragged through the doors and at night she can hear their screams. Somebody should put a stop to such Asiatic lawlessness."

"I mentioned," Mr. Foss continues, speaking for himself, "that there was a certain precedent here for stuff like that."

What will become of the world if one horror becomes a precedent for another?

Secretary of State Byrnes went to the unsuccessful conference of the Big Three in London in September, 1945, and demanded free elections for Rumania and Bulgaria. Whereupon some critics said: "What business has he insisting on free elections in the Balkans when there are no free elections in his native state of South Carolina?"

I do not mind Byrnes' demanding free elections in Rumania and Bulgaria. It makes it easier to demand free elections in South Carolina.

Catholics make Stalin their daily target. But when Moscow criticizes the politics of the Pope they take offense. Communists condemn Chiang Kai-shek for limiting freedom in China. But it does not matter to them that the Soviet government suppresses it completely in Russia.

Our civilization is menaced by cynicism and the abandonment of principle. There has never been a perfect government. My country may be wrong though it is my country. If my government were totalitarian I would try to overthrow it.

I have the same abhorrence of a sin committed by my country as I have of that sin when it is committed by another country. The doctrine of double rejection requires one to think objectively and to judge objectively.

Some have religious feelings about their native country. Some have religious feelings about a foreign country. When they allow those feelings to affect their estimate of world events they sacrifice truth. They mislead themselves. They are thinking and judging nationalistically.

Political thinking is today at a low ebb because men and women are ruled by religious, nationalistic, racial, and party prejudices instead of by a desire for a clear picture of the situation. Having seen how mistaken I can be on occasions, and especially when passion obstructs vision, I have decided to be completely ruthless and merciless with myself. The analyst and observer must have no gods. He does himself a disservice if he has.

This attitude stimulates the will to act. An awareness of pervading evil stimulates a burning desire in me to fight it. Double rejection releases energy for action because it shows how desperately necessary it is to do something which will lift humanity out of its present crisis. Pessimism based on correct appraisal of events is creative. It stirs one to challenge and to act. Optimism about international events in the 1930's was one of the causes of the second world war. The public lulled itself into the illusion that conditions were not as bad as they were painted, that things would work themselves out, that Hitler would settle down and behave. Pessimism and even panic then might have prevented the second world war. Now too a sober view—the double rejection view—would focus attention on the dangers that surround us.

Most persons are, probably without being conscious of it, afraid to engage in double rejection. That might take the floor from under their feet and leave them only principle to stand on. And how many people feel comfortable standing on principle?

One reason why certain Americans idealize Russia is because they must have a heaven. They reject the American system on account of its transgressions. They accordingly grasp an alternative, Russia. If they were told that Russia too is a transgressor they would be unhappy. They would lose their moral crutch.

Acceptance of a far-off heaven which you do not know, or acceptance of a situation near at hand because you know no other, reveals weakness. I reject the evil in Bolshevism. I reject the evil in capitalism. I seek something which is better than either.

Double rejection, therefore, is obviously not negative. It is an affirmative philosophy which exalts change away from the past; it wants progress towards a brighter future.

Those who launch out into uncharted areas may discover a new continent or open up a new world. There is need of a new world. Where is that new world? Where the better future? Neither is easily discernible. It will not come from conformers but from reformers, from protesters with programs, from iconoclasts with ideas, from brave men who walk the straight, narrow path and risk inviting shots from both sides because they have rejected both.

21. *The Crisis*

THERE is a rebel in each of us. Whether the rebellion lasts a night, a day, a year, a decade, or a lifetime, whether it ends with adolescence or begins when old age threatens, whether it is a revolt against the tedium of a job or the boredom of philistine existence or the lie in life or against sobriety or poverty or authority or wealth or sex restrictions or a family or a mother or a father—there is a rebel in each of us.

The maladjusted millionaire sits on his yacht mapping the Communist Eden. The impecunious Negro, without hope, seeks solace in the ecstasy of religious rites; if hope appears, he seeks Zion in Africa or heaven in Russia. British poets of the kind that flirted with Communism in the nineteen-twenties and -thirties now embrace the Catholic church. Another group tries to escape from life into Yoga and Oriental mysticism. Ernst Toller, a gifted, anti-Nazi German Communist poet committed suicide in 1939; Russia had let him down and Spain had fallen. Heywood Broun, a gifted columnist, accepted Communism, then rejected it, and subsequently accepted Catholicism. Louis Budenz, managing editor of the Communist *Daily Worker*, turned Catholic. After Hitler took power, "a large portion of the Communist party, perhaps about one-third, became active Nazis," Saul K. Padover, an Army psychological warfare officer in Germany, reported to the *Herald Tribune* forum in 1945. Doriot, the French Fascist leader, used to be a high official of the Communist International. Laval, the Nazi friend, was once a Communist. A radio commentator speaks for Mussolini in Italy and later speaks for Russia in the United States.

Communism, Catholicism, and to a lesser extent Fascism, offers its own different but complete answer to all doubts about the universe. Anybody psychologically inclined to accept one of these answers may try another if the first dissatisfies.

A Midas son, a Negro, a Jew, a Fascist goes Communist; a Communist kills himself, or goes Catholic, or goes Nazi. It is all a revolt against life as they live it. They reject life as is. They are rebels who go away.

266

In pre-Hitler Germany, young Jews went Zionist, then went Communist, and often drifted back to Zionism again. They were rejecting Germany.

In America, England, and France t're are more persons who were in the Communist party than are in it. They sought an alternative, did not find it, and departed to look for another. Most people need a spiritual home; they want to belong. If they cannot belong fully to their present world they go in search of another world.

This is an age of spiritual insecurity which makes for totalitarianism.

The Communist believes in the infallibility of Stalin and the Communist government of Russia. He has a dogma (Marx), a church (the Party), and is sustained by a faith in the Socialist hereafter on earth. Communism and Catholicism are worlds apart, but temperamentally the Communist takes only a short step when he enters the Roman fold.

The most energetic political rebels of our day have been the Communists and Fascists. The Communist rejects the capitalist world. He accepts Russia which he regards as the enemy of that which he rejects. He does not believe in reforming capitalism. He is a revolutionist. (I am an impatient evolutionist.) He desires a complete change. He sees Russia as the most effective instrument of that change. He fights in this world to get power for himself and Russia to make the change. The Communist party is not an agent of reform; it is an agent of power.

The most essential feature of Communism and Fascism has been the transfer of power from all classes, parties, and persons who possess it to the state which then becomes all-powerful, so powerful that the individual is powerless to rebel. The end of rebellion is the impossibility of rebellion.

In the Soviet Union, men and women join the Communist party for a variety of practical, material reasons, and from tradition, and conviction. Outside Russia, the vast majority of Communists are idealistic rebels. They want a better world. The Communist party is dynamic; it has zeal; it demands sacrifice and devotion, secrecy and discipline. That appeals to a certain type of human being. In the bosom of the Party, Communists find comradeship and work, and balm for their conscience if their conscience troubles them—if, for instance, they are high-salaried Hollywood writers, or heirs to unearned fortunes. Some join because they are lonely, or thwarted, or eager for action, or full of resentment towards society. Party membership means friends, parties to go to, work, and an outlet for energy.

The average Communist is a cleaner, more decent individual than the average Fascist. Fascism attracted and attracts the criminal element, those ejected from society and embittered by it, adventurers who love violence for its own sake, ambitious leaders ready to accept support from the underworld and the upper class, men with passion, men with hate, men without scruples, men without the milk of human kindness, men who rebel by killing, men who revel in death.

Frustration builds passion, and unloosed passion has no principles. Fanaticism destroys repose. Nerves and blood put the brain out of action. The intellect becomes subservient to emotion. Thought is submerged by faith. The end hallows any means. A principle becomes an irritating abstraction, for loyalty to principle precludes opportunistic zigzagging and flip-flops this way and that.

Every democracy is being bombarded with totalitarian germs. The intensity of the barrage has precipitated a world cultural crisis.

A small instance recently came my way. A British publisher printed my book, *Empire*, in September, 1945, and introduced a number of changes in the text. Publishers, especially British publishers, have a high reputation for scrupulousness in this regard. They consult and ask permission. I was not consulted. . . . In one place, I wrote that though Gandhi may not be known throughout India, this was "no warrant for any broad conclusion about India's readiness for independence. Probably not one Russian in a hundred had ever heard of Lenin or Trotzky when the Soviet government was established." The British edition deleted "or Trotzky." In another place, I said: "I do not think in nationalistic terms. I was not pro-Spanish; I was pro-Loyalist and anti-Franco although he was a Spaniard. I am not anti-Russian; I am anti-Stalin. I criticize not Britain but the British policy of holding India in bondage." The words "I am not anti-Russian; I am anti-Stalin" were cut out. Further on, I wrote: ". . . since I arrived in India, almost every fifth person has told me that he has been in jail. Now I have lived for years in Russia and Germany. In those countries one rarely meets anybody who has been in jail; they are in jail. . . ." That was changed to: "Now I have lived for years in Germany. In that country . . ." Finally, I said: "That is why Churchill's 'Hold our own' policy, Stalin's desire to restore Russia's pre-1917 frontiers as well as some of her pre-1917 ideas, and America's support of European reactionaries do not conduce to the new world in which alone there can be peace." The references to Stalin and Russia do not appear in the British edition.

These deletions and distortions were, obviously, made by a Communist or pro-Communist. To him it is all right to criticize British policy and American policy, but Stalin and his policy are touch-me-nots.

This is a minor illustration of a major phenomenon in our civilization. It is new and growing and frightening. It is part of the strategy of totalitarian falsification which manifested itself in the Moscow trials, and manifests itself every day in Soviet publications, in Communist periodicals abroad, and in all Communist arguments. If a Communist is ready to suppress a few unpalatable though quite harmless words of an author why should he respect facts or be honest or have any scruples about the things he himself says and writes? Communists, like all totalitarians, do not respect truth.

Mrs. Eleanor Roosevelt wrote in her column on June 22, 1945: "What I object to in the American Communists is not their open membership nor even their published objectives. For years in this country they taught the philosophy of the lie. They taught that allegiance to the Party and acceptance of orders from Party leaders whose interests were not just those of the United States were paramount. . . . Because I have experienced the deception of the American Communists I will not trust them. . . ."

If you cannot trust them you cannot work with them.

Falsification is a Communist philosophy. Communists mock the very idea of respect for truth. The written and spoken word is for them a weapon to achieve a concrete purpose—usually power—and they bend it to that purpose. They believe in the little lie as well as the big lie, in character-assassination, in smear.

This is the age of smear. Lacking honest argument, the totalitarians sling mud. The smear is a generalization of the pauper mind: "Reactionary," "Trotzkyist," "Fascist." The smear is an emotional short-cut to an unproved conclusion.

The abuse and misuse of words is one of the most widespread diseases of our time. Joseph Goebbels called the Western nations "pluto-capitalistic-Jewish democracies," a cocktail of political cusswords. The Communists called the German Social Democrats "Social Fascists" one year and the next year they invited them to join their United Front. Today, in the mouth of a Communist, everything that is Communist is "democratic" and "anti-Fascist," and everything that is democratic and liberal and therefore anti-Communist is "reactionary." The Tories do exactly the same thing when they call everybody they dislike a "Communist."

These crooked words will be the chains that enslave democracy unless we wake up to the menace. Words are the feet on which ideas move, and ideas move the world, either the right way or the wrong way.

The absence of integrity in Communists and their disregard of truth is a fundamental reason for their opposition to democracy. Since words and ideas must work for an end, how can they be free? How can expression remain free when it must conform to a political pattern?

Yet writers, speakers, and artists, for whom freedom ought to be the breath of life, take their cue from Communists. No Communist party, no trade union or national organization of trade unions, and no citizens' committee or association or magazine in which Communists play an important role would ever tell the truth about Russia, would ever be critical of Russia. They condemn England, France, America, anybody, with gusto. They never criticize Russia. This is plain lying. Nevertheless, Communist-front groups attract many people of the word.

They are variously motivated. Some like to have the backing of bigger battalions than they would otherwise get. Some like to bask in the reflected glamor of stars who join because other stars joined who were told that their lives would be empty and worthless unless they helped a cause. Some like the motion, commotion, activity, and bustling of dinners, petitions, conferences, etcetera.

This is perhaps the key: All about us is evil, and few fight it. A system which has brought freedom and well-being to many millions is threatened with extinction because it has not brought enough freedom and well-being. But the threat does not stir the friends of the system to extend the area of freedom and well-being. It stirs the enemies of the system who would kill all freedom by arousing false hopes of more freedom and more well-being.

In Great Britain, the Communist party is very weak because there is a powerful Labor party. In prewar Austria, the Communists were an insignificant handful because the Social Democrats had a dynamic philosophy and political strength. In pre-1936 Spain, the Communists could get no following because the Socialists and Syndicalists were active and rebellious. In India, the Communists cannot find a large body of adherents because the Gandhi-Nehru Congress party is the standard bearer of the revolt against imperialism.

The British Labor party, the Austrian Socialists, the Spanish Socialists rejected the reactionaries of the Right as well as the totalitarian Communists. Wherever the double rejectors are effective the false rebels who live on falsehood have little chance of success.

The fewer the faults of democracy the weaker the assaults on it will become. The more democracy improves the more it will disprove the strictures of its critics. If democracy abdicates through inaction it cannot blame others for wishing to occupy its place.

Democracy will find dynamic defenders or it will die.

Democracy is challenged by enemies who wish to destroy it. Neither Communists nor Fascists believe in democracy though the Communists always and now the Fascists—those who stole Mussolini's corpse from its grave—call themselves democratic. The Fascists make a direct attack on democracy. The Communists worm themselves into the democratic camp and disrupt it. This weakens the democratic forces and thus fosters Fascism. In several European nations, the advent of Fascism was hastened by Communists. Hitler owed much to the German Communist party. Communist tactics in the American trade union movement diminish its cohesiveness and strength.

An even greater challenge to democracy is the challenge to find within itself the courage, vigor, and vision necessary for its own renewal and re-dedication to high ideals and the happiness of the greatest number. Material suffering or political oppression or racial discrimination anywhere is a limitation of democracy and therefore a danger to democracy.

22. *The Second Aftermath*

WE HAVE seen all this before: small nations overrun by big powers; major nations unable to agree on how to divide the earth among themselves; facade internationalism concealing aggressive nationalism; "defense" as an excuse for predatory imperialism; economic war; financial war; war on rebellious colonials; millions who suffered the tortures of war suffering the tortures of a vengeful peace; the pursuit of power at the expense of justice and people; the helplessness of governments; the helplessness of the public in the face of governments; the readiness of leaders to hide the truth lest the truth drive them from leadership; sick, synthetic official optimism; official trust in luck and drift; widespread collapse of faith in a conscious settlement of problems.

What disturbs is the similarity between the present situation and earlier situations which led to wars.

No honest person can say that the conditions which caused the second world war were removed by the way we fought the war or the way we made the peace. A war is not ended until its purpose is achieved. The second world war is therefore not at an end. The present peace seems peculiar because it is not really peace. The world is still at war.

"The mere conquest of our enemies is not enough," President Roosevelt would have said on April 16, 1945, had he lived.

Hitler, Mussolini, and the Japanese warlords are no more. The wartime German, Italian, and Japanese governments have bitten the dust. These great and necessary achievements, for which so many died and gave their eyes and limbs and health and nerves and tears, would give more comfort if they had become the foundation for a better world. But they have become the opportunity for more national selfishness, territory grabs, high-handed unilateral action, and treaty-breaking.

International relations lack a unifying principle, a moral standard, a common program of action, a common goal, a clear purpose.

Hitler, Mussolini, and the Japanese warlords are no more. But was Fascism defeated? Is totalitarianism dead?

The war lasted over five years. It ruined countries. Yet even to those who live amidst its graves and rubble it is already merely an episode because what followed it is so much like what preceded it.

Where is mankind going? Does anybody in authority know? Is anybody responsible for where it is going? The planets move by cosmic laws which keep them from colliding. Not so nations. They collide periodically. Has postwar diplomacy discovered a law or force that will prevent collisions? It has not. The deadliness of the atomic bomb has apparently taught us little.

The first world war made pacifists of millions. The second world war has made millions of pacifists who advocate militarism. They are pacifists and cynics and militarists; they say: war is waste; war is inevitable; prepare for war.

The war has left one god: power. Big battalions vanquish ideas and morality. Who wins is king though he be a knave. Follow the victor even if he leads you into his prison. Lies, unscrupulous deeds—what do they matter? The goal is power. Communists and Fascists are the chief exponents of this view. "When we get power we will do unto others all the horrors they did unto us"; that is the new ungolden rule. The totalitarians have adopted the *lex talionis*.

"Morals is an indecent word," say the disciples of the god power. "Idealism? In the atomic age? Are you crazy?"

"Gandhi is a dreamer," say the cynic "realists," "Nehru is not of this world. They lack deceit. They say what they think, even about themselves. They believe in the individual."

The totalitarians work for and worship the machine. The machine of power. The power which enslaves and destroys man. The published diaries of Fascist Foreign Minister Ciano show strikingly how little Mussolini cared about human life. Italy was hopelessly short of food, raw materials, and money, but his concern was that Hitler accept more poorly-equipped Italian soldiers to die fighting Russia. He yearned for a share of the "glory." Casualties and cripples were not counted. "Italy," "the nation," was something quite apart from living people. His country verged on collapse, but the Duce schemed to annex another worthless scrap of territory. He wanted a strong Italy full of weak, submissive men. All dictatorships are like that. Totalitarianism desires more power in order to cram more helots into the machine of power.

This is a totalitarian age. It started before 1939. The war did not end it. The war was fought so that arbitrary force, the sole arbiter within dictatorships, would not be the sole arbiter in world affairs. The war destroyed the major Fascist dictatorships. Now arbitrary force is the sole arbiter in world affairs.

Force is always present to give sanction to justice. But force without justice is dictatorship. Force without ideas is nihilism. Force for its own sake is Fascism. The reign of force is the greatest threat to democracy.

If the democracies had been awake to the danger of war in 1936, 1937, even as late as 1938, the second world war might have been prevented. Instead, they were lulled to sleep by lullaby communiqués from "successful" conferences; they were assured that if they did nothing, if they were "neutral" in Manchuria, Abyssinia, and Spain, peace would reign. Then the war came.

Why are the democracies supine in the face of threats to their existence? Why are they given to isolationism, appeasement, and inaction?

Modern democracy is not a movement to achieve something; democracy is a way of life. Democracy is relaxation. The tensions are introduced by personal struggles for a living or for wealth or for other successes.

Modern civilization dulls man's capacity for indignation; perhaps this is a device to protect him from a constant mood of indignation against omnipresent evil. Religion dampens the atmosphere of protest by teaching reliance in the supernatural or by offering balm tomorrow for today's sufferings. Individualism tends to direct each person towards a personal solution.

Dictatorships function in a condition of permanent public mobilization. Totalitarian governments are always summoning their subjects to do. But the normal state of a democracy is collective inaction.

Before democratic society bestirs itself to action it must be goaded by a Pearl Harbor or, as England in September, 1939, by a threat to national existence, or by an economic depression. Truly national acts by the people of a democracy are rare. Usually, it is one section of a democratic community—labor, or a racial minority, or an industry—which desires government action, and before it achieves its purpose it must overcome the opposition, but more frequently the inertia and indifference of the bulk of the democratic community.

The numerous divisions in public opinion and in politics offer democratic governments excuses for doing nothing and sometimes prevent democratic governments from doing anything.

The function of democracy is to protect the majority against a minority, to protect a minority against the majority, and to protect one minority against the other. This conduces to passivity. Democracy means checks and balances. They conduce to passivity.

Democracy tends to break up the community into its smallest units: individuals and families. Democracy thereby demobilizes. Demobilized, it cannot defend itself. Groups like trade unions, cartels, manufacturers' associations, and various lobbies operate to defend or aggrandize themselves. The national community as a whole, the democracy, rarely operates as a unit except through its government whose indecision, temporizing, and procrastination are the result of the balance between one set of forces which pulls in one direction and another, sometimes almost equal, set of forces which pulls in another direction.

The lag between politics and science confirms the dilemma of a free society. Scientists develop the atomic bomb according to the best methods the best brains can devise. But the disposal of the bomb in peacetime is not determined by what the best brains think; the decision is the sum total of innumerable interests, pressures, pulls, fears, lures, hopes. Science would long ago have abolished poverty, empires, and backward regions; but politics perpetuates the obsolete. Politics hesitates to cut off society's vermiform appendices.

It is not necessarily the ablest man who becomes the candidate of his party; it is the best vote-getter. It is not the best idea that always wins but the idea that has the most vociferous support.

Democracy fears a very active, efficient government: it might endanger freedom. Then when great tasks confront a democratic government it is handicapped because it has been inactive and inefficient.

These factors explain the retreat of the appeasing democracies in the face of aggressive dictatorships. They also explain the failure of democracies to solve internal problems.

War opens up latent reserves of democratic determination; danger mobilizes democracies. They can win wars. But demobilization and politics-as-usual are always right around the corner.

The postwar world is full of big, urgent problems; democracy will ignore them at its peril. Speed has made the planet smaller; the war reduced the number of great powers. A crisis in any part of the earth affects many countries and will affect more if a good solution is not quickly applied. Diplomacy is no longer a sideshow in politeness; it is and will be a life-and-death matter, the core of national existence.

Relaxation, aloofness, facile optimism, and dilettantism will lead to a third world war.

Domestic problems have likewise become more pressing. Men and women are demanding a better life. A job is now universally regarded as an indispensable human right. There was full employment in the democracies during the war because there were customers for everything they produced; the customers were Hitler and Hirohito; they had to take what was sent them. Today citizens are insisting on full employment for constructive, peacetime purposes. But private enterprise has nowhere and never provided jobs and security for all. That is why, more and more, the people expect governments to step in and help solve the problems which private business cannot solve.

Private enterprise is losing its sanctified sovereignty. Private enterprise is also a public utility. "We recognize," Sir Clive Baillieu, President of the Federation of British Industries, declared in Manchester on November 30, 1945, "that the control of industry is no longer solely and exclusively a matter for the proprietors." The proprietors' rights are limited by the public's interest. A private owner has no more right to injure the community by the way he runs his factory (through paying low wages or charging exorbitant prices, for instance) than he has to burn a Rembrandt or to make his home a public nuisance. A new concept of human rights has modified the old concept of property rights.

This new concept creates new dangers. When the government, acting as the community's agent, does more it acquires more power and it may, unless watched, acquire power over the community. The history of modern dictatorships is a record of the passage of power from individuals and groups to governments which then become inaccessible to the will of the people. A trend towards dictatorship threatens every democracy.

The dilemma of modern democracy is this: unemployment, insecurity, scarcity, and discrimination are condemnations of democracy and make converts for dictatorship. On the other hand, a do-all government which undertakes to solve economic and social problems may lead to dictatorship.

In a dictatorship there is a job for everybody—at low pay—but no liberty. In the old-style capitalist democracies there was liberty, but also insecurity and scarcity. The problem facing democracy is to achieve economic security and universal prosperity while retaining political freedom. Only if democracy attains this synthesis will it survive in its current struggle with totalitarianism.

Democracy must steer a perilous course between the Scylla of too little government action which leaves problems unsolved, and the Charybdis of too much government action which may bring jobs but banish liberty.

As the richest, strongest capitalist nation, the United States will, for some years, chart a safe mid-channel route between too little and too much government. The least America can afford is what was called the New Deal: overwhelming private enterprise, with a small but growing percentage of government enterprise such as the Tennessee Valley Authority, plus increasing government planning, supervision, and arbitration. More consumers' and producers' cooperatives would add a healthy element. Diehard capitalist resistance to this moderate development will polarize American society and hasten a clash between the extremes.

In Europe, however, the choice is no longer between capitalist democracy and Communist dictatorship. Adolf Hitler, enthroned by German capitalists, Junker landlords, and middle class innocents, and favored by non-German reactionaries as a capitalist bulwark against Communism, killed European capitalism. European capitalism is a humpty-dumpty that cannot be put together again. Europe's alternatives are Socialism with capitalism with democracy, which is social democracy, or Socialism without capitalism and without democracy, which is Bolshevism.

In Asia, Africa, Latin America, and Australia, all undeveloped industrially and agriculturally, governments must likewise play a major part in economic upbuilding. An Indian millionaire manufacturer told me he was a Socialist. A group of Bombay super-capitalists headed by J. R. D. Tata, the steel king of India, has drafted a fifteen year plan of industrial expansion which depends for its success on government enterprise. This is the new trend. Capitalists confess they cannot do the job without socialistic help from the state. Simultaneously, they look to American capitalism for support. The new economy is indeed mixed.

The war smoothed the way toward Socialism. In the first world war, foreign governments got loans in the United States from the banks. In the second world war they got their loans from the United States government through Lend-Lease. Similarly, it was the Federal government, after 1941, which took the lead in planning, financing, and carrying out the expansion of American industry for war purposes. The job of war production was too big to be done without Government aid. As big a job faces the democracies in peace.

Governments are in economic affairs to stay. Winston Churchill, a Conservative, has stated that the world-wide swing towards Socialism is more than a passing phase. "It is definitely a permanent movement," he declared.

Apart from the Soviet Union where capitalism is barred, the question in all countries is no longer: Private Capitalism, To be or not to be? The question is: What percentage of state enterprise and what percentage of private enterprise are required to meet the nation's needs? In other words, how much Socialism will be mixed with private capitalism? What counts is to arrive at the proportion that will guarantee security and plenty without limiting liberty. The fate of democracy depends on the successful outcome of this postwar experiment in symbiosis. The purpose of the experiment is to make man free and happy.

First after the war to enter the social laboratory was Great Britain, most mature of the major political democracies.

Nations seldom get the governments they deserve; Spain, for instance, deserved better than Franco after fighting him, and Hitler and Mussolini, for three years. Yet sometimes, especially in advanced democracies, intuition and commonsense lead a people to adopt a course which is in the national interest. That happened in July, 1945, when the British electorate gave the Labor party a clear mandate to introduce more nationalization into British economic policy and more internationalism into British foreign policy.

Nationalization is necessary to modernize British industry which has grown obsolete. In every British factory I inspected in 1941, the director would say to me after a while "Now let me show you our museum," and it sometimes dated back centuries. England, of course, has many up-to-date plants, particularly in the field of consumers' goods, but capitalism and imperialism have combined to keep British industry generally backward.

Internationalism is necessary in British foreign policy for a simple reason: a nationalistic foreign policy, entailing forceful domination of weaker nations, can have only one, if temporary, attraction: success. It should have no lure for England which, confronted by Russia and, in places, by America, cannot win at the game of power politics,

Old policies are stubborn; they linger on from inertia, habit, tradition, and fear of the new, and they find champions in permanent officials who occasionally carry more weight than elected ministers. But if England can break with her imperialistic, balance-of-power past, and with her capitalistic past, Europe, and later Asia, may look to her for leadership.

It is for this that the British people elected the Labor government to power. British Labor statesmen have indicated that they are aware of the historic opportunity. Time will show whether the ministries located on both sides of Whitehall and on its side street—Downing Street—can take advantage of the opportunity.

Whitehall, the Kremlin, and the Vatican constitute Europe's fateful triangle. Those are the three forces which contend for influence on that hungry, tired, ruined, and bleeding continent, the greatest center of culture despite all the horrors it has experienced.

Whitehall is the symbol of the new British way of life, social democracy; the Kremlin stands for Bolshevism, the Russian way of life. Conservative Catholics, conservative capitalists, royalists, and Fascists oppose both. America's relation to the triangle is crucial.

In the autumn of 1944, Stalin wrote a letter to the Pope about church problems. Stalin proposed friendship between the Kremlin and the Vatican. In fact, he proposed a merger between Russia's Greek Orthodox church and the Roman Catholic church.

Stalin was concerned with Poland. Poland is Russia's bridge to Germany, and Germany is the heart of Europe. Poland is a Roman Catholic country. Stalin knew that he would have trouble in subjugating the Poles. He knew they always had been and still were capable of prolonged resistance to alien rule, even if disguised. Stalin therefore wanted the Pope's assistance. An understanding between Rome and Moscow would facilitate Russia's task in Poland.

Father Orlemanski, a Catholic parish priest of Polish ancestry from Springfield, Massachusetts, announced to the world after visiting Stalin in the Kremlin in 1944, that the Soviet regime meant no harm to the Roman church in Poland. But the Holy Father in the Vatican was less cooperative.

For a long time the Pope did not reply to Stalin's letter. President Roosevelt then took a hand. Edward J. Flynn, the Democratic leader of Bronx county, traveled to Rome, then to the Yalta Conference in

February, 1945, then to Moscow and Leningrad, where he saw much of Stalin, Zhdanov, and other high leaders, then again to Rome. He was sounding out both parties, with a view to a compromise arrangement.

In the end, the Flynn mission failed. The Pope rejected Stalin's offer. Since then, the Soviet press and Soviet agents everywhere have been vehemently anti-Catholic.

The Kremlin and the Vatican are the two great internationals and they are today in a state of ideological and political war. The second world war weakened Catholic political influence in Europe. Italy, a Catholic country, was defeated. Germany, with its large Catholic population, has lost its political status. Catholic Spain and Portugal are Fascist and therefore out of the main political stream. France, formerly a first class power, has sunk to second class. Poland, once a pillar of the Papal political structure, is in the Russian sphere. The Vatican therefore directs its attention increasingly to the Americas. But it has not withdrawn from the fight for power in Europe. Rather it will try to draw the Americas into that fight.

The Tories of the earth are likely to regard the Vatican as their ally against the Kremlin and Whitehall. But in France and Italy, liberal Catholic political groups are conscious of new social ferments; they show signs of adapting themselves to new trends. They may become the allies of Whitehall.

Whitehall and the Kremlin are engaged in an epic struggle. Blows have already been exchanged which are echoing down the corridors of Europe and Asia. This is the decisive battle of the postwar era.

Walter Lippmann, whose articles have applauded spheres of influence and Big Three domination, asserts that since England is a "whale" or sea power and Russia an "elephant" or land power, they can live in peace. But in Asia, England is a great land power. Stalin, moreover, has announced Russia's intention of building a big navy; Russia is moving towards the Atlantic, the Pacific, the Baltic Sea, the Persian Gulf, and the Mediterranean.

The question, therefore, is not whether the "whale" can swim into the "elephant's" jungle. Will the lion lie down with the bear? The lion might be willing. But the bear is full of vim; he is going places. He has no apparent desire to lie down at all and certainly not with old Leo whose mane has grown thin and whose roar is drowned out by cries of pain and protest from his Asiatic subjects.

While writing *The Soviets in World Affairs*, I had many talks with George Chicherin, Soviet Foreign Commissar from 1918 to 1930. Chicherin always manifested a special interest in Iran, Afghanistan, and the East generally. He sent me in 1928 to Professor Snesserev, Tsarist Russia's most outstanding authority on India; I spent many fascinating hours with the old scholar. Chicherin said: "Baku is a finger pointing to Asia." He was Asia-minded and Germany-minded. Consequently, he felt no friendship for England. Chicherin belonged to the Communist party, but he carried on the tradition of the Tsarist foreign office in which he had served.

But Maxim Litvinov, who was Chicherin's assistant before he became his successor, used to tell me that it was far more important for the Soviet government to achieve good relations with Britain than to spoil them by courting the small semi-colonial nations of the Middle East. Litvinov and Chicherin were always at daggers-drawn. Litvinov was dismissed when Stalin reverted to Chicherin's policy. He was dismissed in May, 1939, just at the moment when Russia started on her career of aggrandizement. Litvinov does not believe in the new expansionist Soviet foreign policy; he therefore could not work for it; he is therefore inactive.

In 1936, at the time of the Abyssinian war, I was in Paris and read in a French newspaper that the Abyssinian minister in Paris spoke Russian. This intrigued me and I investigated. I learned that before the Bolshevik revolution, princeling sons of Ethopian *rases* frequently went to Russia at the Tsarist government's invitation to study in the St. Petersburg military academy and to be pages in the Tsar's court. Abyssinia was in the British sphere of influence.

The Abyssinian Christian church is Monophysitic; it believes in the divine, not in the divine and human, nature of Jesus. The Armenian church, which has its headquarters at Echmiadzin, in Russian Armenia, where I several times interviewed the Patriarch, is also Monophysitic, and the Tsarist authorities used the Armenian church to strengthen Russia's position in Abyssinia.

It was Tsarist Russia's policy to be present and irritating whereever the British exercised influence. Today, once more, Russia strives to be present and irritating, and powerful, wherever the British exercise influence.

In 1944, Egypt granted diplomatic recognition to the Soviet government; theretofore the Egyptian reactionaries, self-conscious about their oppression of the hard-working village *fellahin*, had blocked relations with Moscow. In the summer of 1944, accordingly, a Soviet minister arrived in Cairo accompanied by a large corps of secretaries, all of them Moslems. (There are millions of Moslems in the Soviet Union.) Their first official act was to bow before King Farouk and suggest that they would like to participate in his regular Friday morning religious services. Translated out of diplomatic language, that meant: Russia has understanding and sympathy for Egypt.

The Soviets are displaying a renewed interest in Palestine and in the entire Arab world because it is also the world of Great Britain. The Kremlin offers itself to the Arabs, and to other Eastern peoples, as an alternative to the British. Soviet Moslems, Soviet Armenians, and Soviet Greek Orthodox Slavs are busy making friends for Russia in and near the areas of British domination. Their sails are filled with the sentiment of hostility which the colonial nations harbor for British imperialism.

Motives may be open to divergent interpretations. But there is no question that Russian bases in the Dardanelles, Russian penetration into Iran, Russian influence in Greece, Russian control in the Dodecanese Islands, and Russian entrenchment in the North African colony of Tripolitania would undermine the British Empire and cut across England's line of communications to Egypt and India. If Russia needs North Africa for defense then she may also need Uruguay for defense. Then Britain needs the Dardanelles for defense, and the United States needs Poland for defense. Then there is no national defense, and no national security, except in mastery of the whole planet.

I have no objection to the breakup of the British Empire. But if that happens under Russian pressure, the British colonies will fall to Russia and an enlarged Russian empire will confront the United States as the only other power in the world.

It is desirable that the British grant independence to their colonies. With an effective United Nations to protect them, those colonies would gradually develop and cease to be objects of international rivalry. But if the colonies are torn from England as a result of that rivalry they will not become free; they will come within the orbit of Soviet dictatorship. The anti-imperialism of an imperialist power is imperialism.

The countries of central Asia and the Near East will not be passive spectators of the tug-of-war between the British and Russian empires. They will intrigue and take sides and fish in troubled waters. They have started doing it already.

The twentieth century striving of subject peoples for freedom is the new factor in the ancient and now renewed struggle between the Russian and British empires. It is a factor which will operate in Russia's favor unless England lets her Empire go. One way or another, the Asiatic peoples will make desperate efforts to win their liberty. An India increasingly restive and rebellious under the British yoke might invite Russia to help it against Great Britain. But a free India will be hostile to Russia's domination and might look to England or America or an effective world organization for protection against Soviet encroachment.

The appearance in the international arena of an expanding Russia changes every aspect of the problem of Western imperialism. Russia will make herself the champion and leader of the colored colonials.

In his joust with British Foreign Secretary Bevin before the United Nations in London early in 1946, about Indonesia, it did not matter much to Assistant Soviet Foreign Commissar Andrei Vishinsky how the UN voted or what Bevin said or how the British and American newspapers lampooned his performance. What mattered was that throughout Southeast Asia Vishinsky would be hailed as the man who defended downtrodden colonials against the united forces of Western imperialism.

What to do? The peoples of Asia must get freedom so they cease being colonials. Those who need help after that to safeguard their freedom and attain prosperity will rely on an international administration set up by friendly countries.

Every resentful Asiatic is a Russian asset against England and America, and the West generally. The West should abandon imperialism because it is evil, and bad for the moral and material interests of the West. But if the Western powers are too obtuse to understand that then they will act under the impact of the great Russian challenge.

The Soviet government has another tremendous asset in the Communist parties of the world. In May, 1943, Moscow announced that the Third International or Comintern was being dissolved. But there is no proof that the Communist parties which constituted the Comintern have since then acted independently of the Kremlin. No Communist party has ever publicly uttered a word of criticism of the Soviet government or ever indicated the slightest difference of opinion with Moscow. No Communist party has ever failed to support the policies of the Soviet government. A single instance of an independent Communist judgment on Russia would be refreshing and might serve as evidence of a divorce from the Kremlin. There is no such instance.

Sometimes the fact that a Communist party advocates non-Communist programs or ideas is adduced as proof that it is not really Communist and does not take its cue from the Communists in Russia. That is not convincing. Russia is not Communist either except in name. The Chinese Communists may advocate reforms which are moderate and non-Communist. The test is whether they, or other Communist parties, opposed the Soviet government's policy or failed to collaborate with it.

The Soviet government's treaty of April, 1941, with Japan recognized Manchuria as a Japanese puppet state and proclaimed that Russia would be neutral towards Japan. How could any Chinese applaud such an anti-Chinese treaty? But leaders of the Chinese Communist party did exactly that in public. Logically, a real separation from Moscow as a result of the dissolution of the Comintern in 1943 would have brought a change in the Chinese Communist attitude towards Soviet-Japanese relations. But it brought no change because the dissolution was no dissolution.

At the outbreak of the second world war, all Indian parties were opposed to the war. It was more natural for Indians to be anti-war than to be pro-war and therefore, by implication, pro-British. When Russia was attacked the Indian Communist party became pro-war and collaborated with the British government in India. The attachment of the Indian Communists for Moscow was paramount. After the dissolution of the Comintern the Indian Communists remained attached to Russia and remained pro-war.

Italian Communists would normally be hostile to Marshal Badoglio, Mussolini's Chief of Staff. Yet when the Soviet government recognized the Badoglio cabinet the Italian Communists likewise supported him and signified their readiness to enter a government under his leadership. Italian Communists would normally be hostile, as all Italians are, to the surrender of Trieste to Tito's Yugoslavia. But Trieste in Tito's hands would strengthen the Communist dictatorship in Yugoslavia and bring Soviet influence down to the Adriatic. So the Italian Communists immediately sided with Tito against Italy.

Germans generally mourn the cession of German territory. The German Communists object to the cession of the Rhineland and Ruhr. But they applauded the cession of German territory to Russia and Poland.

The Communist parties of the world have shifted policies in strict conformance with changes in Moscow; the identity between Soviet policy and foreign Communist words and acts is too intimate to be in doubt.

Then what was the meaning of the dissolution of the Comintern in 1943? It was part of Russia's retreat from internationalism. It heralded a new role for the Communist parties of the world.

Stalin is the businessman in politics. He, so to speak, keeps a little black book in which he enters profits and losses. When he examined the Comintern's page he found few profit entries in all the years since its inception in 1919. The Chinese Communists had a large army and ruled large territories. But they were never able to alter Chiang Kai-shek's allegiances or his foreign policy. The German Communists had been powerful before 1933 and polled over six million votes. But they could neither prevent the rise of Hitler nor overthrow him. The Communists had developed tremendous activity for Loyalist Spain in England, France, and America. But they could not change the policies of those countries towards Spain. Nowhere had Communists decisively affected government policy.

The reason is obvious and Stalin certainly grasped it. The Communists could stage a big public demonstration; they could capture or destroy an organization; they could publish effective propaganda. But none of those activities ever brought much benefit to the Soviet government because the Communists were operating in the area of protest and the best they could hope for was a successful protest. They were operating in the area of protest where there was no power, and therefore they had no power which they could turn to Russia's use.

By the dissolution of the Comintern, Stalin moved the foreign Communist parties over into the area of power.

Prior to 1943, the only national government outside of Russia which included Communists was the Loyalist government of Spain. Since then, Communist parties—even weak Communist parties—have entered governments whenever they could. They moved into the area of power.

This explains recent Communist activities and gives a preview of the future.

The Italian and French Communist parties can, by resigning, bring the fall of their Governments. As a result of this ever-present threat, neither the Italian nor French government is free to adopt a policy unfavorable to Moscow. France cannot join the Western bloc if the French Communists fight such a step; they do; so does Moscow.

The presence of Communist parties in an increasing number of governments will prevent those governments from saying or doing anything distasteful to the Kremlin. This has much more value to Stalin than protests against capitalism. It is much better for Stalin to have friends inside the council chambers casting votes than outside the building shouting slogans. On occasions, the Communists can do both.

The new post-Comintern Communist party line puts a premium on power and service to Russia's national interests rather than on principle or loyalty to Socialism. The Indian Communists collaborated with British imperialists. The Chinese Communists were ready to collaborate with Chiang Kai-shek whom they had reviled as a Fascist. The Rumanian Communists collaborated with King Michael who had collaborated with Hitler; they collaborated with Rumanian Foreign Minister George Tatarescu, one of Europe's top reactionaries. "Left" and "Red" no longer apply to the Communists; they are Pan-Slavs and upholders of Russian imperialism.

In countries like the United States where the Communists are not numerous or strong enough to get into the President's cabinet, the new Communist line is to acquire maximum influence over members of the Cabinet and over members of Congress, and to burrow into Government departments, the major political parties, capitalist newspapers and radio stations, trade unions, and—during the reign of the deposed Earl Browder—in the National Association of Manufacturers. The older Communist policy of "boring from within" applied with special emphasis to labor and left-of-center groups. But today the object is to gain influence in all institutions that have influence and power.

When this strategy triumphs the least it achieves is a moratorium on criticism of the Soviet government. Organizations in which the Communists carry weight delight in attacking the British government and, of course, their own government. But Moscow is spared; Moscow is the sacred Communist cow.

If the strategy of "burrowing" fails, the American Communist party can always drop a few of its innocent masks and sally forth to slay, or at least sling mud at, the evil Goliath of American capitalism, Russia's worst enemy.

By an ingenious maneuver, accordingly, Stalin has got rid of an embarrassment: officially, the Comintern is dissolved; governments can no longer pin its acts on the Soviet authorities. In addition, the Communist parties are now more useful to Moscow than when they were admittedly connected to Moscow.

The foreign Communist parties are an appreciable asset in furthering Russia's world aims.

The task of the Communist parties of Europe and Asia was at first facilitated by the enormous prestige which the Soviet Union acquired during the war. Russia made the biggest contribution to the defeat of Hitler; Moscow and the Communists minimized and often ignored completely the part played by Great Britain, the United States, China, the smaller nations, and by American Lend-Lease to Russia. Europeans and Asiatics were impressed by Soviet military might; as usual, they attributed virtue to power.

This favorable view of Russia has best stood the test of time in the areas not occupied by Russia.

In America, England, western Europe, Asia, Latin America, and elsewhere, "the truth about Russia" comes in conflicting books, articles, lectures, and broadcasts. But in central and eastern Europe the truth about Russia walked the streets in boots and bought or stole wristwatches. The Europeans were not amused.

Europe saw the poor equipment, the horse-drawn carts, and the ragged clothing of the Red Army. Soviet military units often arrived driving their cattle before them; Europeans spoke of "Asiatic hordes" especially since many Soviet regiments in Europe consisted of Mongols, Azerbaijans, and other Easterners.

No people loves a foreign conqueror, yet it did make a difference that the Red Army, which far outnumbered the American, British, and French armies together, lived off land already impoverished by war, whereas the American Army, for instance, brought its own food and even imported food for Germans and Austrians. Comparing Russians with Americans, British, and French, the residents of eastern and central Europe had to conclude that Russia's standard of living was miserably low.

Moreover, those who encountered the-truth-about-Russia-in-boots remarked the large number of Soviet citizens, and not merely displaced Poles and Balts, who preferred Europe to Russia. The American GI sang one refrain: I Want To Go Home; Englishmen, Frenchmen, even Axis prisoners of war, yearned to get home; but many thousands of Russians, soldiers as well as male and female civilian slaves imported by the Nazis from Soviet territory, asked to be concealed, and used every stratagem to avoid returning to the country which propagandists had painted as "the proletarian paradise." At the Yalta Conference, Stalin asked and Roosevelt and Churchill unfortunately agreed to facilitate the repatriation of such reluctant Soviet citizens. Some were returned forcibly. Some tried to commit suicide as they were being forcibly returned. Something was wrong.

Certain activities of the Red Army men surprised Europe. I can imagine the eager excitement with which European Communists, Socialists, idealists, and plain decent persons awaited the advent of the Red Army. In the working-class districts of Berlin, and of many other cities, red flags were hung from windows and balconies not, as is frequently the case, to obtain immunity, but to express a sincerely friendly emotion for the Bolshevik revolution and for its sons who had liberated them from the Nazis. But the Red Army pillaged and raped in the proletarian districts just as it did in the bourgeois sections. Russian nationalism had replaced the earlier Soviet teaching of internationalism and class solidarity.

Then the Soviet soldiers took to the black market. So did the soldiers of other armies and Germans and Austrians, too, and together they bargained and bartered. Nothing distinguished the Red warriors from the soldiers of capitalist nations except the greater hunger of the Russians for material goods. Those Europeans who expected to see in the Red Army the representatives of a Socialist society which had liquidated private capitalism and private trade and produced a New Man were disillusioned.

Soon enough Europe noticed the long arm and hard hand of the Kremlin reaching into factories, laboratories, stores, grain fields, and homes, and loading the loot on freight trains to Russia. Friend and foe were looted. Not only formerly and formally enemy countries but members of the United Nations like Poland, Czechoslovakia, and China were deprived of possessions. In Austria, the Soviets confiscated Nazi property which the Nazis had acquired by confiscating it from Jews and other anti-Nazis.

In Poland, Czechoslovakia, Rumania, Bulgaria, and Yugoslavia, Red Army officers trained large native armies. GPU agents abounded. Through contracts imposed on the governments of the countries in the Russian zone, Moscow gained control of vital segments of their economy. Everywhere, the Communist party was either officially in command or pulled strings behind the scenes.

It all looked like a permanent marriage between half of Europe, inhabited by about a hundred and fifty million people, and the Soviet Union.

For this reason alone, friction would have developed. The Kremlin had anticipated it and made plans to cope with it.

First, the Russians closed their zone and kept it sealed for months. Later, an occasional newspaperman or group of newspapermen were taken through some areas on a brief, conducted, restricted tour. Foreign diplomats, foreign military men, and correspondents were limited in their movements and in what they could send out by wire. When governments did receive reports from their representatives the material was at times so damaging to Russia that it was suppressed lest Moscow take offense. Governments are often polite to one another—at the expense of the truth and of public enlightenment.

The reduction of information to an occasional trickle has a crucial effect on public opinion. The world knows but forgets that the Russian area is blacked out. When something happens in Greece or Indonesia, newspapers and the radio give the public detailed data on what took place in Constitution Square and how the crowd moved down the avenue to the Prime Minister's house and who said what. But when something similar happens in Yugoslavia, Poland, or northern Iran there is silence. The result is that Greece, Indonesia, and the other countries accessible to the free press loom large in the mind and conscience of the world—as they should—but the Russian sphere of influence becomes a dull blank. Apologists for Russia intensify the blackout by consciously diverting attention from countries where Russia sins, to countries where the United States and England are at fault. At one time, accordingly, Spain and Argentina began to look like the centers of the world, while Russia and her new empire in Europe and Asia slipped out of focus.

Behind the light-proof curtain, the Soviets and their helpers were exterminating those who refused to accept foreign rule and dictatorship. Now and then, news of pitched battles between Polish or Yugoslav government forces and their domestic enemies filtered into the press. Now and then, the political murders perpetrated by Polish and other officials became so numerous that state departments protested openly.

Nevertheless, the liquidation of democrats, anti-Communists, reactionaries, and Socialists continued. Half of Europe has been or is being denuded of the sort of people who in the West lead movements for progress and freedom. First the Nazis butchered the intellectuals and tyranny haters of Europe; then the Bolsheviks assailed the remnant. To make sure of their power to prosecute this ugly crusade, the Communists managed in almost all countries, from Finland down to Albania, to introduce their own men, usually Moscow-trained Comintern officers, as Ministers of Interior; the Ministry of Interior is in charge of the secret police.

But as in Russia so in the Russian zone of influence the Soviet authorities and the Communists supplement police power with propaganda power. Sometimes, propaganda is mightier than the police. The bodies of heroes can defy the sword, but the minds of most men succumb to the uninterrupted, prolonged, repetitive, insidious word-attacks of one-sided propaganda.

Propaganda is the handmaiden of policy. What is Soviet policy in the Soviet sphere of influence? Is the Kremlin engaging in national-istic, imperialistic expansion? Or is Russia building a Communist Europe as a preliminary to a Red Asia?

The answer is that Stalin has too much political acumen to take one line. Stalin's natural flexibility is enhanced by unscrupulousness; he uses many means to attain one end. If the means are contradictory all the better; they win diverse supporters and confuse the critics.

Moscow tells the Slavs that Russia is their big brother and protector against the Teuton menace. Soviet propaganda regularly plays the Slav-versus-Teuton chord. The Czechoslovaks, the Bulgarians, the Yugoslavs, and many Poles are undoubtedly grateful to Russia for liberating them from Hitler. But Germany has crumbled. The psychological dread of a resurgent Germany is present and represents a Russian asset. At worst, however, it is a possibility whereas Russian domination is an onerous, day-and-night reality.

Moreover, Finland, the Baltic countries, Rumania, Hungary, Austria, and Albania are not Slav. The Poles are Slavs but they have a passionately anti-Russian tradition. The Poles are Slavs and Catholics. Pan-Slavism, consequently, would divide eastern Europe.

Pan-Slavism is a reactionary, racist movement supported by the obscurantist Russian church; it is reminiscent of Pan-Germanism. East European liberals and Socialists abhor it. To European Jews, Pan-Slavism, like Pan-Germanism, has always been a nightmare.

Moreover, Moscow's Pan-Slavism raises the specter of an outright or disguised union of Poland, Czechoslovakia, Bulgaria, and Yugoslavia with Slav "Mother Russia" which would end their separate national existence.

To counteract this fear, Moscow recalls that in February, 1944—just as the Red Army advanced into Esthonia and approached Poland —the sixteen constituent republics of the Soviet Union were accorded the right to maintain their own armies and their own foreign relations, and that at Yalta, Roosevelt and Churchill, yielding to Stalin, gave the Soviet Ukrainian Republic and the Soviet White Russian Republic (which no more resemble independent countries than Nebraska) the right to send delegates to the United Nations. But if the Ukrainian and White Russian delegates, or the Polish, Czech, and Yugoslav delegates who vote with Russia at all international meetings, nurse any illusions regarding their freedom of diplomatic action they have been overtaken by a gullibility which is rare among East European politicians. Any official in the Soviet sphere of influence who is reluctant to obey the Kremlin's orders can be ousted by Russian authority or by Communist action.

Moscow knows that these conditions inflame nationalist resentment against Russia and arouse sympathy for the Western powers. The Communists, accordingly, put themselves in the van of the nationalist movements of the several countries. In Czechoslovakia, for instance, it is Czech Communists, "more than anyone else," writes Maurice Hindus after a visit in 1946 to Czechoslovakia, "who insist on a boycott of everything German, even for the present of Beethoven and Schiller. It is they, at least as much as anyone, who are resolved on the expulsion of Germans from the Sudetenland, capitalists as well as workers. . . ." In Germany, however, the Communists are German nationalists. Marguerite Higgins, cabling from Berlin to the *New York Herald Tribune* of February 14, 1946, reports a conference in the Russian zone of Germany where "the Communists, and also the Russians through a spokesman, Colonel Sergei Tulpanov, who gave the welcoming address, launched a series of appeals to the nationalistic feelings of the Germans." These statements are confirmed by the German newspapers which I have been reading since V-E day. The French Communists, on the other hand, agitate against Germany.

Is that the way to get peace in Europe, to stir anti-German nationalism in the Czechs, German nationalism in the Germans and French nationalism in the French? The Russians adopt this questionable strategy in order to capture the nationalist forces in each country and prevent them from going anti-Russian. When the Italian Communist party began losing followers because of its anti-Italian stand in favor of Tito's annexation of Trieste, a quick flip-flop ensued. It was more important to Moscow to have a strong Italian Communist party than to have Italian Communist assistance in the Trieste issue.

Further, Moscow applies plasters of coveted territory to the wounds which its encroachments have inflicted on nationalism in eastern Europe. Poland receives German territory. Yugoslavia demands Greek Macedonia and Italian Trieste. Bulgaria seeks annexations at the expense of Turkey. These map carvings would extend the Soviet sphere of influence. By encouraging them, Russia appears as the champion of ancient nationalist-expansionist aspirations. This diverts attention from what Russia takes to what Russian support may give. In any of these boundary disputes, the Balkan country involved would need Russian assistance. The purpose is to sugarcoat the pill of Kremlin control while enlarging the area under Kremlin control. The result is to keep Europe and the Near East in turmoil.

Foreign diversions are often indispensable to dictatorships: foreign successes bolster the dictatorship. All the Axis powers acted on this impulse, and on one notable occasion, Hitler enunciated it as a principle. Hitler received Franco's Foreign Minister Serrano Suner in Berlin on September 17, 1940, and, according to a captured document published by the State Department, declared: "Many a domestic difficulty that Spain, at the moment, perhaps, still had to face could quickly and easily be overcome by successes with foreign policy. This was an old historical experience. . . ."

Economic setbacks in dictatorships and popular disgruntlement impel dictators to sprinkle the germs of nationalism as a counterirritant. Nationalism stirs an interest in territorial aggrandizement. The resulting international tension enables the police state to call on its people to rally around the government and make further sacrifices for the strengthening and arming of the country.

Seeking to perpetuate itself and to ease its tasks, a dictatorship offers patriotism as a substitute for material plenty, guns for butter. Dictatorships have always advertised their enemies; enemies are among the dictator's dearest assets.

Dictators copy from dictators. The Italian embassy in Moscow had permanent orders to supply Mussolini with material on Stalin's political techniques. Yugoslavs shout "Tito! Tito! Tito!" as the Italians shouted "Duce! Duce! Duce!" as the Spaniards shout "Franco! Franco! Franco!" In important social, political, and economic matters, the East European dictatorships pattern themselves after Moscow.

Governments create new regimes in their own image. Stalin believes—he said it in a speech on February 9, 1946—"that the Soviet social system has proved to be more capable of life and more stable than non-Soviet social systems, and that the Soviet social system is a better form of organization of society than any non-Soviet social system." Naturally, therefore, Stalin aims to introduce that Soviet social system in the countries that have recently come under his sway.

This is not always immediately possible. It can only be done in stages. The speed of the transition to Stalin's Soviet social system depends on the country and on the personnel and politics of its government. These vary.

Tito, schooled in Moscow, has set up a one-party dictatorship. His is a police state with a secret police on the lines of the GPU. Tito accepted non-Communists and political opponents into the Government because at Yalta Stalin, Churchill, and Roosevelt agreed that this be done. Within a few months, however, the non-Communists were expelled.

Hoxha, dictator of Albania, has followed in Tito's footsteps with Tito's neighborly help.

The Rumanian government of Prime Minister Radescu was overthrown by the personal intervention of Soviet Assistant Commissar of Foreign Affairs, Andrei Vishinsky, who went to Bucharest for that purpose. Vishinsky then established a new cabinet of his choosing. He excluded the Peasant party of Julius Maniu, the largest Rumanian party, because it opposed Russian and Communist supremacy.

The Bulgarian government is dominated by the Fatherland Front, organized and led by George Dimitrov, hero of the Leipzig Reichstag-fire trial, former chief of the Comintern who worked for many years in Moscow.

The Austrian and Hungarian governments which came into office when the Red Army entered were overwhelmingly Communist whereas the people were not.

The Polish government was first formed in Moscow, then transferred to Lublin, and finally moved to Warsaw. It is predominantly Communist. Originally, it barred the large Peasant party whose leader was Mikolajczyk, a former Prime Minister of the Polish Government-in-Exile. Through Allied pressure, Mikolajczyk was admitted into the Warsaw cabinet. He hoped to serve his party and his country and perhaps pry the Communists loose from power. He has more political influence and less political power than any Polish leader.

The Finnish government included Communists imposed by Moscow; it was burdened with war reparations payable to Moscow; Moscow ordered trials of high Finnish officials who were sentenced for leading Finland in the wars with Russia. The Finns nevertheless were allowed more freedom than most other countries in the Soviet sphere of influence.

The Esthonian, Latvian, and Lithuanian governments are pure Soviet governments.

The Czechoslovak government retained more independence and democracy than any nation within Russia's orbit. But there too the Communists exercise influence out of proportion to their numerical strength.

In the Russian zone in Germany, Communists, many of them Soviet-trained, form the backbone of the local administration.

Stalin's first step throughout the new Russian empire was to introduce Communists. They give him power. Later, depending on circumstances, the Communists might begin to introduce Communism.

These overwhelmingly Communist regimes did not reflect the pre-war political allegiances of the people. There was no proof that the people had changed their views and gone Communist. Wherever truly free elections took place, as in Austria and Hungary, the Communists were the weakest party. These elections amounted to plebiscites against Russia. The voters cast their ballots against their own Communists but they were voting against Soviet overlordship. The Soviet forces of occupation nevertheless retained complete control. In the Hungarian elections, the Communists received a tiny percentage of the total vote. But, thanks to Russian pressure, the Communists received many key posts in the Cabinet.

Since the Communist or near-Communist governments in the Russian sphere of influence lacked public majorities they had to be kept in office by dictatorships, by secret police systems, and by Russian bayonets.

Inevitably, the extension of Soviet power extends the area of dictatorship in the world. The dictatorships' first move is to shoot, imprison, exile, or otherwise persecute those who, for nationalistic, idealistic, religious, political, class, or economic reasons, wish to overthrow them. The struggle against dictatorship continues and will continue, but the Soviet Union's overshadowing might throughout eastern and central Europe is a decisive factor against political freedom.

"Well, they never had freedom or democracy in those parts anyway," is a frequent interjection. "Everything was feudal and backward."

Such statements stem from ignorance and a white-and-black intellectual approach. Freedom before the war was incomplete; democracy was curtailed by poverty, racial animosities, corrupt, inefficient politicians, Gestapo-GPU type gendarmeries which perpetrated cruel tortures, rotten landlord oligarchies, and obsolete monarchies. Yet in all the countries where the Soviets and Communists now rule, opposition parties existed. The Socialist party of Horthy Hungary was outspokenly anti-Nazi and favored the land reform which Admiral Horthy abominated. In some nations, the opposition has no real power and was often persecuted and occasionally suppressed. But at least it could now and then yell, and state its case in parliament. In all these countries opposition newspapers existed which attacked the government. Trade unions existed; strikes were possible. Individuals could go abroad and return. Foreigners circulated freely in the entire region. Foreign newspapers and literature entered without restraint. The foreign radio was within the reach of many citizens. Nor was eastern Europe a cultural Afghanistan.

I have often criticized the pre-1939 governments of Poland, Rumania, and other eastern European nations. But surely the hope of liberals, progressives, and Socialists was that the limited democracy of East European countries be expanded after the war and not that it be totally suppressed by Russian Stalitarianism.

I do not understand liberals and democrats who applaud the suppression of democracy and who do not cry out against the annihilation of democrats.

With many others, I urged independence for India. Imperialism is a form of dictatorship and I hate it. The British raj in India arrests thousands of people who have committed no illegal act and holds them in jail for years, on occasion, without trial. British warplanes have machine-gunned Indian villages from the air. These reprehensible acts occur in times of stress and political disturbances—in 1942, for instance. Nevertheless, in normal years, which means usually, and even during the second world war, Indian leaders, Indian newspapers, and Indian parties kept up a constant verbal barrage against British policy and British officials and organized to oppose the Government. This is freedom within an unfree country. It is far from satisfactory, but only those who have not been in prison or lived perpetually within the shadow of the tyrant's gallows will underestimate its value. This is a freedom which does not exist in Russia or in most Russia-dominated countries. Russia exports its system wherever it can. The biggest item of Soviet export is repression. Moscow boasts that it has swept away the physical débris of feudalism in eastern and central Europe. But it has substituted a new political and intellectual serfdom which is at least as bad.

Stalin's political wisdom, however, teaches him that in the long run terror cannot hold the Russian sphere of influence unless the Communists gain wider public support from the local population. Therefore, and because they sincerely believe in it, the Russians have, wherever they could in eastern and central Europe, nationalized large industries and divided up large estates. This was designed to deprive the manufacturers and the landlord aristocracy, naturally anti-Communist, of their economic and therefore political strength; the workers and the peasantry who received parcels of land would be grateful to the Russians and Communists.

A land reform to satisfy land-hungry farmers and break the hold of high-living, game-hunting, exploiting estate proprietors on their national governments was overdue in many parts of Europe. But the scope and benefits of the Russian-sponsored postwar land reform have been exaggerated by persons, for instance by some of my old friends on *The Nation*, who do not know the countries affected. Under the spiritual and political impact of the Bolshevik revolution, land reforms were carried out during the nineteen-twenties in Finland, the three Baltic states, Poland, Rumania, Bulgaria, Yugoslavia, and Czechoslovakia, but not in Horthy Hungary and of course not in Germany. (This was one of the causes for the fall of democratic Germany.)

Finland, the Baltic states, Bulgaria, Czechoslovakia, and Yugoslavia became countries of small holders who tilled their own farms. Some estates remained but they did not bulk large in the national economy. In Rumania and Poland, the number of estates was greater. Yet in the Poland east of the Curzon Line, that is, in the truncated Poland of today, approximately eighty-five per cent of the land had been divided among the peasants before the war.

Immediately the Red Army advanced into a country, the land reform was initiated irrespective of the season of the year and of local conditions. The result in Poland, Rumania, and Hungary was to intensify the food shortages and bring suffering to the people. But just as in the Soviet Union during the period of agrarian collectivization, the Bolsheviks ignored human suffering; they were designing a new system.

In Poland, the peasants who benefited from the land reform received eight acres at most, and many of them received as little as five acres. This sentences them to poverty or to emigration to the newly-acquired Polish provinces of eastern Germany.

Anna Louise Strong, a pro-Soviet writer, cabled from Moscow to *The Nation* of February 3, 1945, about the Polish land reform. She described the method of distributing the land and added: "By such processes eight hundred thousand acres formerly belonging to one thousand owners were transferred to one hundred thousand families. . . ." That makes eight acres a family.

The Polish Finance Minister Kwiatkovsky told the Polish Sejm or parliament on December 5, 1935, that Polish peasants who owned twenty-five acres of land spend on the average of eight dollars a year. Yet they were millionaires compared with peasants who owned only ten to twelve acres and who, he said, constituted thirty-one per cent of the population. An additional thirty-four per cent owned even smaller or "dwarf" households. "Ten million persons," Kwiatkovsky reported, "stand completely outside of economic life" because their holdings were about eight acres or more. They earned too little to buy city goods.

Then why the land reform in the midst of the war? Anna Louise Strong gives several reasons. "The land reform," she cables, "not only spurs volunteering for the Polish Army but makes millions of peasants statistically conscious of why they want East Prussia and Pomeranian lands—to give every Polish peasant at least twelve acres." So eight acres in Poland make them want to run away from Poland and fight Germany to get twelve acres in Germany.

Small-scale farming in poor countries is hardly likely to raise individual standards or to enrich the countries.

The land reform which Stalin engineered in eastern and central Europe cannot solve the chief economic problem of that vast area. That problem is the underdevelopment of industry and the shortage of financial credit. There Russia cannot help. Russia is an insatiable market for the manufactured goods of her zone of influence. Russia can supply some of the raw material, as in the case of Soviet cotton to Polish textile factories. But for a number of years, perhaps ten or fifteen years, the Soviet Union will face her own deficiencies in food, housing, clothing, machine tools, and basic materials. Russia cannot be a giver. She will be a taker; she will take the oil of Austria, Hungary, Rumania, and Poland, the grain of Rumania, the meat of Hungary, the consumers' commodities of Czechoslovakia, and so forth.

The Russian sphere of influence in Europe, accordingly, will look to the United States and Great Britain for the economic help without which economic prosperity and, in turn, political stability are impossible. Whether America and England will be admitted into the Russian zone must depend on a larger political settlement with Moscow.

Russia cannot soon solve the economic problems of eastern and central Europe; nor can she solve the nationalities problem of her orbit. The war, Hitler's racism, Russia's policy, and Pan-Slavism which is a species of racism, have intensified nationalism everywhere. The Czechs, probably the most civilized people in that part of the world, have been expelling all Germans and Hungarians in order to create a racially-pure country. Old frontier quarrels between Czechoslovakia and Poland remain alive. The Axis gave Transylvania to the Hungarians as an inducement to fight for Hitler. Stalin gave Transylvania to the Rumanians as a reward for fighting on the side of Russia. But Transylvania is inhabited by Hungarians and Rumanians, so now the Hungarians are resentful. The present arrangement is not a solution; it is a makeshift. In Yugoslavia, during the war, the Croats massacred the Serbs. Tito said in a specially-cabled article in the New York *Free World* of June, 1944, that: "Under German instigation the Ustachi [Croats] killed hundreds of thousands of Serbs. Mihailovitch's Chetniks, incited by Germans and Italians, destroyed tens of thousands of Croats. . . . [We] exerted every effort to prove to the enraged Serbian people and misled Chetniks that not all Croats were villains." The question is whether the enraged Serbian people were convinced. The Serbs have not forgiven the Croats, nor Tito who is a Croat, nor Moscow which supports Tito. The Serbs are the backbone of Yugoslavia, half the population. Nor are the Croats likely to forgive the Serbs. To strengthen the pro-Moscow Croats against the Serbs, Moscow proposes a Great South-Slav Federation uniting Yugoslavia with Bulgaria with Macedonia. In such a combination the Serbs would be outnumbered by anti-Serbs. This again is not a solution of national difficulties. It is a smart power maneuver which means struggle and repression.

No tampering with frontiers, no mass expulsions however cruel, and no patchwork with nationalities can solve the nationalities problem of Europe. Only internationalism can do that. But Moscow is preaching nationalism and practising nationalism. The alternatives, therefore, are nationalist tension and friction, or a United States of Europe, or final absorption into the Soviet Union. Stalin never takes a long leap unless he must. He prefers half-measures and quarter-measures.

In the troubled times that lie ahead of eastern Europe, Germany, and Asia, Moscow must have at its disposal a reliable instrument of maximum utility. The Communist parties are not such an instrument because they have never been able to recruit a sufficient following. The Soviet authorities have adopted various measures to meet this situation. They create a "Fatherland Front" in Bulgaria to entice nationalists. In Iran, they father a "Democratic" party. (How that word "democratic" is abused by dictators and democrats alike!) Elsewhere they form a "People's party." But the disguises are thin.

The Kremlin's chief hope therefore lies in a fusion of its Communist parties with the larger Social Democratic or Socialist parties of Europe. The assumption is that with Russian assistance the little Communist tail will wag the big dog.

The bitter feud between Communists and Social Democrats or Socialists is of long standing. In Russia, it dates back to the split, decades ago, between the Bolsheviks who wanted a proletarian dictatorship by violence and the Mensheviks who wanted democracy with Socialism but without violence. In Germany, it divided the working class and opened the door to Hitler. The Communists, on occasions, supported Nazi measures in German parliaments. They did so because they thought they would gain thereby. For the same reason, they constantly campaigned against the Social Democrats. In the end, the Nazis gained thereby and smashed the Communists as well as the Social Democrats.

The German Social Democrats were moderate. In 1918 they had an opportunity to make real changes in the German social structure which would have eliminated the Junkers and militarists. But they recoiled from fundamental reforms. Their leaders lacked courage and clarity. Ultimately, power slipped from their hands into the ample laps of their class enemies who fostered Hitler.

Both German workers' parties have a sad record.

In 1935, Russia was impressed by the Nazi menace and the need of greater friendship with the democracies. Moscow therefore ordered the Communist parties to seek closer contact with the Social Democratic parties. The Communists, accordingly, tried to form alliances with the Social Democrats whom they had yesterday called "Social Fascists." In some countries, such alliances or united fronts or popular fronts were established.

But in Spain, when the Social Democrats of Catalonia merged with the Communists the fused party joined the Comintern. When the Spanish Socialist and Communist youth organizations merged they became a purely Communist party.

This is what Moscow wanted. In fact, George Dimitrov, the leader of the Comintern, told me in Moscow in May, 1938, that he would like to see the Communist and Socialist parties amalgamate in each country. The result, he thought, would be one Socialist-Communist body to replace the Comintern.

Dimitrov envisaged the dissolution of the Comintern as early as 1938. In the unified Socialist-Communist organization the Communists, he expected, would dominate.

This is now the official, openly-avowed Communist and Soviet policy.

The Communist parties of Europe have striven to unite with the Social Democratic forces. This would end the separate existence of the party which has always commanded more working-class support than the Communists. It would give the Communists a chance of running the one, united workingmen's party. In many countries, such a party could either be the national government or exercise a decisive influence over the government.

In the Russian zone of Germany and in Berlin, Social Democrats have been told by Red Army officers that they must merge with the

Communists; most of them obey. Some who refused have been sent to Siberia. Some have escaped, with the help of the American and British military, to western Germany beyond the reach of Soviet terror.

Moscow is convinced that if its Communists have the upper hand in a single workers' party and in the trade unions then it can rule the Russian sphere through local politicians and make the military occupation less visible and irksome to the local inhabitants. Given the Socialist strength in the American, British, and French zones of Germany, a Moscow-manipulated Communist-Socialist party would be tantamount to Russian control of all of Germany. This is how the Kremlin answers the much-debated question: What To Do About Germany?

The Socialists and Communists can agree in their opposition to capitalist exploitation and to Fascism. But they disagree fully about democracy. This is the cause of the chasm between them. The Socialists want Socialism with democracy. But for the Communists, in the words of Wilhelm Pieck, the veteran German Communist leader, spoken on February 21, 1946, at a Berlin demonstration for the Socialist-Communist merger: "Our goal will always remain the true Socialism as it has found its fulfillment in the Soviet Union."

The Communist fatherland is Russia. German Social Democrat spokesmen have therefore publicly asked the German Communists whether they are a Russian party or a German party. The unimpaired Communist attachment to Moscow as well as the Socialist desire for democracy militate against a united workers' party which would block reaction, royalism, clericalism, and Fascism.

Nevertheless, some Socialists have leaned towards a union with the Communists. Outside the Russian orbit such a tendency cannot be attributed to direct Soviet pressure. It is often due to the threat of rightist conservatism. The Left is more likely to close ranks, despite serious ideological differences, when the Right has power or moves towards power.

That is why Stalin was probably the unhappiest man in Europe the day Churchill was defeated by the Labor party. Churchill, with his sympathy for kings and his ineradicable conservatism, was a valuable asset to Stalin. In the face of Churchill's support of royalism the Communists could call on the workers, the Socialists, and the Liberals to join with them and follow their political strategy. But the British Labor government was no sooner in office than Harold J. Laski—

strange that it should have been the ambivalent Laski who believes in Russia's "new faith"—sought to dissuade the Socialists of the Continent from making common cause with the Communist parties. Laski merely reinforced a powerful existing aversion. Yet in the long run the Socialists can remain free from Communist entanglements and can resist submersion by the Communists only if Europe is safe from rightist reaction. The middle class and the professional classes have been impoverished by war and its aftermath; their cohesion, interest in politics, and dynamism, unless inspired by the church, have been reduced. Before the war in France and before Hitler in Germany, the Socialists, when pressed by the extreme Right, could look for allies among the middle class middle-of-the-road moderates a little to the right of center. But now the moderates are weak. The Socialists, accordingly, must on occasion accept an alliance with the Communists lest the reactionaries otherwise come to power.

Thus, encouragement of reactionaries conduces to Socialist-Communist unity at the expense of the West and to the delight of Moscow. Elimination of the reactionaries, pro-Fascists, Fascists, and royalists will enable the Socialists to resist Communist courtship. The Socialists would then be the moderate democratic Socialists stemming the inroads of extremist dictatorial Communists.

The British Labor government, therefore, must do more than delegate Laski and convincing orators like him to Socialist congresses. It must make Europe liberal, left, and social-democratic. Franco in Spain, Salazar in Portugal, monarchists in Hungary, agrarian standpatters in Austria, ambitious industrialists in Germany, vestigial Fascists and backward-looking friends of the *status quo* in Italy, all become arguments which incline Socialists towards common action with Communists.

Why is it never the other way around, that Communists accept the Socialist program of democracy? Because the Communist party is a strictly-disciplined secret order whose primary loyalty is to Moscow. If a Browder pursues one policy and the Party suddenly engineers an overnight flip-flop which he cannot execute on such short notice he is expelled and branded "a servant of capitalist reaction." A slight sign of independent thinking in a Communist leader immediately makes him "a vicious Trotzkyite" or "a near-Fascist." So no Communist party is capable of any change of policy which does not conform to Moscow's wishes. Moscow frowns on Communist service to democracy and national interests. Communists may talk "democracy" and call themselves "democrats." They mean "Soviet democracy," the kind that is administered by a secret police, by one party, and by a dictator. The dictatorial democrat.

Communist success in wooing the Social Democrats would banish democracy and British influence from Europe and confirm Russia's mastery. Hitler had only force at his disposal. Stalin has politics too.

The ancient struggle between the Russian and British empires has been renewed and extended. It used to be confined to Asia and eastern Europe. It is now raging in every nook of Europe and in all parts of Asia. Nor are more distant regions excluded. New weapons are employed: the Tsars had Pan-Slavism, the Greek Orthodox Church, diplomats, spies, and force. The Bolsheviks have all of these plus dynamic political parties in all countries, a social philosophy which they are attempting to sell, and the appeal of anti-imperialism. Unlike the Tsars who twice inefficiently and abortively moved to conquer India with armies, the Soviets call on colonial peoples to strike off their chains.

Moreover, Britain is weaker than in the nineteenth century and Russia stronger. By virtue of the Stalin-Churchill-Roosevelt peace fashioned at Teheran and Yalta, Russia won a gigantic victory; she garnered half of Europe. Indeed, more than half. In the rump, Englishmen and others advocate a Western bloc led by Britain or by Britain and France as a counterpoise to Russia's sphere of influence.

What are the possibilities of such a Western bloc?

Look at the nations not included in the Russian zone.

Norway, Sweden, and Denmark have a deep tradition of neutrality and an abhorrence of blocs and alliances beyond Scandinavia. Moreover, Norway is now a neighbor of Russia, and so, in effect, are Sweden and Denmark. They could not enter a Western bloc which the Russians oppose.

Holland might well join the Western bloc; so might Belgium. France could not unless the Communists lose their present voting strength. Spain and Portugal would perhaps come in if they established democratic regimes. Italy's decision would depend in considerable measure on the policies of the Communists. Switzerland is the confirmed neutral; its sympathies are with England but it would not take membership in any bloc. Greece is riven by internal dissension. More definite alignment with Britain would exacerbate the domestic antagonisms between Right and Left and create friction with Yugoslavia and Bulgaria; Greece, therefore, will waver. Turkey which is part European, part Asiatic, hopes for salvation from Britain but fears Russian encroachment and would refrain from formal adherence to a Western bloc as long as any prospect of peace with Russia remained.

That is all that is left of Europe except Germany.

Throughout the second world war, innumerable Germans behaved like brutes and beasts. The catalog of German sins against man will long cover Germany with a big black blot. Nothing can excuse or mitigate Germany's war and prewar crimes. Shall Germany go unpunished? Defeat and its aftermath are part of the punishment. The world's horror and bitter resentment against Germany will not soon die down. But in the last analysis there is no adequate punishment for what Germans did because measure-for-measure revenge would so cripple Germany as to cripple innocent Germans and innocent non-Germans outside of Germany and, consequently, retard world recovery. What is to me equally important, any adequate punishment of German crimes would have to be so cruel as to destroy the morality of those who meted out the punishment. This is a situation where, of necessity, evil has to be repaid with undeserved good.

Something is happening to our civilization. Observe Europe and Asia, observe the British, the Dutch, the French, the Russians, the Argentines, the Spaniards, the Chinese. Barbarism is lowering itself over us like a hood over a man to be hanged. But we are not hanged. We walk around directionless with the black hood on our heads. Our civilization threatens to disintegrate. Someone must stop the vicious circle of an-eye-for-an-eye-for-an-eye-for-an-eye. The question is not whether the Germans deserve decency. We need decency.

At a press conference in Washington on June 18, 1945, General Dwight D. Eisenhower said: "You can't build peace with hate or with a club." That is Christian.

During my stay with Mahatma Gandhi in 1942, he said to me: "Your President talks about the Four Freedoms. Does that include the freedom to be free?"

"After the war the world will be better," I replied.

Gandhi looked me straight in the eye and said: "Are you sure?"

"I hope," I said.

"I want to see a change in the hearts of England and America now," Gandhi declared, "if I am to believe that you will be capable of building the kind of world in which there could be peace." There spoke a Christian who is not a Christian, who is a Hindu.

In St. Louis recently, the wife of a minister asked me what the church could do to save the peace. "Make Christians out of Christians," I suggested.

I have traveled in many countries. I have met Hindus who were Christians, and Jews who were Christians, and Protestants and Catholics who were Christians. But I have never been in a Christian country.

The peace will be as good as the people who make it.

The Germans, Japanese, and Italians made the war—with a lot of help from Englishmen, Frenchmen, Russians, Americans, and others. The men of Munich were war criminals. The men of the Soviet-Nazi pact were war criminals. Germans are not the only war criminals in Europe.

Nor are all Germans war criminals. I know Germans in Germany who are better anti-Nazis than many of those who say that all Germans are Nazis. "We have no purpose to incriminate the whole German people," Mr. Justice Robert Jackson wrote in his indictment at the Nuremberg trial in 1945. "We know that the Nazi party was not put into power by a majority of the German vote. We know it came to power by an evil alliance between extreme Nazi revolutionists and the most aggressive German militarists." That is historic truth.

To say that the Nazis could not have remained in power without the approval or at least connivance of the German people is to ignore the essential characteristic of a dictatorship: it does not rule by popular approval and consent. I would not pay Hitler the unearned compliment that he won the favor of all Germans. He won many, all too many, and the others acquiesced, especially during the war, because the alternative was death or imprisonment and because he inflamed the deep German nationalism implanted by his predecessors.

Nothing we could do to Germany or Japan would bring us peace. There is talk of a threatening third world war, the first atomic war. It would not be launched by Germany, Italy, or Japan. They could not start it if they wished.

War and Fascism are not German diseases. They are world diseases. They transcend geography, blood, and race.

Poverty, privations, oppression, discrimination are universal. They make war.

Nationalism makes wars.

Dictators make wars.

Democracy tries to check wars. It is not universal.

The democrats of Germany were timid, Fabian, and usually non-violent. The feudal, militaristic, monopolistic elements in Germany were not deprived of their power for evil. Those who point a finger of scorn at vacillating, inadequate German democrats might do well to look at other democracies too. The Spanish democrats were true democrats if there ever were any—and Teutonic blood in Spain is negligible. Did they, between 1931 and 1936, smash the militaristic, landowning, pro-Fascist and monarchist cliques who were all the time preparing to overthrow the liberal republic? In France democracy was a treasured privilege; Frenchmen voted with the seriousness and solemnity of a church rite. Did the French banish the anti-democrats who undermined democracy before 1939?

How successful are American progressives, liberals, radicals, and democrats in eliminating the domestic enemies of freedom, the haters of Negroes, of Jews, of labor, and of reform? Blame the Germans and then blame yourself.

"There was no German underground against Hitler but there was an anti-Nazi underground in France, Poland, Yugoslavia, Italy, Greece, etc." Is that wholly correct? German concentration camps were full before the war, before foreigners were detained in them. They were full of German anti-Nazis who risked their lives and often lost them. The undergrounds in the Nazi-occupied countries were bigger and stronger because the Nazi terror machine was newer than in Germany and, above all, because nationalist antagonism to the foreign conqueror inspired the underground.

Those citizens of democracies who criticize Germans for not having courted death might ask themselves how much they risk in order to rid their countries of social and political and economic evils. Sometimes they invest a little time and money in a cause. Would they risk their careers, their families, their social connections, their jobs, their necks?

How many Spaniards or Russians openly fight their dictators?

"We have lived and we are living in a rotten world," Sumner Welles said in New York on October 16, 1943. German rottenness was a great part of that rottenness but not all of it. Each country has its share of rottenness.

The roster of Japanese prewar and war crimes is long and ugly. Who can tell whether it is longer and uglier than Germany's? Yet the treatment of Japan has been very different from that meted out to

Germany. The social revolution by the consent of General Douglas MacArthur has been more radical than most people, knowing what American reactionaries had supported him for President, had a right to expect. Persons responsible for Tokyo's anti-democratic terrorism at home and abroad have been excluded by name from participation in public life. A land reform has been instituted. A free press has been encouraged. Political party life is free. There is a central government, but the Emperor has been shorn of his absolute power, of his religious attributes, and of his former prestige. All this was accomplished with no bloodshed and little friction. The people are eager for democracy. They give little evidence of anti-foreign bitterness.

The treatment accorded to Japan has little to do with what the Japanese deserve. It is explained by the fact that the United States was in a position, alone, to fix policy for Japan.

Touring the United States in 1946, Dr. Baeck, Chief Rabbi of Germany, who saw the Jewish people in Germany cruelly butchered by Hitler and who spent years in a concentration camp, was asked whether he believed in the democratic future of Germany. "Certainly I do," he replied. "But all depends on how far the Allies are capable of strengthening the healthy and constructive forces in Germany." The Chief Rabbi counseled against hate. Of course, much depends on Germans themselves. But Germany is part of the world; we are in her and must live with her. Germany cannot "stew in her own juice" because everybody is in there making the juice and stewing in it with her.

What is done with Germany, what the victors have done to Germany, is less a retribution for German misdeeds than the result of American-British-Russian-French competition for the control of Germany.

Germany is the hub of the European problem. Russia began by annexing outright a part of East Prussia. Via annexation by Poland, Russia dominates a fifth of prewar Germany—Silesia, Pomerania, and the remainder of East Prussia—which, for want of the trained manpower and resources, the Poles cannot themselves digest. In addition, Russia occupies one-third of the present Germany. The United States occupies somewhat less than a third, inhabited by approximately seventeen million Germans. Britain and France share what is left.

Obviously, if the Big Powers continue to spar and struggle each will endeavor to use its position in Germany against its rivals.

The policy of Russia in Germany, as in China and, in fact, everywhere is to strengthen that which it can control and to divide and weaken that which it cannot control.

The policy of making Germany a pastoral or overwhelmingly agricultural country is not being carried out by Russia in her German zone. But the Communists and their friends advocate the dismantling of German factories and the destruction of German industries in the other zones.

Measures are necessary to eliminate any possibility of Germany's going to war again. What with foreign occupation, the ruination through war, and the hold which the conquerors have and are likely to keep on Germany, the Germans will go to war only if America, England, and Russia want them to do so. No matter how thoroughly Germany is now disarmed and de-industrialized, therefore, the major countries can reverse the process at any time. Germany began to rearm with Soviet Russia's help in 1922, and thereafter by secret arrangements until 1932 Germany produced on Soviet territory war equipment which the Versailles Peace Treaty proscribed. This can be repeated at any time in that way or some other way.

Having lost the war, Germany is a victim of policy; she does not make policy. Germany cannot start another war. Another war could start over Germany.

Wars in Europe have been launched by the strongest power in Europe; at one time it was Rome, later Spain, later France, later Germany. The reason is simple: only the strongest power can have the illusion that it will win a war. The strongest power is not afraid of being attacked. It attacks because it is not afraid. Germany is no longer the strongest power in Europe and is not likely to become the strongest power.

In these circumstances, the destruction of industries in Germany or the restriction of industrial production in some areas of Germany cannot be a conclusive war deterrent. Even if all of German industry were pulverized, Germans could still be used in a war among their recent enemies. And if those allies live amicably together Germany can do no harm.

Germany was taught aggressive nationalism for over seventy years. During an interview in Paris on June 15, 1945, General Eisenhower said of Germans: "To my mind, a very young child is really of no nationality. A person achieves his nationalistic bent, let us say, through education or propaganda, but he achieves it after he is beyond, let's say, the age of mere childhood." This is perfect anti-Nazism from the soldier who beat the Nazis. Nationalism is not in the blood plasma or corpuscles. It is not inherited. It is the result of miseducation and propaganda. Nationalism bred militarism under the Kaiser and under Hitler. Great industrial strength put wheels on the nationalism. It could go places.

Now certain people say: Deprive Germany of industrial strength. Would it not be better to deprive Germany of nationalism and militarism? Industrial strength, America's industrial strength, for instance, does not produce wars. People who are nationalistic and militaristic produce wars.

The purpose of the victorious nations, if they want contentment and progress in Europe, should be to create conditions which do not conduce to nationalism and armaments, conditions which will cure the German mind and soul. Reducing the German standard of living by pastoralizing Germany will do just the opposite.

To curtail industrial output artificially when Europe and the world are hungry, roofless, ragged, sick, and weary is a modern sin against humanity. The German problem is a difficult problem. It is a growth of decades. It cannot be solved overnight. But it cannot be solved at all by hate, by a club, by revenge, by pulling down factories which could turn out telephones, thermometers, beds, houses, street cars, chairs, and the many other necessities of life.

A sick Germany will make a sick Europe.

A vacuum in Germany stirs up winds of rivalry all around her.

A discontented, harassed Germany will yearn for an extreme solution and for a dictator. A dictator will not be long in arriving; he will be sent by another dictator in Moscow. When a nation is in trouble it despairs and falls prey to charlatans, messiahs, or despots who promise everything to everybody.

Some may say: Having suffered from Hitler for twelve years is not a dictator the last thing Germans would want? That is logical but not psychological. A dictator first kills the people's will and faith in themselves. Tired people are ready to entrust their burdens to a supreme *fuehrer*. When a nation sees itself rudderless, divided, and poor it easily succumbs to the blandishments of the strong man and the strong power. Dynamism has a fatal attraction for the spineless and the weak.

A dictator breeds loathing of dictatorship but kills the capacity to resist dictatorship. The Germans were sick before Hitler, otherwise they would not have had Hitler. Now they are more sick because of Hitler. Germany is the sick man of Europe.

The little man of Europe and Asia and the little and weak countries of Europe and Asia are searching for security and well-being: they are shopping around for friends and ideologies. What was and is appalls them. They want something new and better. Their lives have been churned up by war. They have lost respect for old powers. They listen to siren songs.

In Asia, moreover, the little man and the colonial nations have lost respect for the white man and for the Western powers. They observe the white man's inability to solve his own problems, the problems of peace and plenty. Mankind, to be sure, has made much progress. We have robot planes, radar, penicillin, atomic energy, and plastics. The colored races are impressed by power and ingenuity. But power unaccompanied by morality and justice excites their protest.

The East is in revolt against Western power and Western civilization. Unless the West changes its face it will lose face.

The East's revolt against Western power is fed by Britain's defeats at the hands of Japan in 1941 and 1942, and by Britain's weakness today. France and Holland are weaker than they were in the prewar period. America is far away and less familiar. Russia challenges Western power. The East feels encouraged.

Asia has moved to the footlights of history.

Russia is solidly anchored in the Far East, in central Asia, and in the Near East. Her inhabitants in those regions are Asiatics. The Bolshevik revolution opened new horizons and new economic and social opportunities for them. Before the war, the center of Russia's population and of her industrial activity had been traveling steadily eastward into Siberia and Turkestan. The war, with the necessary evacuation of factories and workers, accentuated the process. It is a permanent trend.

The Soviet Union is a factor in the life of every Asiatic country, of Iran as of Java, of Manchuria as of Palestine. That stems from geography, from Soviet policy, and from big power rivalry, but also from the circumstance that all these countries are tortured by urgent, turbulent, unsolved economic, social, and political problems, and by irksome foreign influence.

The urge of Asiatic peoples to get rid of ancient masters is irresistible and irrational. There was no use telling the Burmese that their new Japanese masters would be worse than the British. They wanted to be free of the British, so they sided with the Japanese against the British.

It is no use telling the Asiatics that Russia is selfish, imperialistic, and more likely to remain and rule over them than the Western nations. Stalin is still operating on the initial capital of the Bolshevik revolution; the Revolution to many Orientals still stands for racial equality, new rights for the oppressed, buoyant economic development, and the ousting of Western imperialism. Soviet Russia is still remembered as the country which relinquished its privileges in China and Iran and went to Turkey's aid in 1921.

Russia's role as an expanding aggressor, as an oil imperialist, as a violator of treaties and of the rights of small nations, as the looter of Manchurian wealth is fast dissipating the political capital which Lenin accumulated in the East. The language of Lenin cushioned the acts of Stalin for a while. But then those acts became too ruthless and raw.

Nevertheless, the real reason for the pro-Russia sentiments of some Asiatics is not Russia's virtues but the fact that she is the rival of the Western powers whom the Orient has long known as imperialists and whom the East can no longer abide. This is a deep emotion and therefore resists argument, logic, and facts.

Further credit accrues to Russia from Communistic advocacy of the distribution of land among peasants. Asia is a leviathan continent of poor, poorly-clad, illiterate tillers of soil and tenders of cattle. In all Asiatic nations, a rich upper class of landlords, merchants, aristocrats, and officials mercilessly grinds the masses. Everywhere, accordingly, movements of protest have sprouted; they are led by young men, often trained in the West or in Moscow, with radical ideas about land reforms.

China must have a land reform, and India too, and Iran, and other countries as well. To people who have lived like animals, a handful of soil, a piece of land is the most important thing in the world. Russia may despoil Manchuria with Chinese Communist acquiescence; but then the Chinese Communists have given land to peasants in areas they rule. The Indian Communists have collaborated with the British imperialists and they flirt with and work with the Moslem League whose membership is overwhelmingly landlord. Yet they organize peasants too and put themselves in the van of any violent protest action like a naval mutiny.

Asia has been miserable for centuries. Whoever has not seen its sorrow and degradation cannot fully understand it. Any little light becomes a bright beacon if all around is black darkness; any kind of water will be swallowed in the desert.

Russia's power, prestige, and past were wind in the sails of the Chinese Communists. But the strength of those Communists rests on more solid ground: Generalissimo Chiang Kai-shek is surrounded by landlords, and many of his officers are landlords or sons of landlords; he has consequently resisted the land reform whereas the Communists have introduced it. The Communists follow the Kremlin line. That gives Russia a hold on China even when her deeds are anti-Chinese.

This is Russia's great challenge to the West.

Asia and Europe want a new deal.

If America, England, France, Holland, Spain, Italy, Greece, etc., reject the new and insist on the past and on the old, on kings, landlords, warlords, and foreign overlords, then Moscow will be Mecca.

23. *America and Soviet Russia*

THE NEGRO leader Walter White, Secretary of the National
Association for the Advancement of Colored People, used to go
down now and then to see President Roosevelt in the White House.
Shortly after Roosevelt died, Walter White went to the White House
for a talk with Truman. As he entered Truman's office, Truman said
to him: "I know what you are thinking. You are thinking how strange
it is that the President isn't sitting here."

Some time later, in a conference with two writers, President Truman said: "I didn't want this job. I don't want this job."

Truman is typical of America. He had greatness thrust upon him.

America does not want the job which its position in world affairs
is thrusting upon it. No demand was so insistent, so widespread, and
so immediately successful as the demand to "bring the boys home"
from overseas service. The American people wanted their sons on
the front porch and on the farm. The American people are not imperialistic. The American pays his taxes loyally and hates it. Nothing
is more popular than the reduction of expenses for battleships and
bureaucrats. Nothing is less popular than "gold braid" and "brass
hats." Anti-militarism is a potent influence throughout the United
States.

The "gold braid" and the "brass hats" want island bases, and a big
navy, air force, and army. Certain interests want Arabian oil. They
have a following among "nationalists" and "patriots." They are a
powerful lobby. The sentiments of millions are sometimes less effective than the wire-pullings of a few.

Okinawa, Saipan, and Truk need not be fortified against Japan; a
new Japanese law, whose enforcement America can compel, rules
out the maintenance of all armed forces. However, the militarists will
now argue that the Pacific islands and Iceland or Greenland and the
Aleutians, as well as bigger armaments, are a defense against Russia.
Depending on world events, this contention may strike a sympathetic
echo in the public.

America is race-conscious and color-conscious. Such intolerance of
differences is neither democratic nor Christian. Yet America is not a

vengeful nation. Under public pressure, chiefly from church groups, the Federal government in February, 1946, permitted relief shipments by voluntary societies to Germany. The average American is pleased with the policy towards Japan; it is cheap and realistic without being harsh. Americans have friendly feelings and admiration for the Soviet peoples. They have a traditional bond of fellowship with the Chinese. They find it difficult to recall that Italians were their enemies.

Whether it is their idealism or religion or their self-conscious sense of guilt for living so well, Americans respond to suffering. They would like to feed the hungry. The same idealism makes them react against aggressors, torturers, and dictators.

Americans like to side with the underdog.

Americans regard freedom as a natural right.

Americans want the world to think well of them.

Americans are good material for a new and better world.

But . . . Americans are afraid of being "suckers." They resent anybody taking advantage of their inexperience and gullibility. They are afraid of being outsmarted by older countries. They prefer to mind their own business and worry when they are minding other people's business. They would enjoy living in a world of nylon stockings, Frigidaires, Havana cigars, horse races, quiz programs, hit parades, steaks, banana splits, detective stories, comics, and new automobile models. They know they are living in a world of atom bombs, Superfortresses, power politics, and problems, problems, problems.

The American brain is thus a bundle of contradictions. America, still trying to get its postwar bearings, is not yet accustomed to its responsibilities as the strongest nation on earth. America is like a child with its hand on the throttle of a mighty Diesel engine; anything may happen.

President Truman said in his first message to Congress on April 16, 1945: "In this shrinking world, it is futile to seek safety behind geographical barriers. Real security will be found only in law and justice." Fine. He said in New York on October 28, 1945: "We do not seek for ourselves one inch of territory in any place in the world." Excellent. But in the next sentence he added: "Outside the right to establish necessary bases for our protection, we look for nothing which belongs to any other power." Truman wants island bases for security although he tells Congress that "Real security will be found only in law and justice."

Why does Truman talk law one day and island bases or war on another day? Because there can be no law without provision for the enforcement of law, and who can enforce law on great nations? The ultimate way, and in most cases the only way, of enforcing a law on a nation is to make war on it.

America is caught in the contradiction of living as a nation in a world that has split the atom and burst the bounds of nationalism. All nations are caught in the same contradiction. That contradiction may strangle mankind.

Stop Russia, certain people insist. But suppose she does not wish to be stopped? Is the only answer another world war, the first atomic war? Russia is a law unto herself, as every nation, particularly every strong nation, is a law unto itself.

The problem of Russia is thus the problem of nationalism in a world that will get internationalism or get itself into another international war.

How could there possibly be a third world war? How could it arise?

Anthony Eden, on the eve of the San Francisco Conference in 1945 when he was still British Foreign Secretary, said in Glasgow: "We have always, though sometimes tardily, as recent history well shows, striven to prevent Europe's falling under the domination of one power. We have never sought such a position for ourselves, and we have never allowed any other state to obtain it, for we knew that if this were to happen our own liberties would soon be gone with those of the rest of Europe. We have fought three great world wars for this end."

The United States has fought two great world wars for this end.

Having fought the first and second world wars to prevent one country from dominating Europe, England and America are interested in preventing Russia from dominating Europe. If Russia succeeded in dominating Europe she would also dominate Asia. The European problem and the Asiatic problem have merged into one Eurasian problem.

Any Russian expansion in Europe or Asia is America's business and at the same time and for the same reason it is British business.

Russian aggression against small or weak states in Eurasia can be regarded by the American and British governments as a step towards Russian control of a billion and a half people and therefore as a threat to the rest of the world.

Hitler aggression and Japanese aggression contained the same threat and caused the second world war.

Hitler argued that Germany went to war in self-defense. The Nazis actually charged the Poles with aggression. The world laughed—and had to fight. In recent years, the Bolsheviks have shared the inverted Nazi concept of aggression. Did not Stalin and Molotov accuse England and France of aggression in 1939? Did not the Communists abroad and the innocents abroad and all fellow-travelers of the Communists repeat this nonsense? Totalitarians are frequently guilty of verbal vulgarity. But they do not become slaves to their own slander; they hope others will.

However disguised and excused, any aggression anywhere may be the signal for a third world war.

The first shot of the second world war was fired on September 18, 1931, when the Japanese seized Mukden. But many people did not hear it until it re-echoed on the other side of the world ten years later, at Pearl Harbor on December 7, 1941.

I have read articles and speeches by seemingly intelligent Americans who say: "America and Russia are so far from one another; they have no territorial differences; why should they fight?" Neither did America have any territorial differences with Germany. Yet America fought two wars with Germany on the one issue of European domination. Those who are comforted by the absence of territorial conflicts between the Soviet Union and the United States pay too much attention to flat geography and too little attention to global politics.

Wars do not commence when a big power attacks a big power. The first world war and the second world war started when big powers attacked small powers. Aggression against Abyssinia, Spain, Manchuria, Austria, Czechoslovakia, Albania, and Poland took boys in Omaha, Liverpool, and Leningrad out of their homes and into graves all over the world.

Aggression against small countries is the beginning of all our woes.

Has Russia been an aggressor?

There is an excellent Soviet definition of aggression, drafted by Soviet Foreign Commissar Maxim Litvinov and embodied in the Convention for the Definition of Aggression signed in London on July 4, 1933, by the Soviet government and the governments of Rumania, Czechoslovakia, Yugoslavia, Turkey, and Lithuania and subsequently by Poland, Iran, Afghanistan, Finland, Esthonia, and Latvia.

This Convention says, in Article 2, an "aggressor . . . shall be considered to be that state which is first to commit any of the following actions:

"1. Declaration of war upon another state.

"2. Invasion by its armed forces, with or without declaration of war, of the territory of another state.

"3. Attack by its land, naval, or air forces, with or without a declaration of war, on the territory, vessels, or aircraft of another state . . .

"4. Naval blockade of the coasts or ports of another state.

"5. . . . support to armed bands formed on its territory which have invaded another state . . ."

The "Annex" to this Convention is even more interesting and apropos than the Convention itself. It reads: "No act of aggression within the meaning of Article 2 of this Convention can be justified on any of the following grounds, among others:

"A. The internal condition of a state, for example: its political, economic, or social structure, alleged defects in its administration, disturbances due to strikes, revolutions, counter-revolutions or civil war . . ."

According to this official Soviet government definition of aggression, the Soviet government has been the aggressor in Finland, Poland, Latvia, Lithuania, Esthonia, and Iran—all of whom signed the Litvinov convention.

It is futile to expect Big Three unity when one of them is expanding. Russian aggression and expansion have put England and America on guard. Unity and aggression are incompatible. Unity and expansion are irreconcilable.

It is equally futile to plead for American-Soviet friendship and simultaneously to condone the Soviet expansion which strains that friendship.

Stalin first asked Poland for Polish territory in December, 1941, when General Sikorski, Polish Prime Minister, visited him in the Kremlin. Moscow told the British in 1943 that it intended to annex the Baltic countries. Moscow asked for Czechoslovak territory in 1943. Russian aggrandizement was confirmed by Roosevelt and Churchill at Teheran in December, 1943, and at Yalta in February, 1945. That was before there had been any serious tension or friction between the three big war allies. That was before the atomic bomb fell on Hiroshima. That was when the peoples and governments of Great Britain and the United States were vociferously and overwhelmingly friendly and helpful to Russia. Stalin's expansion and aggrandizement, therefore, cannot be attributed to the atomic bomb or to Anglo-American hostility.

We fought the second world war in order to introduce some semblance of law into international affairs, for there is peace only to the extent that there is law. But aggression in violation of treaties is lawlessness, the maintenance of troops in foreign countries against the wishes of their peoples is lawlessness, pressure on small nations for concessions is lawlessness—the exact kind of lawlessness which brought war in 1939. The law-breaker robs others of their security and usually, in the end, gets himself into trouble.

In *The Soviets in World Affairs* I wrote a detailed history of Bolshevik Russia's relations with the capitalist world. The Soviet Union was for many years subjected to unwarranted armed intervention, economic boycotts, financial embargoes, and diplomatic exclusions. Its envoys were assassinated, its offices abroad raided.

That was an era. It lasted while Russia was relatively weak and comparatively Communistic. While it lasted Russia was afraid and unaggressive. Now Russia is strong and nationalistic. Now Russia is aggressive. This is an altogether new era. If Russia were afraid she would not be aggressive.

The Nazis did not understand the democracies. They held them in contempt and underrated their determination. Stalin has behaved as though he held similar views. He could say truthfully to himself: "At Teheran and Yalta, Roosevelt and Churchill gave me what I asked for in Germany, Poland, the Balkans, Manchuria, Korea, the Kurile Islands, and Sakhalin. The moment they agreed in principle to my annexation of parts of East Prussia, but before they finally approved of it, I actually incorporated them into the Soviet Union and they did not demur. Then in Rumania, Austria, Poland, and Bulgaria I unilaterally set up governments of my own choosing; this was in contravention of the Yalta agreement ["The three governments will jointly assist the people in any European state or former Axis satellite state in Europe . . . to form interim governments broadly representative of all democratic elements in the population"] and Truman, Byrnes, Attlee, and Bevin know it and have said so but they do nothing about it. In fact, America, under popular pressure, but not without help from my Communist party there, has withdrawn most of her troops from Europe. I demanded the Kars and Ardahan provinces from Turkey and also, at Potsdam, 'a fortress inside the straits' to dominate Istanbul. America and England agreed to keep the straits open and that is fine; but with my fortress I could close the straits. Strange how quietly they took the whole thing. They do not seem to be very dynamic. England is having trouble in the Empire. The Arabs are stirring. China is divided. The American Communist party and its "fronts" have done a good job confusing people and paralyzing the action of liberals and labor. The German Communist party is trying to get the upper hand in all Germany. France is unable to act decisively because of the French Communist party. Europe and Asia are starving. I have built up a tremendous new Russian empire. They have swallowed that camel; will they strain at the gnat? I will see what happens if I turn towards Iran and Turkey."

This psychology together with strident nationalism and the usual tensions within a totalitarian state might produce a war. They produced the second world war.

In these circumstances, some Americans and Englishmen propose that America forego the manufacture of atomic bombs. Why not forego the manufacture of TNT bombs and Superfortresses and super-dreadnaughts? Why not disarm? Why are nations not ready to disarm? Because they see potential conflicts between themselves.

Suppose America stopped producing atomic bombs. Is there any guarantee that Russia would not produce them? Would Russia permit inspection of Soviet plants throughout the country, of power stations and power lines, of laboratories? That question should be put to Moscow. Russia is a police state; for years all Soviet citizens have had to carry passports within the country and register with the police when they move from place to place. Foreigners are under strict surveillance even when, as in the case of foreign correspondents, they merely want to go to a provincial town, see the sights, talk to some men-in-the-street, and get general impressions. Foreign technical experts to peer into every nook of Soviet industry to discover whether atomic bombs were being made? An International Atomic Authority to own and operate uranium deposits and atomic plants in Russia? That is quite inconceivable to anyone who knows a little about the Soviet system. When the United States was giving the Soviet government eight billion dollars' worth of Lend-Lease arms and materials, American military men were not permitted to go to the front or into Soviet factories for more than a brief perfunctory glimpse.

Give the bomb to Russia, some propose.

What would Russia do with the atomic bomb? Use it against Germany and Japan? That is unnecessary; they have been crushed and occupied. Use it against the United States or England? That is no good reason for giving it to her. Use it against a small country for extortion purposes? That is no good reason for giving it to her.

"But Russia will have the bomb anyway," they argue, "and meanwhile the Anglo-American atomic monopoly sows suspicion in Moscow and widens the rift between the two worlds." Perhaps Russia has the bomb; perhaps Russia will get it. Professor Harold J. Urey, prominent atomic physicist, said early in 1946 that the Russians may begin to "produce [atomic] bombs within three years." Other authorities put it at five to ten years. But suppose it is only two years or one year or six months. The map of Europe and Asia is being made every day, and if Russia has the bomb the map may be made to the disadvantage of Europe and Asia. The atomic bomb in Russia's hands would make weak nations in Eurasia quail before her even more than they do already. It would make America and England more inclined to appease Russia than they already are. In this sense, the gift of the bomb to Russia would keep us out of war, as appeasement always keeps nations out of war—for a while. Then the war is worse because of the appeasement.

Would the revelation of the atomic secrets to Russia relieve her of suspicion and fear?

"It is untrue that America has the atomic bomb," I have said. Audiences are startled. Actually, of course, America possesses the bomb. But under what circumstances would America use it?

Speaking at a celebration in his honor in Washington, D. C., Admiral Chester W. Nimitz, Commander of the United States Fleet in the Pacific, made a most astounding statement. "The atomic bomb," he said, "did not win the war against Japan. The Japanese had, in fact, already sued for peace before the atomic age was announced to the world with the destruction of Hiroshima and before the Russian entry into the war. In saying that the atomic bomb played no decisive part, from a purely military standpoint, in the defeat of Japan, this is no effort to minimize the awful power of this new weapon."

If this is correct—and Nimitz should know—then the dropping of the atomic bomb on Hiroshima, certainly the loosing of the second atomic missile on Nagasaki, was the worst single atrocity of the second world war despite the fact that the end of the anti-Japanese conflict may have been hastened thereby.

It nevertheless remains true that the United States government could not conceivably, in peacetime, order an atomic bombing of

Mexico, or Argentina, or France, or England because it wished to extort something from the victim. It is inconceivable so long as the United States is a democracy and so long as public opinion remains virile, critical, and free.

There is a defense against the atomic bomb. It is democracy.

Stalin knows that the United States will not use the bomb for aggressive purposes. He probably hopes that the United States will hesitate to use it in defense of a small country.

I have seen many statements in American newspapers that the Soviet authorities are suspicious of or afraid of the United States. I have seen no proof of it in Soviet publications or in Soviet declarations or in Soviet acts. Indeed, Joseph Barnes, a pro-Soviet writer, told a Foreign Policy Association luncheon audience in New York on December 15, 1945, shortly after his return from a trip to Russia, that he had found "arrogance and bumptiousness" there towards the outside world.

Russia is not afraid and not suspicious for two clear reasons: the British Empire is in decline and on the defensive; America rushed from victory to headlong psychological and military demobilization. Nobody else could attack Russia, not Germany, not Japan, not Iran, not Finland, not China, not France. Britain's weakness and America's unimperialistic demobilization encouraged Stalin. The strong respect strength.

Russia's behavior is explained not by fear of an attack but rather by her certainty that she will not be attacked.

Is my view prejudiced, or unfair to Russia or too kind to America or too friendly to England?

I check my opinions carefully. I have never hesitated to criticize and condemn the actions and policies of the American and British governments. My first loyalties are to freedom, progress, peace, and human happiness; when I think anybody interferes with these I speak up. I do not believe that criticism makes wars. On the contrary, lack of criticism may make wars; the soft-pedaling of dangers and mistakes may hasten wars. Hitler did not send his armies across the German frontier because some person delivered a speech or wrote a book. Stalin does not order mobilization when he reads a sizzling denunciation of the Soviet Union; he merely replies with a sizzling denunciation.

Churchill poured forth fire and brimstone on Nazi Germany yet

Hitler did not attack England in 1939; he attacked grimly silent Poland and tried to avoid fighting Britain. From August 23, 1939, to June 22, 1941, the Soviet authorities not only refrained from criticizing Germany; they fawned on Germany, and then Germany invaded Russia.

The reactionary American newspaper syndicates, radio commentators, editorial scribes, and Congressmen who incessantly crusade against Russia are repugnant to me. But they cannot precipitate a war any more than isolationist propaganda before Pearl Harbor kept America neutral. Propaganda can ripen sentiment or delay the ripening of sentiment, but wars are precipitated by concrete military moves, the marching of armies, the bombing of cities—by aggression.

Has the government of Britain or of America given the Soviet Union cause for alarm and concern?

The American government has been criticized for its reluctance to intervene against the Argentine dictatorship and against Franco. I was actively engaged in the fight against Franco, and I loathe any dictatorship. But I think it would be dangerous to the peace of the world to establish the principle that great powers have the right to intervene with armed force in the affairs of another state which is not at war. One day it might be a liberal government intervening to overthrow a dictatorship, and the next day it might be a reactionary government intervening to overthrow a democracy. In one case, the motive might be honestly anti-Fascist; in another, it might be imperialist.

Foreign intervention rallies the people around the dictator for patriotic reasons even when they are opposed to him for class and economic reasons.

It is significant that those who approve of Soviet intervention and aggression were loudest in urging American intervention in Spain and Argentina. But how could the United States protest Soviet intervention in Eurasia if it intervened itself in Latin America?

Armed intervention in a peaceful state is permissible only in obedience to the voluntary decision of an effective international organization acting under no pressure from the one or two powers that are likely to be chosen as the intervening agents of the organization.

The very fact, however, that the British and American governments avoided armed intervention in Spain and Argentina although they vehemently excoriated, condemned, exposed, and denounced the dictatorships there should reassure Moscow, for it shows how hesitant democracies are in taking military action against weak countries which could only put up a token resistance; how much greater would be the hesitation in attacking a mighty military nation like the Soviet Union.

I see valid ground for censure of the British government's action in Indonesia, but that was a case, as Jawaharlal Nehru wrote, of "one decadent empire [trying] to help another still more ramshackle empire," and the Kremlin probably took comfort from the cracks in the Dutch and British imperial positions which the bloody Java events disclosed. Certainly, Russia is not menaced when colonials refuse to be ruled by Western imperialists.

The British government has been criticized for its actions in Greece. This is a turgid, complicated situation because the domestic affairs of that unhappy, hungry country, as of several other countries, are less a reflection of political alignments within than of the pull and tug of rival foreign powers. "It is tragic," Sumner Welles wrote in the *New York Herald Tribune* of March 6, 1946, "that after liberation Greece should have become an arena for a contest between Soviet and British interests. . . . It has encouraged civil war. . . . The Near East has become the scene of an increasing conflict of interest between the Soviet Union, bent upon an expansion of her influence over that area, and the Western powers, which are determined to keep open to all nations the channels of communications through the eastern Mediterranean, the Suez Canal, and the Red Sea."

If the Communist party or the EAM gained the upper hand in Greece (and if Russia obtained the one-power trusteeship of Tripolitania in North Africa) Turkey would be semicircled, Italy would be flanked by Russian power, and the whole British position in the Near East would be menaced. "Russia is reaching across our throat," British Foreign Secretary Bevin said.

Churchill made the mistake, not surprising in his case, of encouraging the Greek royalists. The Labor government had no sympathy with royalists. It tried to follow another line. But it could not easily shake off its Tory legacy. And it felt compelled to try to keep Russia from seizing one of England's few remaining footholds in southern Europe. Inside, through the EAM and the Communists, outside by Russia's attitude towards the transfer of the Dodecanese Islands to Greece and by Albanian and Yugoslav demands for Greek territory, Moscow is making a bid for the control of Greece; England fights back with poor weapons.

The central fields of struggle between Russia and the Western powers are Germany and China. These nations, as well as Greece, as well as Italy, will not enjoy tranquillity and prosperity until the conflict between Russia and England and America is resolved. Today, each side is endeavoring to draw the defeated Axis peoples, the small neutrals, and China or parts thereof into its camp.

The process is shrouded in much murky and dishonest propaganda. When the American and British military authorities do not denazify their zones to the satisfaction of the American and British Communists, the uproar is terrific. When the Communist daily of Berlin, the *Deutsche Volkzeitung*, of January 31, 1946, proposes allowing "small Nazis" to join the German Communist party, and when Wilhelm Pieck, top German Communist, in the same week asks Nazis to help the Communists in "reassuring a democratic, anti-Fascist Germany," the critics of American and British denazification are silent. When German industrialists are permitted to operate in the Western zones this immediately becomes a preparation for war against Russia. When German industries are restored in the Russian zone it is regarded as smart politics.

Who runs German industry makes a lot of difference. German industrialists contributed to the advent of Hitler and of the war. A natural, and sometimes a financial, bond exists between them and certain conservative groups in the capitalist West. The international liaisons and the domestic actions of the industrialists should be sternly scrutinized and curbed; yet the British contention is not without validity that the restriction of German factory output creates hunger, unemployment, and unrest, and as a result, new difficulties for the Western powers and new opportunities for Communist aggrandizement. Perhaps the escape from this dilemma is German industry without German industrialists.

But the crowning fact of the German situation is that half of Germany has been annexed by Russia or Poland or is occupied by Russia. This area has been sealed off by Moscow and is irretrievably lost to Western influence. In the remaining half of Germany, on the other hand, German Communists and some German Social Democrats who have fallen under the Communist spell and certain pro-Soviet American, British, and French trade unionists are furthering Russia's interests and undermining England's and America's.

The eastern half of Germany has been drawn into the dictatorial orbit. Hitler's concentration camps have been reopened and fly the hammer and sickle. In the western half, democracy is still a weak reed. But there at least the struggle for free speech, free trade unions, free political parties, and free men can go on.

The deterioration of relations between Russia and the West means that Germany will be divided in two.

In Japan and China the Soviet government has a legitimate, power-political grievance. Japan is American-controlled territory. A China united under the rule of anti-Communist Chiang Kai-shek would be solidly ensconced in a mighty American sphere of influence.

"The American armed forces defeated Japan," it might be contended. True, but the Soviet armed forces drove Hitler out of the Baltic states, Poland, Rumania, Bulgaria, Yugoslavia, and Hungary, and shed most blood in crushing Hitler in Germany, and yet Americans object to Russia's preeminent political position in those countries.

What-Came-First:-The-Chicken-Or-The-Egg? debates are always fascinating but usually fruitless. Russia staked out her claims for the Baltic region, Poland, the Balkans, and Manchuria long before United States troops landed in Tokyo Bay and before Japan had been driven out of China. Moscow could reply that it was easy to divine American intentions in Japan and China. And had not Churchill proclaimed that Britain would not liquidate the Empire? Then why should not Russia reach out for empire?

My own attitude is that England should liquidate the Empire, Russia should not acquire an empire, and America should not aspire to empire. Then war and threats of war would cease.

Britain's imperialism is in retreat. American imperialism is not full-fledged. Russian imperialism is dynamic, expansive, and unconcerned with the destinies of the human beings over whom it spreads like a glacier; Iran, the looting of Manchuria, the annexations at the expense of Poland, Czechoslovakia, Japan, and Germany, and the oppressive, Soviet-puppet regimes in Europe prove this. It cannot be said that the United States or Great Britain has annexed any continental areas, or partitioned any countries, or looted any, or set up governments and then prohibited the voters from changing them.

The United States is keeping a strong air force and navy, and seeks more island bases. Russia has kept under arms many millions of men, is building a bigger navy, and is concentrating on the expansion of armaments industries. What is decisive is Russia's absorption since 1939 of a vast empire, still growing, where freedom is dead.

It cannot be proved that America or Britain has any intention of attacking Russia. It cannot be proved that Russia has any intention of attacking America or Great Britain. It is clear that Russian expansion constitutes the world's major problem. Expansion leads to war.

For many months after the victories over Germany and Japan, innumerable Americans, Englishmen, and others gave Russia the benefit of every doubt that tortured their minds. They could only hope that Moscow's moves in Poland, the Balkans, Austria, Germany, and Asia were a passing phase. They held their tongues, and their breath. They praised Russia while fearing the worst.

At all the wartime conferences—Teheran, Yalta, Potsdam, etcetera—Russia's one vote counted for more than the two votes of Great Britain and the United States. Russia could not be antagonized; therefore London and Washington, against their better judgment, gave Russia what she asked.

To make the transition from wartime to peacetime diplomacy, a fundamental change of approach was necessary. In the first postwar conference in London in September, 1945, accordingly, Secretary of State Byrnes and Foreign Secretary Bevin tried to teach Foreign Minister Molotov a lesson in peacetime arithmetic: one is one; one is not more than two. Molotov said that was not so. The disagreement was so complete that they could not even agree on a communiqué stating that they had disagreed. Molotov likewise refused to include France and China in the making of the peace. Molotov wanted the Big Three to dominate and in the Big Three he hoped Russia could dominate by the war-period mathematical paradox of one is more than two.

One is more than two is the arithmetic of dictatorship. One is more than one hundred and ninety million.

Russia's apparent intention to dictate in world affairs disturbed the Western powers and China. Nevertheless, relations with Russia were too crucial and already too tender to admit of frivolous despair. Byrnes decided to make another effort; the three Foreign Ministers met in Moscow in December, 1945. Iran and Turkey, bubbling issues under the surface, were passed over in silence. In everything that was officially discussed, Molotov won.

Restraint and optimism still triumphed over doubt. Then the United Nations convened, for the first time, in London in February, 1946. Bevin jousted fiercely with Vishinsky over Greece and Indonesia, but the Russian rejected talks on Iran where his comrades had established an "autonomous" government of Azerbaijan in territory adjacent to Stalin's Soviet Georgia; the territory was under Russian military occupation. Earlier, Russia had demanded an oil concession in northern Iran, and Teheran had refused.

This precipitated a crisis in Anglo-Russian and American-Russian relations. Senator Arthur H. Vandenberg, returning from London where he served as an American delegate, delivered a widely-commented speech in the Senate, in which he asked "What is Russia up to now?" "Russia," he declared, "is the supreme conundrum of our time." Then Secretary Byrnes, straight from the same UN meeting, revealed his concern in a long address. He referred to "aggression" by Russia and said world conditions were not "sound or reassuring." That same day, another American UN delegate, John Foster Dulles, who on occasions has been the Republican adviser to the Democratic administration, told a Foreign Policy Association audience in Philadelphia: "It is particularly hard to find ways of working together with the Soviet Union, for it seems not to want cooperation."

Columnists, commentators, editors, and the public on both sides of the Atlantic and elsewhere reflected the gathering crisis.

"What to do about Russia?" everybody asked.

Winston Churchill, painter, was in Florida for a rest-cure amply earned in his five great years as Britain's Prime Minister. With President Truman he traveled to the tiny town of Fulton, Missouri. The worried world cocked an ear. Truman introduced Churchill and said: "I know that Mr. Churchill will have something constructive in his speech." He knew because he knew the speech. So did Secretary Byrnes.

"Time is plenty short," Churchill warned.

"Prevention is better than cure," he said.

"A shadow has fallen upon the scene so lately lighted by the United Nations victory," he continued. "Nobody knows what Soviet Russia and its Communist International organization intends to do in the immediate future or what are the limits, if any, of their expansive and proselytizing tendencies."

Serious words.

"I do not believe that Soviet Russia desires war," Churchill declared. "What they desire is the fruits of war and the indefinite expansion of their power and doctrines."

What did Churchill propose?

"The fraternal association of the English-speaking peoples."

"A special relationship between the British Commonwealth and Empire and the United States of America."

"Fraternal association," Churchill explained, "requires . . . the continuance of the intimate relationships between our military advisers, leading to a common study of potential dangers, and similarity of weapons and manuals of instructions and the interchange of officers and cadets at technical colleges. It should carry with it the continuance of the present facilities for mutual security by the joint use of all naval and air force bases in the possession of either country all over the world. . . . Already we use together a large number of islands; more may be entrusted to our care in the near future. . . . Thus, whatever happens, and thus only, shall we be secure ourselves. . . ."

This looks very much like the text of a military alliance.

Churchill and his proposal and the British Labor government were bitterly attacked by Stalin in an interview—a most unusual act. The Soviet press excoriated Churchill with passion. The reaction in America was varied. Some liked his analysis and his projected alliance. Others, including myself, felt that while Churchill had done a service by calling attention to the central problem of our time, his proposal was unfortunate and inadequate.

The peace of the world depends on a steady job at a living wage for all workers, land that yields a livelihood to all farmers, liberty for all individuals of all races and classes, and independence for all countries and colonies. Alliances do not yield these results.

This is not the age of the common man. It is the age in which the common man has commenced to make insistent demands. If he does not get full employment, a full dinner-pail, education, security, opportunity, and surcease from discrimination, he may become an easy victim of the totalitarians who promise him these things and ask him, in return, to forfeit his freedom before they fulfill the promise.

All the imperfections of the democratic world will be used by the Communists to destroy it. Here and there, especially in Latin America, the Fascists will pursue a similar strategy.

Moscow holds up a mirror which reflects and often enlarges the misery of those who choose to look into it. Against that, an alliance or any other power-political mechanism is powerless.

Churchill's proposal is a nineteenth century power proposal. It might suffice to deal with certain aspects of the Russian challenge. It might either prevent a Soviet military move or serve as one possible device of coping with it. But Russia is not merely a nation; it is not merely Peter the Great. Russia is Peter armed with Marx, a perverted, almost unrecognizable Marx, to be sure, but a Marx who nevertheless still represents the revolt against what is rotten in the *status quo*.

Churchill can wrestle with Peter, as he wrestled so skilfully with Hitler. But he has no weapons against Marx. In fact, there is reason to doubt whether he dealt Hitler the final *coup*. Hitler also challenged the whole world; his Panzers and dive bombers would not have leveled Europe so quickly if Europe had not been eaten through with disease. Japan's path to conquest was likewise smoothed by the unhappiness of Asia's colonials—in Java, Burma, China. The ultimate defeat of Hitler and Japan requires the molding of a better world and of a better human being. Otherwise Hitler and the Nipponese warlords will merely have yielded their places to Stalin.

Hitler, Mussolini, and Hirohito challenged the democratic world. We smashed the challengers. Now Russia challenges the democratic world. This is the greatest challenge democracy has ever confronted. It is a challenge to improve or succumb.

It does not matter that the challenger has more room for improvement than the challenged. The subjects of the challenger are not accessible to outside challenge; they live behind the iron curtain which hides the high wall and the inmates within it. The challenger is a challenger not because of his superiority but because of our shortcomings.

Russia or no Russia, there would be death in India, discontent in China, dissension in Greece, republicanism in Italy, and anti-Fascism in Spain. The Soviet government merely makes itself the spokesman and champion of all opponents of what is. It collects them and exploits them.

Organize an Anglo-American military alliance to "Stop Russia"? How would that affect Russia's role outside her borders or outside her zone? March an army into the Soviet Union and smash the regime? How many millions of lives would it cost; would it, even if successful, kill the decay in the body of democracy? It might have the opposite effect.

Churchill attacks the problem on the military and diplomatic level, not on the social, economic, and political level. But the problem is chiefly social, economic, and political.

International politics used to be the relationship between governments. It was "foreign" policy. A momentous change has taken place, and as yet few foreign offices have realized it. Diplomacy has been invaded by the people's problems. America's relationship to China is no longer an exclusive relationship with the Chinese chief of state, foreign minister, and foreign traders. America's relationship to China must be, above all, a relationship to the land reform and industrialization. America's, and England's and France's relationship to Germany is a question of whether the Social Democrats can survive the attempt of the Communists to merge with and devour them. America's relationship to Great Britain involves Socialism, freedom for India, and tariffs.

That is why diplomats in spats no longer belong. Diplomacy must descend from the rarefied realm of *démarches, aide-memoires,* "conversations," and notes, into the peasant's hut, the factory, and the political parties. Diplomacy must deal with the frustrations of the middle class and the aspirations of the hundreds of millions, for these are winds in the sails of totalitarian adventurers.

The foreign policies of America and Britain should be as broad, and deep, and inclusive as human life. Then they will come to grips with the great challenge which Russia has flung out to them.

The expansion of the Soviet Union has already induced the United States and British governments to begin mending their broken military bridges and, wherever possible, to do it together. Continued tension between Russia and the West will produce an Anglo-American alliance in fact if not in name.

But if England and America stop there they will not meet the challenge. Russia will try to split every country in the world. In that atmosphere, the fundamental problems of poverty and democracy will not be solved. On the contrary, the people will bend under back-breaking armament budgets, and freedom will languish.

This is one world geographically. But politically and ideologically the one world is riven; there are two worlds. Perhaps there are three: Russia, England and America, and the remainder where the contest between them rages.

In the present era of heavy foreign and domestic pressures, few countries in Europe or Asia can stand alone. Within all of them, even in those under complete or partial Soviet domination, the two worlds are struggling for supremacy.

Communist wedges have been driven into the Anglo-American

world. Western-world bulges exist in the Russian zone wherever men yearn for freedom and relief from the unbroken tension that characterizes one-party despotism.

The front between the two worlds is irregular. The two worlds overlap. France is two worlds. Germany is two worlds. Where there is health but not great strength, in the Scandinavian area, for instance, an attempt will be made to balance one world against the other, to benefit from both, and succumb to neither.

The front is long and the battle will be long. Battle lines will shift. Lulls will intervene. Armistices will be signed. Prisoners will be exchanged.

Treaties will not help. The path from the first world war to the second world war was paved with non-aggression treaties, peace conferences, solemn and passionate promises to keep the peace, and beautiful descriptions of the benefits of peace.

War is a relationship between nations and it is natural, therefore, that its elimination should be sought by the establishment of a new relationship between nations through treaties, alliances, leagues of nations, and, finally, world government.

The weakness of Poland in comparison with Nazi Germany was the immediate impetus to war. If Poland had had the support of an international organization which, to the certain knowledge of Hitler, would march to Poland's (or any other nation's) defense, the war might have been prevented.

But this truth is an over-simplification of the world situation. The fact is that Poland did not have the support of an international organization and could not have had it at the time because any organization would have suffered from the divisions between the Anglo-French entente and Russia, and from the aloofness of the United States.

The situation is better today because collective security is attainable.

In the sphere where it might be interested in aggrandizement, no practicable combination could stop the United States; but the United States is not likely to go to war for aggrandizement.

England could be stopped from committing acts of aggression.

Given Anglo-American readiness to act, either directly or through an international organization, Russia too could be stopped, at least in the next few years, for Russia is weak from loss of blood and wealth in beating the Nazis. The Soviet government does not want a major war and would try hard to avoid even a lesser war if it knew that such a conflict would grow into a bigger affair by reason of collective-security intercession on the part of other great powers.

Provided Russian territorial expansion does not subject relations within the Big Three to an unbearable strain, the central problem of the next five or six years will not be actual world war but rather the absorption, penetration, and undermining of weak states by big powers in order to extend their spheres of influence; this would later be regarded as a threat by the non-expanding powers and thus might lead to the first atomic clash between nations.

An Anglo-American alliance could very likely deter Russia from invading a foreign country, and a United Nations with teeth—that is, without the veto—would have the same effect. How, however, could that alliance or the UN keep Moscow from tearing at the inner social and political structure of foreign countries?

The unequal strength of one nation can be corrected by allies or by an effective international collective security body. But the unequal domestic, political, and economic development of nations which makes some eager to expand and others incapable of resisting expansion cannot be eradicated by power instruments.

The final key to international politics and to peace is not alliances nor organizations but the domestic policy of nations and the social character of national regimes.

Suppose the United States, Great Britain, and many smaller countries that would follow their lead were prepared to create a world government, and suppose the Soviet Union refused to adhere because it did not want to become part of a capitalist government or because it felt that it would be hopelessly outvoted in such a body? What then?

As soon as the non-Soviet countries are ready for world government—and the sooner the better—they should offer every inducement to the Soviet government to join them in initiating a world state, leaving broad areas of autonomy for the expression of the personality of each country. If Russia wished to remain outside, no pressure and no punitive measures would be applied to her. The non-Soviet countries would merely organize a four-fifths-world government and keep the door always open for Russia.

To obviate the resulting cleavage, some would counsel against world government for the present. That would not end the cleavage. That would simply cover it up. The cleavage already exists. If this were one world we would proclaim it joyously. Since there are two worlds we do well to recognize the fact.

To refuse to organize a world government as long as Russia will not join is to allow Russia to keep the non-Soviet world divided endlessly so that it cannot withstand Russian pressure. It is far healthier for both worlds to admit the division between them than for the democracies to nourish the illusion of oneness—the Bolsheviks have no such illusion—when in fact one part is undermining the other while consolidating and extending its own sphere of influence.

I would rather the world were one world, one decent world. But blindness does not make it so. One World is a great goal, and Willkie, who gave humanity that slogan, was a great man. But one world is not a fact.

The division of the world into two unequal parts does not preclude friendly diplomatic relations between them. Trade, scientific and cultural exchanges, and travel can flourish. The competition of the two worlds can remain non-violent for a very extended period.

What is the nature of this competition? Is it the old Slav, anti-West Messianism harnessed to modern Communist proselytism? Is it that the world cannot be half-slave and half-free? Is it that the Bolshevik leaders are afraid that they cannot indefinitely maintain their present state-capitalistic tyranny if the rest of the world enjoys personal liberty? Is it that the capitalist nations fear they will be destroyed by Communists and radicals oriented on Moscow?

Whatever the reason for the competition and whatever its duration or intensity the democracies can meet it with only one policy: to set their own house in order and make it more attractive and more comfortable to live in. If they say: We have lived in this house for generations; it was all right for our grandfathers and fathers; our sons and daughters and their visitors and the servants will have to like it; then the servant will leave and the younger generation will move out.

A victory of the conservatives, reactionaries, and defendants of the *status quo* who resist repairs, modern improvements, and new wings will make the house uninhabitable to the new generation who will look for other quarters.

The Axis powers were lured into aggression and war and destruction by the physical weakness of their prospective victims and the reluctance of the non-aggressors to protect those victims.

The Soviet regime feels that it may succeed where others failed because it is equipped to exploit an additional weakness in the capitalist world: the unsolved social, political, and economic problems of many nations.

When Russia reaches out to China, the Mediterranean, North Africa, Trieste, Greece, and, through her Communist parties, into every capitalist country, she is moved not only by imperialistic arrogance but also by ideological confidence. This major Soviet offensive is inspired by the defenselessness of weak countries and the appeasement psychology of large countries, but above all by the unrest and discontent within countries, including the unrest and discontent within the Soviet Union. What makes a nation aggressive is what makes a person aggressive: psychological knots inside and suitable objects outside. Sometimes only one of these two factors suffices.

The democracies export their goods and are ready to export their ideas. They prefer freedom to dictatorship; many democrats are convinced that capitalism is best. But the democracies have not crusaded for a long time. Perhaps they have lost faith in themselves. Perhaps they do not believe in imposing ideas by force. They are actually mingling their capitalism with Socialism, which shows a readiness to try something else.

The Bolsheviks, on the other hand, are sure they are right and that their way is best. They have not proved it but they assert it very vehemently.

Stalin's ideological offensive stems from his certainty that he can win it. He is buoyed in that faith by the stupidity of the defenders within the fortresses he expects to assail. They add some bricks and widen the moat. Stalin smiles: "I have friends within the walls; the Churchills make new friends for me every day. Others inside will be too indifferent, or too bored, or too decadent to fight."

An alliance proposal arouses Moscow's ire. "Tough talk" followed by tough acts impresses the Soviet government. But only when Washington and London begin to favor movements for freedom and social democracy throughout the world will Stalin believe that we have understood his intentions and are prepared, by constructive, progressive measures, to block his offensive.

The British Labor government's plans for the independence of Asiatic colonies worry Moscow much more than Churchill's Anglo-American entente. Let the Western powers shift their support from the feudal landlords of the Near East to the impoverished peasantry, and Moscow will know that something important has happened. Let the Chinese Federal government introduced a land reform and Stalin will say: "They are uniting China and driving me out of it." Let the white race give incontrovertible evidence of a new and honorable attitude towards colored people, and Moscow will realize that it is being robbed of millions of potential political recruits. Let the democracies demonstrate that they combat anti-Semitism, and those who compare and judge will conclude that the democracies are anti-Fascist. Let England and America befriend the forces of social change in Europe, and Europe will find new vigor to fight Slav-Communist imperialism. Let the Anglo-Americans shun Fascists, clerical reactionaries, royalists, economic royalists, and militarists, and the freedom-loving millions will flock to the Anglo-American banner. Let England, America, France, Holland, and Portugal abjure territorial, oil, and trade imperialism, and they will acquire a fresh moral power to obstruct any other imperialism. Let the West refuse to intervene forcibly in the affairs of weak countries and it will have clean hands in blocking Soviet intervention. Let the spokesmen for Eastern colonial peoples crusade not only for freedom from outside tutelage but for social justice inside; then they can hope to be fully free.

These are the kinds of weapons that can stop Russia's offensive against the democracies. This is ideological competition with Russia. It is a substitute for war with Russia. If the democracies win there will be no war, there will be no war ever, there will be a world government which ultimately will include Russia. If Russia wins, there will be no democracies.

Inevitably, some will say that this proposal for conscious ideological competition with Russia is "anti-Russian," cuts a chasm between Russia and the rest of the world, and makes war unavoidable. I think the opposite is true. Moscow is now actively engaged in a combined territorial-ideological offensive against the non-Soviet world. Not to resist means to help Russia expand to a point where, alarmed, the two great Western powers will seek to call a halt by the use of force.

There are these ways of dealing with the Russian problem. 1) Fight Russia now. I reject that vehemently. 2) Appease Russia. (Appeasement always includes saying that what you are doing is not appeasement but the only way of getting on with Russia.) I reject that because it will wipe out freedom in many countries and end in war. 3) Block Russia's territorial expansion by an effective international organization and block Russia's ideological expansion by increasing the contentment and cohesion of the countries in her path. I defend that. It will be attacked by those who do not wish to block Russia's expansion.

A foreign policy based on conscious ideological competition with Russia will improve the chances of peace, check the inroads of totalitarian thinking among liberals, fortify democracy, raise standards of living, and give the free world a much-needed moral lift. The alternative to ideological competition with Russia is to accept defeat supinely at the hands of Russia.

But foreign policy is not the whim or plan of a foreign minister. What America does abroad is determined by what America is at home. The same is true of England and of other nations.

"Have we got leaders big enough and wise enough to carry out an internationalist, progressive policy?" This question troubles many citizens. The answer is that leaders in a democracy cannot be much bigger or move much faster than the people they lead.

"Should we send telegrams to our Congressmen?" I have been asked at meetings where I urge the abolition of the veto in the UN or the rejection of anti-labor legislation.

"By all means," I say, "send telegrams to your Congressmen. But the next time, elect Congressmen who will not need your telegrams."

The men and women who make foreign policy, and every policy, are those who sit in legislative halls and behind desks in government offices. They are elected or they are accessible to the will, pressure, and arguments of those who are elected. Thus ballots make foreign policy. Foreign policy, and peace, are made in Peoria, Illinois, in Hamilton, Ohio, in Dallas and Schenectady, in Liverpool, Glasgow, Hull, and Dover, in Marseilles, Bordeaux, and Nice, in every town and village where voters go to the polls in free, honest elections.

Peace, like charity, like every virtue, begins at home.

The mass of the people desire the welfare of the mass of the people in all countries. The average person will make many material sacrifices for peace; he puts peace above the interests of tariff-seeking corporations and privilege-seeking cartels. Normally, the common folks are neither militaristic nor imperialistic.

But their sentiments, views, and interests are not fully reflected in the political life of their country. Reformers, idealists, civic leaders, social workers, internationalists, Leagues of Women Voters, trade unions, societies for the advancement of this and that noble cause are constantly tugging at the coat-tails of politicians. Would it not be better if they were themselves in politics? The gulf between what many want and what they can work for and get accounts for much of the frustration in the public life of the democracies.

Politics used to be a "game." Politics was a matter of who cleaned the streets and collected the ashes and appointed the police inspector. Politics has become the woof and warp of life; politics decides whether humanity is to be sated, employed, happy, and alive instead of dead by bombs.

The establishment of a better world requires the more active participation of the inhabitants of the world in the political affairs of their nations not only by voting whenever the opportunity is present but also by choosing the opposing candidates. That must not be left to party hacks and professional wardheelers.

The average citizen wants to do something about peace or war, freedom or dictatorship, plenty or poverty. He does something by producing, distributing, and consuming material values. He does something by his personal conduct. He must do more as a political unit.

"Go west, young man" was the sage advice of one who foresaw the emergence of a great new country. "Go political, young man and young woman, and older man and older woman" should be the slogan of all who hope for the birth of a great new and free world.

A better America, a better England, a better France, a better Germany, a better Russia, a better India, would work together for a better world. There is no magic formula for freedom and peace. It is a matter of hard work and sweat in each family, in each community, in each state and in each nation.

In a better world, there would be freedom and opportunity for all, freedom from the indignity of unemployment, freedom from soul-cramping discrimination, freedom from want where there could be plenty, freedom from insecurity and fear, freedom from too much government and the obsession of too much wealth, freedom from uncontrollable political and economic masters, and the opportunity to learn, to grow, and to be one's self while serving others. In such a world of peace within man and between men there would be peace between nations.

Index